DRUGS, POWER, AND POLITICS

Drugs, Power, and Politics

Narco Wars, Big Pharma, and the Subversion of Democracy

Carl Boggs

Paradigm Publishers
Boulder • London

All rights reserved. No part of this publication may be transmitted or reproduced in any media or form, including electronic, mechanical, photocopy, recording, or informational storage and retrieval systems, without the express written consent of the publisher.

Copyright © 2015 by Paradigm Publishers

Published in the United States by Paradigm Publishers, 5589 Arapahoe Avenue, Boulder, CO 80303 USA.

Paradigm Publishers is the trade name of Birkenkamp & Company, LLC, Dean Birkenkamp, President and Publisher.

Library of Congress Cataloging-in-Publication Data

Boggs, Carl.
  Drugs, power, and politics : narco wars, big pharma, and the subversion of democracy / Carl Boggs.
     pages cm
  Includes bibliographical references and index.
  ISBN 978-1-61205-870-2 (hardcover : alk. paper) — ISBN 978-1-61205-872-6 (library ebook)
  1. Drug abuse—United States. 2. Narcotics—Political aspects—United States.
3. Drug traffic—United States. 4. Drug legalization—United States.
5. Pharmaceutical industry—United States. I. Title.
  HV5825.B624 2015
  362.290973—dc23

2014035152

Printed and bound in the United States of America on acid-free paper that meets the standards of the American National Standard for Permanence of Paper for Printed Library Materials.

19 18 17 16 15   1 2 3 4 5

To Junior and Sasha, for all their love and support

CONTENTS

Introduction	1
1 Drugs: The Historical Matrix	19

A Contextual Framework 21
Drugs in America 24
From Prohibition to Warfare 30
The Great Moral Panic 35

2 An American Crusade	43

"Threats"—Domestic and Global 45
Drug Hysteria and Culture Wars 50
A Corporate-State Agenda 57
Warrior Myths and Illusions 60

3 Delusions of an Epoch	68

The United Nations Report 69
An Alternative Path? 73
Political Mythologies 78

4 Drug War, Authoritarian Politics	84

From Volstead to Nixon 85
Civil Rights under Siege 87
The Surveillance Complex 90
Prisons: Lockdown Nation 99

VIII CONTENTS

5 Narco Globalism   104

The Criminal Syndicates   105
A Different Face of Capitalism   113
Expanding Battle Zones   122
Drugs and US Militarism   131

6 The Medical-Drug Behemoth   137

The Rise of Big Pharma   139
Medicine, Drugs, Power   149
Drugs and the Cancer Industry   154
Medical Tyranny   159

7 The Medicalized Society   163

Corporate Medicine Today   166
The Many Faces of Addiction   167
Obesity: Food, Drugs, Addiction   176
Modernity, Disease, Iatrogenesis   184

8 The Great Pot Wars   188

The Cannabis Legacy   189
The "Killer Weed" Hoax   192
Political Repression, Social Protest   198
Federal Power, Local Democracy   207
A Great Reversal?   211

Notes   219

Index   247

About the Author   259

Introduction

To critically explore the drug phenomenon in American society, in all its mysterious complexity, the author must be ready to investigate multiple realms of public life, from social policy to corporate power, law enforcement, health and medicine, foreign policy, political ideology, and the role played by government in the lives of more than 300 million people. In the early twenty-first century it has become incontrovertible that the War on Drugs, going back to the early twentieth century and recycled in its current version by President Richard Nixon in 1971—sometimes depicted as "America's longest war"—intersects with all these realms. In certain areas (politics, social policy, medicine, law enforcement) the drug war has been nothing short of transformative. A guiding motif of this book is that the political outlook behind this war—prohibitionist, moralizing, intolerant, deceitful, destructive—carries forward a deep authoritarian logic, as seen in widening power of the federal bureaucracy, police, security state, prison complex, and border operations—all coinciding with a perpetual narrowing of the public sphere.

Driven by an ensemble of wealthy and powerful interests, the drug war has caused more damage—politically, economically, and socially—than could ever be attributed to drug consumption as such. It has done incalculable harm, but this crusade has done nothing to reduce drug use or ameliorate problems of abuse, overdose, and addiction—surely nothing to justify the vast material and human resources poured into the prohibition agenda for more than forty years. Its destructive consequences—lucrative black markets, growth of criminal syndicates, political corruption, elevated crime and violence, worsening addiction and related drug problems—are the predictable result of coercive governmental

2 INTRODUCTION

policy in search of a mythological "drug-free society." Nowhere in American political life is the gulf between illusion and reality, propaganda and fact, pretense and outcome, more flagrant than in the case of drug politics, where public discourse is so colonized by a bundle of platitudes and myths. Sadly, a good deal of the carnage emanating from the drug war has been obscured, lost in a maze of fearmongering narratives and images that saturate American media culture.

Costing in the neighborhood of $20 billion yearly, the War on Drugs nourishes some of the darkest features of American society, having become a crusade heavily reliant on monolithic discourse that subverts the norms and practices of democratic politics. It is a policy built on elevated governmental power, with its silencing of critics, curtailing of personal freedoms, ruining of individual lives, and wasting of massive tax revenues. The very motif of continuous warfare, an enduring feature of US history, is based on a righteous national mission against enemies that must be confronted and vanquished. Warfare demands generous use of institutional power and military force—that is, an aggressive, interventionist politics. This special American undertaking requires the combined resources of federal agencies—the FBI, the CIA, the DEA, the ATF, and Customs, as well as the Pentagon—to confront an assemblage of traffickers, pushers, gangs, and cartels. The large Mexican cartels in particular—organized, affluent, militarized, and globalized—represent the ideal nemesis, a convenient target of drug interdictions, cross-border police raids, crop eradications, surveillance operations, and mass arrests. As United States–engineered warfare spans much of the global terrain, from Colombia to Mexico, Central America, and Afghanistan, the already-swollen national-security state gains new legitimation and power.

The War on Drugs helps reinforce ongoing trends in the direction of authoritarian politics, as military interventions, border mobilizations, counterterrorism operations, high-tech surveillance, and mass incarceration become the norm. A pressing question is whether even the most truncated forms of democracy can survive tendencies that, on the whole, seem to go unnoticed within the corporate media. Warfare against Mexican cartels, which have moved into Central America and parts of the United States, only feeds the militarization of antidrug politics. Counternarcotics activity greatly intensified during the Felipe Calderón presidency, spanning 2006 to 2012, at a time when tens of thousands of deaths resulted from the spread of military combat into the streets of several Mexican cities. For its part, Washington provided generous economic and military aid to Mexican police and armed forces, stepping up antidrug incursions along the borders. High-level arrests took at least fifteen cartel leaders out of circulation—operations touted by American politicians and the media as mortal blows to the syndicates, even as illegal drugs flow outward to meet huge US markets continued apace.

Drug interdiction requires sophisticated intelligence and surveillance work that now includes systematic overflights by unmanned drones and other aircraft. Used widely in Afghanistan, Pakistan, Yemen, and elsewhere for strictly military purposes, drones are now being deployed for information-gathering, domestically and globally. Though in 2014 relatively few in number, the US drone fleet is expected to reach 30,000 by 2020, most planes equipped with state-of-the-art cameras to detect personal identities and movements from 20,000 feet or more. First operated by the Pentagon and the CIA, by 2013 drones were being ordered by the DEA as well as Customs and Border Patrol, used for live feeds to dozens of ground stations. Drones—some likely to be armed—are also set to be deployed at military bases across the United States. According to the Pentagon's "global strike doctrine," remote-controlled planes will soon be capable of engaging "high-value targets" anywhere on the globe. The implications of this technology for expansion of governmental surveillance powers—for bolstering the security state—should be obvious.

As of early 2014, the federal government had seventeen intelligence agencies overseen by the Office of National Intelligence that, working alongside Homeland Security, were charged with detecting and countering military threats, terrorist activities, border challenges, and the illegal drug trade. Could the task of fighting internal political opposition be added to this list? In fact plenty of evidence reveals that the FBI, the NSA, and other agencies are already extensively involved in domestic surveillance. According to such NSA whistle-blowers as William Binney and Edward Snowden, along with critics like James Bamford, this most well-funded and intrusive of all federal agencies has augmented its high-tech intercept work across US domestic society, monitoring electronic communications such as phone calls, email, text messages, and Internet transactions.[1] As is well known, the NSA manages a sprawling operations center where massive data flows are intercepted, stored, processed, and analyzed. American citizens have little protection from this kind of secret eavesdropping, especially when it is carried out in the guise of "national security."

The post-9/11 environment has further given rise to a merger of national intelligence agencies and local police operations, connected through dozens of regional "information centers" involving Homeland Security, the FBI, the DEA, and local law enforcement. Created to serve counterterrorism priorities, these centers—no doubt aided by the NSA—are equipped to monitor virtually any illegal activity, including drug trafficking. The centers have been able to retrieve

4 INTRODUCTION

personal information from such corporations as AT&T, Verizon, Microsoft, and Google. While such operations are presently limited in effectiveness, the threat they pose to individual privacy and civil rights is already fearsome.

A broad look at the drug issue in American society reveals a tightening linkage between government and corporations, both functioning to subvert public debate and democratic governance on matters of social policy. Several giant pharmaceutical complexes—comprising Big Pharma—today exert a powerful influence on the medical system, Congress, state legislatures, federal agencies, and the media. These behemoths (most notably Merck, Pfizer, Abbott, Eli Lilly, and Johnson & Johnson) have accumulated such vast power, resources, and legitimacy, with collective profits in the tens of billions of dollars annually, that their role in reinforcing general oligarchic tendencies can hardly be overstated. Their political lobbying and commercial advertising are perhaps the most aggressive, not to mention efficacious, of any economic sector in the United States. Indeed, Big Pharma constitutes the quintessential example of a modern oligopoly.

Just how far-reaching is Big Pharma's economic and political power? Its huge profits, enhanced by blockbuster sales that for a single drug exceed $1 billion yearly, are generously subsidized and protected by the government, which blocks imports, funds research and development, fights corporate regulations, controls Medicare and related markets, allows private colonization of the FDA and its crucial testing procedures, and permits direct-to-consumer advertising. Such enormous clout helps the pharmaceutical industry secure astronomical returns on investment, a status easily jeopardized were prohibition to be overturned and (some or all) competing drugs legalized. Backed by the federal government, Big Pharma lobbyists are prepared to do anything necessary to keep their privileged markets intact—that is, free of competition from both imports and currently banned substances.

The dramatic postwar rise of Big Pharma coincides with growth in popularity of the "medical model" of health care—heavily reliant on drugs, high-tech procedures, and surgery, and fiercely hostile to preventive, holistic, nutrition-based alternatives. As this model becomes synonymous with American medicine, expensive pills of every sort are prescribed by medical professionals for an ever-expanding list of physical and mental problems: depression, obesity, high blood pressure, sexual dysfunction, insomnia, allergies, pain, and many others. The drug companies have built a cozy relationship with the medical establishment and federal agencies like the FDA, where test results pointing toward risk and harm are routinely watered down or even buried.[2] The companies advertise freely in medical journals and popular magazines that reach tens of millions of people. Prescribed drugs can be obtained with startling ease—through doctors and other professionals, even online—for both "medicinal" and "recreational" purposes, sometimes in dangerous mixtures for which no testing or monitoring exists. It is these substances, found in nearly every bathroom cabinet, that now contribute to the most pervasive drug culture ever known to humans.

It is a great tribute to Big Pharma and its advertising prowess that the American public is largely clueless about the harmful effects of legal drugs, which are indeed many: severe adverse reactions, lethal episodes, explosive mixtures, addictions, overdoses, wrong prescriptions, and induced accidents—all usually trivialized as "side effects." Adverse reactions alone vary from extreme dizziness to high blood pressure, heart attacks, strokes, breathing difficulties, and insomnia. Drug-related hospitalizations (as many as two million in some recent years) and deaths (in the tens of thousands) far exceed those from marijuana or in fact any other illegal substance.[3] The medical model is now such a taken-for-granted part of the American economy and culture that horrific outcomes—even when recognized—are usually explained away as minor nuisances on the road to "medical progress."

A fatal defect of drug-war ideology is the persistent failure to acknowledge the dual properties of *all* drugs: any chemical substance can be taken routinely or occasionally, can be addictive or not, can produce adverse reactions or not, can lead to severe health issues or not—whether for medicinal or recreational purposes, and whether legal or outlawed drugs. Chemical substances taken in mixtures—a frequent practice among seniors—can have wildly unpredictable, often lethal, consequences, while the dividing line between legal and illegal, medicinal and recreational drugs is increasingly blurred. Still, antidrug warriors pretend, against all credible evidence, that "illicit" or banned drugs are uniquely harmful and addictive, whether pot, cocaine, hallucinogens, or opiates. American society is saturated with all-night pharmacies where "meds" like Vicodin, Valium, OxyContin, Viagra, and Zoloft, routinely abused and potentially habit-forming, are sold and resold in the manner of ordinary staples. These products are so widely consumed and so much a part of the medical and social landscape that any reference to "drugs" hardly seems to apply, since "drugs," after all, conjures something exotic, dangerous, and prohibited.

The narrowing of political discourse around drug issues—indeed the nearly total absence of debate regarding the War on Drugs—reveals just how closed the public sphere has become. At a time when dozens of local and state organizations are pushing for more liberalized drug laws, especially for marijuana, the federal antidrug bureaucracy rigidly adheres to its dogma, with alternatives to prohibition still regarded as taboo. The drug warriors are strongly influential within several governmental agencies, a vast network of lobbyists, Big Pharma,

6 INTRODUCTION

key sectors of the medical establishment, and a compliant media. Against this institutional, material, and ideological power those independent organizations and grassroots movements pursuing drug-policy reform are completely out-manned, despite shifting public attitudes. The entire public sphere—Congress, federal government, state legislatures, media, and popular culture—is dominated by corporate interests, beholden to an archaic ideology, and subservient to the pharmaceutical oligopoly.

Despite years of political futility and social disaster, the War on Drugs continues to follow its time-worn platitudes and myths. Warrior tropes are ritually dramatized in the media: drug busts, inner-city violence, cartel horrors, strung-out addicts, interdiction successes, border clashes. "Drug problems" are sensationalized, one reason Americans have for decades placed the "drug menace" near the top of urgent social issues in public-opinion surveys. Those few public figures courageous enough to insist on drug-policy liberalization—for example, the libertarian Ron Paul during the 2012 presidential primaries—are ridiculed, savaged for being ignorant about how drugs "ruin peoples' lives" and "destroy communities." The June 2012 United Nations report, a carefully researched document that called for thorough rethinking of the global drug war, was cavalierly dismissed by the White House, ignored by leading politicians of both major parties, and generally treated as crazy blather within the mainstream media—a development explored in Chapter 3. At the 2012 (as in other) US presidential debates there was mostly silence: no participant—Democrat, Republican, moderator, or commentator—addressed issues of drug policy, aside from Paul's intervention that came mostly outside the official debate format.

When Eugene Jarecki's film condemning the War on Drugs, *The House I Live In*, appeared in late 2012, it attracted little media interest except for a few obligatory reviews in leading newspapers and magazines. Urging an end to the war along with legalization of some banned substances, Jarecki won few allies; most reviews attacked the filmmaker as a delusional "hippie" looking to resurrect the sixties counterculture. A central motif of the documentary, it turns out, concerned precisely this media tendency to employ slogans, stereotypes, and name-calling as a substitute for rational and open debate on the drug war.

The expansion of Big Pharma across the postwar era, with its growing army of lobbyists and heightened advertising presence, is more crucial to understanding the drug-war trajectory than is generally believed. Since the 1930s, when prohibition commissioner Harry Anslinger's fanatical crusaders forged a tight alliance with the emerging drug industry, Big Pharma has taken its place among the richest and most powerful oligopolies in the world, reaping superprofits from drugs marketed for an endless catalogue of human "disorders" that never stop proliferating. Such wealth and power could not be sustained without help from the federal government, which provides aid for research, carries out testing, funds subsidies, and ensures protection from cheaper imports and other potential competitors now outlawed. As with other corporate entities that are oligopolistic in practice while preaching "free market" virtues, Big Pharma spends billions yearly on advertising and contributes generously to (mostly Republican) political candidates. Meanwhile, the media-entertainment landscape itself is controlled by a few corporate titans like Disney, Sony, News Corporation, Viacom, and Time Warner. In this thoroughly commodified setting the only truly "bad" drugs are those decreed illegal by the warriors.

The mode of discourse most congruent with both the medical model and the drug war is either direct advertising or media "coverage" dictated by corporate interests—in other words, communication bereft of empirical substance. Thus, if pot is illegal it must, by definition, be more "harmful" and "addictive" than such legal products as alcohol, tobacco, and pharmaceuticals. Critical voices are rarely heard in the national media, radically skewing public debate over the issue of drug-policy liberalization. Big Pharma naturally wants to preserve its own nonstop marketplace of commodities. In recent years, as noted, the legal drug industry has enlarged its media presence (especially TV), emboldened by more open rules allowing direct-to-consumer advertising of drugs for most any "disorder" that medical researchers can imagine.

As the popular media itself depends more and more on advertising, Big Pharma ends up better positioned to market its vast cafeteria of drugs. The typical American watches TV four hours daily, and thus is more exposed to the inducements of drug marketing. Media critic Jerry Mander writes, "Over the last half century, the combination of television and astronomical advertising spending has effectively reshaped the consciousness of the United States and the entire planet: our self-image, the way we aspire to live, our habits, our thoughts, our references, desires, memories."[4] The goal of such corporate marketeering is to colonize every public space available for commercial messages. Its great success in this has contributed profoundly to development of a large and dynamic American drug culture.

The aggressive marketing of legal drugs, many extremely risky and harmful, has intensified since the 1990s: expensive pills are prescribed to meet (or shape) every conceivable health problem at a time of seemingly ubiquitous mental and physical "disorders." Drugs constitute the quintessential modern-day quick fix—easy to make, distribute, market, and sell—while requiring little change in the user's habits of thought and behavior. The pharmaceutical giants have access to media venues reaching tens of millions of people, from TV to the Internet,

8 INTRODUCTION

magazines, and newspapers, spending billions of dollars on propaganda to convince target audiences that legal drugs are efficacious. TV advertising stokes the popularity of such "blockbuster" drugs as Cialis, Vicodin, Ambien, and Zoloft, each reaching sales of at least $1 billion yearly. These products are now so widely consumed, indeed so taken for granted, that the label "drugs" is often dropped in favor of the more tepid-sounding "meds." The resulting American drug addiction coincides with a social order marked by atomization and passivity, where sedentary lifestyles, fast foods, TV habituation, and quick fixes shape the popular consciousness.

To the extent Big Pharma is interwoven with corporate interests, governmental power, media influence, and the medical complex, it constitutes a focal point in the drug war. The American medical system, a shining legacy of the Enlightenment, exemplifies capitalist modernity at its best and worst—a repository of high-tech, commodified, iatrogenic health care with all the trappings of social progress. The system is driven by technological innovation, a huge administrative structure, and treatment methods geared to surgery, drugs, and technical procedures. While modernized health care can be first-rate when it comes to many difficult challenges—for example, complicated surgeries, transplants, technical devices, and emergency care—it suffers from being bureaucratic, expensive, and closed off to natural alternatives based on either prevention or long-term healing. Although medical costs per capita in the United States remain astronomical, far higher than in any other country, overall national health indicators reported by UN surveys rank the United States near the bottom of all industrialized nations. In 2013 American healthcare spending reached $2.7 trillion, or roughly $8,600 for every person, dwarfing second-place Switzerland by 60 percent, and many other countries (with much better health measures than the United States') by 70 percent or more. By 2020 US health spending is expected to reach about $4.6 trillion, nearly 20 percent of domestic product. Although modernized health care has expanded rapidly in recent decades, it has not produced any commensurate elevation of US health indicators.[5] Not only do these sophisticated methods fail to address either social context or deeper causes of health conditions; they are ultimately compromised by a popular fast-food culture responsible for widespread obesity and associated chronic diseases now plaguing American society. Meanwhile, the increase of wasteful, often-harmful medical practices—including surgeries, technical interventions, and drugs—has aggravated the problem of iatrogenesis, where medicine serves to *worsen* health outcomes.

The tragic increase in medical iatrogenesis in the United States can be attributed in great measure to modernity itself. Here drugs—legal drugs prescribed by doctors—constitute the main culprit of the disaster. According to the *Death by*

Medicine authors, conventional American medicine is responsible for a staggering 783,000 deaths yearly. They report that 2.2 million people per year experience in-hospital adverse reactions to drugs, in a context where unnecessary hospital visits total nearly 9 million and wasteful surgeries another 7.5 million yearly—despite a maze of government regulations, testing, and oversight.[6] As drugs are now probably the major treatment method within contemporary medicine, they are simultaneously the leading cause of harmful outcomes. Harsh reactions to commonly prescribed medications, tens of thousands lethal, occur from routine treatment of such conditions as pain, depression, obesity, allergies, high blood pressure, and sexual dysfunction—all more effectively (and safely) remedied by means of natural, preventive care. Common reactions include everything from nausea, dizziness, skin rashes, and vision impairment to severe addictions and lethal episodes. As for pain medications in the form of opioids, or analgesics, some twelve million cases of serious abuse were reported in 2010 alone, including 475,000 visits to emergency centers.[7] Antibiotics have reached the very top of the iatrogenic list: with more than thirty million pounds sold for humans and animals yearly, extreme overuse gives rise to drug resistance, spread of harmful bacteria, and increased difficulty treating both old and new diseases. Touted as the greatest of all miracle drugs, antibiotics are best understood nowadays as source of a modern health catastrophe. As for chemotherapy on the cancer front, its iatrogenic properties—toxic invasion of the body and assault on the immune system, along with marginal benefits in survival rates—are too well known to require further comment.

The medical model views symptoms apart from social context, ignoring a broad range of nutritional and related lifestyle variables. No one questions whether drugs can provide short-term relief for such conditions as pain and depression, but their long-term success in treating most health problems is hardly inspiring, while adverse reactions are frequently harsh or debilitating. Drugs sold for obesity, hypertension, arthritis, and alcoholism, for example, have shown at best only modest results. Chronic, degenerative conditions require a more natural approach; drug therapy offers little more than a temporary palliative. Legal drugs, of course, are big business, with all-night pharmacies like CVS ($127 billion in sales for 2013)[8] selling potent drugs for everything from colds to headaches, pain, depression, anxiety, and high cholesterol. Outlets like CVS and Walgreens have been reported aggressively pushing drug refills to customers, even sending false claims to Medicare to meet yearly sales "quotas."[9] Corporate domination of American medicine has its parallel in the fast-food industry and purveyors of tobacco, sugar, meat, dairy products, and soft drinks, which all contribute to the proliferation of chronic health problems.

10   INTRODUCTION

The medical establishment celebrates "progress" on a foundation of advanced technology, including drug therapy. While obesity, afflicting nearly 130 million Americans, can be traced overwhelmingly to lifestyle choices—especially diets heavy in calories, saturated fats, and sugar—the medical model embraces surgery and drugs to "manage" what is defined as an intractable disease. Pharmaceuticals such as Belviq and Qsymia—all FDA-approved despite known risk of heart problems—are sold to "treat" problems of excessive weight. Qsymia, marketed by Vivus, Inc., has shown limited benefits as a diet pill, but tests indicate possible adverse reactions such as heart attacks, strokes, and birth defects.[10] Meanwhile, the obesity "epidemic" continues unimpeded, keeping pace with the high-threat American diet and new pharmaceutical "breakthroughs," including "fat burners," expected to dramatically augment Big Pharma revenues.

Given the prominence of drugs in American medicine, an estimated twenty-one million people have reportedly measurable "substance-abuse disorders," mainly correlated with pain killers, antidepressants, sleeping pills, and amphetamines. Still other millions suffer from lesser but still disturbing problems: occasional abuses or overdoses, milder addictions, and nagging adverse reactions—part of a long list of "warnings" that accompanies most pharmaceuticals. "Treatment" of drug-related conditions, moreover, is often simply more drugs—for example, Naltrexone, commonly prescribed for alcoholism.

While the medical sector presently accounts for 16 percent of domestic product, far more than half of this spending entails profits, administration, cost markups for hospitals, insurance claims processing, excessive testing, and wasteful procedures. While technology and drugs help drive up medical costs in the United States, there are diminishing returns on money spent, especially as the system becomes more iatrogenic. The great drug fixation of American medicine ultimately privileges certain kinds of drugs—those sold for "disorders" over those for intoxication or mind expansion, "meds" over recreational products, prescribed over "illicit" substances. Drugs taken for depression, sleep disorders, pain, and sexual dysfunction usually have a professional imprimatur, while intoxicants are deemed contraband and vilified as "street drugs." In reality, such distinctions are impossible to sustain—prescribed narcotics, for example, can be taken for "intoxicating" purposes while illegal drugs like pot and cocaine can satisfy medical needs such as pain reduction. At the same time, many "recreational" drugs are entirely legal, including tobacco, alcohol, and caffeine.

The coercive elements of the medical model merge with the repressive logic of the drug war, both intent on limiting personal choice—even at the cost of basic rights—in the guise of protecting individual and public health. The imposition of such limits runs against traditions that resonate across US history—above all, pursuit of individual freedoms spelled out in the Declaration of Independence, the Bill of Rights, and upheld by a rich legacy of judicial decisions. In fact, this history has been sharply conflicted, pitting authoritarianism against democracy, repression against freedom, oligarchy against local control, and prohibition against individualism. Both the medical model and drug war can be situated within the first, darker side of this legacy.

One reason banning intoxicating drugs is inherently repressive is that the "fourth drive" explored by Ronald K. Siegel in his book *Intoxication*—universal human attraction to mind-altering substances—is natural to social life, to be eradicated only through force, and probably not even then.[11] Further, prohibition has always sought to constrain types of human behavior that, left untouched by coercive policies and laws, are essentially self-regarding—what should be of little interest to others or government. The mode of drug experience aligned with the "fourth drive" might be called existential—pursuit of transcendent meaning, embrace of the visionary, search for creativity, break with social conformity, tearing down of external barriers to self-actualization. The intoxicating dimension of drugs—typically considered "illicit" substances—has long attracted intellectuals, artists, and sundry creative people. Sigmund Freud was known to have used cocaine as a therapeutic, mind-altering tonic; the scientist Francis Crick used LSD as a "thinking tool"; Thomas Edison is reported to have frequently chewed coca leaves; Apple CEO Steve Jobs used a variety of psychedelics for concentrated thinking; Microsoft cofounder Bill Gates consumed LSD as an instrument for "breaking boundaries"; and astrophysicist Carl Sagan said that marijuana profoundly helped his intellectual pursuits.[12]

Of course, such pursuit can be abused and, moreover, often falls short of its potential—yet its mind-expanding potential offers space for "intoxication" to morph into the existential realm. This would seem to have deep roots in American history, going back to the revolutionary period and frontier era, and reemerging in the 1950s and 1960s with the Beat generation, youth counterculture, and psychedelics such as LSD, mescaline, and psilocybin. Dimensions of an existential outlook (visible in the work of Paul Goodman, André Gide, Albert Camus, and Jean-Paul Sartre) merged with such currents as surrealism, film noir, jazz culture, and French New Wave cinema, eventually overlaid by the intoxicating element celebrated in Aldous Huxley's *The Doors of Perception* and the later work of Allen Ginsberg, Jack Kerouac, and Timothy Leary. Against the more repressive Puritanical, corporate, and bureaucratic side of US history, this underground current insisted on a break with convention, new modes of apprehension, and opposition to received wisdom, all potentially corresponding to "existential" aspects of the "fourth drive."

12 INTRODUCTION

Jack Kerouac's 1957 novel *On the Road*, a tribute to the Beat and jazz scene of the period that in many ways anticipated the sixties counterculture, captured profound elements of the "fourth drive." The work celebrated a search for freedom and adventure against the stifling conventions of bourgeois social life—a search fueled by rebellion, novelty, sexual experimentation, and drugs. While *On the Road* was something of an anthem for the Beat generation, its meaning could be universal, the "road" standing for new modes of seeing, for going beyond normalcy to "mind-altering" experiences consistent with Huxley's vision and prefiguring the ideas of Leary, the Yippies, and Theodore Roszak in *The Making of a Counter Culture*, which celebrate the sixties convergence of music, politics, sexuality, and drugs.[13]

The Beat world was drawn to a mix of literary creativity, jazz, black culture, and intoxicating drugs, especially marijuana. Martin A. Lee, in his book *Smoke Signals*, writes, "A key part of cannabis as a social phenomenon has been its boundary-crossing quality, how it leapt like a flame from one culture to another. So did jazz. The music and the weed were fellow travelers, so to speak, joined at the juncture of hip."[14] Lee notes that Kerouac and other Beats first started experimenting with pot at jazz clubs during the 1940s and 1950s, as musicians like Charlie Parker, Dizzy Gillespie, and Charles Mingus were coming into vogue. Lee adds, "To Kerouac and his literary comrades, jazz represented the uninhibited expression of the soul's impulses. They wanted to write like Parker and Gillespie played music. Kerouac, who often composed while high on reefer and Benzedrine, called his writing 'bop prosody.'"[15] Following the poet Arthur Rimbaud, the Beats and jazz musicians embraced creativity, innovation, and transcending the stale conformity of the Cold War era, with "the use of illegal drugs . . . an integral part of their search for transcendence."[16]

Kerouac and Ginsburg, joined by fellow writer William Burroughs and others, forged a dynamic subculture outside hegemonic rules and norms of American society. Lee writes, "The Beats were conscious of their link to the great stoned lineage of European artists, which included the Dadaists, surrealists, symbolists, and others who defied conventions and labels."[17] Here pot and other mind-altering drugs, part of the "fourth drive," helped unleash the power of intellectual and artistic creativity. "They stayed up all night smoking fat marijuana bombers, listening to jazz, reciting poetry, and confiding their deepest secrets, their hopes and fears, in protracted, stoned rap sessions. Marijuana was a truth drug, of sorts, for the Beats."[18] Burroughs, in *Naked Lunch*, took the subversive drug experience further, using mind-transforming chemicals as a vehicle for rejecting a society run by "maniacal power addicts." For him, "addiction" was less a personal vice than an ordinary element of conformist behavior in capitalist society.[19]

The sixties era, with its epic fusion of music, politics, and drugs, could be seen as even a stronger embellishment of the "fourth drive." For more than a decade, the scene resonated with change, creativity, experimentation, and, above all, new musical sounds produced by groups like the Grateful Dead, Jefferson Airplane, The Doors, Santana, Credence Clearwater Revival, and Country Joe and the Fish, and performers like Janis Joplin and Jimi Hendrix. The period was one of nonstop cultural happenings, concerts, parties, and celebrations mixing social protest and psychedelic drugs that, in the aftermath of the Beat era, took alternative lifestyles to new heights. In San Francisco alone, the sixties scene witnessed the appearance of some 500 rock bands, fueled by an explosive mixture of blues, folk, jazz, and earlier rock traditions that enlivened hundreds of clubs, ballrooms, festivals, and parks. These venues were energized by easy availability of such drugs as marijuana, LSD, speed, mescaline, and nitrous oxide. Joel Selvin, writing in *Summer of Love*, comments, "The musicians and the people around them saw themselves as psychedelic settlers living on the frontier of a new wild west."[20] For popular groups like the Dead, Jefferson Airplane, and The Doors, the psychedelic input was hardly peripheral, but rather crucial: an easy supply of drugs boosted creativity and stamina, combined with high levels of musicianship that, in Selvin's words, "captured a time and place on which American music turned."[21] Without the mind-transforming power of drugs, this surely would have been impossible.

As prelude to Nixon's 1971 drug-war crusade, the sixties witnessed the opening salvo of a protracted federal crackdown on "psychedelic" substances (loosely including pot, LSD, mescaline, and psilocybin, along with certain lab mixtures) that many in the counterculture saw as consciousness-raising. LSD, brought into general use only in the early 1960s, was valued within youth circles as a stimulus behind psychic, spiritual, and cultural self-awareness—for some also an inspiration to political rebellion. It was also perfectly legal until it was chosen as a prime target in the drug war. Experiments conducted in the 1960s by Dr. James Fadiman (in Menlo Park, California)—as well as by Leary, Richard Alpert, and others at Harvard—sought to unlock empowering mental properties of LSD and produced highly suggestive results.[22] Research had shown that such intoxicating drugs could exert a positive effect on the mind, expanding the capacity for creative and visionary thought, even helping to solve problems. (The antidrug warriors, then as now, imputed only negative outcomes to such doping, in the absence of supportive evidence.) Meanwhile, some psychedelics came to

14 INTRODUCTION

be valued as therapeutic aids, documented in Fadiman's book *The Psychedelic Explorer's Guide*.[23] LSD appeared especially promising for its contribution to innovative thinking, as Apple CEO Steve Jobs and others would later acknowledge on the basis of personal experience.

The federal government, however, would have none of this: by mid-1960s the FDA had already moved to block additional research as a first step in rendering all hallucinogens illegal. Quite clearly the LSD experiments—with their implicit legitimation of mind-altering drugs—sharply contradicted the medical model and its demonization of substances considered "intoxicating" or "mind-expanding." Associated with the counterculture, these drugs were viewed by the guardians of public morality as threats to rational thinking and, indeed, the entire social order. By 1970 it is estimated that at least twenty million Americans had explored psychedelics, the preference of writers, poets, musicians, and various outsiders, valued as a medium of creative self-activity, a refocusing of personal identity to cope with an alienated social world. Fadiman had observed that "what happens in serious psychedelic work is there's a sudden reframing of massive amounts of worldview."[24]

The great promise of psychedelics—unthinkable for the antidrug warriors— was to take users beyond ordinary states of consciousness, a point emphasized in Roszak's *The Making of a Counter Culture*. Here "mind-alteration" would have both individual and social repercussions: the drugs could be envisioned, as they were by Fadiman, Alpert, and Leary, as a vehicle of dealienation, possibly radicalization. In an American society where the confluence of corporate, state, and military power still dominated the public landscape—matched by a smothering one-dimensionality and conformity at the mass level—the psychedelic experience had life-changing implications, a possible harbinger of deeper antiauthoritarian trends and even social revolt.

As a political expression of the medical model, the War on Drugs works against human impulses and aspirations consistent with the "fourth drive"; the federal crackdown on psychedelics represents warrior ideology in all its prohibitionist, intolerant, antidemocratic thrust. In his "preamble" to a *Lapham's Quarterly* volume on "Intoxication," Lewis Lapham writes,

> The war America has been waging for the last one hundred years against the use of drugs deemed to be illegal . . . cannot be won but in the meantime, at a cost of $20 billion a year, it facilitates the transformation of what was once a freedom-loving republic into a freedom-fearing national-security state. The policies of zero tolerance equip local and federal law enforcement with increasingly autocratic powers of coercion and surveillance . . . and spread the stain

of moral pestilence to ever larger numbers of people assumed to be infected with reefer madness.[25]

Lapham refers to a long history of outsiders, subversives, and radicals—from anarchists and surrealists to the Beats, hippies, and social-movement activists.

At a time when Big Pharma offers up "a cornucopia of prescription drugs—eye-opening, stupefying, mood-swinging, game-changing, anxiety-alleviating, performance-enhancing"—with a total market value of $300 billion, Lapham suggests that "the keepers of the nation's conscience would be better advised to address those conditions—poverty, lack of opportunity and education, racial discrimination—from which drugs offer an illusory means of escape."[26] Although "escape" is simply one of many reasons people consume drugs, Lapham's critique of the drug war as a wasteful intrusion into people's lives is valid enough.

The intoxicating property of drugs not only engages basic human impulses that cannot be extinguished by legal or institutional repression, but signifies something broader—pursuit of noninstrumental modes of consciousness, a major impetus behind psychedelic experimentation in the 1960s. The drug experience signaled a break, however temporary, from the tyranny of social convention, institutional hierarchy, and ideological ritual, opening new mental spaces for finding self-awareness and "access to a visionary state of being" of the sort celebrated by Rimbaud, Huxley, Kerouac, Leary, and other advocates of drug-enabled mind expansion. Rimbaud, anticipating surrealism, the Beats, and elements of the sixties counterculture, wrote, "A poet makes himself a visionary through a long, boundless, and systematized disorganization of all the senses. All forms of love, of suffering, of madness; he searches himself, he exhausts within himself all poisons and preserves their quintessences."[27] As people are so often trapped in their social immediacy, the liberating potential of intoxicating drugs in penetrating those limits was obvious to proponents of the "fourth drive." As for the ongoing legacy of antidrug warfare, Americans nowadays consume so many drugs, which are linked to so many addictive behaviors and myriad harmful outcomes, that governmental coercion directed against pot and hallucinogens, for example, appears hypocritical in the extreme. Further, drugs are now so integral to social life in the United States that the opposition between medicinal and intoxicating, legal and illegal drugs is now impossible to sustain.

Beyond pot and hallucinogens, warfare against drugs like cocaine—vilified as a "hard" drug—is likewise based on false premises and shaky evidence. Coca products have long been a target of moral panic despite their mildly intoxicating properties and the fact that coca leaves have been ingested routinely in large regions of South America for centuries—not only for pleasure but also for treating

16   INTRODUCTION

such health problems as arthritis, diabetes, and asthma, without any of the horrors ascribed to "coke" in the American experience. As Tom Freiling argues in *Cocaine Nation*, "coca products . . . could become a globally recognized health product along the lines of Korean ginseng."[28] A World Health Organization (WHO) study in 1995 concluded that the coca leaf has few adverse effects on human health—a study that was quickly buried after the United States threatened to withhold its financial contributions to the WHO. Of course the coca leaf, like opium poppies and the cannabis plant, can be processed into more concentrated drugs like "crack cocaine," with potentially severe effects, but that is a function of lab technology rather than the substance in its more natural form.

The irrationality of US drug policy, unfortunately, shows few signs of abating: moves toward legalization remain somewhat marginalized or localized (confined to states) within the public sphere, regarded as a threat by many established interests. Those pushing for meaningful policy alternatives are demonized as both crazy and dangerous—though such rhetorical attacks should be less efficacious in the wake of the historic 2012 Colorado and Washington votes legalizing pot. The drug war relies heavily on media propaganda, state power, and the leverage to criminalize behavior deemed illicit. Its commitment to a "drug-free society" is just as laughable as it is meaningless. Freiling writes, "Those in authority are unwilling to admit their addiction to control, or the illusion of control. The United States government should face up to its inability to devise a workable response to the demand for drugs."[29] For governing elites, threats to social order and national security are forever imminent and ubiquitous—perhaps none more so than the evil personified by drug traffickers.

For reasons more fully explored in the following chapters, the warriors hold firm to prohibitionist fantasies despite continuous failure, their dogmatism completely at odds with reasonable political discourse. Meanwhile, drug consumption of every sort is so normalized that even the combined efforts of local and federal governments, devouring ever more resources, will be hard-pressed to successfully prosecute the war. In 2013, a large number of Americans were using illegal substances, including 24.6 million pot smokers, 6.5 million users of nonmedical pharmaceuticals, 1.5 million cocaine users, and 1.3 million hallucinogen users.[30] Prohibition had done little to reduce drug use or contain its most harmful consequences. On the contrary, it had somehow managed to recycle the Volstead Act catastrophe, and in the process "has only made criminality as widespread as drug use and made a mockery of the law."[31] Just tracking, arresting, and prosecuting those involved in the cocaine trade, whether in the United States or abroad, has proven impossible, a tragic waste of public resources. Freiling's *Cocaine Nation* concludes, "Finding a workable alternative to prohibition has to begin in the United States . . . so it rests with young Americans to ensure that future drug policies are grounded in science and the protection of public health and to recognize that knowledge is the prerequisite for free choice."[32]

The War on Drugs is symptomatic of so much that has gone wrong in American society—its harsh neoliberal global policies, its mammoth security state and war economy, its sprawling prison system, its plutocratic economic structure, its crisis-ridden public sector, its steady erosion of democratic norms and practices. In this setting, the antidrug crusade reinforces political authoritarianism along with its reverse side—mass disempowerment and alienation. While the political and media establishment prefers to cast its gaze on what is happening elsewhere in the world—"failed states," global terrorism, the Iran nuclear "threat," drug cartels, etc.—it is the American system itself that merits closest scrutiny: the wealthiest nation in history is deteriorating from intensifying social inequality, poverty, civic violence, militarism, and environmental crisis, not to mention eclipse of democratic politics reflected in the yawning gap between electoral activity and the social reality it fails to address.

At the same time, the drug war has long fed the voracious appetite of American big business: marketing leverage of the (legal) drug industry; funding for law enforcement and prisons; resources for border control, surveillance, and testing; money for an endless array of treatment programs; and so forth. Likewise benefiting are myriad bureaucratic interests, from the FDA, the DEA, the NSA, and the CIA to a variety of federal, state, and local agencies involved in sustaining prohibition. Nowhere is the historic convergence of government and corporations, state and capital, more visible than in the antidrug crusade.

In contemporary American society the familiar boundaries separating warfare and civil life have collapsed, thanks at least partly to the War on Drugs. With consolidation of the warfare state and the security complex, violence enters all realms of public existence: international politics, social policy, law enforcement, popular culture, and daily life. Henry Giroux notes that "violence now runs through media and popular culture like an electric current."[33] As for the drug war, Giroux adds, "What has emerged in the United States is a civil and political order structured around the problem of violent crime."[34] Indeed the entire neoliberal order, despite lip service to freedom and democracy, is based on corporate rule, militarism, punishment, and incarceration. Media spectacles predictably dwell on mayhem, death, guns, civic violence, and of course severe punishment meted out to moral outlaws and everyday criminals. Here warfare, guns, and masculine superheroes naturally take center stage, while drugs become a convenient target for any threats to social normalcy and political order. In this context, moreover, the very drugs commonly administered to military personnel to help smooth

18 INTRODUCTION

over the enormous stresses of combat (and their aftermath) wind up feeding an upsurge in substance abuse for both troops and veterans.[35]

The incapacity of the governing apparatus to alter its drug-war trajectory speaks directly to this worsening condition of politics. Like other stark challenges—poverty, collapse of social services, military spending, corporate power, global warming—problems connected to the War on Drugs remain largely insulated from vigorous public debate and needed political remedy, especially at the national level. "Bipartisan consensus" on drug policy remains the unshakeable imperative of the day, beyond criticism. Here as elsewhere, conventional politics becomes largely irrelevant to the lives of ordinary Americans, who are increasingly disengaged and voiceless. The explanation is disarmingly simple: in a plutocratic order corporate interests, with their lobbies, think tanks, money, and media ownership, overwhelmingly shape the governing process, rendering it closed off to rational decision making. At the same time, given the integration of elite interests, the American public has come to accept, or at least tolerate, this narrow, authoritarian system of rule. One logical consequence of such politics is mass depoliticization, a condition, in fact, eagerly promoted by elites as they celebrate the wonderful virtues of freedom, rights, and democracy.

As politics degenerates further into a spectacle of manufactured elite dramas, the drug war appears as one more arena of social policy over which the American public has traditionally exercised little if any influence—though recent popular victories in the great pot wars could signal a profound shift. Further, sadly, the citizenry in general does not seem to harbor viable expectations of democratic participation. Meanwhile, the endless antidrug crusade—sold on grounds of improving the personal and social health of Americans—wreaks increasing havoc on the social order and political system.

Chapter 1
Drugs

The Historical Matrix

At the time of this writing (late 2014), the seemingly endless War on Drugs has attracted new levels of public interest in the United States and, to some extent, worldwide. A rather ordinary *Los Angeles Times* front-page headline of May 28, 2012, reads "Cartels Push Drug Violence to New Depths," detailing the arrest of Mexican Zetas cartel kingpin "El Loco" (Daniel Ramirez), a long-targeted mastermind behind gruesome killings in the ever-intensifying Mexican drug wars. The story focuses on the piling up of forty-nine mutilated bodies—heads, feet, and hands missing—alongside a northern Mexican road leading to the US border, a narrative that has become far too familiar. Martinez was said to have acted on orders from top commanders of the Zetas paramilitary group, with the intent of sending a message to the rival Sinaloa cartel and its allies. At this juncture we encounter a new phase of wide-open narco combat that has claimed up to 70,000 lives across Mexico in seven years. Sinaloa counts as just one of eight Mexican states riddled with bloody combat involving several powerful drug syndicates, rife with kidnappings, torture, and mass executions—ongoing battles of attrition driven by a War on Drugs centered in the United States, with eager Mexican governmental compliance. Some regions, including parts of Jalisco and Sinaloa, have recurrently been reported as on the verge of civil war as well-armed paramilitary forces operate with surprisingly few limits or restraints. President Felipe Calderón's antidrug program launched in 2006 was at one point declared a success by US officials, but an everyday reality of bloody combat refuted such propaganda: in 2013 drug traffickers were doing more business than ever, as

20   CHAPTER I

cartel networks orchestrated a virtually limitless supply of drugs, weapons, and money, always fueled by a voracious, drug-consuming nation just to the north.

Other newspaper headlines spoke to different facets of the drug predicament, one (in the *Los Angeles Times*) announcing, "Drugs Now Deadlier Than Autos."[1] The chemical substances in question were perfectly legal: as the costly and failed drug war continued full-speed, data gathered by the US Centers for Disease Control and Prevention (CDC) showed that deaths from such routinely prescribed medications as Vicodin, Xanax, Ambien, Soma, and Fentanyl far outnumbered those from all banned drugs combined. With prescriptions for such drugs in the United States rising more than 40 percent since 2007 thanks to aggressive marketing by giant pharmaceutical companies, the dangers from adverse reactions, overdoses, addictions, deadly combinations of two or more drugs, and drug-related accidents have correspondingly skyrocketed.[2] The striking increase in overall American drug consumption—taken in high volume for every conceivable purpose—has given rise to flourishing legal and illegal markets spanning most ages, social groups, and geographical regions. Total US consumption of illegal drugs amounts to at least $50 billion yearly, while pharmaceuticals total roughly $320 billion—in each case amounting (in 2012) to nearly 40 percent of the global market.[3] Other headlines called attention to the rapid growth of a "medicated military," highlighted the failure of the drug war to impede the flow of contraband substances into the United States, and reported on federal attempts to destroy medical marijuana outlets in several states. Such media accounts speak to a complex, often byzantine, legacy surrounding drugs in US history: on one hand, large-scale consumption and marketing of mind-altering substances, and on the other a persistent moralistic drive toward prohibition, with its myriad coercive policies and laws.

Drugs have long been a source of taboos, fears, myths, and warfare, despite being simultaneously integral to American economic and cultural life. As the preceding data suggest, in 2012 the United States led the world in consumption of both legal and illegal substances that we commonly refer to as "drugs," with some twenty-four million Americans reportedly using illegal drugs—a solid increase over the previous decade, despite the best efforts of antidrug warriors.[4] Understood broadly, products that conventionally fall under this label have figured strongly in human life for centuries, a font of pleasure, self-discovery, mood alteration, performance enhancement, and medical treatment—not to mention abuse, addiction, and myriad other harms. Historian Mike Jay points out that "drug cultures are endlessly varied, but drugs in general are more or less ubiquitous among our species."[5] In modern society drugs intersect with virtually every realm of social life, a reality met with misunderstanding, distortions, myths, and outright lies. A more critical, dialectical perspective is needed for a rational politics and social policy; Andrew Weil laments that "our present ways of thinking about drugs are as useless to us as a geocentric theory of the solar system."[6]

A Contextual Framework

Viewed historically, drugs can be seen as natural or synthetic, legal or illegal, medically prescribed or simple commodities—that is, as virtually any substance exerting a biochemical impact on mind or body. In hegemonic American discourse, "drugs" are typically viewed as illicit, harmful, associated with deviant subcultures and criminal activity. In fact humans have partaken of literally thousands of mind- or body-altering compounds going back centuries, although references to "drugs" did not enter common English usage until the early fifteenth century.[7] As medicines, psychological agents, intoxicating substances, and even food, drugs (of greatly varied dosage and frequency of use) have long been part of both traditional and modern cultures. Herbs derived from plants alone run into the many hundreds. In this context drugs can be defined to include not only familiar illegal substances like opiates, cocaine, cannabis, and hallucinogens, but also a wide variety of pharmaceuticals (painkillers, sedatives, antidepressants, sex stimulants, etc.); regularly available products like aspirin and sleep enhancers; commonly used intoxicants such as tobacco, alcohol, and caffeine; and foods including sugar and chocolate. In this sense drug consumption has been, and remains, one of the most ordinary of human activities, little different from eating, sex, culture, and entertainment.

Although the very discourse of drugs can be emotionally charged, simple generalizations have today become more elusive (and worthless) than ever. The degree of risk or harm from drug use ultimately depends on the type of substance consumed, frequency and amount of use, combinations taken, psychological framework of the user, and social context. Few drugs are so innately and powerfully addictive or harmful they cannot be managed by the user, and levels of harm bear little relation to questions of legality or social convention.

The colloquial understanding of drugs generally extends to illegal, "illicit," or street goods—that is, recreational substances with questionable legitimacy, harmful by definition. Pharmaceuticals, on the other hand, are usually viewed as medicinal ("meds") whether prescribed or over-the-counter (OTC), sanctioned within the established healthcare system. A better, more comprehensive and useful framework would identify diverse patterns of drug consumption, whether legal or illegal, that have existed for many decades and, in some cases,

22   CHAPTER I

centuries. What should be immediately obvious is that the cultural, legal, and medical status of what we typically call "drugs" has varied enormously from time to time and place to place, often dramatically. Patterns readily visible today include (1) *medicinal*, pertaining to body (morphine, beta blockers, ibuprofen, etc.); (2) *medicinal*, pertaining to mind (sedatives, tranquilizers, antidepressants, etc.); (3) *recreational or intoxicating* (narcotics, cocaine, methamphetamines, marijuana, etc.); (4) *mind-expanding or psychedelic* (LSD, mescaline, psilocybin, etc.); (5) *social or situational* (wine, beer, spirits, tobacco); (6) *religious or spiritual* (peyote, various mushrooms and herbs); (7) *sexually stimulating* (Viagra, Cialis, numerous herbs); and (8) *food-enhancing* (sugar, salt, chemical additives, etc.).

Overall drug consumption in the United States has long been rather common, and is now so widespread as to be normal, taken for granted, routine. Drugs are easily available at meals, restaurants, bars, hospitals, stores, musical events, military facilities, and sports activities, and, of course, in household cabinets, while pharmacies dot the American landscape by the thousands. Advertisements for costly prescription drugs—used to treat heart conditions, depression, anxiety, sleep disorders, and sexual problems, for example—flood the TV airwaves and Internet sites. Major pharmaceutical companies are keenly aware of the many reasons people use chemical substances, marketing new lines of commodities for hundreds of billions of dollars yearly. Without great benefit of advertising, meanwhile, underground cartels, gangs, and small-time traffickers reap tens of billions more in profits from intoxicating "street" drugs. By far the most lucrative earnings, of course, come from thoroughly legitimate food, alcohol, tobacco, and coffee markets, and these generally turn out to be the most harmful.

Among the eight distinct modalities of drug consumption mentioned above, the prevailing orthodoxy frames as "illicit"—thus innately harmful—only specific types of recreational, intoxicating, or mind-altering substances: opiates, cannabis, cocaine, methamphetamines, and hallucinogens such as LSD. Yet the classification distinguishing *some* recreational products from others—for example, cannabis from wine, opiates from liquor—is rather arbitrary, having no logical relationship to abuse levels, addictive properties, health impact, or social harm. All these drugs have long histories of human consumption and all engage certain psychological impulses, what Ronald K. Siegel calls the "fourth drive" that exists alongside such human needs as food and sex.[8] The same is true for mind-expanding or "psychedelic" drugs that are usually less problematic, less potentially addictive and destructive, than many widely marketed legal drugs. For Siegel, "the pursuit of intoxication is no more abnormal than the pursuit of love, social attachments, thrills, power, or any number of other acquired motives."[9] Compulsive drug-taking associated with dependency and addiction is, as with most other substances, merely one of several possible outcomes—and here not even the most common.

Humans have always explored altered modes of consciousness, in one fashion or another. Indeed "altered states" can be realized through not only drugs but also meditation, hypnosis, dreams, mystical experience, intense exercise, and even foods. Mind-altering substances like peyote and mescaline were long used by native peoples in the Western Hemisphere and elsewhere, with few if any signs of abuse or harm. Today psilocybin mushrooms are found and processed around the world. Within the Amazon tropics can be discovered no fewer than forty hallucinogenic plants regularly used by indigenous peoples, with severe problems rarely encountered. Psychedelic drugs, including LSD, are easily synthesized, packaged, and sold. Dozens of studies, moreover, have shown powerful therapeutic results for such comparatively benign drugs.[10] Mind-expanding substances, when taken intelligently and in moderation, can help people more fully engage their imagination, sense of creativity, and interactive energies. They can facilitate personal catharsis, self-inquiry, and consciousness transformation. In this context Neal Goldsmith refers to the potential for a "revised world view" through judicious use of psychedelics.[11]

Much depends here, as elsewhere, on the general *framework* of drug experiences. Many substances can be used for positive results, whatever their legal, cultural, or ideological status, and most can surely be abused. As for psychedelics, whether a "trip" is good or bad often depends on several variables that are both external and internal, situational and psychological. In the words of one researcher, cited by Weil,

> Conventional forms of psychotherapy often enable people to understand how their habits of thinking about themselves and others produce frustration and pain, but you can spend years in therapy gaining all this insight and keep on being the same frustrated, neurotic person. One good psychedelic session can make you feel what you are doing and show you how to do it differently. In the right hands and settings, these drugs can convince you that the worst problem in your life can be solved by changing your own attitudes and ways of perceiving and can motivate you to make the necessary changes.[12]

What needs to be emphasized here is "in the right hands and settings"—in other words, within a benign or uplifting social context.

It is possible at this juncture to speak of the "phenomenology" of drugs as it relates to the human experience. The great difference between wine-drinking in moderation with meals (common in Mediterranean Europe) and desperate guzzling of alcoholics on skid row should be obvious enough. The same can be

24   CHAPTER I

said of traditional coca-leaf versus modern crack-cocaine consumption, opium poppies versus heroin, painkillers on the battlefield versus a daily OxyContin addiction, pot smoking versus concentrated THC intake, and herbal sleeping aids versus regular or heavy sedative use, possibly mixed with alcohol. The view that particular classes of natural or synthetic drugs are innately destructive or addictive while others are not—the prevailing outlook of the medical-drug complex—does not stand up to close scrutiny. The familiar prohibition ethos substitutes abstract moralizing (drugs are evil) for rational, critical thought informed by an open-minded, empirical search for (both positive and negative) evidence. Within so much contemporary public discourse the topic of drugs is riddled with half-truths, distortions, and myths—nowhere more so than in the corporate media. One much-overlooked reality is that the vast majority of people who consume drugs of even the "hard" variety can live relatively normal lives— or, where problems do surface, manage to contain them over time.[13] (In some cases, of course, chemical substances can help make life more bearable, more satisfying.) Even here, however, those products most frequently abused turn out to be *legal* in status: pharmaceuticals, alcohol, tobacco, and foodstuffs like sugar.

Drugs in America

Although drugs have long been part of the general human experience, nowhere have they been more widely consumed over the past century than in the United States. Chemical substances in their great varieties have found fertile terrain in a society that continues to exhibit a love-hate relationship with any substance labeled "drugs." From the earliest years of national development, Americans have, in fact, had a voracious appetite for drugs—always, however, within a cultural matrix of sharply divided opinions, government prohibitions, media fearmongering, and high levels of addiction. In 2012, more than twenty-four million Americans (9.2 percent of the population) were reported to have used illegal drugs in the preceding year—an increase from 8.3 percent in 2002.[14] A 2008 survey found that Americans were consuming pot, cocaine, and heroin at rates double that of Europeans, with pharmaceutical comparisons showing yet higher levels of US production and sales.[15]

During the late eighteenth and nineteenth centuries Siegel's "fourth drive" no doubt extended to a long list of substances: hemp, tobacco, alcohol, cocaine, opium, morphine, and food products like sugar. Up to the present, repressive government policies (not always seriously enforced) have made little dent in what has become the most flourishing (and lucrative) drug culture ever known.

The early settlers reportedly drank and smoked heavily despite a far-reaching Puritanism. Calls for regulation and temperance coincided with high rates of popular indulgence. Later, drugs became widely acceptable and available within a rapidly industrializing order, likely serving as "therapeutic" antidotes to the mounting hardship, stress, and boredom of urban life. Opium and cocaine, for example, satisfied a common desire for excitement and adventure beyond the dreary routines of modern life. Ordinary drinks like Coca-Cola were laced with such drugs as cocaine and caffeine, while companies such as Merck processed, refined, and marketed the coca leaf. Popular use of marijuana, peyote, and hallucinogenic mushrooms was inherited partly from Indian tribes. Alcohol consumption (and indeed alcoholism) skyrocketed with the steady proliferation of saloons and taverns. Morphine as painkiller came into wide use during the Civil War, with its massive battlefield casualties; by the start of the twentieth century literally hundreds of opiate preparations could be readily purchased at local stores. In the 1890s, the German firm Bayer was marketing not only the everyday painkiller aspirin but various barbiturates and sedatives in the United States as well as Europe.

That a deep Puritanical strain in American life instilled mass feelings of guilt and shame regarding these and other indulgent practices would do little to undermine the popular appetite for drugs; the irrepressible "fourth drive" would remain alive and vibrant. Drugs signified less a phenomenon of "disorder" or "pathology" than of everyday normalcy, as even US presidents (Monroe, Grant, and McKinley to name three) were known for having strong alcohol and tobacco habits. The desire for mood-altering substances, it turns out, was pervasive across most demographic groups. During the nineteenth century even refined sugar was endowed with certain miraculous powers as both medicine and stimulant— beyond its properties as condiment, preservative, and sweetener.[16]

US drug consumption was spurred by the rise of a global drug trade that permitted widening availability of alcohol, tobacco, coffee, opium, cocaine, and sugar, beginning in the late eighteenth century. Drugs of myriad types were becoming highly marketable commodities. Governmental controls were either absent or poorly enforced. The drug trade was vital to the expansion of British imperialism at its peak. In that period drugs (including tobacco, beer, and wine) were overwhelmingly plant-based and most widely cultivated and processed in the Western Hemisphere. Aside from intoxicants, many were used as sources of healing, rejuvenation, or personal therapy. Some types of domestically harvested mushrooms were taken as "liberty caps."[17] Consistent with much progressive thinking, many believed that such new and mysterious chemicals would bestow on humans unprecedented control over their modes of experience and consciousness,

26 CHAPTER 1

including pain and pleasure.[18] Refinements were continuous: nitrous oxide was discovered in the 1770s, morphine was produced from poppies in 1803, caffeine was isolated from coffee beans in 1820, nicotine was refined from tobacco in 1828, poppies yielded codeine in 1832, and coca leaves became the genesis of cocaine in 1860. Many novel and exotic substances were credited with aiding personal creativity in the realms of literature, painting, music, and even philosophy.

It is worth noting that American society was always conflicted between excesses of consumption and a drive toward prohibition, between love of intoxication and its repression, between celebration of legality and coexistence of thriving outlaw cultures. Nowhere has this tense dialectic been more visible than in the realm of drugs. From the very outset, as Peter Andreas writes in *Smuggler Nation*, the United States has been the site of two interrelated but contradictory forces—an influx of contraband goods paralleled by a sprawling law-enforcement system to fight the spread of such goods.[19] More than two centuries after this trajectory was set in motion, the contemporary War on Drugs fits the historical pattern exactly.

Andreas observes, "For better or worse, smuggling was an essential ingredient in the very birth and development of America and its transformation into a global power."[20] Indeed, smuggling hubs were located throughout the early colonies, extending to every kind of trade: alcohol, drugs, finished products, and even slaves. Part of a "hidden history," illicit trade fueled business growth and profits across the economy, with capitalism generating a good deal of its nineteenth-century dynamism from a flourishing subculture of criminality and outlawry. The American frontier became a smuggling haven, involving alcohol, furs, cotton, and imported labor for railroad construction. As would later be the case, formal legality was routinely subverted by the informal reality of everyday behavior, mostly linked to smuggling operations and black markets.[21] With the onset of Prohibition and its supposedly draconian laws and regulations, such outlawry predictably expanded, accelerated by hundreds of smuggling rings making huge profits from rum, whiskey, gin, and beer. Not only alcohol, but drugs, jewelry, watches, and clothing would constitute a large part of the illicit trade.[22] Outlawry, with its huge criminal syndicates, contraband goods, and black markets, continues to shape both the national and global capitalist economies. As prelude to the contemporary drug war, American public discourse was turned toward a moral panic focused on the "vile practices" of an underground capitalism that had long been part of the national legacy.

Despite heightened levels of prohibitionism in the early twentieth century—leading to the Harrison Narcotics Tax Act, the alcohol Prohibition era, and the Marihuana Tax Act—overall forms of drug consumption, legal and illegal, increased across the decades. One factor was that commodification of new chemical substances reached a scope never imagined throughout all previous human experience. Drug-taking for medical and nonmedical purposes evolved into something of an American norm, whether for treatment, excitement, performance enhancement, or mind expansion. In the face of powerful repressive forces, the vast majority of Americans seemed to take the idea of personal rights and freedoms in this area rather seriously, reflecting perhaps on Thomas Jefferson's iconic embrace of "the inalienable right to life, liberty, and the pursuit of happiness" in the Preamble to the US Constitution. Unfortunately, this time-honored ideal would be later sacrificed to new waves of prohibitionist zeal that would culminate in the modern War on Drugs.

The outlawing of alcohol did little to curtail high rates of American drinking even during the 1920s, when saloon life that had been so vilified by the temperance movement simply went underground, where it naturally flourished.[23] Beer, wine, and liquor consumption increased slightly after repeal of the Volstead Act, as did use of tobacco products—until slight declines (especially for cigarettes) were registered by the 1990s. Even then, as US wine production increased dramatically, some alcohol preferences grew in popularity. The Marihuana Tax Act did little to curtail pot use during the 1930s or later, as marijuana use too was driven into outlawry, where it largely remains into the twenty-first century. World War II signaled a profound shift in American drug consumption: morphine, methamphetamines, and antibiotics came into wide use for the first time, especially during combat. Battlefield conditions also encouraged heightened use of antidepressants that, along with tranquilizers, helped fuel rapid growth of the pharmaceutical industry during the 1950s. The drug corporations geared up to vast domestic markets for antidepressants, painkillers, sedatives, and antibiotics—drugs that today underpin much of the still-expanding legal market.

A vigorous underground drug culture has long coexisted with a legal commodity system, continuously adapting to new restrictive laws that come into force. During the 1960s and 1970s, however, sales of a wide spectrum of illegal drugs began to flourish. Youth cultures have often been at the center of drug use for mind-altering purposes, and this period was no exception. Not only marijuana, hashish, and mushrooms but new cycles of domestically produced synthetic drugs (mescaline, psilocybin, LSD) became fashionable on college campuses and among youth. Psychedelics were associated with rock music, social rebellion, new forms of community, and (indirectly) radical politics—a vehicle of critical thought, consciousness transformation, and alternative lifestyles. Writing at that time in *The Making of a Counter Culture*, Theodore Roszak observed, "At the bohemian fringe of our disaffected youth culture, all roads lead to psychedelia. The fascination with hallucinogenic drugs emerges persistently as the common

28 CHAPTER I

denomination of the many protean forms the counterculture has assumed in the post–World War II period."[24] Sixties youth culture was profoundly shaped by an ethos of drug-induced mind alteration, pioneered by such intellectual figures as Aldous Huxley, Alan Watts, Timothy Leary, and some Beat writers, eventually to be celebrated within rock music and social movements of the period. Although use of psychedelics has oscillated in the United States since the 1970s, pot consumption (and for a time, cocaine) later took off and remains firmly embedded in the underground drug scene.

From the vantage point of 2014, it is hardly controversial to note that American society has experienced amounts of drug consumption beyond anything known across human history. The most popular drugs—pharmaceuticals, OTC products, alcohol, tobacco, and food additives—are entirely legal, immune from legal or social sanctions. The biggest (and most profitable) drug commodities in the United States today are manufactured, advertised, and sold by Big Pharma: prescription drug sales in 2012 totaled nearly $400 billion, roughly *eight* times the level of 1990. National spending was expected to surpass $500 billion by 2020.[25] The pharmaceutical giants currently spend a staggering $11 billion yearly on advertising. Americans filled some four billion prescriptions in 2010. The United States easily leads the world in legal drug sales, with Spain a distant second and France an even more distant third. In 2010 nearly 50 percent of all Americans had filled one or more prescriptions; 32 percent filled two or more, while 11 percent filled more than five. Nearly 45 percent of drug users took doctor-prescribed medication to reduce cholesterol levels—double the rate of 1999. Thus in 2010 Pfizer sold $12 billion in Lipitor orders, while AstraZeneca sold $6 billion in Crestor pills, both for high cholesterol readings.[26] Today Big Pharma markets sophisticated chemical substances for a nearly limitless assortment of conditions: pain, sleep disorders, depression, sexual dysfunction, heart problems, chronic infections, and allergies, to name some. According to Sidney Wolfe and associates in *Worst Pills, Best Pills*, at least 180 of the 549 most commonly prescribed drugs are known to have potentially severe adverse reactions, especially when taken in combination.[27] Meanwhile, OTC retail drug sales have soared over the past few decades, from $1.9 billion in 1964 to $17.4 billion in 2011. Today there are no fewer than 700 OTC drugs available that needed prescriptions thirty years ago.[28] Pharmaceuticals now constitute a leading sector of the US economy.

As for the vast range of other legal—but generally nonmedical—drugs readily obtainable in the United States, the most profitable are alcohol and tobacco, and they too occupy a dynamic place in the corporate economy. In 2010 the American public spent $60 billion on beer, wine, and liquor, with beer the most preferred and most vigorously marketed. Per capita beer intake reached 470 pints yearly by 2010. Nearly 70 percent of Americans presently drink alcohol, including 80 percent of college graduates. Alcoholic beverages are advertised across the media landscape, most visibly surrounding sports events, at a cost of nearly $3 billion annually. While drinking-related problems and accidents are known to cost tens of thousands of lives and roughly $225 billion yearly in health problems,[29] there are no signs of a falloff in consumption: in 2012 there were an estimated 135 million regular drinkers in the United States (51.5 percent of the adult population).[30]

Like alcohol, tobacco has a long history in American society, going back to the early years when plantations were yielding large and excellent crops, some for export. The smoking of cigarettes, cigars, and kindred substances was always popular, until recent declines owing to health fears, heavy taxes, educational campaigns, and public restrictions on advertising. Tobacco cultivation in the United States expanded from 300 million pounds in 1860 to 1 billion pounds in 1909 to more than 2 billion pounds in the 1940s. By 2010, however, just 20 percent of Americans smoked (forty-five million), down significantly from 42 percent in 1966. Even so, the tobacco industry currently sells $89 billion in products, with advertising expenditures of $13 billion yearly; a sharp decline in domestic consumption has been overcome by increasing foreign sales. Cigarette use has dropped to 1,200 cigarettes per capita annually in the United States, compared to 1,700 in South Korea and 2,200 in Spain. According to the CDC, annual US cigarette smoking has decreased from 435 billion cigarettes in 2000 to 292 billion in 2011, a sharp reduction of 32 percent.[31] The FDA has managed to regulate but has so far failed to ban tobacco advertising entirely.

Despite its long-standing governmental crusade against "drugs," the United States still has the highest rate (per capita and absolute) of illegal drug use in the world. Though figures are understandably sketchy, in 2010 the aggregate level reached an estimated 9 percent over 2009, even as use of drugs like metham- phetamine and cocaine was falling. A 2008 World Health Organization survey found that 16.2 percent of Americans had used cocaine the previous year—more than three times the rate of any other country. A March 2014 Rand Corporation report found that cocaine use had been cut in half from 2006 to 2010.[32] As for marijuana, the United States easily led all nations: consumption levels stood at 42.4 percent, compared with 19.8 percent for more liberal Holland and 17.5 percent for Germany. The widening availability of medical pot in many states has led to a spike in cannabis use at a time when total marijuana sales in the United States were roughly estimated (in 2013) to reach at least $45 billion.[33] Pot alone had become a leading cash crop in California while underground sales of other illegal drugs were steadily declining.[34]

30   CHAPTER I

Taking into account all types of medical and nonmedical, legal and illegal, natural and synthetic drugs sold in the United States—including many foodstuffs and additives—American society has risen to unchallenged world champion of drug production, sales, and consumption. The drug market is so thriving and profitable, with no reversal likely, that it now constitutes both a dynamic economic sector and a deeply embedded reality of contemporary social life.

From Prohibition to Warfare

Drugs in US history always had a dual and conflicted reality, with vast consumption of hundreds of medical and intoxicating products coexisting with official vilification, bans, and repression of items defined as innately menacing or addictive. Nowhere has the global drug trade established more fertile terrain, yet nowhere has it been met with stronger fear, hostility, and sheer mendacity. The governmental drive to criminalize some types of drugs while allowing others to be sold within established markets characterizes more than a century of American experience. The recurrent waging of aggressive and costly antidrug crusades has, in the end, been entirely futile—and indeed counterproductive.

Conservative forces have long tried to impose repressive policies on a society historically saturated with drugs of every variety. A deep Puritanical strain has surely empowered the moral enforcers—those prepared to use state power to dictate lifestyles, social policies, and laws consistent with their own narrow prejudices and interests. The nineteenth-century temperance movement, prelude to the 1920 Volstead Act outlawing alcohol, was largely driven by antagonism to a working-class saloon culture that was deemed to embellish all kinds of sinful behavior: laziness, drunkenness, violence, wasteful spending, sexual promiscuity—all supposedly egregious transgressions against the work ethic and the nuclear family. The outlawing of alcoholic beverages would be a crucial step toward exorcising the demons of that debauched lifestyle, which had been subverting cherished American traditions.[35]

Although the moral crusaders viewed other drugs as menacing—witness passage of the Opium Exclusion Act of 1909 and the Harrison Narcotics Tax Act of 1914—it was booze that presented the gravest danger to "civilized life"—that is, to traditional social relations and values. As would later be the case with marijuana, narcotics, and psychedelics, alcohol was blamed for a multitude of health problems, home breakups, crime, poverty, and general antisocial behavior. Movements like the Anti-Saloon League (ASL) and Woman's Christian Temperance Union (WCTU) waged holy crusades heavily dependent on fearmongering, myths, and hysteria. Aside from its Puritanical moralism and political authoritarianism, the prohibition agenda was fueled by racist hostility to immigrant groups that frequented the saloons, middle-class contempt for proletarian lifestyles that pervaded the drinking establishments, and small-town rejection of urban culture—the major thrust behind prohibition coming from the South and Midwest. A xenophobic hatred of Germans during and after World War I—the Germans controlled much of the beer industry—also influenced passage of the Volstead Act.[36]

The problem was that drinking alcohol—and the multitude of rituals, lifestyles, and celebrations associated with it—had been thoroughly and ineradicably American, part of a culture that in fact extended beyond the world of immigrants, workers, and men. Authoritarian designs to jettison behavior that was so much a part of everyday life, whatever the (often indirect) links of that behavior to social problems, were sure to fail, especially in a society so wedded to individualism. As the ASL and kindred organizations claimed to be working tirelessly to bring clean thinking and right living to the American public, the everyday reality of Prohibition would confound every one of the crusaders' hopes and promises. For one thing, repression never had the desired result of abolishing or even curbing US alcohol consumption. Underground bootlegging and saloon operations immediately took off after introduction of the Volstead Act: speakeasies proliferated in American cities while distilleries, breweries, and smuggling activities flourished across the country. Mike Gray notes in *Drug Crazy* that "by erecting an artificial barrier between alcohol producers and consumers, the government had created a bonanza that can only be likened to the Gold Rush."[37]

The sordid history of Prohibition is by now too well known to require much further elaboration, beyond stressing its uniquely explosive confluence of antiurbanism, moralism, racism, and authoritarianism that, to varying degrees, would ideologically shape later US antidrug crusades. Worth adding here is that the Volstead Act didn't merely falter on its own terms, but soon produced a culture of outlawry, violence, corruption, and hypocrisy that would remain fully part of the national experience with intoxicating drugs well after Prohibition was repealed in 1933.

While justified as a great benefit to the social and personal health of Americans, Prohibition was more energetically fueled by broad cultural struggles against the evils of indulgence. Indeed the temperance movement erected its political dynamism on old-fashioned Protestant reformist zeal; it was overwhelmingly religious, even messianic, embracing holy combat against lower-class rabble unable to control its insatiable appetite for booze—and of course God was squarely on the side of the crusaders.[38] The Volstead Act was an outgrowth of concerns among

32 Chapter 1

"real Americans" identified overwhelmingly as small-town, white, middle-class Protestants. As Prohibition forced the alcohol trade underground, however, what emerged was a parallel business empire, a flourishing alternative capitalism that survived all the sermons, policies, raids, and arrests that followed the Twenty-First Amendment. Once the popular demand for alcoholic beverages remained at high aggregate levels, there would be no turning back, no extirpation of the intoxicating "fourth drive" associated here with neighborhood gatherings, music, dancing, and daily conviviality in a society riddled with social conflicts, material hardships, and personal alienation. It is often forgotten that the Jazz Age achieved its popular breakthrough precisely during the supposedly booze-free 1920s.

Despite its obvious excesses, saloon life resonated with large sectors of the American public at a time when urban, industrial life was pervaded by workplace stresses, poverty, family breakdowns, and increasing social powerlessness. Alcohol, whether imbibed at the saloons or at home, clearly satisfied a good many psychological needs—one reason state efforts to outlaw drink could not be systematically enforced. That alcohol might be linked, rightly or wrongly, to "sexual promiscuity" probably made saloon life even more appealing for the vast majority of men.

If the apostles of Prohibition claimed the mantle of freedom, good health, family values, and religion, the real consequences of the Volstead Act would be altogether different, including a harsh authoritarianism rooted in attempts to use state power to regulate personal behavior. This motif is graphically laid out in Ken Burns's three-part documentary *Prohibition*. The impetus toward government regulation of mostly self-directed personal choice is endemic to prohibitionist ideology, central to the work of the ASL and WCTU. The goal of monitoring, raiding, apprehending, and jailing buyers and sellers of "contraband" substances was then, as later, intrinsically coercive and counterproductive. While claiming to be defenders of Constitutional rights and liberties, the moral guardians and drug warriors of the period had, in actuality, little respect for those rights and liberties. The Fourth Amendment ensuring immunity from "unreasonable searches and seizures"? Null and void. The Preamble to the Constitution, which states that all human beings are endowed with "inalienable rights of life, liberty, and pursuit of happiness"? Scarcely relevant when it came to confronting the mortal threat of demon rum.

An expansive regimen of social and political controls might have been justified on strictly economic grounds—at least in terms of resources saved from reduced healthcare costs, better work performance, and reclaimed lives. But Prohibition, then as later, would in fact produce just the opposite results. The negative impact of alcohol on personal health was greatly exaggerated or, in any event, difficult to ascertain, as reliable data were then flimsy or nonexistent. One problem, of course, was that American drinking habits lapsed slightly if at all in the context of the new laws. As alcohol went underground, thriving black markets virtually ensured that beer, wine, and spirits would be available in the absence of taxes, tariffs, and antitrust laws, meaning the cost to consumers would be lower while the public sector was deprived of potential large revenues.[39] Meanwhile, requirements of law enforcement, courts, and prisons ultimately imposed *greater* costs and pressures on all levels of government. Local trafficking syndicates and smugglers had no need to advertise products and thus no impetus to pass additional costs on to consumers as competition between rival crime organizations gave rise to urban turf rivalry and outlawry that in turn fed into the upward spiral of Prohibition costs.[40]

The Volstead Act did nothing so much as drastically weaken public respect for legality; a milieu of criminality, including government and police corruption, was the predictable result. Further, tens of billions of dollars in wealth would be transferred to an outlaw subculture able to perpetuate its profit-making within an expanding black market. It was not alcoholic beverages as such that generated the outlawry, but rather government efforts to ban a substance nearly as old as human civilization itself—and long a staple of American social life.

With alcohol legalized in 1933 once the myriad failures of Prohibition became too extreme to ignore, ideological crusaders soon took up warfare against a different category of sinful indulgence—"drugs," or at least those chemical substances deemed uniquely harmful or evil. In this context marijuana became the first, and no doubt the easiest, target. In 1937, following an aggressive campaign against the horrors of "narcotics," Congress passed the Marihuana Tax Act, allowing the federal government to police cannabis and setting in motion future decades of warfare against "demon weed," although pot was actually one of the most benign of commonly used drugs. Even during the relatively drug-free 1930s, government officials, politicians, and the media launched a fear-based campaign against pot, led by Harry Anslinger, who would serve as director of the Federal Bureau of Narcotics from 1930 to 1962. Anslinger and his lieutenants warned of a scourge of violent crimes and family crises resulting from an imminent "reefer epidemic."[41] Building on the Harrison Narcotics Tax Act, Washington politicians moved to stiffen drug controls far beyond the law's initial taxing and regulation initiatives.

From the 1930s to the present, as the political attention to alcohol and tobacco waned, federal mobilization against drugs (meaning narcotics and cannabis) picked up steam as a bipartisan agenda: policies, laws, social stigmas, and popular attitudes steadily hardened over time, eventually culminating in the modern-day War on Drugs. Racial fears and ethnic hostilities played a crucial role, along

34 CHAPTER 1

with revived efforts—always relying on state power—to protect the interests of *legal* sellers of alcohol, tobacco, and pharmaceuticals. The antidrug mania in the United States would over time give rise to the largest prison-industrial complex in the world, incarcerating more than two million people (roughly one-third as nonviolent drug offenders). As with Prohibition, this costly and repressive government agenda turned out to be entirely worthless on its own terms. Jeffrey Miron notes, "There is little evidence that enforcement under current drug prohibition has raised drug prices or decreased drug consumption to a substantial degree."[42] Every postwar US president has lent supreme authority to this disaster, always in the name of fighting the scourge of "drugs." Unfortunately, genuine political debate over this ill-fated agenda—over policies shared equally by Democrats and Republicans—has been woefully absent up to the present.

The tradition of a "smuggler nation" trading in endless varieties of "illicit" products continues into the present, now in a more globalized form that involves lucrative markets in both legal and illegal drugs. Moisés Naim, for example, calls attention to the dark side of globalization, marked by widespread trade in banned goods, counterfeit products, laundered money, guns, and, of course, all varieties of chemical substances. In his book *Illicit*, Naim writes that as much as 10 percent of all global trade falls on the underground side of capitalism, commerce "that breaks the rules—the laws, regulations, licenses, taxes, embargos, and all the procedures that nations employ to organize commerce, protect their citizens, raise revenues, and enforce moral codes."[43] In a word, such global trade today—in which the United States is a major player—has developed a close, symbiotic relationship with legitimate capitalism. Moreover, the Internet has provided space for even more ambitious, far-reaching illicit business, with its vast collection of websites, databases, and marketing centers for every conceivable product. This "deep Web" has provided a haven for vast numbers of thieves, counterfeiters, smugglers, and traffickers.[44]

The great crusade against *some* types of drugs has done severe damage to American society—politically, economically, and culturally. Now fully 100 years in the making, the War on Drugs represents an assault on individual freedom, civil rights, and, in the deepest sense, political democracy. It remains, as always, based on a syndrome of myths perpetrated by government agencies and a compliant media. The vision of a "drug-free America" remains official dogma, while pot use, widespread as ever, has no reported lethal effects and yearly deaths from alcohol (180,000), tobacco (450,000), and pharmaceuticals (150,000)—all perfectly legal—leave their horrific imprint.[45] The question here is surely not whether illegal drugs (or indeed *any* drugs) are frequently misused and harmful, but whether long-standing federal policy makes rational sense.

The Great Moral Panic

The watershed Marihuana Tax Act was ushered into law amidst mounting public frenzy over the ominous American "drug" threat. In the absence of open, rational discourse, fearmongering and ignorance ruled the day—an ideological dynamic that would forever shape political debate (or lack thereof) over drug policy. Such rigidity and intolerance fueled widespread celebration of the crude film *Reefer Madness*, an impressive tribute to media propaganda associating drugs with racial and political outsiders. Despite the lack of reliable evidence that pot was especially harmful, the Marihuana Tax Act was driven by spurious claims that the drug led to violence, sexual abandon, social deviance, and every manner of criminal behavior. During the 1930s and later years the federal antidrug program was deemed a "mission from God" to rid American society of evil intoxicating substances.

Several decades of futility did nothing to blunt later continuation of the same drug-warfare narratives, policies, and laws. In launching his recycled variant of the drug war, President Nixon announced that the struggle for zero tolerance was nothing short of a moral imperative. The War on Drugs was framed as an *ideological* battle against both internal (criminal) and external (subversive) enemies of the social order. For Nixon this war—likened by some to a mighty campaign against vampires—was for the very survival of American society, if not Western civilization.[46] In the tracks of Anslinger, the "drug" scourge was blamed for every conceivable social problem, with health concerns actually far down the list. A few decades later, in November 2011, presidential candidate Newt Gingrich could say, "I think the California experience is that medical marijuana . . . becomes a joke. We need to do more drug testing in the U.S. We need a draconian method like Singapore. They kill people for having pot."[47] That comment echoes the statement of former Los Angeles Police Department chief Daryl Gates, who announced in the late 1980s that "all drug users should be taken out and shot"—a comment lacking any traces of humor or irony.

The federal government, in tight partnership with corporations and supported by a faithful media, has in different ways carried forward its campaign against "illicit" drugs since World War II, a goal embraced across the political spectrum. An extremely costly and authoritarian legacy, it has contributed mightily to the rise of a surveillance state, expanded police operations, and a prison apparatus that today confines hundreds of thousands of drug offenders. "Drugs"—and their producers, sellers, and users—have been stigmatized as evil incarnate, responsible for all manifestations of crime, deviance, addiction, mental disorders, and family problems, possessing supernatural, even demonic powers over

36 CHAPTER I

those weak enough to be seduced. Meanwhile, as the War on Drugs was being vigorously expanded and globalized, the media was increasingly saturated with pharmaceutical ads hawking pills for every imaginable problem: depression, heart conditions, obesity, sexual dysfunction, pain, arthritis, many others. The ubiquitous character of drug advertising—across TV, radio, the Internet, newspapers, and magazines—coincides with the familiar American proclivity for solving big challenges with quick fixes.

American public discourse appears uniquely monolithic when it comes to the topic of illegal drugs: alternative viewpoints, if not altogether ruled out, are ridiculed as crazy, a return to sixties counterculture immaturity. The political culture has always had a certain fondness for the warfare ethos, obsessed with the task of finding and vanquishing diabolical enemies. US exceptionalism rests on the noble mission to defeat all challengers to national power. Political agendas—whether domestic or global—easily morph into ideological crusades to make the world safe for "American ideals," with freedom and democracy, of course, always at the forefront. For more than two centuries, in fact, the United States has been a nation perpetually at war, its population mobilized through a psychological matrix of fear, paranoia, and hostility to outsiders. The War on Drugs can be located squarely within this historical trajectory. A deepening culture of fear helps illuminate the special American preoccupation with "drugs."[48]

Like such threats as terrorism and communism before it, the "drug menace" has come to signify not merely a health or social threat but a more ominous—indeed, ideological—challenge to the social order. This, at least, is how the architect of modern drug warfare, President Nixon (and later occupants of the White House) viewed a select group of intoxicating substances. As contraband goods, illegal drugs were historically associated with foreign threats, "aliens," subversives, cultural deviants, Asians, Mexicans, hippies, political radicals, and blacks. Such xenophobic and racist attitudes are critical to understanding American politics in the realm of drug policy, as in other realms. Here Ziauddin Sardar and Merryl Wyn Davies write, "Without fear there is no America; constant recourse to fear is a motivating force that determines its [the United States'] actions and reactions."[49]

What is true for politics extends to popular culture. Sardar and Davies comment, "Fear looms as a reality within the narrative history, myth, and legends of America."[50] The early white-settler attitude of fear and hostility toward Indians would be replayed again and again, in both politics and culture—toward Asians and fascists in military combat, communists during the Cold War, a long list of subversives in the sixties, and finally terrorists, drug traffickers, gangs, and cartels in the past few decades. As in history and politics, it follows that "fear is the common currency of the American media."[51] This very motif would be recycled endlessly in Hollywood film genres, from Westerns to combat movies to a wide assortment of sci-fi, horror, and action/adventure films—all depicting the saga of noble and enlightened protagonists doing epic battle against unspeakable savagery. As with most evil threats, the danger is viewed as imminent and ubiquitous—a drug "epidemic" in the making. Consistent with the US warfare legacy, massive state power is needed to restore a moral order under siege by enemies that, for the War on Drugs, include an ensemble of pushers, cartel operatives, and gangsters. War consciousness is driven by images of a virtuous nation struggling valiantly to rid itself of cancerous agents, a remarkably easy selling point for the American public. If drugs are a mortal threat to established rules and norms, their very popularity gives rise to moral panic; they are considered a threat to social order, institutional stability, and perhaps even global power. Here marijuana seems to have reached the pantheon of extremely dangerous substances, despite its rather benign chemical properties. Pot fits into the culture of fear for reasons having nothing to do with scientific evidence, popular revulsion, or public harm.

The necessary media contribution to spreading moral panic around the great drug menace cannot be overstated. Neal Gabler refers to a certain lawlike behavior of the corporate media, according to which "it is more acceptable to fail in conventional ways than in unconventional ways," meaning "you can screw up with impunity so long as you screw up like everybody else." Or, put differently, "there is safety in numbers even if there isn't necessarily wisdom." Gabler adds, "Even when you are wrong, you have the defense of working within the consensus. When you are wrong outside the consensus, you have no defense. You are on your own."[52] Gabler writes here mainly about film and TV programming, though he suggests that "lawlike" conformity of this sort extends equally to the political terrain. Thus government and media opinion leaders repeat the same fictions and platitudes about the War on Drugs, year after year, seemingly oblivious to the irrational and wasteful policies that are disastrous for most sectors of American society. The antidrug warriors have found abundant safety in a solid ideological consensus.

Although public fear of the drug menace has been orchestrated for nearly a century, the degree of moral panic has naturally oscillated, depending on targets of the moment—marijuana from the 1930s to the 1950s, hallucinogens during the 1960s and 1970s, cocaine in the 1980s and 1990s, methamphetamines later, and pot once again. Narcotics in their many variants, especially heroin, have long brought special fears, rivaling even communism and terrorism. Both the "dope fiend" and "pusher," forerunners of the contemporary "trafficker" or "cartel

38   Chapter 1

kingpin," have presented larger-than-life villains in popular culture, notably in TV and movies. Scare tactics could always help mobilize resources, especially where victimized children could be the focus of attention. TV could always be relied on to dramatize the combustible mixture of drugs, crime, and inner-city life.

As for mainstream print journalism, just a few examples across the decades should be enough to capture the broad thrust of American antidrug propaganda. In 1938 (one year after passage of the Marihuana Tax Act), *Reader's Digest* featured an article titled "Marijuana: Assassin of Youth"; in 1951 *Time* magazine focused on "Narcotic Addiction among Teenagers" while *Life* turned to "Children in Peril"; in 1958 *Ladies' Home Journal* explored "Our Teenage Drug Addicts"; in 1967 the *New York Times* magazine dramatized "Children on Drugs"; in 1969 *Life* returned to the ever-fashionable "Drug Plague among Kids"; in 1970 *Time* revisited the "Addiction Epidemic among Kids"; in 1973 *Good Housekeeping* asked, "Should We Turn Our Son In?"; in 1985 *U.S. News & World Report* warned, "Teen Drug Use—The News Is Bad"; in 1987 *Reader's Digest* reported "We're Teaching Our Kids to Use Drugs"; in 1992 *McCall's* scrutinized "The New Teenage Drug Danger—Human Growth Hormone"; in 1995 *McCall's* updated the threat to "Drugs in the 1990s: Is Your Child Safe?"; in 1996 *Time* returned to the familiar theme "Kids and Pot" and *U.S. News & World Report* alerted readers that "They're Toking Up in Algebra Class." Hundreds of other examples could be added to this list, continuing into the present. A recent Drug-Free Partnership advertisement warned that "Marijuana is Robbing Youth of IQ, Memory, and Possibly Mental Health."

In the 1980s, as the Reagan era took hold, moral panic fixated on cocaine, with special attention devoted to its "crack" form said (with some exaggeration) to be the preferred drug of inner-city youth. It was "crack" that, in 1986, *Newsweek* announced was taking over American cities, turning its many victims into zombies. Warfare ideology was invoked to frame coke as some kind of modern "plague," its addictive properties so awesome as to be all-consuming, irresistible. The fact that little evidence was put forth to demonstrate the existence of a "plague," aside from a few anecdotal stories, did not deter media outlets from constant scaremongering about wasted youth, "crack babies," demonic pushers, and new crime waves. Most of these accounts were based largely on personal narratives exaggerating the harm from coca products that, in most cases, are relatively benign. These were the years of Nancy Reagan's silly "Just Say No" campaign, eagerly taken up by the opinion makers and news managers. It was none other than President Reagan who, referring to the crack menace, said in 1986, "This epidemic has our children's names written all over it." Drug-horror narratives filled the media, replete with graphic images of violent crime, medical

DRUGS 39

crises, personal breakdowns, and new threats to family life.[53] While the media dutifully took its cue from the DEA and Office of National Drug Control Policy, an accumulation of antidrug messages helped deflect public attention from more pressing social challenges than illegal drugs.

During the 1990s and into the early twenty-first century, moral panic shifted toward methamphetamine, notably crystal meth, which *Newsweek* in 2005 labeled "America's Most Dangerous Drug." The problem of meth (or speed), despite widespread use in the United States going back a century or more, was now reported to be on steep incline, with meth labs proliferating in every town and city—most of them manufacturing crystal meth. TV was saturated with reports of out-of-control "meth freaks" and their emaciated bodies, rotting teeth, broken families, and lost jobs. Here the drug warriors merely substituted meth for coke as the new focus of hysteria, obsessed with a substance reputed to transform its users into frozen corpses. Crystal meth was the very incarnation of evil, so powerful that anyone under its spell would end up an addict-monster. Media preoccupation with the "menace of crystal meth," with its small kernel of truth, ultimately relied more on scare propaganda than actual evidence.

A major ideological conduit of the drug war has been the well-funded Partnership for a Drug-Free America, founded in 1985 and recently renamed Partnership at DrugFree.org. As with so much warrior discourse, the organization overwhelmingly dramatizes teenagers' drug abuse, which it links to a multitude of social problems—crime, poor schoolwork, family conflict, health issues, and personal accidents. Illegal drugs, the organization ritually intones, are inescapably addictive and harmful, leading the user to a descent into hell. Known primarily for its TV and radio ads promising unspeakable horrors to pot smokers, as of 2012 the group had run more than 11,000 commercials during its quarter century of work, mostly directed at inner-city youth and parents. The ads feature nightmarish stories associated with illicit drugs: fatal car accidents, violent outbursts, kids turning into little savages. One of Partnership's more enduring ad campaigns, "This Is Your Brain on Drugs," compares an individual's brain to an egg and shows how using illegal drugs is purportedly tantamount to frying the egg. The group has effectively mounted single-brand advertising campaigns financed by such pharmaceutical companies as Pfizer and Johnson & Johnson and, until 1997, big tobacco and alcohol interests. The DrugFree.org website attracted more than one million visitors monthly throughout 2012.[54] While somewhat deemphasizing its crude antimarijuana ads of recent years, the organization has never retreated from the tired myth of "demon weed."

Drug-related motifs have long pervaded Hollywood cinema, though relatively few popular feature movies have ever dealt systematically or directly with the

40   CHAPTER I

War on Drugs. The narrative thrust is generally that "drugs," understood by definition as banned intoxicating substances, are the source of all evil. One staple of music biopics, for example, is the steep, inexorable downward trajectory of drug-addicted performers, as in *Lady Sings the Blues* (1972), *Bird* (1988), *Round Midnight* (1986), *The Doors* (1991), and *Walk the Line* (2005). None of these personal stories has enjoyed very happy endings.

Many Hollywood films across the decades have dwelled on images and narratives of self-destructive drug use by the protagonists, typically inhabited by the same demons. First, drug use inevitably produces disabling if not fatal addictions, especially where heroin is involved. The habit is extreme, all-consuming, and debilitating to the extent that it takes over an individual's entire life: Jim Morrison in *The Doors*, Charlie Parker in *Bird*, Edie Sedgwick in *Factory Girl* (2006), the two doomed characters of *The Panic in Needle Park* (1971), the daughter of a leading drug fighter in *Traffic* (2000), a tormented heroin addict in *The Man with the Golden Arm* (1955). For these and other victims of such dystopic cinema, drugs loom larger than life, permitting no exit from escalating nightmares. A second, related story line depicts these same characters as completely trapped in a personal/social morass that engulfs everything—family, relationships, work, health, mental stability. In *Sid and Nancy* (1986), for example, the only exit for the two drug-addled main protagonists is tragic self-destruction. A similar fate lies in store for the junkie couple at the center of *Candy* (2006), Sedgwick in *Factory Girl*, Morrison in *The Doors*, Parker in *Bird*, and the kids in *Needle Park*. These movies dwell on the nexus linking drugs, violence, and destruction—an inescapable merger—with nothing left to retrieve. Addiction winds up so overpowering that no mortal being can evade its clutches.

A third Hollywood motif revolves around the grotesquely evil world of pushers, dealers, and traffickers, who in movie scenes predictably receive their due punishment, often death. In *The Man with the Golden Arm*, a sleazy-looking pusher approaches the reformed addict on his release from prison, presenting a diabolical temptation. The big-time dealers in *Rush* (1991) and *Blow* (2001) will stop at nothing, including murder, to perpetuate their barbaric (but extremely lucrative) trade. Even bigger-time traffickers working for Mexican cartels, as in *Savages* (2012), are portrayed as scum-of-the-earth characters ready to torture, to kill, and even to turn against their friends, family, and fellow criminals when it serves their barbaric designs. In such films as *Traffic*, *Blow*, *Savages*, and *Drug Wars: The Camarena Story* (1990), we encounter overwhelmingly foreign, dark-skinned traffickers as monsters who devalue human life in their endless pursuit of riches. The ruthless power of such villainous forces enables the global drug trade to perpetuate its horrifying agenda. There is naturally just enough truth to such crude story lines to endow this sort of antidrug propaganda with an element of credibility.

The descent into personal (or collective) darkness that so prominently figures in Hollywood drug tales often reflects a Hobbesian milieu of chaos and fear, with characters facing a life-world devoid of stable rules, norms, and social relations—in some ways akin to existence on the military battlefield. Human purpose and identity evaporate in a setting where social and political institutions are corrupted beyond repair. Such are the mainstream depictions of "drug culture," dramatized wherever intoxicating drugs come into play. In such a world the drug trade contaminates, dehumanizes, and ultimately obliterates everything it touches. As in Hollywood's film noir tradition, a wide assortment of politicians, government officials, police, even ordinary people—not to mention some counterdrug agents—end up seduced by the sinful and ruinous attraction of illegal drugs. Of course, uncorrupted agents do manage to survive all the mayhem and carnage, as in such films as *Traffic* and *Blow*, but they mostly do so as lonely and embattled outposts in the drug war, where the uphill battle can often seem hopeless.

In *Savages* we encounter a dystopic, Hobbesian world of endless sadistic drug-related violence located in Mexico, where the cartels naturally perpetuate a culture of bloodthirsty nihilism in which everyday killing becomes simply "part of the trade." Here it is possible for even a woman (Salma Hayek) to be placed in charge of the brutal Baja Cartel, its barbarism recognizing no limits to a capacity for torture and murder. After all, as the movie emphasizes, "savages don't make deals," nor do they shrink from an ethos of ruthless, sometimes pleasurable killing. Here again the nexus of drugs, violence, and dark foreigners is strongly established, even at the hands of a progressive filmmaker like Oliver Stone. Other popular Hollywood fare, including such recent teen-centered movies as *Spring Breakers* (2012) and *The Bling Ring* (2013), builds narratives around the fashionable linkage of youthful hedonism, drugs, and crime. In contrast to pictures like *Savages*, *Traffic*, and *Blow*, however, the drug experience here is rather peripheral to the central narratives.

Some Hollywood films, including *Easy Rider* (1969), Cheech and Chong's *Up in Smoke* (1978), and, more recently, *This Is the End* (2013)—tributes to the sixties counterculture—do furnish a more even-handed look at the drug experience, but such examples stand out as aberrations that, in any event, usually limit the positive vibes to marijuana. Meanwhile, present-day US film-industry ratings dictate that movies depicting drug-oriented scenes must be R-rated, although this category is rather meaningless since these movies can easily be viewed by general audiences in neighborhood theaters and through video distribution.

42 CHAPTER I

Today as before, the crucial question for Hollywood—ever fearful of being "soft on drugs"—is not whether but precisely *how* drug use is to be framed in movie scenes. The essentially *unwritten* code, as we have seen, is that movie story lines should frame drugs in the horrific context of *abuse* or *addiction* that, in some way, coincides with personal nightmares and social disasters, always resonant with the antidrug crusade.

A few widely viewed documentaries, however, have subjected the drug war to critical scrutiny, including the aforementioned *The House I Live In*, which addresses mainly how the warrior crusade targets poor and minority groups as it sharply increases the already-swollen prison complex. Still, few films—feature or documentary—have been so bold as to take on Big Pharma or the truly frightening scourge of legal drugs. One recent exception is *Side Effects* (2013), in which a lurid tale of sex, illness, crime, and greed is hitched to the world not of street drugs but of prescribed meds—a powerful satire targeting corporate larceny and the mental-health profession. The female protagonist, depressed and apparently suicidal, is given the latest in sophisticated antidepression drugs by a therapist in partnership with Big Pharma. One of the problematic "side effects" of this powerful new drug, it turns out, is lucid sleepwalking combined with homicidal impulses, played out when the woman kills her husband. Much of the film revolves around whether the wife, whose severe personal challenges are aggravated by meds, ought to be held legally responsible for murder at a time when she is coping with adverse reactions from the prescribed antidepressant. Advertised as a "psychological thriller," *Side Effects* represents one of the few (perhaps the *only*) cinematic excursions into the dark world of pharmaceuticals—that is, the most ubiquitous and harmful drug culture on the planet.

Beneath a veneer of political normalcy, legality, and celebration of personal freedoms, American political culture today has come to represent something rather different—the steady growth of corporate, state, military, and law-enforcement power, disturbing signposts of an authoritarian system in which the drug war occupies a prominent role.[55] American politics is riddled with moneyed interests, in the form of wealthy donors, political action committees, well-funded lobbies, hidden business largesse, and, of course, the routine influence of corporate media. Here the boundary separating government from corporate power has indeed become invisible, just as C. Wright Mills anticipated many decades ago.[56] The present conjuncture is one of a deeply institutionalized state-capitalist order in which citizen participation and governmental accountability—indeed the entire public sphere—are being continuously diminished, corrupted, and emptied of democratic content.

Chapter 2
An American Crusade

The contemporary incarnation of the War on Drugs, launched by President Nixon in 1971, ranks among the most myopic and destructive federal policies in American history. With hundreds of billions of dollars wasted pursuing an ill-fated, mythological "drug-free" society, the crusade has given rise to authoritarian politics, a bloated prison system, draconian laws, heightened surveillance, widespread personal and social misery, and a public discourse riddled with deceit, fearmongering, and hypocrisy. Between 1990 and 2010, roughly six million Americans were arrested on marijuana charges alone, nearly 90 percent for simple possession of what is known to be a relatively harmless substance. After decades of costly warfare, most forms of drug use—legal and illegal—have steadily increased in the United States, placing the country easily at the top of world consumption, with all its resulting problems of abuse and addiction.

This variant of American "warfare" can be traced back at least a century, to earlier political initiatives culminating in the 1914 Harrison Narcotics Tax Act and subsequent measures like the 1937 Marihuana Tax Act.[1] Full-scale prohibition agendas, then as later, were never actually evidence-based, motivated as they were by other concerns: moral hostility to "evil" intoxicants; defense of large business interests; xenophobic hostility to foreigners, immigrants, and "aliens"; and the struggle to combat social deviance. Overtly stated concerns about health risks and public harm associated with *certain* drugs were always secondary to these other priorities. Something of a Holy War throughout its tortured and ill-fated history, by the 1990s the antidrug crusade had finally turned back on itself,

43

44 CHAPTER 2

devouring its own pretenses and feeding into the general descent of American society, including the corruption of its governmental institutions.[2]

Prohibitionist ideology has long targeted racial and foreign groups—Asians, Mexicans, blacks, South Americans—who, as frequent "offenders," are the most regularly (and easily) demonized and subjected to legal sanctions. As a general phenomenon, the US warfare legacy depends on a regimen of punishment, surveillance, and incarceration—the source of an expanding American prison complex that consumes tens of billions of dollars yearly in state and federal revenues. Civil liberties are routinely and arrogantly subverted while antidrug operations bring more surveillance and wiretapping, random arrests, undercover operations, crop destructions, and property seizures that, in most cases, wind up entirely out of proportion to the offenses in question. As the crusade forces certain kinds of drug trade underground, the inevitable black market nourishes a thriving criminal subculture of gangs, cartels, and small-time traffickers immersed in a life of corruption, outlawry, and violence. The same criminal violence that antidrug crusaders claim is endemic to the "drug culture" is in reality an outgrowth of their own intolerance, dogmatism, and prohibitionism. Since Americans are the most voracious consumers of both legal and illegal drugs globally, not only does the vision of "zero tolerance" or a "drug-free society" seem illusory; it also clashes directly with such ostensibly cherished American values as popular sovereignty, individual rights, and political democracy. A central motif of this book is that the War on Drugs has always been intrinsically repressive and authoritarian—nothing less than an assault on democracy—leaving aside questions of its efficacy.

Dystopic repercussions of antidrug warfare are by now common knowledge: deflection of public attention from more urgent social problems, growth of police and surveillance functions, deepening political corruption, shrinking public discourse, waste of material resources, cost in ruined lives, strengthening of Big Pharma and kindred corporate interests, and sharpening of international conflicts. Rational, empirically grounded debates over government drug policy remain largely taboo, as "drugs" in American political culture immediately connote something sinful and alien, an evil temptation that destroys everything in its wake. References to the state of "public opinion" here can be rather misleading, since the vast majority of Americans remain ill-informed about the complexities of drug production, sales, and consumption—mostly unaware, for example, that legal pharmaceutical substances are generally many times more harmful, addictive, and lethal than most variants of "illicit" or "street" drugs. The unfortunate reality is that popular views regarding drugs have been systematically influenced by corporate-media propaganda.

"Threats"—Domestic and Global

Prohibitionist ideology, oriented for the most part toward defense of social conventions and privileged interests, frames drugs as a mortal danger to the established social order posed mainly by outsiders, aliens, and foreigners—a danger nowadays conveniently focused on Mexican cartels, inner-city gangs, and sinister "pushers." A crucial point here is that, while literally hundreds of chemical substances have been used generously by humans for centuries, only recently have governments moved to outlaw and abolish them.[3] The idea of a ubiquitous "drug menace," in fact, goes back little more than a century, associated at that time (in the United States) with temperance efforts to ban alcohol. While demonstrably harmful goods such as tobacco and (when used in excess) alcohol were tolerated during most of American history, less problematic substances such as cannabis, opium, and cocaine (all previously legal) were by the early twentieth century defined as contraband goods imported from Mexico, Asia, and South America; "illicit" and "harmful" were meanings inextricably linked to what antidrug forces viewed as exotic, foreign, and threatening.

During the early decades of the twentieth century the actual number of drug abusers and addicts—obviously difficult to measure at the time—was surely quite small, hardly deserving of moral panic or political hysteria. Marijuana, opium, and cocaine were said to be dire menaces, a view that made sense within a xenophobic worldview that defined *imported* drugs as uniquely menacing. Passage of the Harrison Narcotics Tax Act gained momentum owing less to public-health concerns than to fears that narcotics were the preferred intoxicants of foreigners and the lower classes (as in the case of Prohibition). "Dope fiends" of the period were almost universally seen as the poor and immigrants. Drug outlawry was framed around stereotypes having deep roots in American history, embedded in a national mission to fight and defeat potent enemies by any means necessary.[4] Then, as later, the drug war was being fought to save God-fearing Americans from demonic challenges—and of course such challenges were always in abundant supply. With their darkly suspicious origins, drug traffickers and pushers were likened to vampires, and drug users to zombies in a Hobbesian world of mounting chaos, fear, and violence.[5]

Opiates, cocaine, and other intoxicating drugs were not only legal, but also popular in the United States across the nineteenth century. As opiates were associated with Asia (notably China) and cocaine with South America, however, xenophobic attitudes soon paved the way toward criminalization, culminating in the Harrison Act. World War I intensified jingoistic feelings that led to targeting of not only Germans (beer), but also Asians (opium, heroin), South

46   CHAPTER 2

Americans (cocaine), and Mexicans (cannabis). Americans were conditioned to see the dangers of addiction in these substances, along with the violence, crime, and nonconformity that came to be associated with their sales and use. While the known addict population in the United States in the first decades of the twentieth century was probably fewer than 250,000, moral panic fanned by politicians and the media easily surfaced.[6] It was believed in some quarters that drugs would push "deviant" groups toward social outlawry and political subversion. Narcotics in particular were labeled as drugs of hostility to authority and defiance of social conventions—which, in the case of Asians, Mexicans, and blacks, took on ominously racist meanings.[7]

By the 1920s, as Mexican immigration to the United States increased owing to plentiful low-wage job opportunities, the supposed connection of Hispanics to marijuana had taken an emphatically racial trajectory. Pot was depicted as a source of insolence, crime, and sexual promiscuity—a grave threat to social cohesion and patriotism. Some wanted to connect the drug to anarchism or Bolshevism, which—in the reactionary aftermath of World War I—became part of the fearsome Red Scare. With the rapid development of blues and jazz culture in the 1920s and 1930s, moreover, the common linkage of this music to blacks and drugs further pushed the antidrug crusades toward outright racism, laying the foundation of the Marihuana Tax Act. Later, in fact, illegal drugs would be tied to the international communist "conspiracy," which, of course, produced its own moral panic in the years after World War II.

From the beginning, drug-prohibition efforts revolved around the (mostly contrived) association of "illicit" substances with such problems as poverty, crime, family breakdown, and poor work performance—problems understood as endemic to minorities and the poor. Intoxicating drugs were further linked to laziness, health ailments, and sexual deviance. If the great drug plague was indeed external or foreign in origins, these problems could easily be blamed on evil global threats such as Communism. The fact that many such drugs—pot, methamphetamines, and hallucinogens, for example—were largely homegrown made little difference to righteous drug warriors, who never expressed much interest in facts. Other substances (heroin, morphine) were widely manufactured or processed in European and American labs.

From the 1920s onward, banned substances (notably heroin, cocaine, and marijuana) were identified with a black subculture associated with jazz, blues, inner-city street life, and the bar scene, with its strong underground appeal. From the warrior standpoint, "users" were by definition outsiders, could never lead normal lives, and fit the stereotype of addicts, "fiends," and zombies, inhabiting a world of the "walking dead" or "frozen corpses." Images of violence, depravity, manic behavior, and death resonated across the (contrived) drug landscape, viewed as the site of an endless downward spiral. Legal drugs, for all their addictive properties and side effects, remained securely within the accepted paradigm of thought and behavior; they were legitimate, "normal," even indispensable.[8] One difficulty with this outlook was that, with passing decades, illegal drugs grew in popularity, their "users" undaunted by scary propaganda and the passage of increasingly harsh laws; the actual harm turned out to be somewhat less than fearsome. Because the appeal of intoxicating drugs—that is, sinful and harmful imports—never waned but rather grew over time, the warrior response was to impose new forms of statist, coercive rules and laws. The very notion of a terrible, ubiquitous menace suggests a force that is *external*, beyond human control, outside the realm of conscious decision making. The warriors were fearful that the drug trade would trap new groups of unsuspecting victims. Steven Wisotsky writes, "The impasse in the War on Drugs thus finds its anchor in [the] unexamined, unconscious denigration of the human capacity for responsible choice and self-control in the matter of drugs and consciousness."[9]

While most American drug consumers have been white and middle-class, the "illicit" label conjures images of alien pushers and dark-skinned users inclined toward a life of parasitic crime. Movies and TV programs have long been filled with narratives of heroic cops and FBI or DEA agents fighting inner-city, drug-infected crime. Gangs, cartels, street traffickers, and growers (some labeled narco-terrorists) are recurrent actors in this media-obsessed "plague." As those charged with drug offenses are sent to jail yearly by the tens of thousands, prisons inevitably wind up as part of a sprawling underground subculture.

For President Nixon and his stratum of fanatical drug warriors, the endless cycle of drugs, crime, and racial conflict emerged as a seamless whole, the major threat coming from outside predators and festering among the inner-city poor seen as disrespectful of "American values." The Nixon administration believed widespread marijuana use alone constituted a major "crisis," threatening not only social cohesion but national security. One of Nixon's first initiatives was to lobby such countries as Mexico, Colombia, Thailand, and Turkey to curtail drug exports, a move that achieved only limited success. Domestically, harsher laws and penalties were introduced, bringing prison time for mere possession or small-time sales of an expanded list of outlawed drugs. Nixon's campaign mobilized the resources of the FBI, the CIA, the IRS, and both state and local police behind "zero-tolerance" goals. The DEA ended up central to this crusade after its founding in 1973, assigned to carry out both domestic and foreign operations. At the time of his all-out crusade the president announced that "drug traffickers . . . must be hunted to the end of the earth."[10]

48 Chapter 2

The call for beefed-up law enforcement, longer prison terms, enhanced surveillance, and stricter border controls during the 1970s coincided with pursuit of an aggressive foreign policy in Latin America and globally, which, combined with emphasis on social controls in the wake of sixties turbulence, fit the conservative mood of the period. Despite lip service paid to Constitutional freedoms, rights, and "limited government," Republicans, especially, saw the drug "epidemic" as a pretext for regulating personal and social behavior. Nixon shrewdly wove together ideological elements of an antidrug campaign that gathered widespread appeal in the sixties aftermath: family values, sobriety, suburban lifestyles, patriotism, and toughness on crime. The War on Drugs would be framed as an imperative battle by noble defenders of American values against an assortment of enemies—a popular motif throughout US history. Nixon clearly thought this would be one of his lasting legacies—before it was negated by the disasters of Vietnam and Watergate.

In the early 1980s President Ronald Reagan set out to reinvigorate the prohibitionist agenda with renewed attention to public health insofar as drug addiction was deemed an out-of-control "plague." The crude slogan "Just Say No" arose from the premise that all drugs are innately and equally harmful, with pot generally singled out as uniquely alarming. Nixon had already laid out plans for an international War on Drugs that would enlist the well-funded efforts of numerous federal agencies and perhaps build toward military interventions abroad. In 1982, announcing a new Drug Abuse Policy Office, Reagan stated, "We can put dangerous drug use on the run."[11] As billions of dollars flowed into an expanding antidrug budget, the White House invoked the World War I Battle of Verdun as purportedly an inspirational example for *this* war—a bizarre reference, given the pointless slaughter of hundreds of thousands of European troops during that protracted, ill-fated catastrophe. It was Reagan, in any event, who first militarized the drug war: in the 1980s US armed forces were deployed to intercept flows of illegal drugs from Mexico, South America, and elsewhere, a mission the Pentagon has yet to abandon. The White House mobilized thousands of FBI, CIA, and DEA agents alongside military forces in what was becoming a quasiglobal strategy in pursuit of a "drug-free society."

Reagan understood the drug war as an all-out struggle against national threats little different than communism and terrorism; indeed, for some warriors such evil forces were tightly linked. Real debate over the merits of drug warfare was never tolerated at the summits of power. The War on Drugs was then, as later, entirely bipartisan, embraced by Republicans and Democrats alike. The mere hint that the federal government might pursue anything but total prohibition, or zero tolerance, was confined to the realm of forbidden speech in the political and media establishments. For American politicians, talk of drug legalization (or even modest reforms) amounted to career suicide. Further, at a time when Reagan was waxing eloquently about the evils of big government and bureaucracy, the 1984 Omnibus Crime Bill gave vast new powers to law enforcement, justified mainly by the drive to abolish drugs.[12] In this milieu, as attention focused on daily terrors of inner-city life, drug offenders were likened to rapists, murderers, and terrorists. As before, the tight drugs-crime nexus meant disproportionate targeting of the poor and racial minorities—and of course it was these groups that would flood the prison system. Those presiding over the widening antidrug apparatus, on the other hand, were overwhelmingly white and conservative, with an outlook perhaps best described as morally righteous.

There can be no mistake: the War on Drugs, racist and xenophobic from the outset, has followed the same pattern across subsequent decades—thanks to the role of the Nixon and Reagan administrations. The inner city has long been a target of street sweeps, wiretaps, sting operations, raids, and arrests, with pushers and users treated as equally dangerous felons. Although a vast majority of illegal drug users and dealers in the United States is white, nearly three-fourths of those imprisoned for drug offenses are black and Latino. From 1983 to 2000, for example, the black incarceration rate increased by a staggering twenty-six times, that of Latinos by twenty-two times, and that of whites only 8 percent.[13] Michelle Alexander writes that "in major cities wracked by the drug war, as many as 80 percent of young African-American men now have criminal records and thus are subject to legal discrimination the rest of their lives."[14] As of 2010, though reportedly only 15 percent of illegal drug users were black, 50 percent of those imprisoned for drug offenses at the state level were black. According to the 2012 National Survey on Drug Use and Health, the actual variation in illicit drug use when comparing blacks, Hispanics, and whites is nearly insignificant—amounting to 11.3 percent for blacks, 8.3 percent for Hispanics, and 9.2 percent for whites spanning the years 2002–2012. This is hardly enough to account for vast discrepancies in American incarceration rates.[15] Once convicted, 51 percent of blacks were incarcerated, in contrast to just 33 percent of whites.[16]

The antidrug crusade orchestrated by Nixon and Reagan, and carried forward by later White House occupants, was fueled in part by a backlash against the sixties New Left, counterculture, and the civil-rights movement. Tough law-enforcement agendas would impact minorities especially: in 2010, among 2.3 million people incarcerated at all levels (along with 4.8 million on probation or parole), roughly 80 percent were black or Hispanic. As of 2014, roughly one-third of black men can expect jail time at some point, a punishment that can easily reduce them to second-class citizenship. In 2010 more blacks were

50 Chapter 2

disenfranchised owing to prison records than at any previous time in history. Once people are labeled felons, their life situation is bound to deteriorate markedly, obstructing work and career possibilities, family life, educational hopes, health care, public benefits, and voting rights. Even minor drug offenders can be condemned to a life of poverty and misery.[17]

In her groundbreaking book *The New Jim Crow*, Michelle Alexander develops this argument further, characterizing the drug war as a turn toward expanded social controls over blacks and other disadvantaged groups.[18] Since the 1980s, she points out, drug offenses (80 percent for simple possession) have accounted for two-thirds of new prisoners in federal custody and nearly one-half in state confinement. These figures had little to do, it turns out, with dramatic increases in either crime rates or illegal drug use in the United States—both of which fluctuated during the period in question. In fact when the great "crack-cocaine epidemic" was being sensationalized in the media during the 1980s—neatly coordinated with Reagan's "drug-free" campaign—the focus, as before, was largely on inner-city minority groups even though no significant uptick in drug use among that population had been recorded.

For Alexander, the drug war illustrates how the criminal-justice system and law enforcement help reproduce a "new racial caste system" in American society, with incarceration rates unknown to any other country. A national warfare agenda legitimates elevated spending for state agencies, police departments, Homeland Security, surveillance, and prisons—all eagerly backed by politicians of both major parties fearful of being labeled soft on crime. Alexander comments, "Quite belatedly, I came to see that mass incarceration in the United States had, in fact, emerged as a stunningly comprehensive and well-disguised system of social control that functions in a manner similar to Jim Crow."[19] Targeting aliens, outsiders, and lower-class groups, the War on Drugs remains a virulently racist enterprise.

Drug Hysteria and Culture Wars

Consistent with the targeting of "enemies" to be fought, tamed, and conquered, the drug war—in the tracks of Prohibition—was always something of a moral crusade by ruling groups, with significant mass support, to purge the world of evil. In Arthur Benavie's words, it was and continues to be "America's Holy War."[20] Promoted on the fiction of improving public health and fighting crime, antidrug campaigns came to rely on an ideological righteousness dependent, for popular support, on a syndrome of empty platitudes repeated endlessly by politicians, the media, and government bureaucrats. Warfare initiatives are routinely driven by scary narratives about crime, violence, and family horrors supposedly resulting from illegal drug use. Of course, such narratives deal only with banned recreational substances in a society where legal, widely marketed drugs (tobacco, alcohol, and pharmaceuticals) do far more damage than outlawed ones. The power of abstract moral discourse is that ideological consensus can be sustained without need for rational inquiry, careful investigation, factual evidence, or informed debate.

While the specter of a great "drug menace" first appeared in the early twentieth century, the buildup to alcohol prohibition in the United States spanned earlier decades, in the context of a strong Puritan tradition, class prejudice, and elite response to social crisis. Organizations like the ASL and the WCTU embraced traditional values said to be threatened by intoxicating drugs that the lower strata were hell-bent on abusing. The prohibitionist surge, however, coexisted with an ongoing popularity of alcoholic beverages and saloon life that actually flourished throughout the tortured life of the Volstead Act. If "demon rum" had been viewed as sinful and corrosive by the early crusaders, it nonetheless remained integral to the daily life of the poor, illiterate workers and immigrant "rabble." Saloons were scandalized as centers of waste and debauchery, subversive of stable family and religious life, but they also provided an arena of escape and conviviality for millions of ordinary Americans, bringing sizable profits to underground speakeasies during the 1920s.[21] The moral consensus that temperance partisans so eagerly hoped to create was nothing less than pure fantasy, then and later.

The traditional "alcohol question"—like the problem of narcotics and other illegal drugs—entered the culture wars of the period, a source of authoritarian measures to ban substances considered both sinful and harmful. A new category of alcoholics and addicts was deemed to be the product not only of psychological weakness but of depraved habits. Yet the imposition of Puritanical values, as mentioned, could never work: the Prohibition era soon morphed into the Roaring Twenties, with the alcohol trade taken over by organized crime and the Jazz Age giving rise to vast zones of underground bars, taverns, and nightclubs. Consumption of beer, wine, and spirits actually increased in many American cities, generating enough revenue for crime syndicates to corrupt both police and government officials. The "noble experiment" to abolish the scourge of drink and bring American society back to its (imputed) founding moral principles soon enough recoiled on itself, its explosive contradictions impossible to contain. Alcohol consumption spread to new groups, including young women who sought out new varieties of cocktails popularized during the Jazz Age. Blues and jazz clubs abounded, spreading an ambience of music, drink, dancing, and

52   Chapter 2

socializing that, for the most part, took little notice of the law. By the late 1920s the moral crusade had fizzled.[22]

After Prohibition's repeal in 1933, temperance concerns shifted to other drugs, notably marijuana; "evil weed" supplanted "demon rum" in the pantheon of sinful intoxicants. With the Depression, thousands of police officers and federal agents moved from the Bureau of Prohibition to the Federal Bureau of Narcotics, directed by moral crusader Harry Anslinger, whose obsession during the next few decades would be the increasing "drug menace." Anslinger was concerned mainly with cannabis, which came to be more often called marijuana to stress its presumed linkage with Mexican immigrants, playing on time-honored stereotypes that economic strains of the Depression only intensified. Framing narcotics as a cancerous evil, the Bureau of Narcotics worked indefatigably to toughen drug laws and penalties in a matrix of global prohibitionist moves. In the late 1940s the United States, behind Anslinger's ideological fervor, instigated the United Nations Single Convention on Narcotic Drugs, which obliged every UN member to outlaw coca products, opiates, and cannabis. The rapid growth of international drug markets, however, rendered this convention essentially symbolic and toothless. Enhanced global demand meant accelerated drug sales and higher profit margins, drawing new criminal enterprises into the trade and rendering prohibition illusory.[23]

For Anslinger and his fellow warriors, cannabis and the heavier narcotics represented an evil tantamount to Bolshevism and other subversive political forces. Their project was eagerly joined by William Randolph Hearst and his sprawling newspaper chain, always ready to sensationalize the latest in (usually contrived) drug horrors. Anslinger worked tirelessly throughout the 1930s, 1940s, and later to secure harsh drug legislation, with the intention of expelling drugs (that is, *some* drugs) from American society. The solution to those horrors was government action—that is, stepped-up legislation, policies, laws, and regulations. Anslinger shrewdly mobilized citizens' groups and strong corporate lobbies to influence electoral and legislative outcomes, a path smoothed by tight ideological consensus at the summits of power, which effectively short-circuited public debate. By 1937 the venomous properties of cannabis were simply taken for granted; "reefer madness" assumed control of the political culture.

Since the 1930s cannabis has been a special target of the warriors, some believing it to be the most threatening of all chemical substances. Most troubling about pot to many chemical gatekeepers is its very popularity, easy availability, and (assumed) source of "deviant" behavior. In fact marijuana was always relatively simple to cultivate and process; Anslinger himself noted that it grew "like dandelions" across the United States.[24] The seductive power of "reefer madness" was especially threatening to children and teenagers, as the drug could be gotten cheaply and quickly and then easily concealed. While national phobia over marijuana scarcely existed in the 1920s, Anslinger's relentless campaign turned this generally benign intoxicant into a larger-than-life menace during the 1930s and beyond. Marijuana was said to release inhibitions and restraints, leading to unconventional and possibly violent behavior, above all among minorities and the lower classes. It was also considered a sex stimulant. Mike Gray comments, "Once again the specter of superhuman sex-crazed savages sent a ripple through [the country], and once again it proved irresistible to politicians and the press."[25]

A Puritanical crusader of the first order, for more than three decades Anslinger shrewdly combined a moral evangelism with a law-and-order agenda that transformed recreational drugs from a marginal concern into a dire national emergency. The continuity from Anslinger to modern drug czars, with their aggressive "zerotolerance" agendas, should be readily apparent. The Bureau of Narcotics director aligned his campaign with the ascendant pharmaceutical industry, composed of Merck, Parke-Davis, Eli Lilly, and a few other drug companies. Frightening tales of victims sucked into a world of mayhem and murder while stoned on cannabis were media staples, backed by phony statistics and biased "research." For many years Anslinger pushed for tough antidrug legislation that few politicians dared oppose. Gray notes, "Harry Anslinger was on a mission from God. If he had to cut a few throats to accomplish the Lord's work, so be it."[26]

Following World War II Anslinger worked to mesh his rabid anticommunism with a reinvigorated antidrug crusade, both understood as two sides of the same (anti-American) savagery. Democrats and Republicans alike were perfectly happy to join this ideological mission. Drug nightmares were associated with the Soviet threat and the Yellow Peril symbolized by the Chinese Communist Revolution. For some, the "plague of narcotics" was understood as part of a secret Commie plot to take over the world. The Narcotic Control Act of 1956, bolstering federal powers, was passed by Congress with little debate or opposition—and granted no media attention.[27] Critics of the drug-centered moral panic were villainized as playing into the hands of the "enemy."

President Nixon's own War on Drugs, launching the DEA and strengthening the antidrug federal bureaucracy, was emphatically ideological in its backlash against values associated with powerful social movements of the 1960s and 1970s. Whatever their differences, those movements shared a visceral antiauthoritarianism and rejection of many dominant values. Nixon's epic initiative was surely an impulsive reaction against everything the New Left and counterculture represented—yet another phase in the modern culture wars that remain alive into the twenty-first century. As Edward J. Epstein observes in *Agency of*

54 Chapter 2

Fear, Nixon's war was a systematic attack on challengers to the status quo—and drugs (rightly or wrongly) were placed at the top of that agenda. It is true that certain preferred countercultural drugs (pot, LSD, mescaline, etc.) could be seen as subversive—that is, mind-expanding and in some ways transformative—but their contribution to political radicalism was always questionable. In any event, Nixon's crusade relied more heavily on crude propaganda and inflated data about out-of-control addict populations than on credible evidence of individual or public harm.[28]

For Nixon and later warriors, the terrifying "drug crisis" became an easy pretext for cracking down on progressive activists and even liberals considered "soft on crime." Illegal-drug use was symptomatic of opposition to capitalism, religion, family values, and a strong military. Intoxicating substances—above all, psychedelics—were said to destabilize normal thought patterns, turning even casual users against the established order. Despite its rather moderate properties, pot was deemed uniquely addictive and harmful, even as government reports called for liberal reforms and decriminalization. Referring to one such report, Nixon famously quipped, "I read it and reading it did not change my mind," adding that "traffickers . . . must be hunted to the end of the earth."[29]

Drug issues as a recurrent focus of the culture wars reached new levels during the Reagan era. In June 1982 President Reagan announced his own, more ambitious War on Drugs, appointing Carlton Turner as first director of the Drug Abuse Policy Office and declaring that it was finally time to take down the "surrender flag" in the face of a national drug emergency. Turner, dedicated to the Anslinger legacy, stated, "We have to create a generation of drug-free Americans to purge society."[30] Joined by wife Nancy, President Reagan announced that the war to rid society of illegal drugs was a moral imperative akin to World War II: creating a drug-free society would return America to a sanity that had been undermined by a hedonistic, violent, unpatriotic subculture that devalued lawful behavior. The biggest fear was that drugs of choice (pot, hallucinogens) in the 1960s were destroying the very firmaments of nuclear-family life. Nancy Reagan's simplistic "Just Say No to Drugs" overture told Americans that all drugs are bad and that any talk of decriminalization was "un-American" and downright crazy; even moderate users were villainized as immoral, criminal, and unpatriotic.

Throughout the 1980s both pot and coke became easy objects of public hysteria, with new "epidemics" said to be sweeping the nation; backlash against the sixties was by now in full swing. Cocaine was said to be instantly and lethally addictive, its users damaged forever, while pot not only deformed the personality but served as a "gateway" to even more devastating chemicals—both drugs inexorably leading to psychological breakdown, wasted lives, violence, and even death. Both *Time* and *Newsweek* sensationalized this revived moral panic in several issues during 1986 alone. The Reagan administration called for a "drug-free workplace," stringent testing measures, and tougher punishment for users as well as traffickers and pushers.[31] Those audacious enough to express skepticism about the drug war were dismissed as lunatics. Few opinion leaders seemed troubled by the festering contradictions of everyday reality: there was no valid evidence that pot, hallucinogens, or even coke produced more addictions, adverse reactions, crime, and other public damage than scores of widely available legal pharmaceuticals. Antidrug hysteria obscured abundant evidence that deaths from alcohol, tobacco, and prescription meds—indeed any *one* of these substances—had always far outnumbered deaths from all illegal drugs combined. From this standpoint, could the War on Drugs have been anything but a costly, fraudulent, ultimately counterproductive political crusade?

As drug czar William Bennett took the helm in the late 1980s, antidrug zealotry reached a peak of moral panic and propagandistic bombast. A righteous preacher of "values," Bennett brought special ideological fervor to the vision of a "drug-free America" that would have made Anslinger proud. Bennett and his lieutenants chose to deemphasize health issues, shifting instead to "moral" concerns. For this group, drugs (again *certain* drugs) were bad because—well, they were simply bad. This platitude, of course, extended only to chemical substances arbitrarily defined as contraband, unlawful—that is, recreational or intoxicating drugs listed as "dangerous."[32] There would be no mention of legal drugs, which brought huge profits to corporations that Bennett and his fellow warriors embraced. Terrence Bell, a czar lieutenant, stated, "If you think drugs are bad, that they make people bad neighbors, horrible parents, dangerous drivers, and what have you, then you think drugs are bad. There's a moral dimension."[33] This version of morality, however, never encompassed alcohol, which at that time was linked to more than *half* of all car accidents and murders. This would have to be called selective morality, at best.

Bennett's ambitious "transformation of values" project fixed its sights on a marijuana scourge said to be "enslaving" American youth. What bothered the righteous czar most, apparently, was not so much pot's addictive powers as the disrespect for authority it ostensibly inculcated in regular users; it was the idea of a "radical weed" used by "dangerous felons."[34] Pot was in fact so terrible that even casual users were believed to merit stiff prison sentences, even for a first offense. Like other conservatives who fancied "small government" rhetoric, Bennett set out to enlist the most expansive and coercive instruments of federal power to fight the plague, regardless of costs. Raids, roadblocks, wiretaps, random

56   Chapter 2

searches, testing, arrests, and punitive jail sentences would all be integral to the drug war—and of course all were contributions to the growth of big government. Mobilizing the usual host of federal agencies, the drug czar moved aggressively to enlarge state power at the very moment Reagan was expanding the military-industrial complex (while also promising an era of "small government").

With taxpayers burdened to the tune of tens of billions of dollars in the futile pursuit of a drug-free America, the czar and his group of bureaucrats did everything possible to stave off debate over merits of their punitive, costly, counterproductive crusade. Dissenters were likely to be ignored or treated with extreme disdain, the issue of drugs deemed a closed matter by leading opinion makers. In their preachy and redundant volume *Body Count*, Bennett and colleagues attacked both drug users and sellers for sabotaging "American values" and for embracing "deviant behavior" that was held responsible for every imaginable public harm.[35] At a time when the warriors' crusade was filling federal, state, and local prisons with tens of thousands of mostly nonviolent drug offenders, government policy enjoyed strong bipartisan support in Congress and most state legislatures. Challengers to that policy, as mentioned, risked an almost certain end to their political careers. That consensus has continued into the present, despite an upsurge in popular demand for pot decriminalization and renewed interest in health issues and treatment for addicts. Drug czars retained a federal presence into the early twenty-first century, as jail populations in many states exceeded institutional capacity. In the late 1980s The Partnership for a Drug-Free America began to fill TV and radio airwaves with scaremongering propaganda directed mainly at teenagers and their parents. Republican politician Newt Gingrich would eventually suggest penal colonies for drug traffickers, with Bennett urging broader use of the death penalty in drug cases and LAPD chief Daryl Gates even calling for small-time users to be "taken out and shot." In 1990 alone, more than 260,000 Americans were arrested for simple marijuana *possession*.

At a time when surveys reported that at least seventy million Americans had smoked pot, President Bill Clinton's drug czar, General Barry McCaffrey, was happy enough to follow Bennett's righteous legacy. The level of arrests and incarceration for drug offenses gradually escalated, with the overall US prison count surpassing two million by the late 1990s; meanwhile, Clinton pressed earnestly ahead. More sensitive to the health dimension of drug abuse and addiction, Democrats nonetheless shared the warrior mentality and never wavered from the prohibitionist outlook: the question of even modest reform of pot laws was still considered off-limits. Clinton's press secretary, Dee Dee Myers, said, "The president is against legalizing drugs and he's not interested in studying the issue."[36] In 1996 Clinton pushed a draconian crime bill through Congress, replete with death sentences for several additional categories of drug offenders. Unfortunately, escalating problems associated with alcohol, tobacco, and pharmaceuticals were again either ignored or downplayed.

Despite mounting public cynicism over the efficacy of antidrug warfare, the spread of organizations favoring liberal reform, rising interest in medical marijuana, and increased emphasis on treatment over incarceration for addicts, the culture battles scarcely waned—then or later. The George H. W. and George W. Bush presidencies, along with the presidencies of Democrats Clinton and Obama, have in practice departed little from the harsh Nixon and Reagan legacies. The Obama administration has at times softened its antidrug rhetoric but on the whole remains strictly opposed to any form of decriminalization; treatment options have gained favor, yet American jails continue to be filled (indeed, overcrowded) with drug offenders. Abolitionist ideology clearly holds sway. Prospects for alternatives to futile government policies seem hardly improved, especially in the wake of Obama's decision to stonewall the 2012 UN report calling for fresh initiatives in the global War on Drugs (discussed more fully in Chapter 3).

A Corporate-State Agenda

Any government striving to maintain strict prohibition laws will face significant economic burdens: huge tax revenues are needed to fund government bureaucracies, law enforcement, surveillance, military operations, and the inevitable prison complex. Further, expansion of black markets and criminal syndicates means that tens of billions in annual drug trade will move underground, beyond the reach of tax collections, regulations, and import restrictions. Added material costs result from the violence, crime, and corruption that typically accompany a thriving underground capitalism. As Jeffrey Miron argues in *Drug War Crimes*, even where prohibition is defended on moral grounds, it can never be justified on strictly economic grounds.[37]

There remains, however, yet an entirely different economic underpinning of prohibition—the oligopolistic power of giant corporations. The producers and distributors of *legal* drugs—constituting a global market worth nearly a half trillion dollars yearly—have strong vested interests in keeping "illicit" (that is, competing) drugs off the legitimate market, as do the purveyors of lucrative alcohol and tobacco goods. While such business agendas restlessly seek new profit-making ventures, the War on Drugs serves a clear purpose, as the outlawing of popular goods like marijuana, cocaine, and hallucinogens greatly impedes competition. As is often the case, such crass economic agendas are shrouded in

58 CHAPTER 2

abstract rhetoric about free markets and evils of drugs, sometimes embellished with references to individual or public health concerns.

The conservative dream of a drug-free society, in fact, is perfectly consistent with the profit-maximizing interests of Big Pharma—not to mention those of vast alcohol and tobacco industries. Federal agencies like the DEA, the FDA, the ATF, and the CIA also benefit given their capacity to justify huge budget increases. Since at least the 1980s, legal drugs produced, advertised, and sold by Big Pharma have amounted to one of the most lucrative sectors in the US economy, bolstered by wealthy lobbies, cozy ties with the media, partnerships with the medical complex, and influence over government agencies. The state-capitalist apparatus embedded in a merger of government and corporate operations is probably nowhere more visible than in the antidrug crusade.

While protectors of the public morality never want to relinquish their hopes for a drug-free America, the entire social order—government agencies, businesses, media, advertising, and the medical system—is saturated with promises of miracle drugs said to treat everything from depression to insomnia, high cholesterol to sexual dysfunction, obesity to hypertension. The medical culture is, more than ever, steeped in widespread marketing of both prescription and OTC "meds" responsible for infinitely more adverse reactions, addictions, abuse, and lethal episodes than all illegal substances combined. The media, academia, scientific labs, law enforcement, and the military—the very structures that most vigorously back the War on Drugs—fully partake of what is now the most far-reaching drug culture ever known. The network of bureaucratic, corporate, political, and cultural interests behind the warfare lies mainly outside the democratic process, more dedicated to profits, institutional leverage, and social control than to personal health, public welfare, or social governance.

Big Pharma occupies the very apex of this network, with deep involvement across the public landscape. Could pot—cheap, readily available, and with few adverse reactions—be preferred by most American consumers over such problematic drugs as Vicodin, OxyContin, and Valium? Pharmaceutical companies, no doubt, fear the answer—especially in the event marijuana were to be fully legalized. In fact, as evidence continues to show, the extensive dangers of legal drugs have all too frequently been obscured or covered up, often in the process of testing.[38] In 2009, for example, AstraZeneca recorded $4 billion in sales for the drug Seroquel, only to be later heavily fined for illegal marketing and concealing drug risks, as was Eli Lilly in the case of Zyprexa the same year. While the remedial powers for these and dozens of other mind-altering substances are grossly inflated or even falsified, the warriors still argue that "street drugs" (including pot) are more dangerous than prescribed drugs. Although this falsehood appears to have been persuasive across recent decades, its appeal has begun to erode, as demonstrated by increasing electoral support for the reform of state marijuana laws. While the most active ingredient in marijuana, THC, has been scorned as harmful and useless by the federal bureaucrats, Big Pharma has managed to synthesize and market the drug to bolster its own earnings.[39]

While the drug war benefits corporate interests and government agencies, law enforcement, surveillance operations, prisons, and testing regimens help gorge Big Pharma profits. Pharmaceutical companies rely heavily on public largesse for subsidies, import protections, research and development, and, of course, legitimation. This was true even during the 1930s, when Anslinger took over the Bureau of Narcotics and linked his prohibition efforts with (then-far-smaller) drug enterprises. He had unlimited power to determine who gained entry into what Gray calls the "narcotics monopoly game," with eight major players admitted in 1936, including Merck, Mallinckrodt, Hoffman-La Roche, Parke-Davis, Eli Lilly, and Squibb.[40] This was an ideal scheme for Anslinger, who indeed "was perfect for the insiders in this oligopoly,"[41] as reflected in their later spectacular growth. Gray writes, "This corporate cartel became Anslinger's steadfast ally, and throughout his career, whenever the commissioner needed help on Capitol Hill, the pharmaceutical industry would come running. When he was pushing legislation, they would testify in favor. When he was under attack, they would move behind the scenes twisting arms. This powerful lobby . . . ultimately rendered him unassailable."[42] If this was indeed a powerful lobby during the 1930s, it was merely an embryonic form of what Big Pharma would later become.

The larger political outlook has changed little in the decades since Anslinger's prohibitionist rule, though Big Pharma today exerts much greater influence over government and the media, having amassed nearly unparalleled economic and political clout since the 1980s. While the established marketeers freely and brazenly advertise their outrageously expensive products across TV, radio, and print outlets, antidrug lobbies like The Partnership at Drugfree.org solicit millions of dollars in contributions from Big Pharma and kindred business interests. During the 1990s The Partnership for a Drug-Free America (PDFA) was funded mainly by such interests as Merck, Pfizer, Johnson & Johnson, Bristol-Myers Squibb, Monsanto, Procter and Gamble, and, until 1997, tobacco companies such as Philip Morris. Huge insurance firms like Aetna, Metropolitan Life, and Allstate continue to donate generously to PDFA, which introduces teenagers to scary propaganda spots about the fatal risks of pot and various other "street drugs," offering newer and more harrowing variants of the "killer weed" myth.[43]

During 2011–2012 generous PDFA donors included Schering-Plough, Pfizer, Merck, and Hoffman-La Roche and such nondrug companies as Comcast (which

60 Chapter 2

signed a $50 million contract with PDFA in 2003), MetLife, JPMorgan Chase, and Disney Corporation. Fixated on pot and cocaine, PDFA ads often suggest that "drug abuse" is the most pressing of all challenges—when poverty is rampant, bankruptcies and home foreclosures mount, the public infrastructure collapses, the environmental crisis reaches the famous tipping point, and health costs soar. Forgotten here is the long list of severe adverse reactions associated with legal drugs—tobacco, alcohol, and pharmaceuticals. For PDFA and its sponsors, the crisis of "drug abuse" refers almost exclusively to the "plague of street drugs." In the United States, at least, the War on Drugs is driven by a merger of corporate and governmental forces—the two sets of interests that have long shared a prohibitionist outlook, with its enduring authoritarian consequences.

Warrior Myths and Illusions

The War on Drugs, like earlier prohibition crusades, is destined to run aground on its own contradictions. The reason is disarmingly simple: devoid of solid empirical supports, the warriors must rely on a regimen of deceitful propaganda that daily experience will sooner or later reject. The guiding warfare assumptions dissolve after even limited investigation. In the United States today it is easy enough to see that drugs of every conceivable type—legal and illegal, natural and synthetic, medicinal and recreational—are consumed (often in extremely potent mixtures) routinely by tens of millions of people. As a taken-for-granted phenomenon of daily life, drug use (and abuse) is mediated through a complex interplay of factors: long-term versus short-term use, dosage, the user's nutritional habits, interaction with other drugs, social context, and, perhaps most critical, the psychological state of the user. Experience indicates that drugs can have a wide variety of positive or negative outcomes, none especially determined by issues of legality. Drug-related problems have long afflicted American society, with no sign of reversal as the United States remains awash in both legal and illegal chemical substances that rank among the most lucrative products on the planet.

Attempts to precisely *measure* the harm (individual or social) from specific drugs are impressionistic at best, as so many complexities, mediations, and variables must be taken into account, while assessment criteria turn out to be subjective and arbitrary. Still, a few basic indicators can be helpful—for example, the number of hospital admissions from overdoses and severe addictions, total of lethal episodes, and number of drug-related accidents. (Looking simply at *these* indicators, legal drugs are generally far more dangerous than illegal ones.) Even here, however, there is always the crucial matter of adequate *reporting*: given professional risk and stigma involved, there is the question as to what percentage of negative episodes from doctor-prescribed drugs, especially at hospitals, is likely to enter official statistics. The task of isolating the impact of any single drug within such calculations, moreover, is nearly insurmountable in a milieu where users often combine two or more substances.

The identification of "good" versus "bad" outcomes for drugs, however, falls short of addressing deeper problems concerning the role of government in defining, regulating, and prohibiting what people decide to consume. Where does "measurement" begin, how should it be carried out, and what should its applications and limits be? Much socially harmful behavior is, of course, subject to legal rules and sanctions: driving while intoxicated, domestic violence, public drunkenness, selling alcohol to minors, etc. Outlawing goods that individuals willingly choose to buy, possess, and consume, on the other hand, falls under an altogether different category—one that might be argued is distinctly "self-regarding" (a term John Stuart Mill used, distinguishing "other-regarding" from "self-regarding" types of human activity, the latter occupying a realm—harmless to other persons—that should not be subject to government laws and regulations).[44] Matters of personal choice ought to fall outside the realm of state politicians and administrators to dictate. After all, the harmful consequences of eating sugar, meat, and fast foods (all documented extensively) are typically deemed, rightly so, to be a matter of personal choice outside the purview of government. The same could be said, even more emphatically, for such products as alcohol, tobacco, and prescription meds—yet these are freely available and heavily marketed, with few if any stigmas attached. The move to outlaw and criminalize food, drink, and other substances of individual preference has deeply authoritarian implications for public life.

The American political system is historically grounded, at least theoretically, in a broad matrix of rights and freedoms, many contained in the US Constitution and ritually celebrated as basic to citizenship. These, however, have been excluded from the realm of drug consumption going back to at least the 1914 Harrison Act. Put differently, some categories of drugs have been randomly kept beyond the scope of these rights and freedoms on the premise that governmental power can and should be used to regulate what human beings put into their bodies. Politicians and bureaucrats have come to occupy a special niche in determining what is harmful, how harmful it is, whether it should be outlawed, and what punishment should be meted out against violators of an official code. The system of authoritarian controls here is in fact highly *selective*—that is, while some human

62 CHAPTER 2

behavior is outlawed and punished severely, other (often more harmful) behavior is arbitrarily given freer reign, as in the case of guns and legal drugs. And such controls, as we have seen, are hardly governed by consistent or rational criteria.

Antidrug warriors, most claiming to identify with classical American ideals of freedom and democracy, have, in fact, shown little regard for Mill's classical theoretical argument. The purchase and consumption of drugs for individual recreational or medicinal use clearly fits the "self-regarding" category, as Mill himself (and many later thinkers) clearly recognized. Further, the crusaders appear indifferent to a political—indeed moral—linchpin of the Declaration of Independence affirming the basic right to "life, liberty, and the pursuit of happiness," later incorporated into the list of rights contained in the 1948 United Nations Universal Declaration of Human Rights, which some Americans (including Eleanor Roosevelt) helped author. The War on Drugs directly conflicts with precepts of individual freedom and human rights laid out in these (and other) documents.

The coercive underpinnings of the drug war not only subvert ideals of freedom and democracy, but run up against the long history of human experience with drugs, which demonstrates that no single, uniform, abusive pattern can be established for *any* drug, whatever its legal status. Official attempts to force (illegal, illicit) "drug use" into a single human modality run counter to everyday-life understanding and quickly turn repressive, not to mention counterproductive. If Ronald K. Siegel is correct about the universality of the "fourth drive"—a basic human desire for mind-altering substances—then state prohibition is no less authoritarian than the banning of particular foods, social gatherings, and sexual behavior on supposed moral or health grounds.[45] Further, in giving rise to increased levels of criminal activity and promoting an underground economy, prohibition fosters the very socially alienating, destructive outcomes it claims to oppose; criminalization never solves, but rather exacerbates, drug-related problems of health, public welfare, and crime.

As for addiction, since drug use is mediated in so many ways, there is the intractable problem of identifying endemic habit-forming properties for specific products or behaviors, although tendencies do vary, naturally. Such tendencies, however, cannot be fully grasped with reference to strictly legal definitions, criteria, and boundaries. Alcohol, tobacco, caffeine, OTC products, prescribed medications, and even foodstuffs can be habit-forming and, of course, harmful to consumers. The complex process of addiction development unfolds within a social totality that includes individual psychological factors, health status, environmental context, work situation, and amount and regularity of consumption. No strictly legal or political discourse can fully encompass this totality. While some within the medical establishment and treatment industry—along with antidrug crusaders—argue that specific drugs (pot, cocaine, and heroin, for example) are innately addictive and have especially harmful consequences, data showing less than 10 percent addiction among users of these and other illegal substances contradict such facile generalizations.

The thorny problem of addiction is best approached on empirical rather than moral or ideological terms. Confusion reigns when people who use certain drugs on a regular or even daily basis—wine at dinner, evening cocktails, morning coffee, ritual pot-smoking, Vicodin for constant pain—might reflexively be labeled addicts or alcoholics, without closer scrutiny of the social context. The warriors often make simplistic assumptions about drug-related harm, which can be daunting to measure or even conceptualize. An obvious measure is rate of lethal episodes, but that would show that illegal drugs such as pot are less problematic than hundreds of widely consumed legal goods. To date no "expert" has managed to identify the constituent properties of outlawed drugs in a manner that clearly distinguishes them from legal substances on the question of harmful outcomes.

Official declarations regarding the problem of addiction are not very helpful—nor is one likely to gain much better understanding from such texts as the *Diagnostic and Statistical Manual of Mental Disorders* (the latest being DSM-V). According to the National Institute on Drug Abuse (NIDA), "as a result of scientific research, we know that addiction is a disease that affects both brain and behavior." NIDA reports typically emphasize this very perspective—that is, a medical model with "disease"-theory reference at its center. While NIDA statements generally offer little empirical guidance to understanding addiction, the "disease" label furnishes a ready-made, catch-all framework in which psychological and social variables are downplayed if not entirely overlooked. Those with dependency problems are victims of a "disease" that somehow invades and transforms body and mind; social context, with its crucial filters and mediations, is essentially dropped from view. To say that particular substances (alcohol, sugar, fast foods, pot) exert an impact on "brain and behavior" is nothing more than a truism, having little to say about the character, intensity, and duration of the ostensible impact. To conclude, however, that an individual is "dependent" on a given substance (daily coffee with pastry, wine with dinner) gives little information about the nature and ramifications of dependency.

The degree of social harm produced by any substance (drugs, food, or otherwise) is scarcely related to its "illicit" status, contrary to official statements indicating otherwise. Issues of abuse, dependency, and addiction are dialectically interwoven with factors embedded in a social totality, reflecting not so much an isolated or discrete *thing* as an ensemble of linkages and interactions. Issues

64 CHAPTER 2

of *legality* are socially constructed—that is, determined by some combination of economic interests and ideological or political rationale. Further, the warrior concept of "drug addicts" totally bereft of self-control as they proceed to lose jobs, homes, families, and sanity—victims of their own crazed behavior—has at best only episodic bearing on everyday reality. In the United States alone, tens of millions of people regularly use marijuana, alcohol, and large varieties of medical and/or intoxicating drugs without visibly disabling outcomes. Tens of millions of others routinely eat junk food and become obese, with high probability they will encounter health problems such as high blood pressure, heart disease, diabetes, and cancer—yet few politicians or media commentators argue for banning such products, nor should they. In fact no one dies from pot consumption and relatively few perish from cocaine or hallucinogens, while hundreds of thousands die annually from legal drugs and, less immediately, junk foods. As is well known, the annual death toll from alcohol and tobacco products combined runs well into the hundreds of thousands—a grizzly toll from addictive behavior not involving illegal drugs.

Aside from the matter of personal harm, coercive drug policy is ostensibly meant to curtail the destructive *social* consequences of illegal drugs: black markets, criminal behavior, underground syndicates and gangs, family breakdown, health costs, teenage misery. It is often claimed that drug use brings personal alienation, despair, and breakdown. Taken at face value, such arguments have some validity, yet closer investigation suggests something deeper at work—the consequences of prohibition itself. As happened with the Volstead Act, efforts to outlaw popular consumer items merely drive markets for such items underground, giving rise to the very social harm warriors insist is endemic to illegal drugs as such. If beer, wine, and tequila were suddenly outlawed, turned into contraband substances, those very outcomes (crime, violence, corruption, etc.) would quickly surface. The drug war generates harm of its own making; indeed a "zero-tolerance" program constitutes the ideal recipe for creating what it theoretically rejects. Unfortunately, US drug policy has never been informed by any semblance of cost-benefit analysis.

The trajectory of *any* drug use has multiple sources, contexts, dimensions, and outcomes. The same holds true for consumption of other products, including many foods, which can readily fit patterns of abuse, dependency, and addiction. When chronic health problems surface and worsen over time, long-term eating patterns can surely be implicated, yet people still adhere to deeply ingrained habits whatever the likely severe damage to mind and body. Such dietary patterns can only be described as highly addictive, as the same destructive behavior continues while health conditions deteriorate. (Ignorance here can never be a viable excuse, since reliable information about just what foods create predictable harm—obesity, for example—is readily and cheaply available, especially in the Internet era.) Where lack of awareness is involved, the problem is probably best understood as one of "willful ignorance," a state of mind where the same debilitating habits are repeated without seeking healthful, rational alternatives.

The steady rise of obesity (and resulting health problems) in the United States since World War II can be traced to growing popularity of fast foods (rich in fatty items, meat, and salt), a McDonaldized regimen of cheap, standardized, easily available meals that are aggressively marketed in the popular media.[46] These foods, thanks to vigorous advertising, pervade American society, from schools to workplaces and in communities, homes, the media, and popular culture. While scarcely regarded as addictive, they are deeply implicated in the "epidemic" of obesity, responsible for higher rates of hypertension, diabetes, cancer, and arthritis. Research in 2010 showed that nearly 40 percent of Americans were overweight, leading to high rates of hospitalization and premature deaths.[47] Failure of habitual consumers to alter important choices despite threats to mind and body reflects stubborn patterns of dependency similar to those among severe alcoholics and addicted cigarette smokers.

The negative impact of fast foods on health is aggravated by sedentary lifestyles typical of modern society, including passive TV watching, the Internet, and heavy reliance on cell phones—which just happen to coincide with the growing fashion of easy medical fixes (pills, surgery, machines) to treat virtually every ailment. As fast-food and other harmful diets give rise to obesity, new cycles of expensive statin drugs marketed by Big Pharma are now the preferred method for lowering cholesterol levels, with many such meds having achieved blockbuster status. Pills give the illusion of medical empowerment while allowing users to retain the old habits and lifestyles—surely an easier choice than shifting to a more healthful diet that many insist (wrongly) is too difficult, too costly, or too bland. A descending cycle of bad decisions and worsening health outcomes can be self-perpetuating; Big Pharma is always ready to take full advantage, with its endless assortment of colored pills. While fast foods have an undeniably debilitating impact on health, depicted in such widely viewed documentaries as *McLibel*, *Super Size Me*, and *Food, Inc.*, the McDonald's brand (among others) enjoys almost iconic status in American society.[48] Despite the media and medical lip service paid to the obesity "epidemic," no War on Fat or War on Meat has ever been launched against the powerful fast-food industry; indeed, for this aggressively marketed sector, it remains business as usual with profits of tens of billions of dollars yearly.[49]

Much the same can be said about products like refined sugar—a harmful substance found abundantly in most processed and restaurant foods. In 2012

66 CHAPTER 2

Americans were consuming an average seventy-seven grams (twenty teaspoons) of sugar *daily*. Scientific evidence, widely found in dozens of nutrition and health books, demonstrates how sugar weakens the immune system, damages the pancreas, interferes with mineral absorption, causes tooth decay, worsens viral infections, aggravates cancer, and contributes to severe mood changes, potentially leading to cognitive impairment and depression.[50] Daily sugar intake can give rise to body imbalance, making the system acidic and more vulnerable to disease. As is well known, sugar also contributes greatly to obesity. So far, however, no guardians of public welfare have decided to carry out "warfare" against this toxic substance that, when consumed regularly, can be strongly addictive. To date the sugar industry, represented by a well-organized lobby, has successfully fought governmental regulations that could undermine its sales and profits.[51]

Looking at the general historical and social context, it is worth re-posing the question as to whether anything resembling a "drug-free society" is realizable—or worth investing vast human and material resources to achieve. This question looms all the more salient once we grant that *any* form of drug warfare is ultimately an assault on basic psychological impulses aligned with the "fourth drive" that has pervaded human societies for many centuries. Not merely logic but also historical experience testifies to the futility of this prohibitionist agenda. Enlisting the most coercive instruments of state power, this agenda is innately authoritarian—a violation of individual freedoms, human rights, and, in the final analysis, political democracy. As Wisotsky observes, "The War on Drugs will emerge in its true character—a war on one-third of the American people, or more accurately, a stupid and futile attack on their satisfaction of a fundamental human desire."[52] The result, as we have seen, is more crime and violence, widening political corruption, a swollen prison population, huge material costs, escalating violations of privacy and human rights, and precipitous corrosion of the public sphere.

Some observers close to the war zone and open to critical thinking now argue that radical drug reforms, including legalization of many or perhaps all currently banned substances, must occur to avoid further disaster. Among these, Norm Stamper, former police chief of Seattle, comments, "It's not hard to explain why I morphed from drug warrior to drug policy reformer. For more than three decades, I watched the drug war destroy values that, as a cop, I swore to uphold. I observed unnecessary suffering, justice gone wrong, and widespread corruption within the police. I witnessed the physical deterioration of whole neighborhoods—streets, homes, and schools made less safe."[53]

The War on Drugs has been sold by the supposed guardians of public morality as an epic crusade to defeat "evil"—yet the harmful "evils" have resulted precisely from this entirely counterproductive legacy. To date no warrior has ever been able to demonstrate how use of banned drugs has threatened either the public welfare or national security. Every official rationale behind this crusade has been shown to be fraudulent. In the end, we are left with other, more ideologically and economically charged interpretations of such authoritarian policies: elite warfare directed against threats to established social conventions, vested bureaucratic interests, and transnational corporate power.

Chapter 3
Delusions of an Epoch

The 2012 United Nations World Drug Report on the urgent need for basic changes in global drug policy appeared as a great step toward enlightenment framed against the darkness of repeated failures and disasters in the War on Drugs. From the early 1960s onward the UN has been under relentless pressure from the United States to maintain the drug war—an extension of the holy crusade initiated by Harry Anslinger and his prohibitionist zealots during the 1930s. After several decades of calamitous results, however, the UN—through its Global Commission on Drug Policy—authored a harsh critique of this agenda, driven by hopes that rational alternatives might be taken up by forward-thinking government leaders. Its well-researched conclusions were meant to force systematic rethinking of the coercive, punitive (and ultimately undemocratic) approach to drugs that has long gripped American society and, indeed, much of the world. Despite the constructive implications of its analysis and recommendations, the report was met in the United States (including by the Obama administration) with a mixture of deadening silence and blind rejectionism.

The report was assembled by nineteen commissioners—two from the United States, several from Europe, and a few from other countries. The chair of the report and the commission was former Brazilian president Fernando Henrique Cardoso. The executive summary of the report goes directly to its central thesis; it argues that "the global war on drugs has failed, with devastating consequences for individuals and societies around the world," concluding that "40 years after President Nixon launched the US government's war on drugs, fundamental reforms in national and global drug control policies are urgently needed."[1] The report says that "vast expenditures on criminalization and repressive measures directed at producers, traffickers, and consumers of illegal drugs have clearly failed to effectively curtail supply or consumption." Apparent gains in one region are soon negated by the emergence of other sources and conduits. The report calls for an end to the criminalization and marginalization of people engaged in generally harmless drug use, and urges governments to consider "legal regulation of drugs" as an alternative to coercive and destructive law-enforcement policies.

Urging a rapid end to "the taboo on debate and reform," the UN commission pointed out that "arresting and incarcerating tens of millions of people in recent decades has filled prisons and destroyed lives and families without reducing the availability of illicit drugs or the power of criminal organizations." It found that "just say no" platitudes and "zero-tolerance" approaches have simply never worked, and proposed a shift toward "educational efforts grounded in credible information that focuses on social skills and peer influences." Law-enforcement resources should be devoted to reducing harm to individuals and communities rather than striving to "reduce drug markets," the report adds. The problem is that drug policy, especially but not only in the United States, has long been fueled by a rabidly conservative, authoritarian ideology in conflict with strategies designed to improve health, security, and human rights. What could also have been mentioned is that the War on Drugs, in targeting only "illicit drugs," largely ignores the harmful consequences of perfectly legal substances such as alcohol, tobacco, and pharmaceutical goods.

The United Nations Report

Viewed historically, as mentioned earlier, global patterns of illegal drug consumption have resisted even the most determined efforts of prohibitionist groups to achieve significant reduction in either use or abuse. In the present era, from 1998 to 2008 the international market expanded dramatically—by 34.5 percent for opiates, 27 percent for cocaine, and 8.5 percent for cannabis.[2] (The demand for legal drugs has simultaneously skyrocketed, a problem to be more fully discussed elsewhere.) Antidrug crusades carried out under diverse banners assume that strict law-enforcement methods targeting producers, distributors, and consumers would shrink the contraband market, driving it further onto the margins. In reality, however, the scale of these markets—dominated by organized crime syndicates, large and small—has expanded steadily over this very period.[3] Key policy-making bodies continue to ignore this reality, however, preferring a

70 CHAPTER 3

well-worn strategy rooted in myths and illusions, refusing to acknowledge that "the global drug problem is a set of interlinked health and social challenges to be managed, rather than a war to be won." This misguided warfare outlook, as we have seen, spans much of American history.

Hoping for a more empirical, balanced, humane model, the UN report surveys risks associated with drug use of all sorts, legal and illegal, based in part on findings contained in a 2007 issue of the British journal *Lancet*. While heroin and cocaine are ranked as slightly more dangerous than such legal substances as alcohol and barbiturates, other reputedly terrible drugs are further down the list: amphetamines (seventh), cannabis (tenth), LSD (twelfth), and ecstasy (sixteenth). The report deems the latter drugs, objects of recurrent media horror stories, "low risk" or even harmless.[4]

The report concludes that, in contrast to the bankrupt warrior model, "drug policies must be based on solid empirical and scientific evidence," with primary measures of success dependent on reducing everyday-life harm to individual and public welfare. Prohibitionists devote too little attention to "the complexities of the drug market, drug use, and drug addiction," with the current strategy obsessed with "the number of arrests, the amounts seized, and the harshness of punishments." Refusal to take seriously an objective harm index is simply another indication of warrior myopia and futility. Considering the impact of drug policies on the incidence of HIV/AIDS cases among those who inject drugs, it is precisely the countries with the most "comprehensive harm-reduction strategies"—Britain, Switzerland, Germany, Australia, and Holland—that have reaped the greatest success. Conversely, nations trapped in the warrior model have had far poorer outcomes.[5]

The report further sharply criticizes the warrior obsession with "drug trafficking," noting that the vast majority of people involved in the global drug trade are themselves victims of violence and/or poverty, and many are also dependent on drugs. Unlike the bosses who run huge criminal enterprises, these participants in the market usually have no violent criminal history and look to earn money for survival or to fund their own drug habits, motivated by a combination of social and economic pressures. Villainization and punishment achieve little under such conditions, but the prohibitionists remain undaunted. The commission states that where dependency is an issue, as is common, drug abuse and addiction are far better seen as a "complex health condition that has an ensemble of causes—social, psychological, and physical—including harsh living conditions or a history of personal trauma and emotional problems." Efforts to "solve" this predicament by means of punishment and incarceration will more likely aggravate than ameliorate matters.[6] It is this larger social context of the drug phenomenon that leading proponents of the drug war have chosen to ignore.

Turning to the question of drug control, the report authors believe the demand for a system based on strict international enforcement "has all too often become a straightjacket that inhibits policy development and experimentation." In particular, the International Narcotics Control Board (a tool of the United States) has worked strenuously over the past fifty years to impose the same zero-tolerance approach on all nations, oblivious to their divergent histories, cultures, and politics. For the warriors, flexibility means nothing more than being "soft on drugs." Harm-reduction programs, including steps toward decriminalization, have been largely kept outside the realm of public debate. With formulaic US agendas in mind, the commission observes, "The idea that the existing international drug control framework is immutable, and that any amendment—however reasonable or slight—is a threat to the integrity of the entire system is short-sighted."[7] The report urges that drug conventions, like other binational and multinational agreements, be subject to rethinking in light of new conditions, evidence, and challenges.

The report also cites a "current example of this process (what may be described as 'drug-control imperialism')"—efforts by the Bolivian government to remove the traditional practice of coca-leaf chewing from sections of the 1961 UN convention prohibiting all nonmedical uses of the drug. In the face of studies revealing that the indigenous practice of coca-leaf chewing is associated with none of the harms of processed cocaine, and that a clear majority of Bolivians (and others in the Andean region) want open drug policies, the big cocaine-using nations, led by the United States, moved to block such revisions. No alternative to zero tolerance and its coercive politics can be accepted as part of rational debate. The UN report suggested that "national governments must be enabled to exercise the freedom to experiment with responses more suited to their own circumstances, in contrast to a model that insists upon uniform laws, restrictions, and programs."[8] The War on Drugs constitutes a prime example of cultural blindness and political manipulation on the part of the most powerful capitalist nations.

The warrior program transgresses universal human-rights principles in its repression of cultural traditions, its criminalizing of mostly victimless behavior, its reliance on cruel and excessive punishment, its violations of individual privacy, and its unreasonable confiscation of personal property. The UN report finds troublesome a history of treating users and low-level sellers as dangerous felons, distinct from ordinary people trapped within their own social immediacy. Basic human rights were first enshrined in the 1948 Universal Declaration of

72 CHAPTER 3

Human Rights, which inspired later international treaties and agreements. In fact, a general foundation of rights had been established in the US Declaration of Independence, which affirmed the right to "life, liberty, and the pursuit of happiness." "Of particular relevance to drug policy," the UN report states, "are the rights to life, to health, to due process, and a fair trial, to be free from torture or cruel, inhuman, or degrading treatment . . . and from discrimination."[9] Yet human-rights violations have become a routine feature of global drug warfare, especially in Mexico and Colombia, where rights are fully subordinated to drug-control conventions and operations. The report concludes, "Individuals who use drugs do not forfeit their human rights. Too often drug users suffer discrimination, are forced to accept treatment that both criminalizes the person and denies basic freedoms."[10]

The global drug war has left in its wake one disaster after another for populations everywhere, with millions of people targeted and apprehended as traffickers, pushers, money launderers, and simple users of contraband goods. Warriors see the battle as one against crime and criminals. The report notes that in many US locations and across the world research has found that stepped-up police efforts to stifle drug markets are correlated with higher rates of murder and other violent crimes—exactly what the drug war claims to be fighting. Thus, "Of all the studies examining the effect of increased law enforcement on drug market violence, 91 percent concluded that increased law enforcement actually increased drug-market violence."[11] Further, enhanced police intervention has been shown to hardly reduce gang and syndicate violence, or even the flow of illegal drugs. Typically, where drugs are intercepted or blocked in some areas—as at border crossings—the trade merely shifts to other areas, the so-called "balloon effect."

The UN report observes that prohibition agendas—not drugs as such—constitute the main problem. Thus, "it is the illicit nature of the market that creates much of the market-related violence—legal and regulated commodity markets, while not without problems, do not provide the same opportunities for organized crime to make vast profits, challenge the legitimacy of sovereign governments, and, in some cases, fund insurgency and terrorism."[12] The War on Drugs eventually leads to "a kind of 'arms race' in which more ambitious enforcement programs actually strengthen the organizational and military power of the traffickers, as the most ruthless and violent trafficking groups usually thrive on the competition within black markets. Unfortunately, this seems to be what is currently happening in Mexico and some other parts of the world."[13] The drug war gives rise to conditions in which the most authoritarian institutions gain ascendancy: police, border patrols, intelligence agencies, the military, and prisons. The report notes, "repeated studies have demonstrated that governments achieve much greater financial and social benefit for their communities by investing in health and social programs, rather than investing in supply reduction and law enforcement activities."[14] In this context, the resulting marginalization of the World Health Organization (WHO) and kindred national bodies on drug policy has been an especially worrisome outcome.

The ideological rigidity that guides the drug war has, over several decades, obstructed rational dialogue and alternative strategies. Antonio Maria Costa, former executive director of the UN Office on Drugs and Crime, has identified no less than five harmful outcomes: (1) growth of a sprawling criminal black market that ensures bloated profits from illegal drugs; (2) "extensive policy displacement" where scarce public resources are devoted to law enforcement; (3) "geographical displacement," with drug production shifting locations to effectively avoid police intervention; (4) "substance displacement," or movement of consumers to new, often more potent substances as their drug of choice becomes more difficult to buy; and (5) coercive targeting and marginalization of millions of drug users, with health and social options thoroughly undermined.[15] Nowhere are such trends more visible than at the epicenter of antidrug warfare: Washington, DC. While politicians and officials refer to such repeated disasters as "unintended consequences," hence trivializing them, the disasters emanate from irrational social policy that adversely impacts communities around the world.

An Alternative Path?

The UN report is laden with recommendations for basic departures from long-standing antidrug strategies that have not worked. A gateway to new initiatives must be the opening of political debate, a break from archaic ideological biases and platitudes. The public sphere must be broadened to overcome the weight of deeply embedded myths, illusions, and deceits. Here the commission lays out its demand for an alternative course, fueled by new ideas to "prevent and reduce harms related to drug use and drug-control policies." All national governments should welcome independent research with hopes of reversing those negative consequences identified by Antonio Maria Costa. The report persuasively argues, on the basis of lengthy historical experience, that coercive and punitive methods are futile—that "the war on drugs has not, and cannot, be won."[16]

What seems evident, according to the commission, is that governments must "replace the criminalization and punishment of people who use drugs with the offer of health and treatment services to those who need them." Many nations (including the United States) have already been undertaking initiatives along

74   Chapter 3

these lines, yet troublesome coercive mechanisms remain largely intact. Countries that abandoned the warfare model have been most successful in reducing both individual and social harm associated with illegal drugs. The report further states that a key underpinning of the War on Drugs—that harsh punishment deters people from using (or abusing) drugs—lacks credibility according to both scientific evidence and political experience. Conversely, "decriminalization initiatives do not result in significant increases in drug use" or in elevated levels of violence and crime. In fact, the results are precisely the opposite of what the antidrug crusaders have long claimed.[17]

A third initiative contained in the report looks to stimulate "experimentation by governments with models of legal regulation of drugs (of cannabis, for example) that can subvert the power of organized crime and safeguard the health and security of their citizens." The War on Drugs, as with other efforts at prohibition, simply opens the terrain to criminal gangs and syndicates while contributing to the spread of lucrative black markets. So far, unfortunately, "the debate on alternative models of drug-market regulation has too often been constrained" by ideological homilies, entrenched institutional norms, and economic interests, closing off new avenues of thought. Thus, "It is unhelpful to ignore those who argue for a taxed and regulated market for currently illicit drugs. This is a policy option that should be explored with the same rigor as any other."[18] That means, above all, a readiness to learn from diverse national experiences, especially those based on health-oriented, harm-reducing, nonrepressive policies. Recent progressive alternatives undertaken in such countries as Portugal, Australia, and Holland point toward more rational (and less harmful) outcomes—but not until the public sphere is enlarged to accommodate broader debate.

The report calls for new indicators in shaping drug policy—that is, better criteria for measuring and judging human outcomes. The current system is deeply flawed, geared as it is to arrests, confiscations, eradication processes, targeting of cartel kingpins, and so forth. None of this, as mentioned, has served to weaken illegal drug markets, curtail demand, or alleviate crime and violence. Long-term warfare against syndicates and traffickers, as in Mexico and Colombia, has produced few results even in the narrowest prohibitionist terms.[19] Eradication of such crops as cannabis, opium, and coca sooner or later forces cultivation elsewhere, keeping law enforcement on the run. New measures of policy success would turn toward health and social programs, optimally within a context of the regulated legalization of currently illegal substances. Outlawed drugs would be marketed, controlled, and taxed much like beer, wine, liquor, and pharmaceuticals today, freeing law enforcement to pursue other, clearly more serious, threats to public security. The report also observes that, at a time of economic downturn and fiscal austerity, massive investment in the drug war—largely a waste of resources in any case—makes little sense.[20] In the United States, where questions of fiscal crisis and debt burdens have gained a sense of political urgency, such arguments would seem to be especially compelling.

Any major policy shift will require new directions in public thinking on drugs *in general*—no easy task given the thoroughly entrenched character of warrior ideology. The report states, "Currently, too many policymakers reinforce the idea that all people who use drugs are 'amoral addicts,' and everyone involved in drug markets is a ruthless criminal. The reality is much more complex."[21] According to UN figures, there are now more than 250 million users of illegal drugs worldwide, with hundreds of thousands engaged in production and distribution. Aside from what is known empirically about the everyday character of drug consumption, common sense dictates that treating so many human beings (most involved in victimless activities) as predatory outlaws is backward social policy.[22]

The observable reality of drug production and consumption has never corresponded to warrior stereotypes and media scaremongering. UN data indicate that, among 250 million illegal drug users globally, less than 10 percent can be classified as "addicts" or "abusers," and even here prevailing images do not hold as the problems are not innately linked to nightmarish outcomes sensationalized in media culture.[23] The actuality is that drugs of every conceivable type have today become an integral part of everyday social life, above all in the United States. According to the commission, "factors that influence an individual's decision to start using drugs have more to do with fashion, peer influence, and social or economic context than with the drug's legal status, risk of detection, or government prevention messages." Patterns of dependency, meanwhile, have more to do with important contextual factors than with "moral weakness or hedonism." As for producers, "Most people involved in the illicit cultivation of coca, opium poppy, or cannabis are small farmers struggling to make a living for their families. The idea of destroying their only means of survival, especially when alternatives are dreary or nonexistent, makes little sense."[24]

Regarding the undeniable global problems of drug abuse and dependency, the commission urges a broadening of media and political discourse to allow for critical voices and fresh approaches. Thus, "It is not possible to frighten or punish someone out of drug dependence, but with the right sort of evidence-based treatment dependent users can change their behavior and be active and productive members of the community."[25] In cases where users are arrested and branded "felons," alternative models wind up extremely difficult to implement. Where less punitive and more harm-reducing strategies are introduced, as in Portugal, Australia, and Holland, more positive results can be achieved with

76 CHAPTER 3

far less expenditure of public resources. A harm-minimizing policy, moreover, is especially compelling where drug markets are diverse and well established, as in the United States. Under these conditions "preventing drug use by stopping supply is not a realistic objective."[26]

The report upholds a move toward decriminalization for the vast majority of users and sellers, with at worst only modest sentences for small-time and first-time dealers. It states, "The majority of people arrested for small-scale drug selling are not gangsters or organized criminals. They are young people who are exploited to do the risky work of street selling, dependent drug users trying to raise money for their own supply, or couriers coerced or intimidated into taking drugs across borders."[27] The problem is that such individuals are often prosecuted as if they were organized and violent criminals—that is, given severe, ruinous punishment that serves no conceivable public good. Small-time offenders are usually the most visible and easiest to apprehend, and generally lack means of adequate defense. "The result is that governments are filling prisons with minor offenders serving long sentences, at great cost, and with no impact on the scale or profitability of the market."[28]

The key challenge now, according to the commission, is for governments to pursue diverse methods for dealing with small-time offenders, which means amending laws to render clearer and more proportionate distinctions among different actors on the global drug scene. Decriminalization ought to be the supreme component of a rational drug policy. At present, in the United States and some other countries, drug offenders can be subject to life imprisonment or even the death penalty—in flagrant violation of international human-rights norms and statutes. The report adds, "To show their commitment to fighting the drug war, many countries implement laws and punishments that are out of proportion to the seriousness of the crime, and that still do not have a significant deterrent effect."[29]

The report calls for expanded health programs, social supports, and *prevention* efforts designed to curb abuse and addiction: large numbers of people will always gravitate toward intoxicants, so resources are best devoted to curbing harm rather than pursuing hopeless zero-tolerance crusades. Nations with strict prohibitionist laws tend to fail across the board, as problems linked to black markets and criminal syndicates naturally intensify.[30] The report stresses that "the energy, creativity, and expertise of civil society and community groups are of particular importance in the design and delivery of these programs. Scarce public resources will have to be shifted from the warfare model to a more balanced, innovative, holistic approach. It follows that governments will need to "offer a wide and easily accessible range of options for treatment and care for drug dependence, including substitution of heroin-assisted treatment with special attention to those most at risk."[31]

For any of such recommendations to take effect, the report urges the United Nations itself to "provide leadership in the reform of global drug policy . . . [which must be] based on evidence."[32] To date there has been only limited reconsideration of failed initiatives, delaying new departures based on the best scientific findings and political experience of countries having adopted progressive harm-reduction strategies. The commission finds special fault with the US antidrug establishment, since "for most of the last century it has been the U.S. government that has led calls for the development and maintenance of repressive drug policies."[33] Some hope was invested in the Obama administration, which in 2008 seemed to acknowledge the need for alternatives to strict prohibitionism. However, there has been little evidence that Obama or the Democrats were ready to shift course—to end reliance on punishment and incarceration as crucial instruments of drug policy. Skepticism along these lines was confirmed by Obama's dismissive response to the UN report; its main findings and recommendations were essentially stonewalled by the White House.

Finally, and most centrally, the commission proposes an immediate move toward genuine drug-policy debate. The main problem here is one of powerful economic interests, an entrenched federal bureaucracy, and rigid ideological biases, as "policymakers understand that current policies and strategies are failing but do not know what to do instead. There is a temptation to avoid this issue."[34] New departures will depend on some combination of approaches—decriminalization, legalization, healthcare measures, and social programs—that hidebound politicians and sundry opinion leaders reflexively find taboo. The report calls this an "abdication of policy responsibility—for every year we continue with the current approach billions of dollars are wasted on ineffective programs, millions of citizens are sent to prison unnecessarily, millions more suffer from drug dependence of loved ones who cannot access health and social services, and hundreds of thousands of people die from preventable overdoses and diseases contracted through unsafe drug use."[35]

The UN report concludes with a moral imperative: "Getting drug policy right is not a matter of theoretical or intellectual debate—it is one of the key policy challenges of our time."[36] That challenge, as mentioned previously, is now being taken up by several countries, generally with beneficial results, pointing toward even more enlightened solutions once warfare ideology is critically scrutinized and, eventually, jettisoned. In Portugal, for example, the first European nation to fully decriminalize use and possession of all currently illegal drugs, overall drug consumption has remained stable while heroin use (the key concern) has

78   CHAPTER 3

sharply declined. One important study revealed that "removal of criminal penalties, combined with alternative therapeutic approaches for people struggling with drug dependence has reduced the burden of drug law enforcement on the criminal justice system and the overall level of problematic drug use."[37]

Prevailing conditions in such nations as Holland, Switzerland, and England—with long-standing liberalized drug strategies—are much the same: less drug abuse, reduced pressures on law enforcement, decreased public expenditures, declining levels of violent crime, far less drug-related public harm. In Holland, where "street drugs" are relatively cheap and easily available, the amount of individual and social damage resulting from drugs is today among the lowest in the world. Addiction is rare and the percentage of heroin users, for example, is extremely low. Scare rhetoric of the sort common in the United States about decriminalization leading to out-of-control drug abuse, with escalating crime and violence, has been fully disproven.

Political Mythologies

Viewed in political context, the UN report could be seen as directed overwhelmingly at the American drug warriors—long the catalytic force behind the global War on Drugs. In fact the report was decidedly liberal in outlook, hardly radical in its motivations, findings, or proposals. Among other limits, the commission never addressed the problem of legal drugs that remain a far greater source of destructive health outcomes than all banned substances combined. Legal products, of course, include not only pharmaceuticals and their myriad offshoots but also alcohol, tobacco, caffeine, sugar, and other widely consumed goods. The report failed to investigate deeper questions of drug abuse and addiction. While the commission urged the White House and its antidrug apparatus to alter course from the warfare model, its discourse generally followed mainstream assumptions, especially in holding to the (untenable) distinction between legitimate and illicit, legal and illegal drugs. In its decidedly moderate and optimistic tone, the report gave encouragement to many drug-war critics hoping that the Obama administration might be ready to shift focus and jettison its moribund strategy. On becoming president in 2009, after all, Obama did suggest that "fresh thinking" would be needed to ameliorate the "drug problem."

Such hopes would be quickly dashed, however, and the White House eventually met the UN report with a dismissive shrug; Obama and some leading administration voices responded that "legalization was off the table."[38] The claim that long-standing drug policies had "failed" was surely too much for any US president to entertain, as this would mean revisiting basic assumptions concerning law enforcement, public health, foreign policy, the drug industry, and social programs. The drug war had become a virtually sacred element of American political culture, with clear dividing lines separating "good" from "bad" policy. While a certain openness to change was deemed worth considering—as in channeling more resources into treating drug offenders—the summits of power continued to embrace law enforcement as the unmovable centerpiece of US drug policy. The ink on the report was barely dry when the federal drug-war apparatus moved into full swing: Rafael Lemaitre decreed the War on Drugs a great success, insisting that "drug use" in the United States was in steady decline. Any talk of decriminalizing banned substances was decreed to be a "nonstarter."

In his off-handed rejection of the report, Obama reaffirmed US commitment to the global drug war "out of recognition that drug use strains our economy, health, and public safety," repeating that "legalization remains a nonstarter . . . because research shows that illegal drug use is associated with voluntary treatment admissions, fatal drugged driving accidents, mental illness, and emergency room admissions."[39] He claimed that legalization would do nothing to reduce Mexican cartel activity, profits, and violence. Nonetheless, Obama's drug-control strategy was advertised as something of a departure from the past, as it embraced a shift toward prevention and treatment while framing addiction as a "disease" instead of a moral failing. This ostensibly more "balanced" and humane approach, however, hardly signified a retreat from prohibition, nor did it augur fewer resources allocated to drug interdiction, crop eradications, raids, arrests, surveillance, and the prison complex.

The corporate media, immersed in the warfare mentality, was quick to denigrate the UN report as unrealistic, dangerous, and counterproductive. A *Time* magazine article by Mark Benjamin echoed a familiar American sentiment: just ignore the report as an exercise in utopian dreaming. Benjamin wrote that the report was filled with nothing but "nutty ideas," predictable enough given a commission made up of a "bunch of hippies" along with some other "no-name pinkos" with a fondness for crazy proposals.[40] (The "hippies" and "pinkos" presumably included such members as former Federal Reserve chair Paul Volcker, former secretary of state George Shultz, and former Mexican president Ernesto Zedillo.) The much-researched UN conclusion that global drug warfare had dismally failed—that prohibition and coercion should give way to harm reduction—apparently did not merit political debate.

Meanwhile, after the White House declared that the War on Drugs was making enormous gains, Obama earmarked (for 2013) yet another $26 billion for domestic and foreign prohibition operations—profligate increases in

80   CHAPTER 3

federal spending at a time of fiscal crisis and deep government cutbacks. As for the report, even its modest proposal to legalize marijuana as a relatively benign substance—identical to widespread reform efforts in the United States—was mocked by Obama and his drug warriors in a series of public meetings. The War on Drugs, it appears, is so deeply woven into the American public fabric that, despite its horrendous failures and costs, prospects for enlightened thinking within the political and media establishments remain dismal, though opinion shifts in state-level politics have been duly registered, as with several 2012 electoral outcomes favoring legalized marijuana.

In April 2014, Obama said (regarding pot), "I think it [taking marijuana] is a bad idea, a waste of time, not very healthy," adding, "I don't think it's more dangerous than alcohol"—a truism that brought the wrath of the drug warriors down on the White House. Obama went on: "If marijuana is fully legalized and at some point folks say, 'Well, we can come up with a negotiated dose of cocaine that we can show is not any more harmful than vodka,' are we open to that?"[41] The problem here is that the facts regarding pot addiction hardly justify the stubborn refusal to remove marijuana's ridiculous classification as a "dangerous drug," as the UN report strongly advocates. Further, if pot is no more dangerous than alcohol—in fact it is dramatically *less* dangerous—the very basis of governmental paternalism (which Obama appears to embrace) is entirely undermined.

The bankruptcy of US global drug policy was embarrassingly visible at a May 2013 meeting of the Organization of American States (OAS) in Bogotá, where Latin American leaders almost unanimously called for an end to the drug war, seen mainly as a boon to traffickers and cartels responding to American demand. The OAS consensus was for a political strategy centered on public health and social priorities, as coercive policies had dismally failed—a stance consistent with the UN report. Virtually alone, the Obama administration stonewalled such proposals, refusing to even discuss constructive alternatives to the warfare model.

The idea of a "softer" drug policy (more emphasis on prevention and treatment) does indeed suggest policy changes at a time when the old paradigm remains firmly entrenched at the federal level; prohibitionist ideology will be hard to dislodge, though cracks in the edifice have become visible. Some thirty million Americans have been arrested for drug offenses since the early 1980s, filling local, state, and federal prisons with mostly nonviolent offenders. Obama's 2013 budget allocated more resources for prevention and treatment than in the past, but funding for law enforcement, border patrols, eradication, surveillance, raids, and prisons has likewise been increased. Generous stimulus money has been devoted to this area of drug control. Thousands of additional police officers have been deployed around the country, many linked to such projects as Community

Oriented Police Services (COPS). As before, arrests are concentrated in minority areas. Well-funded lobbies behind the drug war—prison unions, private lockup corporations, law enforcers, Big Pharma—are in fact stronger today than ever.

Michelle Alexander notes that antidrug narratives in the United States have always fixated on the wrongdoing of outsiders and "aliens," drugs and criminality being associated with blacks, Hispanics, immigrants, and foreigners. Whoever occupies the White House, this targeting of "others" in effect serves the interests of corporations, the security-state, and drug-war bureaucracy. She writes, "Whether one believes . . . that Obama's drug war is actually worse than his predecessors, one thing is clear: Obama is in no hurry to scale it back to any significant degree, much less end it. The drug war is now too deeply rooted in our nation's political and economic structure to be cast aside. The war rhetoric may have ended and the song may have changed, but the system hums along."[42]

What, then, about the White House contention that illegal drug consumption in the United States has dropped, proof the War on Drugs is working? Of course the reference to "drugs," as usual, ignores the much larger *legal* drug markets, as pharmaceuticals alone account for more than $300 billion yearly in revenue. Americans consume 60 percent of all drugs, legal and illegal, worldwide. The former—including not only prescribed medications but OTC products, alcohol, and tobacco—are responsible, by conservative estimates, for roughly one million deaths each year, along with such harmful outcomes as adverse reactions, overdoses, addictions, and drug-related accidents. Compared to this nightmare, damage from illegal drugs (including perhaps tens of thousands of deaths from overdoses) must be viewed with less urgency. Still, within American public discourse allusions to harmful drugs rarely go beyond those products sold and bought outside the legitimate market, as they are by definition "illicit."

A key question remains: has *illegal* drug consumption actually fallen in the United States, as government officials contend? The answer: hardly. In fact, this claim—advanced by warriors across the decades—is nothing short of preposterous, handy for stonewalling information such as that contained in the UN report. It is particularly useful for closing off public debate. According to a 2011 report by the Substance Abuse and Mental Health Services Administration (SAMHSA), illegal drug use in the United States rose to its highest level in nearly a decade, fueled by a sharp increase in pot consumption and a similar rise in methamphetamine use. Office of National Drug Control Policy director Gil Kerlikowske called this trend very disappointing, a function of "eroding attitudes" about the dangers of banned drugs and the widening influence of medical pot outlets. He said, "I think all of the attention and the focus on calling marijuana medicine has sent the absolute wrong message to our young people."[43] The SAMHSA

82   CHAPTER 3

report found that 22.6 million Americans twelve and older had used illicit drugs in 2010—roughly 9 percent of the population, an increase from 8 percent two years earlier. In 2012—at the time of the UN report's release—the United States easily had the highest rate of combined legal and illegal drug use in the world. Despite a recent slight drop in cocaine purchases, Americans were still four times more likely to indulge in that prohibited drug than any other country's population, including in nations with far more permissive laws. Per capita marijuana consumption in the United States dwarfs that of countries like Holland and Portugal, where criminal penalties have been abolished. Ironically, it is tobacco use that has fallen most sharply—an entirely legal drug that has been regulated and taxed more heavily, targeted as well by negative media coverage. The UN report, backed by findings at the WHO, reveals a striking tendency: nations with the most stringent antidrug laws are among the highest in their incidence of both use and abuse. Meanwhile, Americans consume nearly 80 percent of the global supply of painkillers—more than eleven tons of pure opiates—yearly, as the prescription-drug epidemic veers out of control.[44]

The official claim that the War on Drugs has been won—or even is winding down—is ludicrous in the context of Obama's refusal to so much as discuss the UN report and of escalating (if futile) law-enforcement efforts to crush the medical-marijuana movement. In California during 2011 and 2012 hundreds of cannabis dispensaries were forced to close after federal prosecutors moved to crack down on even those outlets conforming to state laws. In July 2012 federal actions forced closure of the Oakland-based Harborside Health Center, the nation's largest medical pot dispensary and one regarded as a model enterprise. Earlier, in April, federal agents had raided several California businesses operated by marijuana activists that were legalized, taxed, and supported by local politicians. Indeed marijuana—not heroin, cocaine, or amphetamines—now constitutes the main target of the warriors' antidrug crusade.

The pharmaceutical industry, about which both the UN report and White House response were silent, has evolved into the most profitable business in the United States. Its corporations are perfectly free to market and advertise their often-harmful goods openly. Big Pharma enterprises like Pfizer, Merck, Abbott, and AstraZeneca sell hundreds of billions of dollars' worth of drugs as medications, most riddled with potentially severe adverse reactions, but also as ingredients in food, toxic agents in water, and substances fed to animals. The chemical makeup of legal drugs usually differs little from that of most illegal drugs—a key contrast being that the former is deemed "safer" because it has a doctor's imprimatur. In 2012 the United States remained the only major country with direct-to-consumer advertising of prescription drugs, which currently saturates most TV outlets.

Filmmaker Eugene Jarecki's searing attack on the drug war in *The House I Live In* (2012), Grand Jury Prize winner at the Sundance Film Festival, depicts how a political crusade mired in lies and myths has been so immensely destructive to American society. Jarecki emphasizes, far beyond what is contained in the UN report, how the War on Drugs tramples basic human rights enshrined in the most cherished of US documents. He contends that we are dealing less with a war on drugs than a war on *people*, especially on the poor and minorities. "We are now in many ways a laughing stock for the rest of the world due to the enormity of our prison population," says Jarecki. "So it seems to me that the moral bankruptcy of the War on Drugs would be something that really should be a central topic [of political debate]." It follows that such "moral bankruptcy" would seem to demand a more radical approach than "policy reform" or liberalization of existing laws—but of course such a departure is anathema to American politicians and the corporate media, a view shared, unfortunately, by the UN critics. After more than four decades of disastrous outcomes, it seems increasingly obvious today that the entire drug-war machinery must be dismantled.

CHAPTER 4
DRUG WAR, AUTHORITARIAN POLITICS

The War on Drugs both reflects and contributes to increasing authoritarian trends in American society, at work beneath the surface of venerated liberal-democratic institutions and practices. Such trends are both ideological and structural, visible in the growth of a federal antidrug bureaucracy, widening law-enforcement powers, a sprawling prison-industrial complex, an expanding surveillance network, and, ultimately, erosion of Constitutional freedoms and rights. As the drug war becomes militarized, moreover, the national-security behemoth gains added dominion and legitimacy. At present several federal agencies carry out important tasks within antidrug warfare: the FDA, the DEA, the IRS, the FBI, the CIA, the DHS, Customs, Border Patrol, the Department of the Treasury, and the Pentagon. The drug war perfectly fits the larger US warfare trajectory, going back to the early postwar years and perhaps even the first days of the republic. In recent years, strong antidemocratic impulses consistent with the general rightward direction of American politics since at least the early 1980s run parallel with the growing concentration of power in transnational corporations, Wall Street, government bureaucracy, far-flung intelligence operations, and, of course, the world's largest military. Political outlooks nourished by superpatriotism, "free-market" capitalism, religious fundamentalism, the gun culture, and "traditional values" remain on the ascendancy—reflected in the explosive spread of Tea Party politics—while general anxiety, social fragmentation, and mass depoliticization are also on the rise. Here the War on Drugs—a political crusade ostensibly against sinful behavior and harmful substances—performs crucial functions of social control and ideological manipulation.

From Volstead to Nixon

Since drug consumption in its myriad forms is natural and ubiquitous, never to be eradicated from human society, prohibition agendas must sooner or later turn coercive and repressive. Such is the well-known legacy of the Volstead Act, inspired by a cleansing war to rid the United States of evil alcohol—a legacy so tortured and futile that mainstream politicians brought it to a halt within little more than a decade. The Puritanical desire for a sober world ultimately collapsed under its own weight, though not before social problems that Prohibition was expected to solve actually worsened: crime and violence, for example, reached new peaks during the 1920s as many American cities became combat zones.[1] Repression gave rise to expanded corruption and criminality, which in turn simply generated more repression. As for demon alcohol, its manufacture and consumption were simply driven underground, with perpetual raids, harassment, and arrests scarcely denting the flow of spirits or spread of black-market capitalism. Nor did harsh laws serve to dampen public attitudes toward bars, saloons, and speakeasies, which remained very much at the center of daily life, especially among immigrants and the working class. The contemporary War on Drugs has in effect recycled this disastrous national experience, as if nothing had been learned, predictably leading to more crime to match widened police operations in the decades after President Nixon launched his great crusade. It was obvious from the outset of the revitalized prohibition campaign that political elites had learned virtually nothing from the past. Those victimized by draconian antidrug laws, police crackdowns, and severe jail sentences were overwhelmingly poor and minorities—a pattern that continues as the American prison complex, like its military power, now stands as the largest, and surely most damaging, in the world.

In the aftermath of the Vietnam War, sixties rebellions, youth counterculture, and new social movements of the 1970s, Nixon moved toward what might be referred to as a restorative politics in which the drug war would come to figure prominently. The historic 1970 Comprehensive Drug Abuse Prevention and Control Act was followed by a series of policy initiatives targeting both traffickers and users, framing the "drug threat" in a manner designed to serve conservative priorities: the security state, law enforcement, large corporations, and the medical complex.[2] The federal antidrug apparatus championed longer prison terms for consumers as well as sellers, including mandatory minimum terms central to the 1984 Sentencing Reform Act, a 700-page document that would lay the foundations of rapidly swelling inmate populations during the 1980s and 1990s. Federal and state prosecutors were given unprecedented powers. The

86 CHAPTER 4

death penalty took on renewed emphasis, notably in the context of federal drug offenses. First-time offenders could receive up to sixty-eight months in jail.[3] By the mid-1990s roughly one-third of all prisoners in US jails (nearly two million total) would be convicted of drug-related crimes.

With congressional passage of President Clinton's tough Omnibus Crime Bill in 1994, federal authoritarian initiatives gained further visibility.[4] Intended to combat terrorism as well as drugs, this legislation laid out thirty-eight new categories for the death penalty, mostly drug-related. Armed with broadened coercive powers, law enforcement had new flexibility to pursue a War on Drugs that had little success, even on its own (purported) terms. In this milieu drug czars were able to win new power and legitimacy. At the same time, evidence showed the vast majority of drug offenders (mainly users and small-time pushers) were socially disadvantaged, poorly educated, and people of color: 65 percent of inmates had never finished high school, 33 percent were jobless, and 32 percent had annual incomes below $5,000. Blacks comprised no less than 35 percent of those prosecuted for drug offenses—and their incarceration rates were by far the highest.[5] Given such reality, it seems clear the War on Drugs furnished conservatives with a class-based rationale for ramping up broader ideological agendas.

Today the federal antidrug bureaucracy includes, above all, the DEA—along with such agencies as the FDA, the ATF, the CIA, the FBI, the IRS, Customs, the Coast Guard, and other sectors of the Pentagon—joined regularly by state and local police departments. Its single-minded announced goal is maximum destruction of the illegal drug trade. Various statistical targets are set up as indicators of success: number of seizures and amounts seized, forfeitures, arrests, indictments, convictions, and jailings. Such aggressive warfare, however, has never seriously undermined the flow of drugs, which for many decades has remained large-scale, international, and lucrative. It does, however, contribute significantly to the growth of governmental power, mainly its coercive and bureaucratic side—not to mention the steady erosion of legal protections and individual rights. Steven Wisotsky observes, "The net result of the War on Drugs is gradually, but inexorably, to expand enforcement powers at the expense of personal freedom."[6]

Antidrug operations, whether conducted inside the United States or outside its borders, cannot be isolated from the more far-reaching national-security state (NSS) and its global war machinery, with its profound impact on the economy, politics, culture, and foreign policy. The NSS seems hardly on the verge of shrinking domestically or retreating internationally: in 2013 the United States was spending more on its military forces (nearly $1 trillion) than all other nations combined, with hundreds of bases scattered across the planet, the world's largest navy and air force, a nuclear arsenal of several thousand warheads, and satellite-based intelligence networks with no parallel anywhere. With the long US history of perpetual warfare and hegemonic aspirations that frame the world as a frightening place, no funding cuts in the warfare system are imminent, owing to a priority shared by the major parties even in the midst of supposedly grave fiscal crisis. A swollen NSS ensures that the United States will continue along the path of military-driven agendas and an interventionist foreign policy, despite moments of relative quiet. As old wars (Iraq, Afghanistan) have consumed less US attention, moreover, new threats (Somalia, Yemen, Iran, Syria, North Korea, terrorist groups like Al Qaeda and ISIS) appear to keep Washington at a high level of armed preparedness and vigilance.

The warfare consensus that permeates the summits of American power also enters the realm of mass politics: the vast majority of ordinary Americans remain infatuated with military prowess, guns, violence, and wartime combat, despite occasional talk of isolationism.[7] The very image of national greatness held by large sectors of the public is embedded in a romanticized view of the armed forces that saturates the corporate media, popular culture, and political discourse. Historically, American identity has often been reaffirmed in the context of bloody and protracted foreign wars. Whether confronting terrorism, rogue states, geopolitical challengers like Russia and China, or the illegal drug trade, the United States seeks a regimen of "order" and "stability" enforced by maximum (full-spectrum) American global power.[8] The decades-old drug war cannot be understood apart from this broader NSS trajectory.

Civil Rights under Siege

Conservatives never tire of praising long-standing American virtues of individual rights and political freedoms, yet the War on Drugs they pursue is overwhelmingly statist and bureaucratic, in the end scarcely respectful of those virtues; the Bill of Rights has suffered immeasurably from the antidrug crusade. Nor have the familiar principles of "life, liberty, and the pursuit of happiness," contained in the Preamble to the Constitution, enjoyed much resonance within US drug policy, as the very goals of prohibition, zero tolerance, and drug-free society militate against this vital core of American political ideology. The "fourth drive" that underlies so much drug use, whether medical or recreational, is in fact consistent with the Preamble, which theoretically valorizes basic human freedoms even where personal choice violates established social norms and rules. Nothing within the basic concept of rights/freedoms dictates boundaries of what should be legally or politically sanctioned. Government efforts to regulate personal

88 CHAPTER 4

life—whether in religion, sexual behavior, drugs, or food—conflict with any system based on rights and freedoms. Since the federal government should have no role in dictating religious, sexual, or food choices, the War on Drugs clearly violates political ideals aligned with the Preamble and the Constitution.

Antidrug laws are inevitably punitive—long sentences for mere possession, severe punishment for even first- and second-time violators, lives ruined over essentially victimless crimes, horrendous jail conditions, intrusive surveillance methods, and so forth.[9] Those arrested on drug charges are stigmatized as criminals, even when, on rare occasions, they wind up exonerated. Infringements of the Eighth Amendment (due to cruel and unusual punishment, all too frequent in drug cases) have become sadly routine: jobs can be lost, careers ruined, savings accounts emptied, property lost, and reputations smeared—all in the service of prohibitionist morality. Property such as homes, cars, boats, cash, and land can be seized without even the pretense of due process. Defense attorneys can be targets of harassment and threats. Local governing statutes can be arbitrarily overturned in cases where they conflict with federal edicts.

Further, sections of the Fourth Amendment have come under attack, or simply been ignored, notably relating to bans on unreasonable searches and seizures. The threat associated with pot arrests is particularly salient as cannabis—though less harmful than most legal drugs—is listed as a fearsome Schedule I controlled drug, subject to extreme penalties even for possession. In fact, civil forfeiture statutes have been most commonly invoked for small-scale pot offenses, although modest reform does finally appear on the horizon.[10] According to federal policy, marijuana use anywhere in the United States is strictly forbidden (except for medical purposes), as the drug enforcers falsely insist there can be no safe level of consumption. Nearly 90 percent of marijuana arrests have been for simple possession, and offenders face jail terms of up to twenty years in such states as Louisiana and Oklahoma.[11]

Forfeiture laws stipulate that arrest for even first-time pot offenses can subject individuals to seizure of real estate, vehicles, jewelry, and other property, often without so much as a hearing. In most drug cases there is no "reasonable doubt" and little due process: property can be confiscated even when a person is only *charged* with a crime. A house can be seized where nothing more than a single joint is found—even if the defendant is later found innocent. Convicted pot offenders face revocation or denial of federal benefits, including professional licenses, welfare entitlements, small-business loans, and farm subsidies. In twenty states the maxim "smoke a joint, lose your license" is invoked to suspend the driver's license of anyone merely arrested for a drug crime. In a period of mounting fiscal crisis, governments at every level—driven by urgent budgetary demands—are inclined to view arrests, fines, and seizures as means of raising money, a form of corruption that has rarely gotten much media attention.[12]

As the American antidrug crusade gained momentum and legitimacy, such activities as police surveillance, house raids, searches, sting operations, and arrests took on features of daily normalcy, as did drug testing at workplaces, in government, and in sports. Drug-sniffing dogs aided law enforcement in the search for banned drugs at high schools, airports, public parks, community centers, and urban streets. In many states anyone possessing a mere joint of marijuana could be arrested and jailed, their livelihood and careers thrown into jeopardy.[13] Workers could be suspended or fired for nothing more than possession of banned substances. Raids and searches were carried out randomly across the country, on the pretext that (illicit) drugs constitute a major health threat to individuals and society. Drug testing escalated during the 1980s, one response to the warrior vision of a "drug-free workplace," consistent with a zero-tolerance policy for society as a whole. Hundreds of labs were set up to monitor American drug consumption.[14] Enforced through bipartisan consensus at the centers of power, urine testing became nearly automatic, even where no grounds for suspicion existed—ostensibly in the interests of public safety. Corporations were free to conduct drug testing more or less at will, which amounts to a violation of the privacy rights enshrined in the Fourth Amendment.

In 1998 the Drug-Free Workplace Program became federal policy, endowing government and corporations with added leverage to conduct testing based on the questionable employee-at-will doctrine, eventually upheld by state and local courts. A positive result—outweighing privacy and due-process issues—could get a worker fired summarily. Then, as later, failed drug tests would be virtually impossible to challenge, as drawn-out legal processes are costly and waged in an atmosphere where those charged are presumed guilty. At present the warrior goal of a drug-free workplace remains very much alive, driven by lobbies for testing laboratories; corporations like Hoffman-La Roche; and politicians eager to target schools, government offices, the military, and welfare systems. There is lucrative business in the sales of testing kits for employers, pressures to "test 'em all"—though, of course, only for "illicit" substances, rarely for alcohol and other legal drugs.[15] As of 2012, more than 80 percent of US businesses had implemented some form of drug testing, often even surpassing programs adopted in professional sports. Hopes for universal mandatory testing—viewed by some as a moral imperative—remain high, especially for beneficiaries of a multibillion-dollar industry, such as LabCorp, Abbott, and Hoffman-La Roche.

Meanwhile, legal guarantees for most workers remain murky, as do general criteria for what is to be tested and how. Urine testing (like blood testing) is still

90 CHAPTER 4

a rather poorly developed technology, in which false positives, faulty procedures, and contaminated samples do occur from time to time. What exactly constitutes a "problem" for work performance is also at issue: not only outlawed drugs, but alcohol and pharmaceuticals can easily interfere with workplace efficiency, not to mention such common difficulties as sickness, depression, and family conflict. As of spring 2014, the American Society of Addiction Medicine was calling for *expanded* drug testing throughout society, meaning no realm of daily life—workplaces, communities, schools, universities, government entities—will be free of an aggressive monitoring regimen. Testing, moreover, can extend to other areas of the body: not only blood and urine, but nails, sweat, saliva, hair, and breath. In attacking human behavior that is generally innocuous and harmless, the testing zealots are taking yet another step toward the end of privacy.[16]

The War on Drugs proceeds in a social milieu where offenders can often be treated worse than rapists, burglars, and even murderers—a matter of cruel and unusual punishment amounting to yet another violation of Constitutional rights. Warrior propaganda about the horrors of drug use underpins a campaign that, all too often, targets victimless crimes involving little if any public harm since, after all, evil behavior must be harshly punished, whatever the broader social consequences. It is often forgotten that the vast majority of underground drug transactions, targeted by surveillance, sting operations, raids, and arrests, are usually *consensual*, with no force or deceit involved, little different from what takes place in everyday market exchanges. Tens of millions of otherwise-law-abiding Americans are subject to being labeled, harassed, targeted, and even ruined simply for exercising the right to indulge certain types of pleasure, to pursue the "fourth drive," to experience some mode of "happiness." That state and federal courts have consistently validated government policies and laws that violate the Bill of Rights only further legitimates repressive modes of rule.[17] That such costly, failed, and unconstitutional policies are supported by most politicians from both major parties reflects the poverty of rational decision making in contemporary American society.

The Surveillance Complex

Recent developments in surveillance technology—leading toward what some have called the "total surveillance society"—have accelerated in the wake of 9/11, the war on terrorism, and growth of the homeland-security apparatus.[18] Less well understood is the extent to which the drug war itself has contributed to such Orwellian tendencies, given its role in the expansion of federal bureaucracies, law enforcement, military power, and border operations—all reinforced by highly sophisticated forms of technology.

The US surveillance regime, as Ray Pratt argues, has a long history in many ways symptomatic of the dark side of American politics, reflecting not only deep fear of ubiquitous enemies but also something of a paranoid style that still infects so much of public life. For most of this history surveillance has targeted disruptive social and political forces—primarily though not exclusively on the left.[19] It follows that Constitutional protections for citizens have always been fragile, tendentious, at times readily disposable, as during the post–World War I Red Scare, 1950s McCarthyism, and 1970s COINTELPRO machinations. As Pratt notes, moreover, the main ingredients of a modern surveillance state—politically charged law enforcement, technological monitoring, state secrecy, covert actions, suspension of due process—are fully embedded in the postwar national-security state.[20] Going back to World War I, perhaps earlier, Americans have been subjected to government elites who lie, engage in cover-ups, and maintain secret agendas. The work of the FBI, the CIA, the NSA, the DEA, and sometimes even local police is largely hidden from view, probably nowhere more so than in the War on Drugs. Indeed the antidrug crusade enlists the highly secretive operations of many federal agencies, consistent with the logic of a powerful, unaccountable NSS. The "drug" preoccupation has done much to broaden avenues of social control and political repression at a time when heightened surveillance helps perpetuate a mass ethos of cynicism, paranoia, and distrust of government.

Since the late 1940s the NSS, erected on a confluence of government, corporate, military, and law-enforcement interests, has embraced a view of the United States as being in a state of perpetual warfare against an assortment of enemies, foreign and domestic—fascists, communists, rogue states, and, since the 1970s, an ensemble of terrorists, drug traffickers, urban gangsters, and cartel kingpins. Such threats were always seen as a mortal challenge to "American values," understood to encompass individual rights and freedoms—the very rights and freedoms routinely placed under attack by the drug war. Indeed, with the collapse of the Soviet bloc, the War on Drugs (often linked to counterterrorism) has provided a crucial ideological rationale for the ever-expanding security-state apparatus. The DEA alone, with its 11,000 employees, $3 billion budget, and far-reaching domestic and global capabilities, intersects in many ways with other federal agencies. Ambitious DEA initiatives—monitoring drug flows, crop eradications, house and field raids, surveillance, interrogations, sting operations, arrests—obviously require ongoing high levels of vigilance and cooperation. Owing greatly to work of the DEA, more than 900,000 people were arrested in the United States for pot violations alone between 2002 and 2012.[21]

92   Chapter 4

Surveillance, naturally, has always been indispensable to the drug war, never more so than in the present high-tech milieu, where new threats to civil liberties and individual privacy seem virtually unstoppable. The DEA, with other federal agencies and local police, has carried out thousands of drug sweeps and kindred operations over the past decade. Citizens face a matrix of electronic monitoring, video cameras, traffic stops, sting operations, and computer-based information gathering. Arrests for drug possession are routinely entered into local and federal data systems, remaining there for many years, while databases do not always reveal the judicial outcomes of drug cases. This Orwellian tracking of human activity, always essential to conduct of the drug war, can easily be accompanied by racial profiling. Michelle Alexander notes that any legal constraints are ritually tossed aside in the service of "larger goals"—that is, drug-bust quotas. She writes, "The absence of significant constraints on the exercise of police discretion is a key feature of the drug war's design. It has made the roundup of millions of Americans for nonviolent offenses relatively easy."[22] The profoundly authoritarian legacy of the drug war—and the surveillance order in general—is only likely to expand as technology becomes ever more refined. Police rely on sophisticated electronic methods to track and search suspects more or less at random, in many cases without actionable evidence, as airports, trains, buses, and cars can be searched on the flimsiest of pretexts.[23]

This political machinery gains momentum (and perhaps legitimacy) from rapid development of surveillance technology that is now thoroughly *global* in its reach. Data for multiple purposes—tracking bank activities, locating terrorist groups, ascertaining political attitudes, monitoring gang movements, tracing drug transactions—can nowadays be processed more rapidly and efficiently, aided by ultraspeedy supercomputers. The familiar elite pursuit of social control through advanced technology is so rationalized, and thus normalized, that popular limits to concentrated power are virtually impossible to sustain.[24] After 9/11, moreover, the Department of Homeland Security (DHS) rapidly came to prominence as another pillar of the NSS—heavily dependent on intelligence and surveillance functions. With a budget of $14.1 billion in 2002, operations from the department ballooned to $42.7 billion in 2007 and a staggering $85 billion in 2012. The political consequences of this sprawling bureaucratic network cannot be exaggerated. As Nick Turse notes, "The post-9/11 creation of an entire industry and culture of 'homeland security' has ushered in an era of military-industrial transformation."[25]

While ongoing threats of terrorism—combined with US military interventions abroad—justify homeland-security preparedness, added impetus comes from the drug war in its myriad expressions. Federal agencies routinely share agendas and information, collaborating in such realms as intelligence, surveillance, and border control. (The NSA, for example, is known to share its massive data collection with a variety of government units, including the DEA.) Some federal programs, moreover, including Power Geyser and Joint Task Force Six, target drug interdiction in such international regions as Mexico, Central America, Colombia, and Afghanistan.[26] As with terrorism, the War on Drugs easily blurs any distinction between domestic and foreign targets, which in reality often merge seamlessly. Accumulated databases on the activities of US citizens are extensively shared throughout government agencies.[27]

Domestic surveillance gained a substantial boost with congressional passage of the USA PATRIOT Act following 9/11. Constitutional rights to privacy and due process were placed in greater jeopardy as federal authorities gained broader surveillance powers, including easier access to wiretaps, searches, camera setups, and electronic monitoring. Such capabilities could be activated even where, as mentioned previously, no reasonable suspicion of criminal behavior is demonstrated. What could be applied to matters of general domestic security, moreover, could just as easily be implemented for the drug war.[28] After all, several US presidents, beginning with Nixon, had warned that drugs were indeed an issue of national security.

Nowhere is surveillance power more intrusive or threatening than in the work of the reputedly supersecret National Security Agency (NSA). By far the largest of all intelligence agencies, it is charged with intercepting electronic messages around the world—mostly outside US borders, but increasingly within domestic society as well. As of early 2014 the NSA had a workforce of more than 33,000 located mainly at the Fort Meade headquarters, much larger than the Pentagon. The NSA intercepts and processes millions of transmissions daily, aided by a labyrinthine network of supercomputers, collecting and storing information that can also be valuable to the DEA, the FBI, the CIA, and other agencies engaged in the drug war. The agency has long worked closely with such corporations as Microsoft, Google, and Apple, extending the partnership between big business and government to yet another realm. As longtime NSA critic James Bamford writes, "Another mission that draws valuable dollars, equipment, and personnel away from critical operations is the use of the NSA in the endless drug war."[29]

The NSA has the capacity to intercept more electronic transactions than any other governmental agency, armed with its supertechnology, access to satellites, and sophisticated listening posts around the planet and in space. Its role, until recently when agency whistle-blowers like Edward Snowden came forward with new information, had been largely hidden from public view; such entities as the FBI, the CIA, and the DEA readily commanded more media and political

94   CHAPTER 4

attention. Where the NSA has episodically come into view, any problematic behavior has typically been understood as confined to the *international* arena, yet as Bamford and the whistle-blowers have reported, *domestic* surveillance has increasingly entered the NSA domain.[30] Still, while the NSA clearly possesses the most powerful high-tech resources in the world, its work inevitably runs up against limits, as there can never be enough analysts to thoroughly process and interpret the mountains of data at the agency's immediate disposal. Similar obstacles constrain intelligence operations of such agencies as the CIA, the DEA, the IRS, and Customs.

Surely no federal agency more reflects the high-tech surveillance order—or the threat to individual privacy—than the NSA, which is empowered to accumulate exhaustive databases from processing a vast range of electronic transactions, through such mysterious programs as PRISM and Stellar Wind. An insular elite stratum of intelligence operatives, scientists, and technicians is given unlimited powers of data mining and citizen monitoring, with little oversight or accountability. Hardly anyone in government has the knowledge or skills to properly follow, much less engage, the global scope of NSA operations. Despite the whistle-blower revelations about widespread NSA violations, including domestic surveillance, Congress has repeatedly backed off from setting limits. Even judging by its own acknowledged store of information, the NSA has done little to effectively track real terrorists; failures leading up to the 9/11 attacks are well known, documented by Bamford and others. As for supposed Foreign Intelligence Surveillance Act (FISA) safeguards, that court has evolved into a virtual rubber stamp for government surveillance requests: only federal lawyers can appear before FISA, and demands for wiretapping and other electronic intrusions are ritually approved—though reforms in that area could be on the agenda.[31] Meanwhile, leaked documents show that the NSA (no doubt working jointly with such agencies as the DEA) has overstepped its legal authority thousands of times just since 2011.[32]

The US surveillance order is reinforced by the deepening integration of two "wars"—one against terrorism, the other against drugs. While both have been given exaggerated global importance, elites view both as grave threats to social order and national security. Privacy safeguards legislated during the 1970s, in the wake of the COINTELPRO scandal and other federal infringements on the Bill of Rights, have been steadily undermined, Congress exhibiting little vigilance in dealing with new encroachments of the surveillance order. For many years the FBI carried out wiretapping, monitoring, raids, and arrests—some legal, some illegal—to fight terrorism, drugs, and organized crime, all the while facing little in the way of democratic opposition.

The drug war took off in earnest roughly a decade after Nixon's "warfare" declaration, when Reagan chose to frame "drugs" as an ominous threat to US national security. Given the large-scale trafficking of coke, pot, and other contraband drugs from south of the border (mostly from Colombia and Mexico), the menace of "narcoterrorism" was born, linking two epic battles well before the attacks of 9/11. By the late 1980s, the DEA was depicting the illegal drug trade as a "subset of terrorism," a political shift leading to militarization of some antidrug operations in Latin America, accompanied by stricter monitoring and policing of borders. The War on Drugs had become simultaneously domestic and global, both a policing and military enterprise; the gathering and processing of information would be increasingly technological, streamlined, and collaborative, with personal movements and transactions more easily monitored.[33]

Surveillance technology has become more rationalized and invasive with the wider use of the Global Positioning System (GPS), ubiquitous camera setups, and introduction of unmanned drones by police and military that, in the coming years, will permit the United States to extensively monitor every corner of the planet. The DEA has especially fallen in love with GPS tracking systems, which it can employ (often with phone-company assistance) to locate individual cell-phone coordinates—ideal for policing drug transactions and flows. While both the American Civil Liberties Union (ACLU) and the Electronic Privacy Information Center (EPIC) have pressured Congress to legislate enhanced privacy safeguards against GPS and aerial drone overflights, the DEA (with some other agencies) has fiercely opposed such legislation, always hoping for the fewest constraints on the drug war. The prevailing government dogma is that such technology is a purely benevolent instrument serving public welfare and should be immune from congressional oversight. Thus, according to DEA literature, "If a tool is used to transport contraband and it gives off a signal that can be tracked, certainly police [ought to be able to] track the signal."[34] Partnering with local police departments, the DEA issues tens of thousands of requests each year for GPS-related data, and the information (assuming no flagrant legal transgressions) is readily obtainable and convenient to use. The reality is that privacy concerns within enforcement circles are dismissed as rather arcane, hardly worthy of public debate. GPS systems allow for elevated government spying on everyday personal movements, often with peak levels of accuracy. Even those well-publicized ACLU and EPIC challenges, furthermore, are directed not so much at the *legitimacy* of high-tech surveillance methods but rather at the problem of *excesses* in the context of special court warrants.

As for DEA operations in general, most surveillance is naturally conducted in secret, with little if any judicial or government oversight, which renders the

DEA a potentially greater threat to Constitutional rights than either the FBI or the NSA. In fact, more than forty years of active DEA surveillance, investigations, raids, and arrests have been effectively hidden from public view.[35] In a series of investigative articles published by Reuters (August 2013), John Shiffman writes that DEA agents have for many years been trained to conceal or obscure their work, going so far as to set up "parallel constructions" where false alternative tracks are laid to deliberately mislead the public where drug operations are involved.[36] As Shiffman reports, the most aggressive DEA work is often conducted through its Special Operations Division, which has close ties to at least a dozen agencies, including the NSA. Evidence gathered at the DEA is shrouded in mystery, not so much as a matter of national security as of simply cracking down on illicit drugs. The bulk of information gathered by the DEA, according to Shiffman, is actually illegal—a violation of the Fourth, Fifth, and Sixth Amendments to the Constitution. The agency is empowered to do pretty much whatever it chooses; flagrant misuse of authority is rationalized through a moral fervor over drugs, as leading DEA figures casually defend nefarious methods in the service of the great crusade.[37]

As surveillance takes on bigger priorities for government agencies like the DEA, the DHS, the CIA, the FBI, and Border Patrol, drone technology becomes the ultimate tool for information gathering. Unmanned aircraft provide clear advantages in the drug war: they can fly at very high altitudes (even above 30,000 feet), are usually very small and hard to detect, can be highly maneuverable, and carry sophisticated tracking systems to minutely survey land, homes, vehicles, human movements, even tiny objects. Equipped with infrared cameras, heat sensors, and GPS devices, drones are the perfect instrument for surveillance and espionage—which, of course, means they are likely to pose the most far-reaching threats to individual privacy.[38] As of 2013 most unmanned aircraft had been deployed by the Pentagon and the CIA, but other federal agencies—joined by local police—are expected to rely more heavily on drone operations in the future. In 2012 the FAA gave out 257 drone licenses for American domestic air space, followed by 373 in 2013,[39] and that number is projected to reach 30,000 by 2020, if not sooner. Unmanned aircraft are ideal for tracking boats, submarines, planes, and ground vehicles used in the clandestine shipment of drugs. As of 2014, the Wasp, Raven, and Puma drones, weighing no more than fifteen pounds and remotely operated, were already scheduled for domestic activity, viewed as the best method for homeland-security operations (directed in part against the illegal drug trade).[40]

Pilotless aircraft have already become central to surveillance for border and immigration agencies, charged with monitoring cross-border immigration, terrorism, and drugs. In 2013 Predator overflights were taking place in the Caribbean and Central America. US Border Patrol agents, working with DHS, rely increasingly on drones to locate illegal drug shipments from Mexico into the United States, especially the Southwest. The US and Mexican governments have combined to set up a variety of surveillance measures directed mainly at drug trafficking. During the Calderón presidency alone the United States helped install more than 100 high-tech monitoring stations along the border, with hundreds more projected to follow. In Washington, meanwhile, Congress has been awkwardly silent about the threat that such technologies pose for individual privacy and personal rights.

The drones prove especially useful for border surveillance, as they cover remote areas relatively efficiently, cheaply, and usually without detection. One of the largest drones, the Global Hawk, has become the perfect instrument for scanning the lengthy, winding US-Mexican border. As Washington devotes more resources to "border security," a confluence of several objectives takes shape: homeland security, immigration controls, counterterrorism, general law enforcement, and the drug war. It is around these border areas, perhaps more than anywhere else on the planet, that sophisticated technology (including robotics) is at the service of state power. Indeed, drones now constitute an important "growth sector" for the Pentagon and federal agencies engaged in border controls, terrorism, and drug interdiction—massive profits accruing to such corporations as General Atomics, Raytheon, Boeing, and Northrop Grumman.[41] One enduring advantage of drone technology is its great capacity to maintain secrecy while eluding congressional oversight.

One factor explaining congressional timidity here is that high-level tracking, monitoring, and controlling of local populations have been long-standing features of US efforts to achieve full-spectrum domination across the planet. We have perhaps reached a phase of expanding governmental reach—a phenomenon ignored by "small government" champions in the Tea Party—that Christian Parenti labels the "society of security," where high-tech monitoring seems rather ubiquitous.[42] The ritual "checks and balances" formula that might weaken such powers is nowhere to be seen, thanks to an enduring "bipartisan consensus" at work in Washington. The War on Drugs plays a crucial, though often ignored, role in perpetuating this authoritarian logic.

Postwar US global ascendancy, the latest stage of national exceptionalism, has given the surveillance state new scope and meaning. The power of high-tech surveillance to heavily influence future development is hard to overstate. Alfred W. McCoy writes, "The American surveillance state is now an omnipresent reality, but its deep history is little known and its future little grasped."[43] The forces

98　Chapter 4

helping to strengthen this behemoth are many—economic pressures, militarism, counterterrorism, the drug war. The traumatic events of 9/11 provided more institutional and ideological leverage to an already-powerful national surveillance order. It might be argued that the two celebrated "wars"—against terrorism and against drugs—constitute something of a mutually reinforcing dynamic.

As dozens of federal agencies carry out various types of monitoring activities, often jointly, enhanced governmental intrusions into private life seem inevitable: video cameras invading public spaces, aerial photography, new facial-recognition technology, databases accumulated from every conceivable form of electronic scanning. This not only represents a giant leap forward for law enforcement, but renders ever more precarious the status of basic rights, freedoms, and judicial due process. The historic convergence of several phenomena—imperial power, the warfare state, corporate interests, advanced technology—underpins a surveillance order threatening to erode what is left of American democracy.[44] This threat is heightened by the seeming absence of counterweights to authoritarian rule, whether from Congress, state governance, the media, or popular movements. The apparent death of privacy depicted in such Hollywood films as *Closed Circuit* (2013) turns out to be no exaggeration—a trend that the vast majority of Americans seem to presently take for granted. Revelations concerning the enormous scope of NSA surveillance indicate virtually unfettered (and unaccountable) government monitoring of the entire world. In the wake of Snowden's NSA information leaks, protests erupted in both Europe and Mexico over systematic US wiretapping and email hacking of political leaders.[45]

Meanwhile, the situation drastically worsens with each passing year. By 2014, as Julia Angwin documents in her important book *Dragnet Nation*, the daily movements and activities of people were being more efficiently and minutely tracked and recorded, leaving the hallowed Fourth Amendment in tatters. Law enforcement in every American city now has the capacity to conduct surveillance through a creative variety of instruments: ubiquitous cameras, cell phones, credit cards, GPS systems, and license-plate scanners. Data-collection agencies and tracking companies, often working with the military, intelligence agencies, and local law enforcement, are proliferating.[46]

While Republicans carry on about the virtues of "small government" and personal freedoms, they have few problems with the permanent-war economy or the security state. The great "fiscal crisis" simply drops from view when it comes to spending trillions for "defense." Neither the War on Drugs nor the bloated surveillance apparatus poses any serious problems for these ersatz libertarians. As this bureaucratic, costly, and repressive order gains more leverage over social life, the actuality of big government (distinct from conservative fantasies about "individualism") ends up as an immovable reality. "Enemies," of course, must always be identified, located, and fought—and these naturally include a large universe of drug traffickers. While Democrats have less to say about the perils of big government, in practice they differ little from Republicans: in May 2011, for example, President Obama approved a four-year extension of the PATRIOT Act with its roving wiretaps, expansion of global surveillance, and heavy reliance on federal agencies' (including the NSA's) monitoring of *domestic* electronic transactions. Drone warfare and other surveillance operations were earmarked for added funding, as these features of governmental power become an increasingly durable element of American public life.[47]

Prisons: Lockdown Nation

Nowhere is an authoritarian system of control more visible, or more egregious, than in the American prison complex—which in 2013 housed nearly 2.3 million federal, state, and local inmates. With broadened law enforcement, thanks in great measure to the War on Drugs, the United States now has seven million people jailed, on parole, or on probation—a number (total or per capita) unmatched by any other nation. For most years, somewhere in the vicinity of one-third of this criminalized population comes from drug offenses: in 2012, for example, there were 1,552,432 arrests in the United States for drug offenses, 82.2 percent for possession of an illegal substance.[48] In 2010 alone, some 830,000 people were arrested on drug (mostly pot) charges, the vast majority for simple possession. The sprawling prison system consumes enormous public wealth—tens of billions of dollars yearly, not to mention elevated funding for law enforcement, intelligence, and the largest court system in the world.

Prohibitionism is in great measure hitched, now as before, to an ethos of abstract moralism, where "drug use" automatically equates to "abuse," possession is seen as addiction, and sales amount to "trafficking"—the discursive basis of a criminalizing regimen geared to coercion and punishment.[49] More jails and longer sentences have created a huge criminal underclass, high rates of recidivism, a culture of poverty, and indeed wider use of illegal drugs. Warrior ideology states that drugs are responsible for crime, violence, family breakdown, poverty, and personal calamities—yet history shows that these very conditions are immeasurably worsened by what the drug war produces—swollen black markets and harsh prison sentences often meted out for minor offenses. Like the War on Drugs itself, the prison system especially damages the life chances of blacks and Hispanics, who comprise nearly 70 percent of all inmates. As the

100   Chapter 4

prison complex expands, moreover, problems of overcrowding, violence, racial conflict, sickness, and recidivism escalate.

What Joel Dyer calls the "perpetual prisoner machine" is sustained by a huge lobby network—by those who run the prisons, of course, but also by unions, law enforcement, drug warriors, and the many businesses that profit from large inmate populations.[50] Tough-on-crime agendas, including three-strike laws and mandatory minimum sentencing, are the stuff of manifestly conservative interests, including the National Rifle Association (NRA), police departments, and media outlets like FOX. Those "dangerous elements" the system chooses to incarcerate typically have low levels of education (65 percent never having finished high school), are poor (32 percent earning less than $5,000 yearly), and jobless (32 percent).[51] Many have suffered from extreme mental or physical disorders, while others serve long terms (five years or more) for nonviolent offenses. As mentioned, people convicted of felonies—common for drug charges—can be stripped of basic citizen rights. Meanwhile, incarceration strategies provide added resources—institutional, material, and ideological—for social control, while making little if any dent in illegal drug consumption.

New prison construction, record numbers of inmates, and vast public expenditures pouring into the criminal-justice system—slowed only moderately by the "fiscal crisis"—are nowadays generally embraced by Americans as indispensable to "fighting crime." This worsening situation has elicited no mass protests—only isolated actions in opposition to the death penalty, along with a few prisoner insurgencies. In California (with by far the largest state prison system), spending on jails skyrocketed from $440 million in the late 1970s to $8.7 billion in 2011, consuming 10 percent of the state budget at a time when higher-education spending decreased from 15 percent to 10 percent of total allocations. Such profligate spending has not, however, kept state prisons across the United States from being overcrowded, violent, and miserable places for inmates.[52] Nor have Tea Party advocates of "small government" and reduced public spending come forth in protest.

Prisons, whether federal, state, or local, are surely the most coercive institutions in American society. Those who administer hundreds of lockup centers have virtually limitless power to manipulate, punish, and in some cases even torture or kill inmates. Gangs, including neo-Nazi groups, often run wild. Drug smuggling, pimping, rape, extortion, and racial warfare have become increasingly normal facts of life behind bars, in all areas of the country. Prisons constitute an elaborate, rationalized system of confinement, where even brief sentences often lead to psychological disability. Christian Parenti argues that intensified anticrime agendas and swollen prison populations coincide with the demands of neoliberal development: a growing subculture of outsiders (mostly jobless) is absorbed, controlled, and pacified within a vast incarceration system. Criminalization is one elite strategy for regulating the misery, discontent, and chaos that inevitably result from a regime of austerity, cutbacks, and deindustrialization.[53] Thus, "the criminal justice crackdown, and its attendant culture of fear, absorbs the dangerous classes without politically or economically empowering them."[54]

If the ruling forces frame drugs as a mortal threat to civil order and national security—and if pushers and traffickers are the equivalent of terrorists—then the politics of incarceration favored by antidrug warriors seems to logically follow. Aside from advancing Big Pharma interests, the drug war has always fulfilled certain Keynesian functions insofar as the prison complex furnishes an economic stimulus or engine of "growth" that readily finds support in both major parties. Federal and state governments benefit materially and ideologically from the drug war and the moral panic it recurrently generates.

Alexander sees the politics of incarceration as fueled by the targeting of designated "bad elements" within society, labeling and stigmatizing them, then removing them from public life. Many such "bad elements," of course, are sent away for years thanks to harsh sentencing laws first passed in the early 1980s. In most drug cases, those arrested and charged are typically assumed guilty, with due process reduced to a dispensable luxury—made easier by the stereotyping. Given a crowded and overburdened criminal-justice system, full-length trials today rarely take place; the accused are usually poor with few resources for defense, while police officers frequently lie and plea-bargaining pressures are irresistible given the strong penalties involved. As the "bad elements," moreover, are overwhelmingly black and Hispanic, they are far less likely to gain respectful treatment, much less judicial fairness.[55]

Once arrested on drug charges, especially where sales are involved, defendants are hard-pressed to win freedom: the accused are often condemned to languish in jail. Alexander notes, "The crucial point is that thousands of people are swept into the criminal justice system every year pursuant to the drug war without much regard for their guilt or innocence."[56] (It should be emphasized that "guilt" might pertain to nothing more than *possession* of a banned substance for individual use.) Unduly long sentences, including mandatory minimum terms, have been upheld by the US Supreme Court. Once people are stigmatized as "drug offenders," the label easily follows them throughout their lives: a convicted felon faces not only many years of harsh confinement but additional years of being monitored while in a state of desperate poverty, good jobs obviously being extremely difficult to find. That is why, within three years of release, nearly 70 percent of ex-convicts in drug cases end up returning to prison.[57]

102   CHAPTER 4

One of the great paradoxes of the American prison complex—filled as it is with a wide variety of drug offenders—is the recent upsurge in use of potent psychotropic drugs to control inmate populations that, repressed and angry, can easily disrupt the authoritarian regime—witness the lengthy, at-times-violent 2013 California hunger strike spread across numerous state prisons. The drugs are administered freely for several interrelated purposes: as antidepressants, mood stabilizers, sedatives, anticonvulsants, and painkillers, all to rein in disruptive or violent behavior. The drugs are relatively cheap, of course, eagerly supplied by large pharmaceutical companies and energetically backed by warrior groups (law enforcement, doctors, psychiatrists, and government agencies). Psychologically numbing substances, with their myriad side effects, are many: Dilantin to control rage and violence; Zyprexa, Risperdal, and Lithium to fight acute aggressive tendencies; Haldol (100 times as powerful as Thorazine) to reduce depression; Altivan and Nadolol for outright sedation. Other drugs, including Prozac, Xanax, and OxyContin are regularly prescribed by prison authorities. This epic fusion of modern penology and medical drug treatment—another legacy of the drug war—has given rise to one of the most ambitious social-control projects ever, with its goal to produce an inmate population of zombies.[58]

It might be argued that the War on Drugs was never meant to be "won" on its stated terms, whatever the lofty official declarations in favor of a "drug-free America" put forward for public consumption by government officials, politicians, and the media. The crusade is better understood as an exorbitant, authoritarian, and corporatist agenda carried out in the service of an expanding state-capitalist power structure. Several decades ago C. Wright Mills, in his classic *The Power Elite*, argued that corporate, government, and military power had merged to constitute a state-capitalist system relegating party competition, elections, and legislative activity to a great political spectacle having little to do with the world of concrete decision making.[59] Today Mills's thesis pointing to the deeply oligarchical and authoritarian character of American public life seems even more valid, at a time when the war economy and security state dwarf the power they had accumulated during the Eisenhower era.

The Orwellian potential of this awesome power structure is indeed frightening: with growing technological capabilities, the NSA and the DEA (to name just two agencies), working jointly with corporations and the Pentagon, law enforcement, and dispersed intelligence groups, are taking the security apparatus into a universe of total information awareness. An eventual goal of those who rule this system is to determine where people of interest are located, what they are doing, even what they are thinking—all far removed from any public knowledge of what is taking place. Such possibilities, only vaguely anticipated by Mills and dimly glimpsed in the 1998 Tony Scott thriller *Enemy of the State* (and the more recent *Closed Circuit*), suggest a range of domination that has no historical precedents. The confluence of bureaucracy and technology obviously strengthens the surveillance order, in the process narrowing the public sphere and threatening to eviscerate what remains of democratic politics. The War on Drugs, from Nixon to the present, coincides perfectly with this authoritarian trajectory. In the meantime, the established machinery of government, with its institutionalized rules, norms, and procedures, has become even more entrenched—perhaps an irreversible development in the age of an imperial presidency, a war economy, and the security state. Within what has taken shape as a global surveillance network, interests at the summit—corporations, government, military, intelligence, law enforcement—converge to further integrate and solidify an authoritarian state driven by expanding wealth, power, and violence.

Chapter 5
Narco Globalism

With its global reach, the War on Drugs—increasingly reliant on military operations—has long been a factor in the flexing of US imperial power. The United Nations report discussed in Chapter 3 called Washington policy makers to account for their many egregious drug-war failures, but ignored the ways in which prohibitionism helps serve American international designs, above all in Mexico and elsewhere in Latin America. While little has been done by any government to interrupt the global flow of drugs, as most illegal substances (cocaine, opium, cannabis, etc.) are now integrated into patterns of economic trade and social life around the world, the drug war continues to buttress federal power along with an interventionist foreign policy.

The drug war coincides with a protracted legacy of US warfare that shapes the political culture, as armed intervention to defeat menacing villains is framed as both inescapable and virtuous, a moral imperative for an exceptional, noble country. Warfare is nothing less than a deep sacred mission—a rather marketable concept in a nation that, from its very inception, has been riddled with fear and insecurity. As Ziauddin Sardar and Merryl Wyn Davies observe, "America's response . . . is to fall back upon the structuring metaphors of the American experience, to rely on the themes of its public myth: to fear, to understand its adversaries as implacable enemies, to seek a violent armed response that will eradicate the problem."[1] That "problem," requiring an incessant public vigilance informed by a superpatriotic ideology, has been recycled endlessly in many genres of film, including Westerns, combat, sci-fi, action-adventure, and horror movies.

The driving motifs of American history, politics, and culture are ideologically consistent with the underpinnings of the global drug war.

The language and ethos of warfare have underpinned an American obsession with drug prohibition for well more than a century, culminating in the 1970s crusade initiated by Nixon. Political elites define the scourge of "drugs"—with its threatening image of pushers and traffickers—as an abominable evil to be extirpated by force where necessary. As with the early nation builders and frontier settlers, modern antidrug warriors become the bearers of a civilizing mission that, more often than not, demands vigorous law enforcement and military action.

The Criminal Syndicates

If coercive methods to enforce drug prohibition in domestic society have brought repeated failure, the global result has been no less disastrous. Criminalizing an international drug trade that goes back centuries inevitably gives rise to outlaw syndicates, government corruption, civic violence, and terrible costs (human and material), while doing little to reduce illegal drug consumption. Most of all, the War on Drugs has benefited law enforcement, government bureaucracy, military power, arms trade, and huge underground economies controlled by powerful cartels. Such insanity extends not only to Mexico but to other regions of Latin America, Afghanistan, and neighboring Middle Eastern nations.

The bankruptcy of domestic prohibition applies equally to the global scene: contraband markets flourish, funneled into an extended world of gangs and criminal syndicates. We have seen how the Volstead Act generated a large black market for alcohol at a time when illegal distilleries, delivery systems, and speakeasies proliferated across the urban terrain. Criminalization of beer, wine, and liquor brought vast wealth to black-market capitalists trading in goods that could never be effectively regulated, monitored, or taxed. Prohibition not only cost governments material resources needed for law enforcement and jails; it deprived them of otherwise generous tax revenues. Within underground capitalism, as Jeffrey Miron points out, syndicate competition for turf and markets often took violent forms, leading to a sharp increase in street crime that prohibition was supposed to alleviate.[2] As for the contemporary situation in Mexico and elsewhere, drug criminalization, coercive methods of drug interdiction, and development of black markets have taken prohibition far beyond this earlier American catastrophe.

106   Chapter 5

While American media outlets seem amazed at the horrors associated with the global drug trade—reserving special outrage for violence carried out by Mexican cartels—the situation ought to be predictable enough when framed against the backdrop of international drug production, consumption, and sales. National boundaries are generally quite porous, rendering efforts to block the flow of contraband substances inevitably futile. Indeed drugs of many varieties—including tobacco, alcohol, sugar, opium, cocaine, cannabis, and mushrooms, not to mention lab-produced chemicals for both medicinal and intoxicating uses—have been manufactured and sold for centuries.[3] Tobacco markets, for one, were a vital part of economic trade in the United States from the outset—as indeed they were to daily life, despite their harmful consequences for health. Not only were hundreds of substances (spirits, plants, mushrooms, flowers, and processed drugs included) marketed openly and easily across borders; they were fully integrated into the social life and cultural traditions of people around the world, which tempered most efforts at prohibition. As Mike Jay observes, historical attempts by some governments to ban drugs were entirely counterproductive, negated by the far stronger pull of global markets.[4]

Today, the US-orchestrated global drug war targets contraband markets in a context where "illicit" trade has become a durable, widening pattern within the international economy. Underground commerce now constitutes at least 10 percent of all global transactions, extending far beyond drugs to money, guns, medicines, and every type of counterfeit product imaginable. As Moisés Naím points out, "In defiance of regulations and taxes, treaties and laws, virtually anything of value is offered for sale in today's global marketplace."[5] Such transactions, moreover, cannot be defined as strictly underground: not only established banks and corporations but also government agencies (including Customs, the Treasury, and police) are deeply involved in the illicit economy. Among many examples, the large Guadalajara cartel in Mexico has developed increasingly close ties with business and government elites. At a time when national borders become more difficult to monitor and control, sophisticated technology permits greater speed and efficiency for international transfers of both goods and money. The global system has become a paradise for counterfeiters, smugglers, traffickers, and money launderers.[6]

Naím writes that "illicit trade pushes the world beyond the capacity for control. It empowers those who are little interested in democracy."[7] In economic terms, globalization means that all forms of production, trade, banking, and technology easily surmount national boundaries and legal barriers—an ideal environment for sprawling networks of illicit activity. Further, loosened financial and corporate regulations (central to neoliberalism) have encouraged the rise of contraband businesses, including the drug trade, which benefits enormously from rapid spread of counterfeit goods now more easily transported from country to country. Hundreds of criminal groups operate more or less freely in most industrially developed nations—Russia, Japan, China, Europe, and the United States, as well as Mexico. It is no wonder that the drug war, with its massive interdictions and seizures, has exerted no impact on flourishing international drug markets. It is worth restating here that the United States is not only the leading warrior nation but also the leading consumer of drugs. Peter Andreas observes, "The American-led global antidrug campaign has . . . contributed to extraordinary levels of crime, violence, corruption, and other ills. These supply-focused policy initiatives endlessly chase the symptoms rather than the source of the problem at home. Blaming foreign drug traffickers and migrant smugglers is politically easier than confronting America's twin addictions to mind-altering substances and cheap migrant labor."[8]

Of course consumption patterns across nations and cultures regarding what we normally label "drugs" have always varied greatly, but one generalization seems inescapable: the use of both intoxicating and medicinal substances is basic and universal, impossible to deny or repress. Legal strictures based on ideological taboos and false narratives bring more harm than they can hope to extirpate. If, as Ronald K. Siegel, Andrew Weil, and others argue, the drive to consume "recreational drugs" corresponds to a fundamental human impulse like eating and sex, then coercive measures by law enforcement to block drug flows across borders are bound to collapse. "Warfare" of the sort preferred by Washington elites and moral crusaders might serve government agencies and corporations, as well as political careers, but will inevitably fail to impede the international drug trade.

Most crucially, the War on Drugs ensures the growth of criminal oligopolies—an alternative capitalism—embedded in a power matrix linking sectors of government, cartels, law enforcement, and (in some cases) the military. In Mexico and other Latin American countries engulfed in the drug war, a cycle of violence and corruption is fed by American consumers, whose demand for illegal substances far surpasses that of any other nation. In the face of prohibition, a 2008 World Health Organization survey found that 16.2 percent of Americans had used cocaine, more than triple the consumption of any other country (with Mexico at a distant 4 percent). As for cannabis, the US level stood at 42.4 percent, easily outdistancing demand elsewhere: Holland at 19.8 percent, Germany at 17.5 percent, and Spain at 15 percent.[9] Clearly, the War on Drugs

108   CHAPTER 5

has done little to subvert the international trade, the bulk of which is centered in the United States. In global terms, UN statistics reveal (as of 2011) that 272 million people worldwide between ages fifteen and sixty-four had used banned substances—in fact a large increase over the previous decade. Cannabis alone had been consumed by more than 200 million people, with no signs of weakening demand. Generating a (roughly) estimated half trillion dollars in revenue yearly, there is no evidence that thriving drug markets were likely to decline, prohibition or not. A coercive drug policy merely shifts business activity into the syndicates while the trade—forever lucrative—continues to flourish.

It is worth revisiting the Obama administration's reaction to the UN report on drugs: any rethinking of the drug war is ruled out, owing to "recognition that drug use strains our economy, health, and public safety."[10] The empirical evidence, however, contained in UN materials and many other sources points to just the opposite—rigid adherence to *prohibition* is most harmful to personal health and public safety and forces the drug trade into black markets. Obama added, without supporting data, that "the bottom line is that balanced drug-control efforts are making a big difference."[11] If so, the sprawling and lucrative Mexican cartels have yet to receive the word. Close investigation of international drug flows will reveal that the decades-old US-orchestrated campaign for a "drug-free world" has been a dismal failure even on its own terms. To date, as noted, hundreds of billions of dollars have been poured into an essentially un-winnable war: all efforts at eradication and interdiction—all raids, arrests, and jailings—have scarcely impacted the availability of illegal drugs for an always-insatiable American market, which totals at least $50 billion yearly. Production and transit venues are closed off in some zones only to reappear (and possibly expand) in others. US antidrug programs, often relying on military force, have targeted many nations, including Colombia, Peru, Ecuador, Bolivia, Panama, Honduras, Guatemala, Afghanistan, Pakistan, and, of course, Mexico. Yet the supply of coke, heroin, pot, meth, and other contraband substances continues more or less uninterrupted.

In Mexico, intensified antidrug warfare under President Felipe Calderón beginning in late 2006 (with strong US pressure) only served to bolster the vast networks of organized crime dominated by such cartels as the Gulf, Zetas, and La Familia. The cartel operations have long been interwoven with sectors of government, law enforcement, the military, business, banking, the labor force, and indeed the cultural scene, a development emphasized by Anabel Hernández in her book *Narcoland*. Law enforcement protects gangs, operatives, and cartels through an elaborate system of bribes. In a spring 2014 interview, Hernández went so far as to suggest a close relationship between many cartels and the DEA, a contention fiercely denounced by DEA leadership.[12] The cartels have developed into yet another face of capitalism, much like the mafia at other times and places, what Ioan Grillo in *El Narco* refers to as a "brutal mafia capitalism" that follows the irresistible logic of money and power no drug war can hope to extirpate. In Grillo's words, "In a globalized world, mafia capitalists and criminal insurgents have become the new dictators and the new rebels."[13] As drugs pass through transit corridors from Mexico to the United States, where the final product is usually consumed, the price markups are stratospheric—as much as 6,000 percent for such street-level goods as cocaine. The cartels stand atop one of the most profitable businesses on the planet.[14] Meanwhile, they have moved toward diversification, finding new profits in extortion, kidnapping, oil theft, pirating, and smuggling of other contraband. Rather than fighting the lawlessness, government and police often find it easier to simply join the operations, happy to share in the bourgeoning largesse. Spoils of the cartel trade—not only in Mexico but elsewhere in Latin America—have become too vast for many within the establishment to resist, including law enforcement and government officials on the take, business interests looking for a share of profits or protection, bankers involved in money laundering, and youth and street people earning money within the long chain of supply and trafficking.

Mexican elites—government, business, military, law enforcement—have for decades been fully entangled in the work of the drug cartels.[15] In Guadalajara, a city of 4.4 million people, the syndicate-state-corporate linkage has grown especially tight, as criminal operations (drug processing, trafficking, money-laundering, etc.) proceed smoothly in an atmosphere far less chaotic and violent than the one that pervades Ciudad Juárez and Tijuana. Moreover, even as the old capos disappear new cycles of leadership arise, usually looking for a more peaceful milieu in which to conduct business. The shift from Calderón to the Enrique Peña Nieto presidency in 2012, however, has witnessed only a slight downturn in the rate of kidnappings and murders. (In March 2013, for example, more than 1,100 cartel-related deaths were recorded, far below the Mexican record but still a horrific thirty-five per day.)[16]

In cities like Ciudad Juárez, where what Howard Campbell labels the "drug war zone" (DWZ) has become a durable reality, drugs in all their dimensions have entered the web of economic, social, and political power.[17] They shape the ideological terrain, where the ongoing activities of drug producers, organized crime, government officials, law enforcement—even the media—seem tightly interwoven. In this byzantine milieu the drug phenomenon takes on meanings—pursuit of wealth, protection of turf, everyday survival, relations with the North—far removed from common myths and platitudes disseminated as part

110   CHAPTER 5

of the drug war. More than ever, Mexican society is pervaded with drugs and the drug trade, locus of a thriving underground capitalism, a source of economic survival for many tens of thousands of people.

In Ciudad Juárez and other big cities, the cartels operate within a Hobbesian world of chaos and poverty, consistent with the workings of a neoliberal global economy in which a "narco culture" hardly seems an aberration. The intricate network of alliances—traffickers, syndicates, local pushers, law enforcement, etc.—shifts constantly but rarely departs from ways of life centered on the drug trade with its ever-present seductions, risks, and dangers. Like the classical mafia, drug-based cartel capitalism is ruthless, secretive, and efficient as it operates within a changing maze of illegal activities. Owing to the drug war, the El Paso–Cuidad Juárez corridor has become a lucrative smugglers' paradise. The DWZ has forged its own culture, open spaces, and social codes: drug surveillance, raids, and arrests (even at the highest levels) make little difference to this expansive zone, despite claims made by the DEA and the FBI.[18] Further, once the DWZ becomes an established reality, no public space is immune to the culture of outlawry, even where thousands of army troops are deployed, as the recent history of Ciudad Juárez, Tijuana, and other drug-trafficking centers demonstrates. Resistance to DWZ agendas has been routinely met with intensified violence.

In the DWZ it could be said that the United States is exporting many of its own social contradictions, its own repressive economic and drug policies—part of a self-perpetuating war culture—as drug flows northward continue unabated. Mexico offers the best but not the only laboratory test for how global prohibition fails, even on its own terms, at great cost in human lives and material resources.[19] Calderón's post-2006 stepped-up antidrug crusade, with a staggering loss of up to 70,000 lives, reveals how the War on Drugs worsens virtually every social problem. The Mexicans, sadly, continue to pay an excruciating price while the cartels reap billions in profits from the insatiable US drug market. If the Mexican case represents the most dystopic outcome of drug-war failures, it is hardly the only case—witness similar disasters in Central America, Afghanistan, and other regions impacted by Washington-driven antidrug policies.

Beginning in the 1990s, drug cartels based in Mexico became increasingly globalized, with tentacles not only in many US cities but also in Central American nations such as Honduras, Guatemala, and Panama. Their presence is marked by the familiar turf wars, economic conflicts, and local paramilitary squads bringing increased violence, social chaos, and political corruption. The DWZ typical of Ciudad Juárez and Tijuana has been exported to Central America, where deep poverty makes available large populations happy to find survival income from the drug trade, whether as producers (farmers, lab operatives, etc.) or as low-level traffickers, cartel enforcers, or simple couriers.[20] Economic dependency on the drug trade, from top to bottom, renders the official targeting of "drug offenders" in these settings mostly futile.

The drug calamity in Afghanistan parallels that of Mexico—without, however, the same massive casualty count. For several decades the Afghan economy has been hugely dependent on the global drug trade, its underground economy tied to poppy cultivation and the opium/heroin market. Like cannabis in many parts of the world and cocaine in South America, Afghan opium crops are virtually ubiquitous, making them nearly invulnerable to removal. Although in recent years, as a counter to the Taliban insurgency, the United States moved to impose its drug-war policy on resistant Afghans, a few decades ago—to serve US foreign policy—Washington used drug profits to aid Mujahideen forces against the Soviets. Here, as elsewhere, during the 1980s the CIA worked closely with drug traffickers in the fight against communism while the domestic War on Drugs was moving ahead full-force.[21] The Afghan drug supply generated up to $65 billion yearly in profits, with a kilo of heroin selling for $3,000 locally and fetching up to $50,000 in the United States.[22]

After 2001, with the US-supported Hamid Karzai government combating the Taliban insurgency—and tens of thousands of American troops stationed in the country—the drug war was revisited, with predictably disastrous outcomes. As in Mexico, many thousands of poor people had come to depend on the drug trade as growers, processors, couriers, dealers, and smugglers, often working at great personal risk. The drugs are moved through Turkey and Iran toward destinations across Europe and the United States. As Fariba Nawa reports in her firsthand account, *Opium Nation*, the Taliban managed to persuade Afghan farmers to convert from more traditional crops to poppies, the insurgency aligning itself with local mafias, bandits, and smuggling operations to finance their operations.[23] As of early 2013 the Taliban stood at the apex of a thriving "narco state," despite Western efforts to criminalize the most flourishing (and lucrative) crop in Afghanistan.

Afghanistan has no sprawling Mexican-style cartels—just a proliferation of growers, processors, dealers, and smugglers doing business with dozens of global syndicates. United States–inspired efforts to remove the leading capos and their lieutenants (often called drug lords or kingpins) have had little impact on the general trade, as police, military troops, and government officials usually share in the profits, upon which so much of the Afghan economy depends. Not only drug production and sales, but also drug *consumption* has reportedly increased across the country. Recent programs to eradicate poppy fields have met with failure; as in Mexico, success in one locale merely pushes operations elsewhere.

112 CHAPTER 5

From a cultural standpoint, there is no belief among Afghans that opium production is criminal or sinful. As of late 2013 the poppy fields, along with labs for processing opium, were more plentiful than ever.[24]

The lengthy Afghan-Iran border is today fortified by the mechanisms of antidrug warfare, as Iran is perhaps the one country more strongly attached to prohibitionism than the United States. Having spent tens of billions to fight drugs, Iran stations nearly 100,000 soldiers along 600 miles of barbed-wire fences, canals, trenches, and cement barriers in a mostly vain effort to stop the flow of narcotics from Afghanistan. A rudimentary electronic surveillance network has been built. While the Iranians do seize hundreds of tons of opium each year and traffickers are punished harshly, the market nonetheless thrives.[25] At the same time, drug use in Iran itself has skyrocketed: Nawa reports that in parts of Tehran opium smoking is just as common as cigarette smoking. Not only opium, but such banned substances as hashish and liquor are readily available on many Iranian city streets.[26]

With US military intervention in Afghanistan beginning in late 2001, the two global wars—one against terrorism, the other against drugs—organically merged as part of a broadened geopolitical agenda. Tens of thousands of American troops (joined by smaller NATO contingents) were deployed to ostensibly fight Al Qaeda and remain, as of 2013, in even larger numbers after Obama's 2009 decision to escalate the US presence (ultimately followed with reductions by 2014). Neither effort (to crush the Taliban/terrorism or eliminate the drug trade) has been remotely successful. On the contrary, the US presence—heavily reliant on military force—has been entirely counterproductive, a major source of blowback.

As the Afghan insurgency began using drug money to buy weapons, the United States set up a large counternarcotics compound in Kabul—the National Interdiction Unit, composed of ten groups of operatives from the military, the DEA, the CIA, and such private contractors as DynCorp.[27] The idea was to destroy opium production through combined law enforcement, material enticements, interdiction, and crop eradication. Drug kingpins, traffickers, and processors would be captured and jailed, a reprise of the domestic antidrug crusade. Nothing worked, however: ten years later the poppy fields and opium labs would remain plentiful. Drug warfare harmed families and communities hoping for material benefits from drug markets, which often brought ten times the returns of wheat or potato crops. The struggle for survival, to provide food, clothing, and shelter for an overwhelmingly poor population, readily trumped the moralistic Western campaign against "illicit substances."[28]

The vast sea of purple-and-white flowers was not only a traditional part of the natural landscape; it had fueled an underground economy, as had happened in Mexico and Colombia with their different crops. Opium profits are consistently high, and of course alluring. Attempts at crop eradication, haphazard and crude as they were, gave rise to scattered local protests. Prospects for locating—and destroying—scores of local heroin-processing labs were predictably dismal. Corruption remains a taken-for-granted feature of Afghan institutional life: as in Mexico, police, troops, and government officials are happy to share in the lucrative proceeds of drug cultivation, processing, and smuggling. The National Interdiction Unit squads, laughable among the Afghan population, have faced a hopeless situation, especially as the drug trade reaches all the way to the top of the (US-puppet) Karzai government.[29]

In provinces like Helmand, within the famous "golden crescent" where the Taliban boasts majority support, the local drug trade enjoys close to a safe haven; though illegal, opium is sold and bought everywhere. Here the Mujahideen legacy, a 1980s creature of the CIA and its billions to aid "freedom fighters," survives fully intact. Nawa writes, "The pioneers of the booming heroin business are the former Mujahideen, and their alliance with the United States and NATO has allowed them to solidify their hold on the business and their power over entire regions of the country."[30] The US-Mujahideen partnership allowed for a *tripling* of opium production during the anti-Soviet holy war.[31] Under CIA aegis, warring Afghan factions competed for the flourishing drug markets, as drug lords, heroin labs, and traffickers operated more or less openly. The DEA, in fact, merely stood by as observers to business-as-usual. At that time, most drug flows moved through Pakistan, which had become the largest conduit of heroin to Europe and the United States. In some areas of Pakistan the producers and traders enjoyed nearly total immunity.[32]

A Different Face of Capitalism

The popular media in recent decades has fixated on the expanding role of criminal syndicates, or cartels, with their pervasive influence across Mexico and other regions of Latin America. Swollen with enormous drug profits, the syndicates are rightly depicted as business enterprises dedicated to the pursuit of wealth and power by any means available—enterprises well known for their massive waves of crime and violence. What receives emphatically less attention, however, is the distinctly capitalist nature of these syndicates, their dominant modus operandi

114   Chapter 5

converging in many ways with that of ordinary big business: profit orientation; structural hierarchy; obsession with growth and diversification; a drive toward globalization; and unyielding competition for resources, terrain, and markets. Such an alternative capitalism, with its precursors in earlier mafia operations, differs from modern corporate power mainly in its more ruthless, lawless use of violence to advance its interests—but even here the contrast is largely one of degree.[33]

Global drug markets have for decades, indeed centuries, been driven by the enormous revenues to be made from chemical substances, whether legal or illegal, always in wide demand. The drug trade, whether in tobacco, sugar, alcohol, opium, or cannabis, has long been an entrenched feature of most national economies and cultures, making it integral to capitalist trade relations. The flourishing of such markets has often been met with determined counter-responses: prohibitions, penalties, "warfare" against contraband substances. The undeniable popular demand for both medicinal and intoxicating drugs seems to contain its own ideological negation or political opposition; it is schizoid to the extreme. As Jay writes, "Although this process was driven by a universal and seemingly insatiable demand, it was also resisted vigorously from the start."[34] One outgrowth of this divided legacy has been the spread of an alternative, or underground, form of capitalism.

It is now common knowledge that prohibition in the United States during the 1920s fueled the rise of a complex, thriving system of criminal syndicates that were able to take over the alcohol trade from legitimate business. When the Volstead Act was passed, alcohol production and consumption simply moved underground: markets remained vigorous, profits soared, quality declined, syndicates competed on the black market, and of course crime rates escalated. Lawlessness took over major American cities as the syndicates built their own parallel network of codes, laws, and operating principles aligned with bootleggers, smugglers, speakeasy owners, drivers, bodyguards, and syndicate managers.[35]

Prohibition, whatever its stated moral aims, guaranteed the rise of an underground economy. Mike Gray writes, "By erecting an artificial barrier between alcohol production and consumers, the government had created a bonanza that can only be likened to the Gold Rush."[36] Criminal operations required few actual skills, experience, or even capital; clandestine distilleries, traffickers, and taverns could be sustained by thousands of manual workers untroubled by "moral" arguments against illicit alcohol. Tens of millions of dollars flowed into the hands of operatives grateful to earn a good living through the black-market trade. Mobsters took over an emergent, dynamic criminal subculture in which violent warfare and political corruption were accepted as the norm. Even before the sensationalized business exploits of Al Capone and Chicago gangsters—and later those of Dutch Schultz, Lucky Luciano, Meyer Lansky, and Bugsy Siegel—Chicago operative Johnny Torrio surfaced as a shrewd underground entrepreneur benefiting from the Volstead Act. Indeed hundreds of such criminal outfits appeared during the 1920s, forerunners of contemporary drug syndicates that would eventually lay claim to international markets.[37]

In his book *Prohibition*, Edward Behr surveys the achievements of perhaps the most astute of all 1920s syndicate heads, George Remus, reputed to have made some $40 million a year from bootlegging operations. His Death Valley Farm enterprise, thoroughly capitalist, built its empire in Chicago and across the Midwest. Writes Behr, "Remus was to bootlegging what Rockefeller was to oil. In the sheer imagination of his plan, in the insolent sweep of his ambition and power with which he swept upward toward his goal, Remus can bear comparison to the captains of industry."[38] His operation recruited an army of well-organized producers, shippers, bodyguards, accountants, and drivers working parallel to the legitimate market structure, trading not only beer and whiskey but gin, vodka, champagne, and even drugs sold as "medicinal," part of a sprawling business network that would tap into international trade. Like other syndicates, the Remus apparatus would forge a symbiotic relationship with not only local government officials but established banks and businesses. Thus, "while bankers and entre-preneurs on both sides of the Atlantic got rich on the proceeds, a new mythical hero emerged as part of prohibition folklore: the risk-taking, devil-may-care rum runner."[39] Remus's activities would be duplicated many times throughout the United States, exemplified by the vast bootlegging conglomerate built by Roy Olmstead in Washington State. Like Remus, Olmstead could rely (for a brief period, at least) on police protection.

Prohibition not only failed to alter the drinking habits of Americans; it ensured the success of outlaw conglomerates like the Consolidated Exporters Corporation, Remus's Death Valley Farm, Olmstead's bootlegging empire, and the Capone syndicate. A thriving underground capitalism meant the public would grow hardened to the nefarious activities of criminal operations associated with urban mobsters, racketeering, and corruption. With repeal of the Volstead Act in 1933, therefore, it follows that underground "mafia" operations were able to move into new venues such as gambling and related sources of wealth and power. Criminal syndicates would continue to thrive as local, national, and global networks. The legalization of alcohol would soon prompt a turn toward other contraband goods, including drugs.[40]

By the 1960s, international drug markets—above all for cocaine, opium/heroin, and cannabis—had begun to surge for several reasons: increased demand

116   CHAPTER 5

rooted in the youth counterculture, rising economic globalization, decline of social obstacles, and refined modes of transportation. Barriers to the flow of goods, resources, and money were effectively circumvented. So were taboos against consumption of some drugs, including marijuana, cocaine, and hallucinogens. At this historical conjuncture, moreover, underground capitalist enterprises ("the mafia") were gaining economic and institutional strength, expanding operations, building strategic alliances, and even achieving wider public tolerance. The rise of large drug cartels in Colombia, Mexico, Central America, Russia, Japan, and elsewhere is best understood in this context. As always, the syndicates and ancillary organizations were driven by insatiable demand for illegal drugs, mainly in North America and Europe.

In this context, the newer clandestine drug operations represent a more rationalized version of classical mafia infrastructure—a parallel system of (capitalist) power. Based in Sicily and southern Italy at the end of the nineteenth century, local mafias sought wealth and power through an "alternative"—underground, criminal, black-market—economic network. As described in Eric Hobsbawm's seminal analysis (*Primitive Rebels*), mafias developed as part of a complex mosaic of syndicate activities (extortion, smuggling, and various rackets) within a parallel system of laws, codes, and practices reinforced, in many cases, by close involvement with legitimate power structures.[41] Like subsequent incarnations, the first Italian mafias drew heavily from the ranks of the poor and marginalized, were led by tough young outlaws, created their own social rituals, and built an apparatus of hierarchy, loyalty, and violence. Some modicum of legitimacy came from pockets of local support that allowed for development of an "institutionalized system of law outside the official law."[42] As Hobsbawm makes clear, however, such legitimacy was not to be confused with democratic participation: "For most Sicilians all that happened was that the 'parallel system' and the official government merged into a single conspiracy to oppress."[43] For the classical mafia, anticipating the future growth of a local underground entrepreneurial stratum would have deeply authoritarian consequences.

As Hobsbawm observes, parallel local power erected by the mafia depended on "control of community life by a secret—or rather an officially unrecognized—system of gangs."[44] The underground syndicates strove for a milieu of internal quiet and external power.[45] An elaborate machinery of professional or semiprofessional outlaws was always crucial to mafia success leading, inevitably, to outbreaks of criminal violence.

Hobsbawm's analysis of classical mafia operations anticipated the later rise of drug-centered underground capitalism linked to cartels in Mexico, Colombia, and elsewhere—organizations more profitable, diversified, globalized, and, for the most part, ruthless. Turning to the present, the United States has mobilized tens of thousands of National Guard troops, border agents, and DEA personnel to fight the global drug war, yet the drug flow northward has continued unabated, as Hobsbawm might have expected. Combined US-Mexican government crackdowns have resulted in the arrests of many drug kingpins, other high-level operatives, and thousands of ordinary Mexicans involved in the drug trade, while trafficking proceeds at ever-higher levels to keep pace with unyielding American demand. The cartels smuggle 90 percent of all cocaine entering the United States, along with more than half of all pot and methamphetamines, flows that find their way to dozens of cities in the United States and Canada. At up to 600 percent in profits—and an estimated $250 billion or more in annual revenues as of 2013— the illegal drug business is among the most profitable enterprises on the planet.

The War on Drugs, boosting as it does international markets in contraband goods, provides stimulus to high-level traffickers that dwarfs Prohibition-era business empires. The North American Free Trade Agreement, passed by Congress in 1995, gave cartels freer maneuverability to conduct smuggling as the exchange of goods and services across the United States–Mexico border was loosened; drug flows benefited immensely from "free trade."[46] Growth of modern crime syndicates is driven by a virtually limitless supply of drugs, money, arms, and other valued items within the globalized economy, as money and power—not ideology—motivate the protagonists.

Based in Mexico but with expanding operations in Central America, the cartels work within an oligopolistic system that includes the Sinaloa, Gulf, Zetas, Juárez, La Familia, Michoacán, and Beltrán-Leyva organizations. Business transactions revolve around drug trafficking and money laundering within defined geographical boundaries that, over time, have grown more blurred. The kingpins recruit hundreds of lower-level operatives from the swollen ranks of the poor and jobless. As violent competition usually follows cartel efforts to expand, the work—especially that of criminal enforcers and couriers—is carried out by young men, as with the classical mafia. Where the cartels rely on such practices as extortion, kidnapping, and murder, as in some parts of Mexico, the brawny contributions of local gangs are frequently enlisted.[47] In some cases paramilitary squads are formed, ready to battle police and even military units. Given the vast US arms trade, weapons (including sophisticated military types) are naturally easy to procure. In Mexico the drug trade alone has come to rival that of oil exports, as constant raids, arrests, and drug seizures scarcely impede the drug flow northward. Given their scope, wealth, and technical sophistication—not to mention their capacity for extreme violence—the cartels have proven virtually impossible to dismantle. The difficulties mount owing to widespread corruption:

118   CHAPTER 5

government officials, police, and the military are vulnerable to bribes and other pressures made possible by the syndicates' superprofits.

As with legitimate business interests, competition among syndicates fuels expansion, diversification, and ruthless combat. In recent decades, as mentioned, some cartels have moved into criminal activities beyond drugs: kidnapping, extortion, protection rackets, smuggling of contraband, pirating of DVDs and similar products, and even theft of government oil. In this milieu the oligopoly has given rise to a more powerful underground network.[48] Diversification allows for deeper entrenchment in the economic, social, and political life of the country, especially in states where cartel power is most firmly embedded. Given the evolving character of both drug markets and the larger economy, moreover, underground trade relations have become increasingly *globalized*.[49]

Cartel struggles over turf have been fierce and violent, despite ambitious joint US-Mexican efforts to take out the leadership of the organizations and weaken their infrastructure. The Zetas syndicate, with its hundreds of well-trained gunmen, has been uniquely adept at expanding operations—in this case, across northeast and central Mexico. Combat with rival cartels such as the Gulf Cartel has been particularly ruthless: kidnappings, torture, mass murder, and dumped bodies along roadsides have been common occurrences. The Zetas's gradual takeover of the central region was met with public silence, evidence of the cartels' power to intimidate journalists and officials by means of bribes and threats of violence. However expansive the warfare zones, trafficking organizations have encountered little difficulty in general recruitment or leadership replenishment. Thus thirteen of twenty-four fugitive cartel leaders placed on a bounty list in 2009 were captured or killed, yet little has changed. As one former US official familiar with the Mexican drug war noted, "The problem with arresting criminal leaders is there are ten waiting to take their place."[50]

As Mexican cartels—and kindred organizations elsewhere—morph into systems of parallel authority, similarities between mafia capitalism and the established corporate system become increasingly visible. Both cartels and corporations expand according to a comparable logic: relentless pursuit of profits built on a perpetual growth machine tied to shrewd investments, hierarchical organization, an all-consuming competitive drive, and recruitment of an exploited labor force. For black markets no less than other markets, the impulse toward globalization is basic to the quest for profits through growth. The familiar capitalist drive toward accumulation of wealth and power applies to both the drug cartels and established corporate giants that dominate the international landscape.

Like transnational corporate power, the cartels are run by a relatively small stratum of aggressive elites—the infamous kingpins rather than CEOs—whose control over a manipulable work force is largely total and unaccountable. In both cases the particular markets (whether drugs, retail goods, oil, or fast foods) are managed within the orbit of a few economic structures—that is, an oligopoly. Indeed the role of seven large Mexican cartels is markedly similar to that of oligopolies in the media/entertainment, pharmaceutical, beer, oil, and banking industries. In both instances, profit-driven enterprises prefer to do business in an environment of poverty and low wages.[51] Like many corporations (banks, insurance companies, retail enterprises, etc.) the criminal syndicates actually *produce* little, if anything. For their part, the Mexican cartels simply facilitate the transfer of contraband goods—aside from whatever mayhem they create.

Other parallels are visible: corporations and cartels both accumulate super-profits and are managed by an insular elite that unilaterally decides matters of investment, logistics, communications, and labor relations. As these institutions expand and globalize, they become increasingly oligarchic in structure and unaccountable to any public, rendering democratic input a fiction. The transnational corporate system, composed of the world's 2,000 largest enterprises, commands no less than $103 trillion in assets overseen by a few thousand business moguls controlling a workforce of roughly seventy million people.[52] This pyramid of wealth and power is naturally concentrated at the top, the bulk of it located in the United States, Europe, and a few Asian countries. Business elites wield enormous power over governments, law enforcement, the media, smaller enterprises, and local communities. It is probably accurate to say that cartel kingpins want to emulate their more "legitimate" counterparts as they compete in the far riskier, more violent world of drug trafficking and other criminal activities. All global drug cartels together control no more than a half trillion dollars in yearly revenue. One might argue that the underground conglomerates, with their ruthlessly antisocial character, will differ from mainstream business enterprises that, after all, operate in a milieu of laws, regulations, and constraints—yet this is hardly the case. The cartels are the main driving force behind a culture of crime and mayhem that has reduced several Mexican urban areas to Hobbesian zones of chaos and violence.[53] Drug kingpins have no moral qualms about the bloody consequences of their underground business ventures; the flow of profits dictates everything. Questions of the public interest, social development, the environment, and workers' health are irrelevant to decision making about drug trafficking and other syndicate agendas.

For the established corporate realm, the same incessant pursuit of wealth and power must ultimately defer to civilizing motifs of freedom and democracy—to regulatory policies and constraints typical of liberal capitalism. This might be true, but only to a limited extent: the problem is that global capital itself recognizes precious few social, ethical, or ecological limits. Coercive and

120   CHAPTER 5

destructive policies foisted on workers, consumers, local communities, and the environment have long been systemic. Commodity production, moreover, does everything in its power to sidestep or eviscerate laws and regulations that stand in the way of profits—a standard feature of global capitalism. One need look no further than Ciudad Juárez, Mexico, a thriving haven of the underground drug economy: hundreds of transnational companies (*maquiladoras*), taking advantage of weak regulations and labor rights, have done far more than the drug cartels to transform large sections of the city into a violent, tortured, miserable mass of humanity. These corporations, mostly United States–based, hire workers at poverty wages, fight unions, pollute the air and water, and leave in their wake massive outbreaks of cancer and other diseases in a setting where celebrated values of freedom and democracy scarcely matter.[54] Legitimate capital, no less than its underground variant, pays scant attention to priorities viewed by elites as external to the dictates of profit maximization.

The Ciudad Juárez calamity, unfortunately, represents only a small part of this global phenomenon. The legacy of giant oil conglomerates (Chevron, ExxonMobil, Shell), with their devastating impact on the global ecosystem and local communities in Africa and South America, persists. The same applies to the fast-food industry and its "McDonaldized" regimen: worldwide production of foods harmful to human health, sustained exploitation of a labor force confined to low-wage work with few benefits and no unions, environmental damage and material waste caused by meat-centered agriculture, and the horrors of slaughterhouses and other "processing" venues. Here it is worth mentioning the horrendous record of such retail industries as Walmart, in 2013 the largest, most profitable corporate entity in the world—its superprofits generated from a mass of impoverished workers.

As Nelson Lichtenstein shows in *The Retail Revolution*, millions of workers face terrible conditions at Walmart and similar outlets where low-end jobs are the norm.[55] Walmart alone operates nearly 5,000 stores internationally, where workers earn little more than minimum wage, have few benefits, carry out union organizing at severe risk, and deal with high-tech surveillance tracking every move. As in the fast-food industry, built along classical Fordist lines, workers are trained to function as interchangeable robots, whether at stores or at sprawling warehouse complexes. Walmart symbolizes the authoritarian model of twenty-first-century corporate power, in which the processing and marketing of goods swiftly, cheaply, and efficiently is paramount. Such power is naturally debilitating to prospects for democracy, human rights, and ecological sustainability. Can the notorious drug cartels, in all their ruthlessness, be any more destructive to the public domain than transnational capital?

What, then, about the drug phenomenon as such? Here the criminal syndicates must surely exceed Big Pharma in their brazen treatment of the populations they impact. At this juncture broader contextual analysis is in order. The US-centered medical-industrial complex, including Big Pharma, is among the most profitable networks of corporate power in the world, dwarfing the international drug cartels. For 2010, prescription-drug sales in the United States reached a staggering $600 billion, with global revenues at nearly $850 billion—compared to a loosely estimated $50 billion for the Mexican syndicates. Revenues for several leading pharmaceutical companies *each* were roughly equivalent to the cash flows of all cartels *combined*: Pfizer at $58 billion, Novartis at $42 billion, Merck at $40 billion, and so on. Big Pharma itself constitutes a vast oligopolistic structure, with the leading ten corporations reaping no less than $711 billion in profits during the past decade, $84 billion coming in 2012 alone, according to a 2013 report by Health Care for America Now (HCAN). Pharmaceutical income, especially, has skyrocketed since 2004.[56] Moreover, while cartel business in recent years has been relatively stagnant, with only small growth annually, established drug-industry markets continue to expand dramatically, thanks to stepped-up advertising and rising demand in Europe, India, and South America as well as the United States.

At a time when the drug war has stimulated black markets and the accompanying violence, it is worth noting that marijuana amounts to more than 60 percent of illegal substances transported from Mexico northward. The remaining contraband (coke, meth, opiates) is worth a maximum $20 billion yearly, less than half the drug trade managed by Pfizer or Merck alone. Further, while cartel-related violence since the 2006 crackdown has been responsible for perhaps 70,000 deaths, the reality is that violence (including murder) elsewhere in the Western Hemisphere is often far worse than in Mexico, with higher rates in Honduras, Guatemala, Colombia, and Brazil. As for high-powered weapons used to kill in Mexico, the ATF has reported that no less than 90 percent can be traced to the US arms trade. Meanwhile, the flow of goods and people across the US-Mexican border continues unimpeded; with 23.4 million visitors, 2011 turned out to be a record year for tourism in Mexico.[57]

Given its far greater international reach, could the harmful impact of Big Pharma actually surpass that of the criminal drug networks? As during earlier US Prohibition, mafia capitalism tied to the drug trade is indeed a bloody affair: black markets naturally breed widespread violence and mayhem, most often the result of turf battles. Legal drug empires proceed along entirely different lines, their operations generally (though not always) within legal parameters. Big Pharma does not hire squads of gunmen—nor does it need to. Its repercussions

122   Chapter 5

are more general and diffuse, part of the everyday workings of "legitimate" economic and governmental activity.

In the United States, where the medical complex is dominated by banks, insurance companies, and sundry large corporations, taxpayers subsidize the cost of most pharmaceutical research, testing, and production, then pay extravagantly for medicinal drugs—up to 60 percent more than in other industrialized countries. While Pfizer, Merck, Eli Lilly, and others accrue between 15 and 30 percent return on investments—and while their CEOs can have incomes of several million dollars yearly—the markup for widely prescribed medications skyrockets, as more than half of all costs go to a combination of advertising, administration, and profits. Describing the general disaster of American medicine, Donald L. Bartlett and James B. Steele comment, "Since the 1980s America's health-care bureaucracy has mushroomed into one of the nation's fastest-growing industries. But this new industry is not designed to serve consumers or to improve the delivery of medical services. Rather, it is driven solely by the need to manage the process of referrals, billing, and reimbursements among the nation's thousands of health plans."[58]

For Americans, drugs are widely marketed for every conceivable physical and mental problem. As discussed elsewhere in this book, Big Pharma looks incessantly toward blockbusters—best-selling drugs marketed for depression, anxiety, allergies, obesity, sleep disorders, and sexual dysfunction, to name the most lucrative targets. In 2011 nearly $4 billion was earmarked for the advertising of legal drugs. Vigorously marketed pills, however, often do more harm than good, especially when used habitually—the source of adverse reactions that yearly send as many as two million people to hospitals and more than 200,000 to their graves.[59] If such estimates are even remotely accurate—and the likelihood of even larger numbers from unreported episodes is more probable—the death count laid at the doorstep of Big Pharma far exceeds that of the Mexican cartels spanning *several* years. While the black-market trade does go entirely unregulated, the pharmaceutical giants (nominally monitored by the FDA) usually find ways to neutralize or circumvent formal regulations, thanks to the power of well-funded lobbies.

Expanding Battle Zones

As mentioned, the drug trade—illegal as well as legal—is deeply embedded not only in the life of particular nations but in the global economy. It impacts diverse areas of human activity: politics, the economy, social relations, culture, foreign policy—as has the drug war itself, which inescapably brings to the fore crucial questions related to the exercise of American global power. That power, of course, has long relied heavily on military force—and the drug war, it turns out, often fits the established pattern.

Globalization in the form of transnational corporate hegemony has been framed by US leaders and the media as harbinger of a "new world order"—that is, a stable international system of economic, political, and military power transcending nation-state interests. While credible in some respects, the trajectory of global capital has a darker side: growing class polarization and poverty, heightened authoritarian controls, a weakening of state power *outside* the domain of a few leading nations. This crisis-ridden system, in which drug production and consumption have found a welcoming and lucrative environment, is rife with tendencies favoring militarization and even fascism. Probably nowhere is this dynamic more visible than in recent US-Mexico relations, where the two sides of drugs—public demand and elite prohibition—come directly into conflict. Here the oligopolistic cartels have built lucrative empires on a foundation of several trends: a mounting overall drug culture in the United States, systemic economic crisis, social deterioration on both sides of the border, and decline of Mexican state power.

The joint US-Mexican warfare strategy against the criminal syndicates, all fully militarized, should be viewed in this context. Escalating police and military crackdowns under President Calderón, from 2006 until 2012, despite limited results, were in part a response to the dual expressions of globalization: mounting crisis and disaggregation that coincide with solidification of elite power. While US-orchestrated drug wars unfold in other settings—Central America, Colombia, and Afghanistan, for example—it is in Mexico where combat has reached peak levels of militarization. The historic 2006 Mérida Initiative, launched under US pressure, identified Mexico as "ground zero" in the global War on Drugs, setting in motion more urgent policies and stratagems—elevated surveillance; large-scale troop mobilizations; wider deployment of federal agents and police backed by the Pentagon, the DEA, and the CIA; strengthened financial measures; a steady wave of interdictions and raids; and ongoing arrests with the goal of "decapitating" the syndicates.[60] The United States provided armed helicopters to the Mexican army and dispatched x-ray vehicles, sniffer dogs, and eventually drones to help intercept drug flows.

In the United States, antidrug hysteria has conveniently fixated on Mexico, viewed by the media, politicians, and law enforcement as a "failed state" where national-security interests are gravely threatened. Drugs are at the center of a different mode of warfare conducted by "narcoterrorists" whose sinister endeavors—drug trafficking, money laundering, murder, kidnappings, and general

124 CHAPTER 5

mayhem—have "spilled over" into American cities, bringing untold horrors to the country. Since the sophisticated drug trade follows no geographical borders, a new strategy of high-tech warfare, with abundant military involvement, is urgently needed. Toward this end, the United States and Mexico entered into the Security and Prosperity Partnership of North America, dependent on both military and policing resources. The enormous and aggressive US war lobby has revved up its pressure to further militarize the drug war—a lobby composed of armed-services contractors, intelligence agencies, disparate corporate interests, conservative think tanks, and drug warriors at the DEA and elsewhere.[61]

Several Mexican states and a few major cities (Ciudad Juárez, Tijuana, Monterrey) have seen an influx of military troops since advent of the Mérida Initiative— not only to fight the drug war but to bolster authority where legitimate public structures had weakened. Numerous states and cities were deeply corrupted by pervasive syndicate and gang influence. Violent battles have increased along the corridor running from Monterrey to the border near Nuevo Laredo, both sides heavily armed as the supply of guns and money from the United States flows mostly uninterrupted. Street battles involving cartels and Mexican troops—and among rival cartels—are frequent and increasingly militarized, as all sides possess an array of sophisticated weapons, including Barrett .50-caliber antiarmor rifles, an inventory of semiautomatic weapons, and both M-16 and AK-47 assault rifles. Roughly 90 percent of these military-style weapons are imported from the North. In this context, the drug trade, cartel power, and escalating warfare become inseparable.[62]

As we have seen, the DWZ in such locales as Ciudad Juárez and Tijuana has given rise to social and political chaos, ensuring government repression. For the United States during the George W. Bush administration, antinarcotics intervention was conducted through the combined resources of the Pentagon, the CIA, the DEA, the ATF, and other federal agencies. Directed not only at Mexico but also Central America, Colombia, Afghanistan, and Pakistan, such intervention is managed by the multibillion-dollar Counter Narco-Terrorism Program Office (CNTPO), merging two "wars" at the core of US foreign policy—against terrorism and drugs. Like the Mérida Initiative, CNTPO would target local insurgencies where US geopolitical interests are aligned with the established power structure, relying on extensive military aid, logistics, training, and surveillance—with direct military operations usually limited.[63] Nowhere, however, has such intervention done much to impede underground drug markets, though quite possibly this was never the decisive objective.

Calderón's war gained momentum after 2006, but the major cartels stood their ground, with violence spread across several Mexican states, from Sinaloa to Durango, Zacatecas, Guerrero, and Jalisco: indeed massive troop deployments only motivated cartel leaders to buy and stock more arms. Urban zones became battlegrounds. Meanwhile, Washington pushed Mexico to augment its counterinsurgency operations in the form of army mobilizations, attack helicopters, stepped-up surveillance, high-tech weaponry, and large-scale searches and arrests.[64] As troops flooded Mexican cities and towns, the syndicates deftly shifted operations from one locale to another while in regions of declining civil authority, ongoing criminality such as theft, prostitution, rape, and personal assaults was increasing. In an article for *Harper's*, Cecilia Ballí describes a Mexican population traumatized by fear and insecurity.[65] At various sites along the border, military-style weapons have become plentiful, cheap, easy to purchase, and just as easy to transport.

Mexican drug-war militarization, of course, bears a strong US imprint, involving not only several billions of dollars in direct aid but also a steady flow of helicopters, vehicles, and technology for "interdiction" and "border control." Armor-piercing handguns have become more available in Mexico and along the borders. US military advisers work closely with the Mexican army, as in Colombia and Afghanistan. Calls for US troop deployments to smash the cartels have come from American politicians, a stratagem the Obama administration resists. Texas governor Rick Perry stated in 2011, "We must show the cartels that Washington will no longer tolerate their terrorizing and criminalizing the border region."[66] For decades, United States–sponsored antidrug warfare has merged with broader economic and political interests, nowhere more so than in foreign policy—above all in the Western Hemisphere.[67]

We have seen how, in Afghanistan, the United States took advantage of the drug trade to help the Mujahideen fight the Soviet Union, only to reverse course in 2001 when a counterinsurgency against those same forces (including the Taliban) gained primacy. In Colombia, US policy has long converged around two targets—cocaine trafficking and political insurgency, each considered a threat to national security. The Reagan administration turned its attention to Colombia in the late 1980s, convinced that large-scale coke smuggling posed a challenge to US interests in South America, especially as large coca fields were adjacent to oil deposits where FARC (Revolutionary Armed Forces of Colombia), an insurgent movement with deep roots in the countryside, was also strong. By 1991 Washington was sending military detachments and CIA personnel to what had become a globalized drug war, a prelude to Plan Colombia (in 2000) when the United States earmarked $1.3 billion for counterinsurgency, interdiction, and crop eradication, sending out helicopters to spray fields with highly toxic chemicals.[68] Fumigation strategies intensified from 2000 to 2003, targeting

126   CHAPTER 5

380,000 hectares of coca cultivation with pesticides. President George W. Bush later broadened US economic and military operations in the region under the Andean Counterdrug Initiative.

The George W. Bush years brought further expansion of Plan Colombia, with new deployments of military advisers, stepped-up covert actions, and widening presence of eradication teams. Counternarcotics units were dispatched to the countryside, working jointly with private contractors like MPRI and DynCorp attached to the Pentagon and the State Department. Several right-wing paramilitary groups, aligned with the Colombian armed forces and backed by Washington, were responsible for killing thousands of FARC members and their allies and supporters going back to the late 1980s. The drug war only fed the violence, left behind vast polluted areas, and provoked social breakdown while doing little to destroy coca production, as growers usually moved to more remote zones—or even to neighboring countries such as Peru and Bolivia. During the 1990s, in fact, coca production in Colombia increased nearly threefold, while counternarcotics activity simply bolstered the most repressive forces—police, armed forces, death squads—at a time when Plan Colombia was sold to the American public as a step toward democratization.[69]

When Bush strengthened the Andean Counterdrug Initiative in 2001, antidrug warfare began targeting new countries—Bolivia, Peru, and Ecuador—where coca production was also thriving. Eradication and interdiction efforts gained new momentum. With the larger cartels (Medellín, Cali, etc.) dismantled across the region, markets became more dispersed while ties with Mexican syndicates (a key conduit of coke transfers) expanded. As for Plan Colombia, militarization did finally achieve results: peaking at 163,000 hectares in 2000, coca growing declined to 80,000 hectares by 2004 and even smaller amounts by 2010. However, as mentioned, when attacked or destroyed in one zone, coca production (coca being a mobile crop) easily relocated elsewhere—in this case, to Peru, Bolivia, Ecuador, and even Mexico. Whatever the Andean situation, there has been no measurable drop in cocaine flows to the United States since the 1990s, as supply consistently meets demand. Meanwhile, South American drug-war militarization offers the ideal pretext for US intervention behind long-standing economic and geopolitical ambitions.[70]

As in the United States and Mexico, illegal drug markets farther south create a bonanza for growers, criminal syndicates, money launderers, and gangs that reap tens of billions of dollars yearly in profits. Like Mexico, Colombia has long been a site of banned agricultural goods, processing labs, transit routes, and money-laundering venues protected by armed groups. Neither the Mérida Initiative nor Plan Colombia ever managed to demolish a drug trade that has traditionally saturated much of the Western Hemisphere, mostly to feed North American appetites for coke, pot, meth, and opiates. In Colombia, the drug war has targeted both left-wing rebels and drug traffickers, as violence throughout the countryside persists, involving (as in Mexico) extortion, kidnapping, and murder. In both Colombia and Mexico, moreover, a militarized drug war has provoked state repression extending to widespread human-rights abuses.[71] Further, as might be predicted, government agencies have been corrupted in no small measure by the growth of mafia capitalism.

While Plan Colombia did serve to reduce the drug trade (and cartel power) in some regions, counterinsurgency efforts against FARC were less successful. In fact, by late 2012 "peace talks" were under way between the government and FARC—with prospects of giving the rebels, still a popular force, representation in the political system, perhaps ending the fifty-year insurgency. For years FARC was depicted in the United States as a narcoterrorist organization despite its deep roots in the countryside. Allied with a popular movement, Marcha Patriótica, FARC leaders called for human-rights guarantees along with extensive agrarian reforms that, presumably, would bring an end to the toxic eradication programs.[72] With struggles composed of several grassroots organizations with broad rural support, democratic reforms were proposed that would curb the very police and military power that Plan Colombia helped create and sustain.

Meanwhile, the Mexican cartels remained not only powerful but global in scope, surviving intensified joint US-Mexican efforts to destroy the organizations. Arrests of drug kingpins have generally signified little more than changes within leadership, while the criminal work remains largely unimpeded. A celebrated drug-war "breakthrough" came in October 2012, when Zetas chieftain Heriberto Lazcano was slain by Mexican special forces acting on US intelligence in the wake of arrests of several key cartel leaders. Some observers speculated that military attacks on the Zetas might eliminate this most violent of all underground syndicates. More likely, the Zetas were in the process of dissolving into smaller, more dispersed groups—precisely what happened in Colombia and in other Mexican locales.

Lazcano, it should be noted, served in the Mexican army during the 1990s, learning sophisticated military skills that were useful to both the Gulf Cartel and the Zetas, which split from the larger syndicate before expanding operations in southern Mexico and Central America. Under Lazcano, the Zetas moved into regions aiming to take over such criminal rackets as drug trafficking, extortion, kidnapping, and, in some cases, the sex trade. The cartel assisted in a few of the largest prison breaks in Mexican history. Often protected by the ruling PRI (Institutional Revolutionary Party), as in Coahuila State, the Zetas were

128   CHAPTER 5

allowed to conduct business with little threat of political crackdowns. Calderón's revitalized drug war, however, targeted the Zetas and other cartels with military force but failed, as noted, to visibly undermine northward drug flows. Instead of de-escalating the drug war, the Calderón years witnessed heightened levels of combat between cartels and government—and between the cartels themselves, especially along the lengthy Mexican border with California, Arizona, New Mexico, and Texas. Several cities (notably Ciudad Juárez, Ciudad Victoria, Matamoros, Nuevo Laredo, and Reynoso) experienced a steady increase in criminal operations, civic violence, and corruption after the Mérida Initiative was set in motion. Dawn Paley comments that the people of Mexico "have been abandoned, losing their loved ones and living in fear and silence as their cities are transformed into battlegrounds, in the shadow of Texas."[73]

The War on Drugs has led to continuously stepped-up efforts to facilitate the flow of heavy arms into Mexico, control border traffic, and monitor electronic communications at the summits of Mexican corporate, government, and military power. The fact that Mexican elites are so often entangled with the business of organized crime has only exacerbated this crucial development. US security agencies—above all the NSA, the CIA, the DEA, and Border Patrol units—have gained unprecedented access to high-level activities in Mexico, as revealed by Wikileaks and NSA whistle-blower Edward Snowden.[74] Such access led to the apprehension of Sinaloa drug kingpin "El Chapo" Joaquín Guzmán in Mazatlán in February 2014. As of early 2014, the powerful Sinaloa operation had extended its activities—going well beyond drug smuggling—to more than fifty countries, from North America to Europe and Africa. An outlaw hero of sorts, Guzmán hid with ease among the local population while still helping to orchestrate brutal territorial wars until agency operatives were able to arrest him at one of his "retreats." It is unlikely that Guzmán's arrest will make a dent in the work of Sinaloa, much less other cartels.[75]

Mexican syndicates remain a vital conduit of cocaine flows northward to meet US appetites. While Colombia production, as mentioned, has declined modestly, the slack was easily picked up by growers and processors in Peru and Bolivia, countries now ranking first and second in the global cocaine trade—marketing 358 tons and 298 tons in 2011, respectively, compared to 215 tons for Colombia according to US reports (though a UN report listed Colombian output at 380 tons).[76] At the same time, while US demand for cocaine products has declined somewhat in recent years, markets in Europe and Asia have been decidedly on the upswing. Today antidrug warriors in Washington claim Plan Colombia as a splendid victory in the War on Drugs, but evidence to support such official triumphalism is nowhere to be found. In any event, militarized antidrug campaigns are actually part of a broader US geopolitical agenda to counter efforts throughout Latin America to subvert US hegemony in the region.[77]

As of 2013, Afghanistan, where the United States was fighting wars against both terrorism and drugs, supplied more than 90 percent of European, North American, and Asian drug markets. One of the poorest nations—with a government overtaken by corruption and outlawry—it employs an estimated 750,000 people in the opium trade, for which few alternative sources of income exist. It is a trade, moreover, that extends to the bordering countries Pakistan, Iran, and India. The drug war in Afghanistan has often turned into a violent assault on local farmers, poor tribal members, and various organizations directly or peripherally active in opium processing or trafficking. As in Mexico and South America, large-scale interdiction programs operated by the military and the CIA, along with several private contractors, have not worked; nor have eradication attempts. Much of the failure, as elsewhere, can be explained by deep involvement of the Afghan military, police, and government in the drug business.[78] No amount of US intervention has managed to alter this reality.

My contention here is that the domestic War on Drugs meshes with and indeed reinforces US global ambitions—that is, the drive toward economic, political, and military supremacy. A militarized drug war is a logical outgrowth of these ambitions, whether in Mexico, other regions of Latin America, or the Middle East. Historical departures from this pattern are duly noted, as in the case of Afghanistan (mentioned earlier) where US intervention was originally aligned with the drug trade exploited by the Mujahideen against Soviet power. But Washington shifted to the more familiar drug-war scenario after 9/11. Peter Dale Scott has shown how the CIA was engaged in drug running in Southeast Asia throughout the 1950s and 1960s in the service of US-backed anticommunist forces.[79] Similarly, Gary Webb in *Dark Alliance* revealed a CIA plan to smuggle cocaine in support of Contra efforts to overthrow the Sandinistas in Nicaragua in the mid-1980s.[80] Along these lines, Alexander Cockburn and Jeffrey St. Clair, in their important book *Whiteout*, document the role of the CIA and other government agencies in using the drug trade to advance US interests in Latin America.[81] Deeply indebted to Webb's seminal work, they reveal an even larger matrix of drug trafficking and money laundering often associated with US covert activities.

Without doubt a variety of economic interests and social forces—left and right, insurgent and status quo—have utilized the global drug trade to serve political ends. The overriding postwar reality, however, has been convergence of antidrug politics and (US) imperial goals. As shown by the Mexican events, the *domestic* War on Drugs quite naturally coexists with an *international* prohibition

130   CHAPTER 5

agenda, a trajectory explored more fully in Chapter 3. From this standpoint, far too much has been made of Webb's correct findings regarding the CIA-Contra cocaine linkage, as this was more an aberration than general pattern. CIA drug pushing in fact covered a rather brief period (mostly 1986) and involved exclusively Contra operations—although, as Cockburn and St. Clair show, CIA participation in global drug markets extended also to Afghanistan and parts of Latin America during the 1980s.[82] But there is no evidence that such practices continued beyond the late 1980s. And the argument that CIA trafficking in cocaine, in California or elsewhere, gave rise to inner-city "crack epidemics" is preposterous. The amount of coke involved at the time (several hundred kilos) was minuscule when viewed against the backdrop of much larger, decades-long global drug transactions. Further, the great increase in American consumption of intoxicating drugs goes back to the 1960s, when large amounts of illegal substances (hallucinogens, pot, meth) were in fact home-produced.

This reality, however, should not obscure the shameful record of US government agencies in covering up or supporting a lucrative trade in money, guns, and drugs benefiting a ruthless Contra operation in the mid-1980s—a record Webb in particular detailed at some length. Cocaine dealing, much of it centered in Los Angeles, where local gang involvement was extensive, was the preferred medium not only to secure large profits—crack distribution was especially cheap and easy during that period—but to achieve political goals: the Reagan administration was obsessed with destroying the Sandinista regime. Here, as in Afghanistan at roughly the same time, all the moral platitudes about illicit drugs were essentially honored in the abstract, even by the DEA. As Webb notes, "Internal government memos show that the CIA, White House, the Defense Department, and the Contras' congressional supporters knew that the Contras had no hope of defeating the Sandinistas. [Yet] . . . they could continue spending CIA funds despite the Boland Amendment [prohibiting US aid to the Contras]. If the Contras were given money for one purpose—arms interdiction—and decided to use it another way, well, that wasn't the CIA's fault, was it?" As Webb shows, the flow of money came, at crucial moments, from CIA-sponsored drug dealing.[83]

For a brief period, at least, coke dealers in Los Angeles (including the infamous Ricky Ross) were processing as much as 150 kilos of cocaine weekly, amounting over time to perhaps $5 billion in cash—a great potential boon to US-backed groups like the Contras.[84] Thus, "even if nothing could have been proven conclusively about the CIA's involvement in the Contra drug ring, the agency was supposed to be the nation's primary intelligence-gathering arm, and its responsibilities specifically included monitoring the international narcotics trade. A plea of ignorance about the dope dealing by its own paramilitary forces would have looked as bad as proof of complicity."[85]

Webb's findings in *Dark Alliance* that a group of Nicaraguan exiles, close at one point to the Somoza dictatorship, helped set up a cocaine ring in California with ties to Los Angeles street gangs—the profits going to CIA-backed Contras—have a strong basis in historical evidence. From all indications, this was an ambitious (though clearly short-lived) criminal enterprise that operated at odds with the War on Drugs. The claim, however, that the "crack plague" had roots in such Contra dealings is rather far-fetched: by all accounts, the coke trade has a much longer and wider history, rendering CIA machinations little more than a footnote to a much larger narrative. Moreover, the idea that the CIA-Contra drug connection was anything more than an aberration from the *general* pattern of US global policies immersed in the drug war is entirely misleading.

The War on Drugs, more accurately, fits the contours of both a neoliberal economic model and a militarized foreign policy long embraced by US ruling interests. Both trajectories buttress an authoritarian logic at work in the corporate-state system, reflected in the continuing incarceration of minorities and poor at high levels, not to mention vast resources for law enforcement, prisons, and the military in a period of the much-agonized "fiscal crisis." Within this matrix, shared by Republicans and Democrats alike, the public sphere declines as democratic processes shrink further. Oligarchical interests predominate thanks to the power of Big Pharma, the Pentagon, Wall Street, corporate lobbies, the insurance industry, and myriad government agencies—fully consistent with established drug-war agendas. It is precisely this authoritarianism—not terrorism or drugs—that defines the great plague of contemporary American society.

Drugs and US Militarism

If the drug phenomenon exerts a powerful influence on American public life, it also deeply impacts the nation's international behavior. As discussed previously, a political culture immersed in perpetual warfare has long been a driving force in the American experience. At present Washington maintains more than 800 military bases around the world, not to mention unsurpassed naval and air forces with enough nuclear weaponry to destroy the world many times over. This US military reach, reinforced by vast economic and political resources, is managed through a combination of worldwide surveillance, covert actions, a network of private contractors, proxy wars, and a phalanx of federal agencies (including the

132   Chapter 5

CIA, the DEA, the NSA, the ATF, and the DHS). To varying degrees, these instruments are central to the War on Drugs. As is well known, the United States devotes more funding to its armed forces than do all other nations combined. Despite such heavy costs and repeated failures, warfare has become a way of life, an addiction, at the summits of Washington politics. As Tom Engelhardt observes, "Military actions have become the tics of an overwrought great power with the equivalent of Tourette's Syndrome. They happen because they are engraved in the policy DNA of our national security complex."[86] The consequences for those hundreds of millions of people subjected to the myriad operations of the warfare state are indeed far-reaching.

Those who find themselves within this imperial orbit face a litany of problems—one being the increasingly closed, authoritarian character of power relations in all sectors of government. Military life in foreign countries can be harsh and alienating, as troops must deal with the challenging terrain, strange languages and cultures, distance from friends and family, lack of personal freedoms and mobility, periods of intense boredom, and in many cases hostile local populations—all exacerbated by the risks and hardships of combat. Battlefield conditions produce the horrors of witnessing death and destruction, compounded where troops return for two or more tours of duty, common for the US military in Iraq and Afghanistan. While combat is a savage experience, those in the field often see little moral purpose or psychological investment in "victory" for warfare that is conducted among or against (mostly poor) local populations. Alienation and demoralization can quickly overcome soldiers (as well as sailors and airmen) with limited support networks and no influence over life-and-death decisions.[87]

Under such conditions, combatants can be easily drawn toward any drugs that are available, for many reasons—to kill pain, fight infections, overcome boredom, temper depression, or just escape the oppressive routines of military life. Not only are many banned substances (pot, coke, opiates, meth) generally within easy reach, but prescription drugs are routinely given to armed-forces personnel just for the asking. In this context, rampant drug use (often leading to abuse or addiction) is predictable, with few options for either treatment or alleviation of everyday stress. Further, there are few stigmas involving drugs (even extreme consumption) in the military environment. US military operations in Vietnam, Iraq, and Afghanistan—with their lengthy, difficult troop deployments—have, predictably, given rise to widespread problems associated with both legal and illegal drugs.[88]

In Vietnam, where roughly six million American troops were stationed for more than a decade, no fewer than 700,000 military personnel were reported to have experienced serious drug problems.[89] Pot use was nearly universal in combat zones, daily consumption being rather normal. Opium, meth, hallucinogens, and heroin were readily available and rather cheap, with antidepressants and painkillers freely handed out by medics. The GI world of intense fear, anxiety, and depression was so inescapable that military discipline frequently broke down; entire army companies were known to come under the influence of drugs, their capacity to fight obviously eroded.[90] In later stages of the war, drug use helped fuel an antiwar counterculture as revolt spread among the lower ranks. Since pot was grown locally, moreover, it was remarkably easy and inexpensive to purchase.

By the time the Vietnam War ended with humiliating US defeat in 1975, hundreds of thousands of American troops had fallen victim to severe drug addictions, the majority to heroin, which could be purchased for as little as two dollars for a plastic vial typically available near US bases. Both the South Vietnamese government and military—not to mention the American CIA—were deeply involved in the opium and heroin trade, just as the CIA would be later in Afghanistan.[91] The proceeds here, as elsewhere, would be directed toward a variety of anticommunist political forces. Although GI addiction to hard drugs was rife in Vietnam, it was typically overcome once people returned home and their environment drastically changed. A Washington University study found that only one in eight former GIs became readdicted once they departed the combat zone; addictions were simply outgrown.[92]

Later wars gave rise to similar traumas, alienation, and psychological breakdown not only during but after combat—mostly afflicting men and women between ages eighteen and thirty. More than two million US troops served in the Iraq and Afghanistan wars, many returning for two or more tours of duty. Emotional and physical scars of war are severe and lasting for hundreds of thousands of personnel as well as their families. Combat-related nightmares naturally feed into personal and social conflict that carry well into civilian life. Under such conditions, should abuse of alcohol, prescription drugs, and banned substances like pot and opiates be shocking—especially where a smorgasbord of "medications" (antidepressants, sleeping aids, pain relievers, stimulants, etc.) can be accessed as easily as a glass of beer or a cup of coffee? Should anyone be astonished to find connections between military-related problems and "civilian" issues like domestic violence, divorce, joblessness, and addiction?

In Iraq and Afghanistan warfare has been such that violence—and threat of violence—is rather ubiquitous: the "enemy" can appear on any road, in any village, in any town, where there are no clear battle lines. Traumas resulting from combat savagery are taken for granted within daily life. The flood of physical and mental casualties has expected outcomes, including widespread alcohol and drug use that can often follow troops into civilian life, one cause of the familiar

134   CHAPTER 5

post-traumatic stress disorder (PTSD). Pharmaceuticals routinely prescribed in Iraq and Afghanistan (Zoloft, Vicodin, Ambien, oxycodone, etc.) are powerful, with extreme adverse reactions that can include psychological changes in the direction of aggression, violence, and suicide. According to some reports, many troops in Iraq used potent mixtures of drugs and alcohol, even while on duty.[93] The physical and mental consequences of such mixtures have rarely been studied, inside or outside of the military.

If the easiest way to treat combat-related stress or depression is by prescription medications, then pill use in the military is sure to be common. In contrast to Vietnam, however, where drugs of choice were mainly pot and heroin, the more recent cases of Iraq and Afghanistan involved a preponderance of legal drugs consistent with trends in American society as a whole. After all, prescription meds in combat zones are basically free, readily obtained, not likely to be contaminated, and essentially without taboos. In many cases officers were inclined to pacify difficult or recalcitrant soldiers with soothing, mood-enhancing medications. One problem is that drug "cocktails" involving a mix of substances have also been made available to troops, putting users at even more severe risk of adverse reactions that have never been studied or monitored by the FDA or the Pentagon. Widely prescribed Seroquel cocktails (combining painkillers and sedatives) were eventually found to produce violent behavior linked to homicidal or suicidal impulses. Drastic mood swings, paranoia, lethargy, depression, and sexual dysfunction are common. And, of course, Big Pharma is deeply complicit here: Seroquel alone brought roughly $5 billion to AstraZeneca in 2009.

As drug toxicity builds over time, veterans bring home their addictions and adverse effects after they leave the military, even though—as mentioned—the majority tend to "mature out" of dependency. Suicides that reached high levels during wartime (935 attempts were recorded in Iraq, for example, during 2007) continue into civilian life. Data naturally remain hazy since few definitive studies are undertaken, but the incidence of violent episodes associated with psychoactive drugs appears remarkably high.[94] By 2011, the Department of Veterans Affairs was coping with a steady flow of trauma victims whose condition, in many cases, was exacerbated by psychotropic drug use—which is now, in fact, part of PTSD treatment. The VA was dealing with a backlog of no fewer than 600,000 postcombat casualties as of late 2013.

The military drug problem cuts across age, gender, racial, and other social lines, with deep roots in the larger American drug culture, where pills of infinite varieties are easily available for every condition. This is another example of iatrogenesis, or medically induced harm. Despite the official War on Drugs, the taking of psychotropic substances in the United States has become rather fashionable, immune to criticism even as such drugs are massively overprescribed and are the source of abuses and addictions. In 2011, more than 110,000 army troops were reported to be using powerful antidepressants—the drugs coming in no fewer than *nine* varieties—most of the users seemingly unaware of the potential harm. Many of those 110,000 were given the enormously potent antimalarial drug Mefloquine, linked to strong impulses toward anger, rage, paranoia, and suicide.[95]

The general problem of medical iatrogenesis is built into a pharmaceutical drug culture ensuring a flow of profits into Big Pharma. The predicament is simply more extreme and more concentrated in the military, where drug regulations and monitoring are weak or nonexistent. The issue of multiple-drug overdoses and severe reactions, referred to as "polysubstance-induced syndrome," is especially rampant in the US armed forces. Widespread drug abuse of the sort visible in army units deployed to Iraq and Afghanistan was already well known among the American civilian population. Monitoring is a greater challenge when prescriptions are written by different physicians, each unaware of potential polysubstance effects. Those Seroquel cocktails given to soldiers (usually by one doctor), combining such potent drugs as trazadone, propranolol, and fluoxetine, have their forerunner in civilian mixtures involving Xanax, Soma, Fentanyl, OxyContin, and kindred substances that have contributed to thousands, perhaps hundreds of thousands, of violent episodes. Such cocktails are more dangerous than most illegal drugs, as users think they are perfectly safe (with manageable risks) given their official medical imprimatur. Those unschooled in the toxic menace of pharmaceuticals are likely to believe that doctors, as medical experts, are always correct—the ultimate source of iatrogenesis, whether civilian or military. Medical harm results in part from a distinctly American impulse to view pills—drug fixes—as a central treatment modality. As noted, the United States accounts for more than *half* the world consumption of legal drugs (more than 90 percent for such medications as Vicodin), prescribed for such problems as obesity, sleep disorders, sexual dysfunction, depression, anxiety, and eating disorders. One consequence of this American pill mania has been the roughly two million cases of *reported* adverse reactions yearly.[96]

The enduring problem of a highly medicated military places in greater relief the widely lamented (but generally misunderstood) phenomenon of drug addiction. American society has witnessed the steady growth of addictive behavior in its diverse forms—one result of pervasive alienation, material hardship, and social disempowerment. Such addiction extends to both legal and illegal drugs,

136 Chapter 5

as well as alcohol, tobacco, sugar, and fast foods. The many antidrug crusades, going back to the Harrison and Volstead Acts, remain out of touch with this historical reality. Where anxiety, depression, and pain appear rather normal, we can expect similar "normalcy" when it comes to drug consumption, abuse, and dependency. In this context, addiction is best understood as a *cultural* or social phenomenon as well as a psychological one.[97]

Chapter 6
The Medical-Drug Behemoth

Widespread drug consumption—of chemical substances that in different ways impact mind and body—has been a feature of human societies for many centuries. Drug cultures and subcultures have taken root and expanded, probably never more so than at present. Distinctions between "legal" and "illegal" drugs have scarcely been a concern of human beings throughout history. As drug historian Mike Jay notes, "Drug cultures are endlessly varied, but drugs in general are more or less ubiquitous among our species."[1] Psychoactive substances have been used for an infinite variety of purposes—as intoxicants, painkillers, antidepressants, sex stimulants, sleeping aids, and medical treatments of every sort, to name some. It is precisely as medications, however, that drugs have become the most profit-making of all businesses in the United States—now among the most powerful and aggressive corporate structures ever to span the planet. A crucial force behind economic oligopoly and big government, what has come to be known as Big Pharma now occupies the apex of a sprawling medical-pharmaceutical-industrial complex.

The American drug industry, dominated by an ensemble of giant corporations, has become a celebrated element of "free-market" or "private" health care ritually championed by politicians, economists, business elites, academics, and the popular media. It has virtually unparalleled legitimacy, as more than 200 million Americans consume prescribed drugs every year, with long-term and multiple simultaneous use of "meds" nowadays common. The medical system—modernized, high-tech, bureaucratic, ultraprofessional—is a more than $3 trillion enterprise, at a time when health indicators for the general population

138   CHAPTER 6

rank among the lowest of major industrial nations. There is little indication that President Obama's liberal healthcare reforms, despite advances in coverage, will significantly alter this reality. The ongoing growth of large-scale medical enterprises—Big Pharma, insurance companies, hospitals, clinics, research institutions—helps explain not only the perpetuation of a deep healthcare crisis but the increasingly closed, authoritarian, inegalitarian features of the system.

The vast material resources, sophisticated technology, and human skills invested in technocratic medicine have not kept the United States from becoming perhaps the sickest nation on earth—a nation afflicted with extremely high levels of obesity, heart disease, cancer, diabetes, and other chronic diseases, such as arthritis and osteoporosis. The death rate from cancer has risen from fewer than 100,000 in the 1950s to nearly 600,000 in 2013, with roughly 1,660,000 new cases expected in 2014, according to the American Cancer Society[2]—decades after President Nixon declared his ambitious and much-ballyhooed "war" on cancer. Disorders both physical and mental are now such an ordinary feature of American life that the United States leads the world by a significant margin in consumption of prescribed drugs. Americans are a grossly overmedicated population by any measure, not only because of what doctors give patients in their offices, clinics, and hospitals but also due to what consumers purchase over the counter. Domestic pharmaceutical sales reached nearly $400 billion in 2011, with the ten leading companies reaping greater profits than all other Fortune 500 corporations combined, as profits exceeded 15 percent return on investments, roughly triple that of Walmart.[3] Over the past three decades Congress has given Big Pharma virtual carte blanche to operate in any manner the market will tolerate, legitimized by a "free enterprise" dogma—meaning deregulation and no price controls—that since the Reagan era has defined the healthcare industry to a degree even greater than the larger economy.[4]

In *Overdosed America*, Dr. John Abramson argues that the US medical system has been systematically corrupted by its very modernity—namely, by a hypermedicated system favoring symptoms over causes, technical shortcuts over durable solutions, and treatment regimens that minimize all-important *contextual* factors such as lifestyle, nutrition, family relations, economic pressures, and the general environment.[5] For Abramson, the system is emphatically iatrogenic, as it does more harm than good—a thesis borrowed heavily from such critics as Ivan Illich in *Medical Nemesis*.[6] For Abramson and other critics of American medicine, the best indicator of iatrogenesis is the drug industry, which now exercises virtual hegemonic influence over the corporate-medical complex.

Such trends reflect nothing less than the corporate takeover of American medicine, a development consistent with the broader trajectory at work in society as a whole. The critiques of Marcia Angell, Donald Bartlett, and James Steele explore the pernicious effects of just such a corporate juggernaut in which marketing, advertising, and lobbying have come to predominate over the age-old tradition of healing, at a time when the agendas of Wall Street and Madison Avenue overwhelm basic consumer interests.[7] While this trajectory might appear to some as rather novel, it has deep roots in an American history shaped during the past two centuries by capitalist industrialization. The rise of large-scale corporate medicine goes back to the dynamic Rockefeller project set in motion at the end of the nineteenth century. Expanded and rationalized across many decades, the corporate-medical complex was driven and legitimated by the innovations of science and technology, then transformed by a managerial ethos adopted by doctors, hospitals, insurance companies, the drug industry, medical schools, and government agencies, profits taking precedence over all other concerns.[8] Under the Rockefeller aegis, as E. Richard Brown observes, business and government elites converged around a "union of corporations, philanthropy, the managerial stratum, the universities, and science spawned by the Rockefeller Medicine Men and their new system of medicine."[9]

The Rise of Big Pharma

The pharmaceutical industry has grown into the largest business enterprise (aside from food) on the planet, and it continues to expand with each passing year. Fuller explanations for why so many Americans are taking drugs—legal and illegal, medicinal and recreational—in the modern setting are reserved for later discussion. The most lucrative of all drug sectors, best described as a corporate oligopoly, influences virtually every realm of life: the economy, scientific research, health care, psychological issues, culture, politics, and family life.

In the United States alone, pharmaceutical sales have risen sharply since the early 1980s, after the 1984 Bayh-Dole Act gave drug sellers freer room to maneuver, largely insulated from public scrutiny and democratic accountability.[10] By 2006 doctors were prescribing roughly 150 medications for every 100 office visits, for such routinely experienced conditions as depression, pain, anxiety, insomnia, sexual dysfunction, high blood pressure, excessive cholesterol levels, and arthritis. One-year supplies of medications could easily cost several thousand dollars. Doctors, pharmacists, therapists, psychiatrists, hospitals, clinics, insurance companies, and government programs like Medicare were all tightly linked to Big Pharma, which was legally empowered to advertise its products everywhere—in newspapers and magazines, on TV and the Internet, through

140   CHAPTER 6

mailings and medical journals—promising the wonders of modern chemistry for happiness, longevity, physical vigor, mental acuity, good relationships, and sexual vitality. The rise of biotechnology as simultaneously science, medicine, and business, with its cozy relations among corporations, government, universities, and the medical establishment, has inspired this biggest-ever leap into American drug culture.[11]

As Big Pharma superprofits accumulate, however, evidence shows that remedies offered by the drug giants commonly fail to deliver on their promises. Benefits are exaggerated, and adverse reactions are ignored or downplayed—not only in advertising but, more disturbingly, in the purportedly scientific world of biomedical research. Critics such as Abramson, Angell, Steele, and Harriet Washington call attention to a situation in which prescriptions are usually written for conditions (obesity, high cholesterol, cardiovascular problems, etc.) resulting from underlying causes that pills might temporarily ameliorate but cannot remedy.[12] Short-term medication for immediate pain relief or treatment of severe depression has obvious justification, but the remarkable fact is that more than 90 percent of drugs are prescribed long-term, often in potentially harmful, even lethal combinations, nowadays known as "cocktails." As Angell writes, "we have become an overmedicated society. Doctors have been taught only too well by the pharmaceutical industry, and what they have been taught is to reach for the prescription pad."[13] And consumers, for their part, often feel cheated if they leave the doctor's office without permission (indeed encouragement) to buy drugs.

In recent decades Big Pharma's overriding goal has been to produce "blockbusters"—drugs bringing at least $1 billion in revenue yearly. Specific consumer populations are targeted: arthritis patients hoping to conquer pain, middle-aged men seeking greater sexual potency, children with attention-deficit disorder (ADD), seniors with high blood pressure, middle-aged women hoping for hormonal rejuvenation, and anyone battling anxiety, depression, or allergies—in other words, a large percentage of the American public. Many "new" drugs that reputedly innovative research and development (R&D) brings to market—including some blockbusters—turn out to be recycled versions of older compounds, referred to as "me-too drugs." Further strengthening Big Pharma is the fact that drugs approved by the FDA for specific conditions can then be prescribed by doctors for *other* conditions. Millions use two or more drugs simultaneously, often for months and years, although the synergistic and long-term effects of such drug mixtures were never tested or monitored by the FDA. In the wake of huge marketing efforts and revenue bonanzas, the drug industry can sustain these practices thanks to collusion of the medical profession, insurance companies, and government agencies such as the FDA.[14]

In the United States today an endless supply of mind-altering drugs is readily available, prescribed—often indiscriminately—by doctors, clinics, hospitals, and therapists, typically with little regard for adverse reactions. Many of these drugs can be easily ordered through Internet sources. Ten variants of antipsychotic drugs include Thorazine, Stelazine, Haldol, Zyprexa, and Risperdal. No fewer than thirteen varieties of antidepressants include Prozac, Paxil, Zoloft, Norpramin, and Elavil, all with potent consequences for mind and body. Eleven types of tranquilizers can be found on the market: Librium, Valium, Prosom, Halcion, and others. Antipain medications (thirty-nine in all) include codeine, morphine, ibuprofen, naproxen, tolmetin, cortisone, prednisone, and salsalate. Such drugs, often consumed in tandem with others, can be bought through prescriptions to satisfy "patient" habits and addictions.[15] These and other drugs (including Adderall and Vicodin) can be readily ordered from Internet sources when they cannot be quickly obtained from doctors or street dealers. Where fatal overdoses are involved, doctors might be charged with criminal violations; in most cases, however, such medical drug dealing goes entirely unnoticed and unpunished.[16]

The United States remains the only industrialized nation that does not regulate drug prices, owing to Big Pharma's lobbying power in Washington, DC, and state capitals. Older institutional and legal restraints to protect consumers have been mostly gutted. The FDA, supposed watchdog over the industry, has become colonized by the very economic interests it was assigned to monitor. A corporation like Pfizer or Merck could aggressively market a blockbuster drug like Celebrex, touted as "super aspirin" although it was known to have severe adverse reactions and to work no better as a painkiller than cheaper OTC drugs such as ibuprofen.[17] As public awareness of price gouging began to spread, Big Pharma moved to fight increased competition from abroad by means of ambitious lobbying and advertising campaigns. With import restrictions, hundreds of thousands of Americans have resorted to buying drugs from abroad, as "pill tourism" in Mexico and Canada mounts in popularity.[18]

The huge pharmaceutical companies often manage to file lawsuits against smaller generic drug makers to maintain high prices. In some cases Big Pharma simply buys off the competition or takes over financially, as in the case of Sandoz becoming a subsidiary of Novartis. The intent of the historic Hatch-Waxman Act of 1984 was to allow cheaper generic drugs to reach the market sooner, thereby saving consumers tens of billions of dollars yearly, but the financial and lobby power of the larger drug industry has frequently nullified that legislation. Indeed drug prices in the United States follow no logic or reason, having little to do with costs of production and oscillating wildly from one venue to another. Purchasers of such drugs as antibiotics can experience a pricing roller coaster as

142   CHAPTER 6

they visit such outlets as CVS, Target, and Walgreens. Thus in 2012 a small vial of the antibiotic doxycycline could range in cost from $4 to a staggering $165 within roughly the same geographic region. A popular blood-clot blocker could cost just $21 at one locale and nearly $400 at another. In the end, many drug prices were simply numbers made up by large sellers, hoping to charge whatever the market would tolerate.[19]

The spectacular rise of Big Pharma coincides with intensification of the War on Drugs that, of course, targets only "illicit" substances—a set of policies ostensibly meant to protect Americans from physical and mental harm; that is, from themselves. This claim, as we have seen, is more laughable today than ever. As mentioned, the total adverse reactions (including fatal ones) from illegal drugs are minor compared to those from pharmaceuticals, tobacco, and alcohol. While overdoses from cocaine and heroin might account for a few hundred deaths in a given year, the figure for marijuana and hallucinogens is close to zero. Further, prescribed drugs can account for as many as *two million* severe reactions and more than 100,000 deaths—and these are just officially *reported* cases.[20] Meanwhile, as the horrors of demon pot and coke are routinely sensationalized in the media, this same media relentlessly advertises pharmaceuticals, cigarettes, beer, wine, and hard liquor—the very interests that contribute so much to the drug-war frenzy.

In a hypermedicated society like the United States, people ritually buy drugs at local pharmacies that are far more potent and addictive than pot and other banned substances. Even OTC drugs can be disarmingly habit-forming. The governing discourse around "narcotics" in American society is shrouded in fear and ignorance, in a milieu in which legal medications shape an addictive culture where pills serve as chemical fixes for dozens of problems, including new ones "discovered" by the medical establishment. One paradoxical result of the War on Drugs is that youth have more frequently turned to legal mind-altering substances to get high: painkillers, antidepressants, amphetamines, and drugs like Xanax, Vicodin, Valium, and OxyContin. With overall drug sales up roughly 400 percent from 1990 to 2010, use and abuse of prescription medications among youth aged twelve to sixteen has kept pace, with 15 percent of high-school students reportedly "pharming" for recreational purposes.[21] Legal doping naturally has its advantages, as drugs are easier to find (often in the family medicine cabinet), costs are negligible, adulteration concerns vanish, and legal risks are minimized.

Problems related to prescribed drugs, typically soft-pedaled by the media, doctors, and politicians, dwarf those of street drugs, the damage far exceeding what are misleadingly called "side effects." Adverse reactions extend far beyond (minor) side effects like nervousness and indigestion to include accidents, overdoses, wrong prescriptions, long-term or combined-use problems, and severe allergies

THE MEDICAL-DRUG BEHEMOTH   143

that can result in death. The number of *reported* such cases is undoubtedly much smaller than the actual number of all episodes. Aggravated harm comes from lengthy use of substances otherwise regarded as safe in more limited or short-term applications, with dependency heightened in cases of sustained intake of one or a combination of drugs.[22] The number of famous political and cultural figures to have experienced terrible legal drug problems, including fatal episodes, is very large—from Judy Garland to Edith Piaf, John F. Kennedy, Marilyn Monroe, Elvis Presley, Elizabeth Taylor, Brittany Murphy, and Michael Jackson. For these and many other victims, prescriptions for a variety of potent substances, including sleeping pills, meth, antibiotics, painkillers, and antidepressants, were routinely available from doctors.

According to Sidney M. Wolfe and associates, at least 181 of the 549 most prescribed medications should never be taken under *any* circumstances.[23] On their strictly prohibited list are such familiar drugs as Valium, Restoril, Elavil, Vioxx, Celebrex, and Darvon, to name a few blockbusters. Aside from problems of extreme dependency, the authors point to some frightening results: at least 166 drugs are implicated in serious depression, 156 produce hallucinations, 129 cause sexual dysfunction, 77 lead to dementia, and 59 give rise to extreme dizziness responsible for falls and other accidents. Adverse reactions occur at rates of several million yearly, all worsened by prolonged use. Various types of opioids, taken as painkillers, account for roughly 75 percent of all lethal episodes from pharmaceutical abuse or overdose—consistently the leading source of legal drug problems. As for the medical profession, surveys reveal that 70 percent of American doctors have flunked exams testing their knowledge of drugs.[24] Among other problems, prescriptions are commonly written before a patient's complete history is taken into account. Where the problem of obesity, for example, is not addressed when treating conditions like high blood pressure, excessive cholesterol levels, and liver or kidney disorders, the pills end up as another temporary fix at best.

Despite FDA oversight, horror stories linked to Big Pharma's obsession with bringing drugs quickly to market never seem to end. Hormone-replacement therapy (HRT) has been given to millions of women looking to stave off the effects of menopause. By 1995 the HRT compound Premarin had become one of the best-selling medications in the United States, touted as a miracle remedy and endorsed by the FDA. Disturbingly, however, the drug was still being praised and sold long after independent tests showed its regular use boosted risk of heart disease by 50 percent and breast cancer by 66 percent, with few significant benefits. As with dozens of pharmaceuticals, saturation advertising campaigns wildly exaggerated the benefits of HRT while largely overlooking the dangers. In 2001, Premarin, sold by Wyeth-Ayerst, remained the third most prescribed

144 CHAPTER 6

drug in the United States.[25] Many such examples can be cited since the 1980s, with hundreds of deaths attributed to such medications as Rezulin (for kidney treatment), Avandia (for diabetes), Celebrex (a painkiller), Vioxx (for pain), and Viagra (a male sex stimulant).

Big Pharma exerts such leverage over the FDA, the NIH, medical schools, and professional journals (all reliant on drug advertising) that flagrant conflicts of interest have come to appear quite ordinary. The work of Angell, Abramson, Washington, and Wolfe et al. is filled with examples of this sort, reflecting deep flaws in so much of the academic research used to justify marketing of specific drugs. As Abramson writes, "Studies repeatedly document the bias of commercially sponsored research, but the medical journals seem powerless to control the scientific integrity of their own pages."[26] Many articles favorable to medicinal drugs are ghostwritten by pharmaceutical agents or lobbyists. Indeed, as Washington observes, the very notion of an objective, scientific "evidence-based" medicine seems rather questionable, as corporate interests have billions of dollars at stake in research outcomes.[27] In September 2014 the federal government, through the Physician Payments Sunshine Act (passed by Congress in 2010) revealed that American doctors and teaching hospitals had more than $3.5 billion in financial ties with drug companies and medical-device makers during just the last five months of 2013. The bulk of this money was earmarked for research.[28]

Pharmaceutical giants battle over market privileges to "treat" common health problems like high cholesterol—conditions reversed more effectively, more durably, and surely more cheaply by natural or preventive remedies that, however, are staunchly dismissed as "unscientific" within the medical establishment. Pills in the category of statins are marketed to reduce cholesterol and, by extension, treat cardiovascular disease. Statins constitute the largest family of replicative drugs: Lipitor from Pfizer, Crestor from AstraZeneca, and Lescol from Novartis, among others. While each medication is promoted as the best solution for lowering cholesterol, active ingredients in each drug often remain essentially identical: pill colors and shapes often vary most. When tested at higher intakes to provide maximum "effectiveness," such drugs outperform placebos but at such large dosages that the risk of harmful reactions increases dramatically.[29]

Known to aggravate the risk of brain and nerve damage, statins have long been aggressively pushed not only in medical journals but on TV and across the media, often directly to consumers, as frequently *long-term* medications for chronic problems. Pill consumption in the United States represents not only a seductive panacea but a chemical shortcut that can deflect attention from vital dietary and lifestyle changes needed to *prevent* or *reverse* heart problems as part of a durable shift in healthcare practices. Further, in the midst of such illusory treatments, those heart ailments are being exacerbated by the McDonaldization of American dietary patterns. Risks associated with use of statins, according to Wolfe and colleagues, include mood disorders, memory loss, cognitive damage, amnesia, sexual dysfunction, immune suppression, and reduced liver function.[30] Such risks could easily be avoided by relying on cheaper and safer natural substances like coenzyme Q-10.

Several heart-disease studies cited by Abramson and others demonstrate that severe cardiovascular problems are rooted in unhealthy lifestyles such as poor nutrition that typically lead to obesity—one product of the fast-food culture. The drugs in question do not reverse underlying causes of illness or disease, which ultimately demand *contextual* solutions. As Big Pharma does everything possible to make drug "remedies" even more fashionable, at great cost to consumers, factors producing high cholesterol and heart disease remain stubbornly in place: Americans consume far more calories and fats than needed for good health, a situation worsened by sedentary lifestyles rooted in such technological addictions as TV and computers. Not only do people eat a daily excess of 500 calories on average, but the calories derive overwhelmingly from animal products, fast foods, and sugar. Some 440,000 deaths yearly are reportedly linked to obesity, usually resulting from those conditions identified earlier—none of which are especially amenable to drug therapy.[31] Yet more than 95 percent of healthcare resources spent in the United States are devoted to biomedical intervention, with drugs and surgeries at the top of the lists.

The familiar virtues of "free enterprise" are ritually invoked by American politicians, corporate elites, and the media when describing the US economy, referring to its model of production, consumption, and resource allocation— nowhere more so than for the medical system. During the 2009 debates over Obama's healthcare reforms, moderate by world standards, the public was treated to a steady diet of fearmongering over the perils of "big government" and the purported "socialist takeover" of medicine, attacks that continued into 2014. A free market, however, involves the relatively open flow of goods, resources, services, and communication—that is, an exchange system grounded in a matrix of self-regulating economic mechanisms and processes. By such measures the US economy operates, today probably more than ever, to manifestly *subvert* free-market principles that, in reality, have never existed outside the fantasies of conservative economists. The system is best described as a state-integrated, corporate-dominated, profit-driven oligopoly in which market relations exist only within tiny enclaves of local activity.[32] Economic and governmental power, for the medical system as elsewhere, is concentrated in a small elite stratum that effectively controls the flow of resources, capital, goods, services, and labor.

146   CHAPTER 6

In the case of pharmaceuticals, the picture is even more sharply focused: fewer than a dozen corporations (some foreign, mostly American) dominate the market landscape, an ensemble powerful enough to shape the contours of manufacturing, sales, trade, and pricing. These include Pfizer, Merck, Johnson & Johnson, Roche, AstraZeneca, Bristol-Myers Squibb, and Novartis—all mostly identical in their operations, all fixated on lucrative US markets where readiness to purchase drugs of all sorts has long been unlimited. This system relies on government patents for exclusive marketing rights as well as public absorption of R&D costs, along with legislation protecting the industry against competition, imports, and price fluctuation. With its remarkable wealth and power, Big Pharma is able to cast enormous influence over Congress, state legislatures, the medical profession, government agencies, political campaigns, and academia.[33]

Over the past few decades US medicine in general has descended into something of a freewheeling Wall Street operation. Bartlett and Steele devote many pages to this transformation and show how a continuous wave of mergers, acquisitions, hostile takeovers, consolidations, and bankruptcies has revitalized an empire built on technocratic medicine, deregulation, stock-market maneuvers, and superprofits. The result has been program cutbacks, deskilling of the work force, lowered wages, and decline in healthcare quality for many—all exacerbated by the post-2008 economic crisis. These trends have been accompanied by a reshaping of the medical system into a sprawling assemblage of bureaucratic, unaccountable structures less vulnerable to challenge or reform from outside, including Congress and state legislatures.[34]

With global sales in 2013 of roughly $840 billion, Big Pharma has sufficient clout to surmount any political obstacles to its profit-making machinery.[35] In the early 1980s Congress passed several laws designed to open up the marketing terrain for the legal drug industry, with legislation permitting tax-supported research to be quickly turned into new products. The Bayh-Dole Act allowed universities to patent discoveries from NIH-sponsored testing—the NIH being a key distributor of tax dollars for R&D—and then grant exclusive licenses to pharmaceutical companies. This ensured not only market exclusivity but huge federal subsidies for testing procedures, meaning higher profit margins (though less "free-market" cachet). As mentioned earlier, Bayh-Dole shifted the trajectory of health care in the United States, freeing corporate giants from public regulation while bringing crucial sectors (hospitals, HMOs, insurance companies, doctors, government, institutes) into the Big Pharma orbit, still advertised as part of a mythical free-enterprise system. Such change has unfolded almost entirely outside the realm of public debate and intervention, another sign of increasingly undemocratic trends.

THE MEDICAL-DRUG BEHEMOTH   147

With its endless supply of capital and its army of lawyers, lobbyists, and public-relations agents, the drug industry has steadily expanded its power within American medicine. Corporations can stretch out monopoly rights for brand-name medications over many years, including patent claims with little basis in creative research or innovation (often the domain of public universities). When patents expire, corporations can simply refine the drug and extend sales for purposes quite different from what the FDA originally approved. In one famous case, Eli Lilly altered its marketing of Prozac (a blockbuster) from treatment of depression to another familiar condition—obesity. Such practices correspond to a disturbing fact: Big Pharma spends three times as much on advertising, public relations, legal affairs, and lobbying as on basic R&D, but R&D is its main justification for price gouging.[36] Firms not only routinely overcharge for products but make false advertising claims, offer kickbacks and "free samples" to doctors, collude to keep generic and foreign drugs off the market, and spend billions of dollars yearly to propagandize about the miraculous lifesaving role of drugs.[37]

The conventional belief that Big Pharma carries out the bulk of its biomedical research does not pass close scrutiny: of seventy-eight drugs approved by the FDA in 2002, for example, only seventeen had active new ingredients, the remainder falsely advertised as new and improved. In the decade spanning 1992 to 2002, some 415 "new" drugs were introduced but only 14 percent turned out to be useful discoveries. Consumers targeted according to specific health disorders find a wide array of "choices," yet behind different labels and pill colors they end up buying roughly similar if not identical products. (Currently *seven* roughly identical drugs are prescribed for a single health problem, high blood pressure.) Meanwhile, Big Pharma manufactures a larger percentage of its drugs abroad, where labor and other costs are lower; Pfizer, for example, has sixty-two plants in thirty-two countries. By 2011, moreover, the bulk of R&D and even testing was being conducted abroad.[38] Since profit-seeking corporations depend so heavily on the public sector for both R&D and testing, the costs of production end up heavily socialized. Angell shows how the drug industry routinely conceals its huge marketing and administrative costs under an accounting umbrella that grossly overstates research and testing expenses.[39]

One of the most popular cancer drugs in history, Taxol, offers a prime example of how the drug industry operates—how it manipulates the public sector for its own interests. Active ingredients in this drug were derived from Pacific yew tree bark in the early 1960s, then researched by the National Cancer Institute (NCI) for thirty years at a cost of $183 million in public funds. In 1992, after the FDA approved Taxol for treatment of ovarian cancer, Bristol-Meyers Squibb was given exclusive marketing rights. NIH-funded scientists at Florida State University

148   CHAPTER 6

developed a method for synthesizing the yew bark, leaving the company the simple task of mass-producing and marketing what would become an extremely lucrative drug—all profits, of course, going to Bristol-Myers Squibb. By 2000 worldwide sales of Taxol totaled nearly $2 billion yearly; in 2005 a one-year supply of the drug could fetch up to $20,000, which, according to Angell, was a twentyfold markup over production costs.[40] With its monopoly rights extended another three years, Bristol-Myers Squibb had sold more than $9 billion worth of the drug by 2003.

Another telling example concerns the ayahuasca plant, grown in the Amazon basin and called *yagi* by indigenous people who for centuries used the plant as a therapeutic hallucinogen. It is usually taken under direction of a shaman who guides the user's experience. As Washington notes, Westerners had for many decades known of the great healing powers of ayahuasca, for them a drug "that promises health and heaven."[41] In 1981 an American, Loren Miller, claimed to discover the plant and decided to patent it so that his company, International Plant Medicine Corporation, could arrange with a pharmaceutical firm to market the plant as a magic tonic. The US patent office granted Miller exclusive rights to grow and distribute ayahuasca, leading to years of protests by indigenous groups—protests that were simply ignored in the United States. Miller's patent finally expired in 2003 but the case demonstrates, in the words of an indigenous leader, "the total disrespect of the white world towards our beliefs and culture."[42] It also demonstrates the ruthless capacity of Western interests to steal and commodify virtually anything that can be marketed as a drug—in the very midst of their moralistic antidrug crusade.

The ayahuasca debacle has been repeated endlessly across the world, with predictable results. Looking for diversity in the drug trade, scientists, medical professionals, and corporations have turned increasingly to the developing world. American interests in particular are ready to go anywhere on the globe: Ethiopia alone is home to a rich diversity of some 6,500 plant species, roughly 800 of which are used as medicines. Brazil and China are goldmines of natural substances. As Washington notes, "Researchers and pharmaceutical companies have designs on the diverse biological riches of poor countries because so much of the biodiversity of the West has vanished, having fallen victim to the short-sighted agricultural behavior of industrialized nations."[43] While the antidrug warriors—backed by Big Pharma—rail against "illicit" substances, the number of drug and biotechnology patents secured in the United States skyrocketed in the 1990s and later. In fact such plants are the source of 40 percent of medicines currently used in the United States. Meanwhile, nations like Brazil do not patent new drugs since, as Washington observes, their "cultural heritage does not include monopolistic claims on living things for profit."[44] The patents, of course, are concentrated in the hands of wealthy and powerful corporate interests anxious to transform exotic and illegal substances into legal, profitable ones.

Medicine, Drugs, Power

Big Pharma and kindred interests can push through their agendas because, as is generally true of American political life, these interests have effectively colonized the public sphere, including election campaigns, federal and state legislatures, government agencies like the FDA and the NIH, court decisions on medical issues, and the popular media. No sector of the American economy is more powerful than medicine, which tirelessly works to maintain and legitimate the profit-driven, technocratic healthcare apparatus.

Since the early 1990s the vast majority of congressional members and every White House administration, Democratic and Republican, has enjoyed a tight relationship with Big Pharma. The trade association PhRMA is among the largest interest-group umbrellas in Washington, DC, and as of 2013 the drug industry deployed roughly 150 lobbying firms with 675 operatives and an annual budget of $500 million—more than is spent by either banking or insurance lobbies. Drug operatives comprise more than two dozen former members of Congress. Pharmaceutical interests gave lavishly to the Bush presidential campaigns in 2000 and 2004, the McCain campaign in 2008, and the Romney campaign in 2012. Groups like Citizens for Better Medicare, masquerading as grassroots organizations, were set up to facilitate Big Pharma priorities such as fighting price controls and imports. Angell notes, "The pharmaceutical industry supports a variety of front groups that masquerade as grassroots organizations. One of these is Citizens for Better Medicare, supposedly a coalition of senior citizens groups."[45]

The far-reaching goals of Big Pharma—strict patent enforcement, import restrictions, deregulation, bans on "illicit" substances—are routinely aided by that supposed enemy of free enterprise, big government. Megacorporations continue to enjoy market exclusivity despite (or because of) their oligopolistic status. They receive such massive tax breaks and research subsidies that the most larcenous firms in the world pay just a tiny fraction of revenues to the very government that underwrites their superprofits. They secure legislation to keep American consumers from buying cheaper drugs from abroad—an agreement extended by the Obama administration in 2009. The 1997 FDA Modernization Act relaxed standards and timetables for new drugs introduced to market. Doctors retain legal power to prescribe medications for whatever condition they

150 CHAPTER 6

choose.[46] In 2003 the United States was the lone holdout among 143 countries in opposing World Trade Organization efforts to relax patent controls—a move that would have lowered drug prices worldwide. Further, the 2003 Medicare Modernization Act paved the way toward even richer pharmaceutical bonanzas by prohibiting Medicare from using its vast purchasing clout to guarantee lower prices for seniors.[47]

The jagged legacy of the FDA, set up in part to monitor the drug industry, perfectly illustrates how government agencies can easily be taken over by corporate interests, a motif central to Phillip Selznick's classic analysis of the Tennessee Valley Authority (set up in the 1930s as a public enterprise but later colonized by private interests).[48] Theoretically independent, the FDA has served for much of its history as an adjunct to Big Pharma, a relationship solidified by the Bayh-Dole Act. In 1992 Congress enacted the Prescription Drug User Fee Act, authorizing drug companies to pay "user fees" to the FDA for required testing, fees meant to expedite drug approvals, often cumbersome and time-consuming. But at $310,000 per application this soon amounted to *half* the entire FDA evaluation budget, meaning the agency became dependent on the very industry it was assigned to regulate. For Big Pharma such fees amount to small change and, as Angell observes, they can be offset by added income from sending products to market with fewer delays and roadblocks.[49]

Unfortunately, a faster approval process often means that tests will be less thorough and reliable, allowing a larger number of potentially harmful drugs to reach the public. In fact, since the user-fee mechanism was introduced numerous prescription drugs were taken off the market after causing hundreds, in some cases possibly thousands, of deaths. As drugs reach consumers more quickly, meanwhile, the understaffed FDA faces new difficulties in monitoring drug safety, ensuring standards, and regulating advertisers. One major disaster involved the GlaxoSmithKline drug Paxil, a blockbuster antidepressant grossing nearly $3 billion in 2003. In June 2004 the New York Attorney General sued GlaxoSmithKline after tests showed the drug to be ineffective while sharply increasing risks of depression and suicide. The case was settled in August 2004, when GlaxoSmithKline was forced to pay a meager $2.5 million fine while its executives avoided criminal charges and even disciplinary actions. The European Union included Paxil on its list of most dangerous drugs, followed by a British government warning that the drug (along with other blockbusters, like Zoloft and Effexor) should be used with extreme caution. GlaxoSmithKline was ultimately forced to arrive at an $88 million settlement over Paxil.[50]

FDA vulnerability to Big Pharma is reinforced by the manner in which its many standing advisory committees on drugs normally function. Composed of medical specialists, these committees review new drug applications and make recommendations to the agency, which are routinely accepted. The problem is that committee members often have financial ties to corporations with drugs under review, even though this is formally prohibited. Conflict-of-interest rules ostensibly work against bias, but rules are frequently ignored on grounds that expert advice is indispensable. "Consulting fees" granted by the industry, as mentioned, are usually lucrative. Wolfe and associates reported in 2005 that in their thirty-three years of monitoring the US drug business "the current pro-industry attitude at the FDA is as bad and dangerous as it has ever been. In addition to record numbers of approvals for questionable drugs, the FDA enforcement over advertising has all but disappeared."[51] From a peak number of ninety-seven enforcement actions to stop illegal prescription-drug ads in 1998, the number decreased to twenty-four in 2003 at a time when advertising volume was dramatically rising. The FDA section that oversees Big Pharma advertising has paltry resources, but the bigger problem, according to Wolfe and associates, is that "it has also been thwarted by marching orders from higher up in the agency to, effectively, go easy on prescription drug advertising."[52] This trend has only escalated since 2003. Further, Congress recently passed legislation greatly weakening FDA capacity to protect consumers, with millions of harmful drug reactions yearly speaking loudly to the success of "higher-up" power brokers.

A well-known case of Big Pharma malfeasance involved Vioxx, a painkiller sold by Merck and prescribed mostly for arthritis. FDA approval in 1998 was followed by scores of deaths from heart attacks among Vioxx users, matched by test findings that revealed serious cardiovascular risks—findings that both the FDA and Merck were later accused of covering up. Vioxx was pulled from the market in September 2004 after congressional testimony by Dr. David Graham, the agency scientist in charge of drug safety. Graham said the Vioxx disaster was symptomatic of FDA failure in its watchdog role owing to its close ties with drug interests. For his whistle-blowing, Graham, a twenty-year veteran of the agency, was accused by FDA leadership of "scientific misconduct" and reassigned to administrative duties. An article on Vioxx in *Lancet* reported the medication contributed to as many as 140,000 cases of heart disease, including some 56,000 deaths from heart attacks and strokes.[53] Lower doses were shown to increase risk of heart attack by 50 percent, with higher doses pushing the incidence to a staggering 358 percent. Merck had sought to conceal this information to protect its blockbuster profits.[54]

In *Worst Pills, Best Pills*, Vioxx (rofecoxib) was listed in the "do not use" category since its adverse reactions obviously more than offset any purported short-term benefits.[55] Citing a VIGOR (Vioxx GI Outcomes Research) study

152   CHAPTER 6

pointing to severe heart-attack risks, the authors mention a host of additional side effects, including strong abdominal or stomach pain, cramping, nausea, indigestion, and vomiting of blood. The same report mentioned that people suffering from arthritis could eliminate these risks by opting for the OTC drug naproxen or even aspirin, but such information was disturbing to Merck, which charged more than $100 monthly for Vioxx (compared to the $18 cost of naproxen). Abramson details how both Merck and the FDA manipulated test findings to conceal a host of worrisome data.[56] Vioxx remained a top-selling drug in 2004, and in February 2005 an FDA advisory panel voted to lift the short ban. At the same time, the *New York Times* reported that ten panel members involved in the Vioxx decision (and that of another dangerous painkiller, Celebrex) worked as consultants for pharmaceutical companies with stakes in the outcome.[57] Here again the FDA had subordinated itself to the Big Pharma quest for profits.

In an article published in *Vanity Fair*, Bartlett and Steele point out that drug-testing by American corporations is increasingly conducted overseas, thus further minimizing FDA oversight.[58] They detail how the drug giants take control of crucial testing procedures—devising their own rules for trials, helping to prepare reports, even ghostwriting articles for medical journals. The results, as might be expected, can be disastrous: for example, the cancer drug Avandia, produced by GlaxoSmithKline, reached billions of dollars in sales at a time when (between 1999 and 2007) it was known to have caused at least 83,000 heart attacks and was banned in Europe.[59] Riddled with conflicts of interest, the FDA again failed miserably to carry out even minimal regulatory obligations.

In one astonishing—but perhaps predictable—development, President Obama in late 2010 appointed Michael Taylor, former Monsanto head, to take over the FDA. A combination of agricultural, chemical, and other corporate interests lobbied heavily for Taylor's appointment. As is well known, Monsanto has long been at the forefront of a food-centered biotech regimen that has brought harmful changes to American (indeed world) agriculture, including milk, wheat, and numerous vegetable crops.[60] Chemicalized food production has been responsible for widespread allergies, nutritional deficiencies, and toxic dangers. The question here is, could a corporate executive so deeply embedded in these interests and biases ever rise to the level of independent protector of consumer rights at such a massive federal agency as the FDA?

Biomedical research is often conducted at major universities and public institutes or clinics, with an eye toward promoting various types of drug therapy. Psychological studies are often geared toward sales of expensive and sometimes harmful antipsychotic drugs. Lucrative medications heavily marketed in the 1990s and later include Risperdal, Zyprexa, Seroquel, and other blockbusters, prescribed

THE MEDICAL-DRUG BEHEMOTH   153

widely for such conditions as depression, anxiety, ADD, bipolar disorder, and insomnia. It turns out that, despite FDA "monitoring," these drugs were no more effective than earlier versions but did cause many of the same adverse reactions. In 2009 Eli Lilly was forced to pay $1.4 billion in litigation for illegal marketing and hiding the risks of Zyprexa. AstraZeneca later paid $520 million in fines and damages based on similar charges, in connection with its sales of Seroquel. In these and other cases testing results were often either hidden or distorted.[61] Yet another questionable practice has been the targeting of seniors told by pharmaceutical companies that declining health and sexuality can be reversed by consumption of expensive magical pills. Abbott, for example, has marketed the drug AndroGel to help older men regain peak sexual energy, made possible by an uptake in testosterone. Indeed the FDA has approved an entire medicine cabinet full of drugs for seniors, in the form of gels, pills, patches, and lotions. One problem: evidence of improvement is minimal, while risks of stroke and heart attack have been greater than either the government or corporations are prepared to concede.[62] Meanwhile, Big Pharma maneuvers continue: between 2009 and 2011 the drug industry spent no less than $700 million to lobby the FDA and related government agencies.[63]

Viewed against the backdrop of a long cycle of criminal and civil settlements spanning 2011–2014 alone, Big Pharma has emerged as one of the largest defrauders of federal revenues in the post-WWII era. The biggest pharmaceutical companies, in fact, paid roughly $30 billion in penalties during the previous two decades, a prelude to the several billion shelled out in 2011—for such offenses as illegal marketing, bribing of doctors to prescribe selected drugs, and overcharging of Medicaid programs in many states. Illegal activities were rampant at a time (as in 2010) when Big Pharma collective profits had reached nearly $90 billion and when corporate executives responsible for such gross malfeasance escaped both fines and imprisonment.

In 2014 two counties in California (Orange and Santa Clara) moved to bring a massive lawsuit against several of the world's largest narcotics producers— Actavis, Johnson & Johnson, Purdue Pharma, and Cephalon—for their long-term "campaign of deception" aimed at boosting sales of commonly harmful painkillers such as OxyContin. These counties have been hit hard by a cycle of overdose deaths, hospitalizations, and addictions while the corporations involved continue egregious business practices, including false advertising and efforts to conceal potential adverse reactions to their drugs. Big Pharma has reaped blockbuster profits in a context where painkillers are being dispensed for virtually every mundane health problem, including headaches, back pain, and general soreness.[64] Meanwhile, thanks in part to all the deceit, fraud, and cover-ups,

154 CHAPTER 6

painkillers were the source of more than 16,000 deaths in 2013—a figure that is likely to increase as the American use of narcotic substances soars. In recent years, moreover, painkillers have been made more widely available through reckless prescriptions on the part of doctors, as well as theft, street sales, and simple personal access. Pills stolen at such chains as CVS, often fetching great street value, enter the black market in greater volumes with each passing year.

Not only painkillers and related drugs but cancer drugs too have come under increasing scrutiny and legal challenge. In April 2014 a federal jury awarded plaintiffs $10.4 billion after finding that the drug companies Eli Lilly and Takeda had marketed the cancer drug Actos while knowing about its severe risks to consumers. This drug, heavily marketed since 2001 in the United States, had been outlawed in France and Germany. Research found that people who used Actos for at least one year were 40 percent more likely to experience bladder cancer; many encountered serious heart ailments. Health problems associated with Actos consumption had (as of 2014) brought no fewer than 3,000 lawsuits.[65] According to Wolfe and associates, Actos must be placed in the strictly "do not use" category due to a long list of potentially severe adverse reactions: liver damage, heart problems, bladder cancer, fluid accumulation, and significant weight gain, among others.[66]

Drugs and the Cancer Industry

A striking example of how corporate-based medicine dominates the American health scene is what Ralph Moss has called the "cancer industry," centered on the escalating drug-based "war" against the most fatal of all diseases. The current prevailing approach to cancer reflects the power of big business to shape health agendas, the corrosive legacy of distorted science, and the failure of medical intervention to curb the worst plague in American society. Since the 1970s the situation has in many ways worsened despite orthodox medical researchers' repeated promises of new "cures," as cancer now accounts for nearly 500,000 deaths yearly in the United States alone.[67] After being fired from the Sloan Kettering Institute in 1974 for refusing to accept falsified data on the efficacy of unconventional cancer treatments, Moss wrote *The Cancer Syndrome*, exposing the pernicious influence of corporations and their lobbies on cancer research and treatment; the book has gone through six editions. This was followed by *The Cancer Industry*, where Moss extended and refined essentially the same arguments.[68]

Moss was able to show in some detail how corporate behemoths like Mobil, IBM, Exxon, and Union Carbide—along with agribusiness, the food industry, financial interests, and Big Pharma—had come to dominate the medical sector, their influence extending to such venerable institutions as Sloan Kettering, the Mayo Clinic, the NIH, the FDA, and the American Cancer Society (ACS). The medical-scientific edifice was, and remains, so dominated by business interests that its practitioners could never get beyond the orthodoxy (surgery and drugs)—or take into account prevention, dietary factors, the environment, and alternative treatment modes. Over the decades the incidence of most cancers has grown despite hundreds of billions of dollars earmarked for research and treatment. For Moss and later critics, like Devra Davis, John Robbins, John McDougall, T. Colin Campbell, and Samuel Epstein, the major hospitals, clinics, institutes, and agencies set up to fight cancer ended up serving corporate agendas to the detriment of general health needs.[69]

After working many years at the ACS, Davis wrote *The Secret History of the War on Cancer*, an insider's critique of an industry she argues has done more to block than to advance efforts at understanding the real causes of cancer.[70] The industry's impact has been nothing short of pathbreaking. Following Moss, she paid close attention to the influence of corporate interests—dishonest advertising, expensive lobbying, takeover of government agencies, scientific spin, political machinations—that focus on symptoms, stress technical intervention over natural remedies, and emphasize surgery and drugs to the exclusion of preventive or holistic approaches. The difficulty with natural modalities, of course, is that far less revenue is generated for profit-driven businesses. Thus the ACS, itself riddled with corporate interests, spends less than 10 percent of its budget on independent studies, seemingly worried that more lucrative outcomes might be compromised by the "wrong" findings. At centers like Sloan Kettering as well as the ACS, cancer is uniformly seen as an invading agent, as opposed to a long-term internal *process* of health deterioration resulting from diet, lifestyle, and other contextual factors.[71] The disease is often conceded by medical experts to be the "price of modern life"—though usually somewhat amenable to drug therapy.[72] While the media often celebrate new innovations (typically drugs) in the "war on cancer," this particular disease is paradoxically understood as either a natural occurrence of daily life or a genetic disorder.

No major center established to fight cancer—the ACS, Sloan Kettering, the NCI, major universities—devotes much attention to larger social and environmental *contexts* of disease formation, or to lifestyle factors such as nutrition. At best these factors appear as afterthoughts, peripheral to the "scientific" interpretive

156 Chapter 6

framework. Little attention is devoted to the fast-food diet, shown by dozens of studies to be strongly implicated in most types of cancer.[73] In 1997 the American Institute for Cancer Research (AICR), joined by the World Cancer Research Fund, issued a report on the basis of 4,500 studies for the WHO, concluding that up to 70 percent of all cancers stem from lifestyle-related causes—above all, consumption of animal products. These findings were strongly reinforced by Campbell's seminal volume, *The China Study*, based on exhaustive comparative analysis of diets and other lifestyle factors, but the US medical-scientific establishment behaved as if the study had never appeared.[74] Other independent research has demonstrated that vegetarians suffer less than half of the cancer episodes of habitual meat-eaters.[75]

In 1998, the NCI announced that a breakthrough in cancer treatment had arrived in the form of a potent drug used for chemotherapy: Tamoxifen, said to help millions survive many years after first cancer diagnosis. Endorsed by the FDA and the NCI, the drug failed to deliver on its heady promise but did cause adverse reactions in large numbers of users. Sold by AstraZeneca, the drug (like most other chemical treatments) had at best temporary success, as it only targeted the symptoms of cancer. The drug maker's parent company, Imperial Chemical Industries, is one of the world's largest pesticide manufacturers. Yet despite weak evidence of remedial properties and abundant data showing adverse reactions, Tamoxifen soon became the best-selling anticancer drug in the world.[76] As Robbins observes in his exploration of cancer and diet in *The Food Revolution*, the price paid by the American public for corporate distortion of cancer research—reflected, for example, in the stonewalling of that crucial 1997 WHO assemblage of studies related to cancer—can likely be calculated in the millions of deaths.[77] Long before Campbell's massive and compelling study, scientific research had shown an undeniable connection between high levels of meat or dairy consumption and cancer, yet the vast majority of Americans, thanks to corporate lobbying and influence, remain ignorant and therefore disempowered when it comes to cancer prevention.

Campbell's *The China Study* illustrates this linkage more systematically than any previous work—a project based on data gathered in China and elsewhere, reinforced by massive clinical research. The work concluded that nutritional factors play a key role in explaining different cancer rates even where environmental or social conditions might be implicated: high intake of animal proteins and fats activates and accelerates bodily processes that can lead to cancer.[78] Obstacles to this line of thinking are erected by corporate interests (food, agribusiness, medical, pharmaceutical) that work to block or distort independent research findings. Campbell mentions the watershed 1980s congressional McGovern

Report, warning about the hazards of meat consumption, roundly dismissed by the political, medical, and media establishments, with public debate largely squelched. The report's dietary goals—less meat, more plant-based foods—were attacked by the National Academy of Sciences, an institute dominated by meat and dairy interests that had long extolled the virtues of high-protein, high-fat diets.[79]

The prestigious American Council on Science and Health (ACSH), promoted as a consumer interest group yet dependent on meat and dairy producers for nearly 80 percent of its funding, nowadays adheres to the same paradigm. The ACSH touts meat and dairy foods, denouncing critics as a bunch of conspiracy theorists and quacks. At the AICR, moreover, nutritional issues receive no attention within an organization supposedly dedicated to uncovering the sources of cancer, as this mode of research conflicts with mainstream drug, medical, and food agendas. Scientific attempts to broaden work in the field are routinely met with intimidation, personal smears, and lies of the sort both Moss and Davis exposed after spending years at the heart of the cancer establishment.[80] The very idea of cancer prevention was always ridiculed at the AICR as well as at the ACSH and ACS. Notes Campbell, "In the world of nutrition and health, scientists are not free to pursue their research wherever it leads. Coming to the 'wrong conclusions,' even through first-rate science, can damage your career."[81] Following Moss, Campbell refers to this corruption of medical research as the "science of industry." The American food, medical, and drug corporations remain today among the most powerful and profitable in the world, and they stand to lose most from any fundamental shift in cancer treatment.

These corporations, lobbies, marketing operations, and public-relations firms—with the government agencies they often dominate—monitor and influence the bulk of health-related research. They also help shape much of university work, including grants, conferences, journals, workshops, and medical-school curricula. Rarely at any of these sites does linkage between lifestyle and cancer receive much attention, as overwhelming emphasis is placed on drug research and treatment. The Federal Nutrition Board itself welcomes to its governing circles representatives of such firms as Burger King, Dannon, Taco Bell, Coca-Cola, Nestlé, Pfizer, and Roche, all long resistant to new directions in medicine; recommendations of such agencies typically go no further than their moneyed entanglements will allow.[82] As for the all-important NIH, with its twenty-seven participating institutes and centers, nowhere does its far-reaching work encompass the social, nutritional, or environmental dimensions of health, and no funding for alternative research is generally made available.

Commonly prescribed drugs with the highest incidence of adverse reactions—some involving lethal episodes—include heart medications, analgesics, antibiotics,

158   CHAPTER 6

and chemotherapy. Chemo treatments for cancer promised strong results in the 1940s and 1950s, embraced then and later by the medical establishment as a "breakthrough," a giant step forward in the "war on cancer." From the outset many scientists and health practitioners questioned the efficacy of chemo, given its toxicity and limited (mostly short-term) benefits. In fact no form of chemotherapy has yet been developed that would attack and kill *only* cancer cells; the treatment wears down the entire body, including the immune system. While up to forty such drugs have been administered to cancer patients, those suffering from the most common types of the disease respond little if at all.[83] Numerous studies have shown that chemotherapy enhances five-year survival rates by only 2 to 3 percent—even less for such frequent cancers as lung, brain, and breast. Further, the treatment has been associated with secondary outbreaks of cancer even where the first condition has entered into remission.[84]

Moss, a staunch critic of this orthodox approach, asks, "Given the generally poor performance of chemo, its often horrendous side effects, and the limitations built into its very nature, why do orthodox doctors continue to promote this form of treatment as the wave of the future, as a proven method of treatment?"[85] The answer is painfully simple: economic pressures—including those from Big Pharma, which derives huge profits from widespread use of chemo treatments. Moss could have added the power of the corporate media, which functions as something of an adjunct of Big Pharma in its triumphalism regarding chemo and kindred drugs. Positive reports on alternative methods of cancer treatment— and there are many—have long been taboo in the popular media. Ideological consensus underlying drug therapy is nearly total, despite its well-documented limited benefits and harmful consequences. Gary Null and colleagues write, "The reason the medical establishment can continue to betray the public trust is because there are no sufficient consequences for killing or maiming patients."[86]

And "killing or maiming" is precisely one of the terrible legacies of chemotherapy in the field of American medicine. It takes little investigation to demonstrate the severely iatrogenic consequences of many cancer drugs: patient health can deteriorate even where (usually temporary) disease reversal occurs. One problem is that, with the advent of Big Pharma's contribution of "user fees" to FDA testing, drug-review time has shrunk to the point where new chemotherapies can be approved in as quickly as four months. Less attention is devoted to monitoring and correcting adverse reactions that accompany so much anticancer drug treatment. Thus the chemo drug Mitotane, prescribed mainly for adrenal cancer, is known to produce harsh allergic outbreaks—breathing difficulties, dizziness, nervous-system problems, and high fever, among other debilitating reactions. Some other successfully marketed chemo agents—Cisplatin, Doxorubicin,

Etoposide—are no less harmful, even giving rise to new cancers such as leukemia when used long-term or combined with other drugs.[87] Despite such extensively reported harm, chemotherapy in the United States continues to be embraced by the cancer establishment with almost evangelical zeal.

At present the vast majority of scientists, doctors, and healthcare practitioners remain attached to a medical-industrial apparatus where "private" and "public," business and government sectors, converge within a network of concentrated power. The role of Big Pharma in this manifestly antidemocratic process would be difficult to exaggerate. Challenges to the dominant paradigm have been routinely marginalized—witness the resounding silence accorded the McGovern Report on nutrition, *The China Study*, and the UN report on the global drug war, not to mention years of independent research. After frustrating decades of working in biomedical research, Campbell writes, "I have come to the conclusion that when it comes to health, government is not for the people; it is for the food industry and the pharmaceutical industry at the expense of the people."[88] As mounting evidence reveals the professional limits and ideological rigidity of standard approaches, the system continues its merry way along the same technocratic, iatrogenic, authoritarian path. Meanwhile, in the early twenty-first century the wealthiest country in the world—possessing the most expensive medical system—can boast of the highest cancer rates, matched by extreme levels of such chronic diseases as diabetes, arthritis, and heart conditions, symptomatic of a society afflicted by deteriorating medical and political health.

Medical Tyranny

The 2010 documentary *Burzynski: The Movie* features a lengthy interview with Dr. Li-Chuan Chen, a medical scientist at the NCI during the 1990s whose research on alternative treatments of cancer roused the medical establishment and drove him from the profession. For Chen, native of an authoritarian Taiwanese society, the supreme irony was that the United States—a reputedly thriving model of political democracy—was the locale of a closed, intolerant, monolithic healthcare structure. He found that the open pursuit of truth in the service of optimum healing was surprisingly off-limits, obstructed by arrogant experts at the NIH and the NCI, where money, careers, and egos prevail over public-health interests supposedly central to the medical vocation. He found an ideological orthodoxy so tight it called to mind the far-reaching power of a ruling party in control of an entire country, nothing less than a "medical tyranny." When Chen complained that "the medical system in the U.S. is very undemocratic—to put

160   CHAPTER 6

it mildly," he was thinking mainly of the cancer industry and the place of Big Pharma within it.

In a different vein, and after many difficult years working within the medical system, Angell said she wrote her book to "show how the [drug] industry, corrupted by easy profits and greed, has deceived and exploited the American people."[89] Like Abramson, Davis, Moss, and Bartlett and Steele (the latter won a 2004 Pulitzer Prize for their book), Angell laid out careful arguments illustrating the bankruptcy of capitalist health care and the many fictions of "free-market" medicine.

Although these critics generally failed to articulate the full economic and political ramifications of their powerful attacks, they did frame a narrative as to how the early 1980s witnessed a shift toward unfettered corporate profit-making bolstered by deregulation, privatization, and freeing up of capital mobility. Matters have only worsened across the intervening years, exacerbated by the post-2008 economic downturn. Behind the ideological façade of market relations, the corporate edifice has grown steadily more globalized, expansionist, and oligopolistic, fueled by a gradual stripping away of Keynesian public agendas and the social contract inherited from the New Deal and the Great Society. By 2010, with the rapid ascendancy of the Tea Party, it seemed right-wing American politicians were prepared to commodify everything—government, public services, culture, social life, education—purportedly in opposition to "big government." Gorging on superprofits and driven by a medicalized culture tied to expensive quick fixes, the pharmaceutical industry managed to permeate all realms of American society, including the military, owing to its enormous financial power and institutional leverage. To maintain its hegemony, the industry created a public-relations, advertising, and marketing empire rivaled by none, spinning grand myths about the curative powers of the hundreds of potent but frequently harmful drugs, all within the fictional construct of "free enterprise."[90]

The corporate-medical system has corrupted democratic politics to a degree probably beyond any other sector, evident not only in the dismal character of health care but in the restrictive public discourse surrounding it. From this standpoint, the low level of "debates" at the time of Obama's 2009 healthcare reforms should come as no surprise. Prospects for significant changes within American medicine—the only system lacking universal coverage in the industrialized world—seem dismal, whatever the status of "Obamacare." The president's hope for overhaul of a crisis-ridden system is progressive enough on the surface, but daunting obstacles remain: aggressive lobbies, a media complicit with orthodox agendas, members of Congress dependent on medical-sector funding for their election campaigns, and Obama's own tepid liberalism and indebtedness to big business for his presidential campaigns. Big Pharma and insurance companies had invested tens of millions of dollars to protect their profit-making machines. Within months of Obama's ascent to the White House, only watered-down legislation (much of it preapproved by Big Pharma) was within reach and the "public option" (or extension of Medicare to everyone) had been jettisoned as too radical. Unyielding opposition to genuine reforms moved along four tiers— corporate lobbies, grassroots resistance (the Tea Party), continuous talk-radio blitzes, and Republican hostility to the long-feared "government takeover" of American medicine.[91]

In 2009 the Obama administration had cozied up to Big Pharma and insurance companies to win crucial backing for its measures; any legislation was destined to favor these interests—and that indeed was the outcome, still denounced as "socialist" by Republicans. While Obama as candidate blasted the drug and medical lobbies for their contribution to astronomical healthcare costs, as president he altered course, moving closer to the drug industry and its agents, including chief lobbyist Billy Tauzin, a frequent White House visitor during 2009. Working with Tauzin and leading CEOs from Merck, Abbott, Pfizer, and other drug companies, Obama arranged to block cheap imports, fight against price caps, and ensure continued government subsidies in return for Big Pharma support of the reforms. These deals, greased by tens of millions of dollars in campaign spending, narrowed the debate and helped shape the final outcome. James Lowe, speaking for nonprofit health care, remarked, "Since Obama came into office, the drug industry has received everything it wants, domestic and foreign."[92]

The drug giants spent $110 million lobbying Congress in 2009, as Democrats and Republicans alike catered to an industry pulling in more than $40 billion in profits yearly, while prices for brand-name drugs rose a record 9.3 percent.[93] Meanwhile, the White House welcomed lobbyists from insurance companies like WellPoint and Health Net, along with such operatives as America's Health Insurance Plans president Karen Ignani and American Medical Association president Dr. J. James Rohack, all hoping to sharply curtail the legislation.[94] In the end, the reform process was not so much "co-opted" as constrained by deeply embedded economic interests already at work. The result was predictable enough—a legislative package composed of a few important measures (such as ending limits tied to preexisting conditions and lifetime caps on coverage) but a boondoggle for corporate interests that would be awarded large government subsidies for tens of millions of new customers.

The medical-industrial complex remained fully intact as its supporters in Congress shepherded through reforms bereft of any public option, stricter controls

162 CHAPTER 6

over Big Pharma, binding insurance rules, and universal healthcare guarantees. Passed by Congress in 2010, the reforms would continue to meet conservative political and legal challenges, though the bulk of the Obama legislation was declared constitutional by the Supreme Court in 2012. In fact there was little in the reforms that would undermine the capacity of medical oligopolies to reap outrageous profits. And, of course, healthcare costs for the average consumer would continue to soar, as we have seen.[95]

As of late 2014 this tightly administered, costly, disabling medical complex remained a seemingly immovable fixture of American society. As for Big Pharma, pill consumption would continue to be the order of the day—with profits amounting to a staggering $711 billion worldwide in a decade spanning 2003 to 2012, as drugs became increasingly central to the healthcare regimen in the United States and elsewhere.[96] The more problems to treat medically, and for the longest periods of time, the more profitable for those who thrive on the great pill industry. Despite the supposedly controversial Obama reforms, therefore, this is a system that for tens of millions of people remains dysfunctional, bureaucratic, and costly. Three decades ago, Ivan Illich wrote prophetically about the perils of a "disabling profession" ruled by technocratic experts and corporate managers and driven by power, money, and status, with arrogant claims to specialized knowledge that legitimate a regime of domination.[97] Today the medical system is perhaps the most undemocratic realm of American public life. A self-proclaimed repository of truth, wisdom, and healing, the healthcare industry—Big Pharma at the forefront—resists every progressive alternative as it reproduces authoritarian politics and social relations across the entire public landscape.

Chapter 7
The Medicalized Society

Capitalist modernity today is shaped increasingly by evolving forms of technological rationality—a dimension of ideological hegemony that, in the United States, is especially powerful in the realm of medicine, which has become intertwined with the general economy, health care, food production and consumption, the environment, science, and culture. In this context, capitalist rationalization develops alongside of—and coincides with—what might be called the medicalization of American society. At the center of a historical process giving rise to technological rationality, anticipated many decades ago by such theorists as Max Weber, Antonio Gramsci, the Frankfurt School, and Herbert Marcuse, is an expanding medical-pharmaceutical behemoth—commodified, bureaucratic, dysfunctional, iatrogenic—that pushes the matrix of ideological domination to new levels.[1]

The War on Drugs and the steadily expanding role of Big Pharma in American society are twin expressions of a progressively hypermedicalized system in which social progress is hitched to the corporate-technocratic growth model that has driven postwar US economic development. A moralistic crusade against "drugs" coexists with the lucrative production and marketing of drugs favored by the medical establishment. What might be viewed as an addictive culture is located squarely on both sides of this trajectory—legal and illegal, medicinal and recreational, synthetic and natural. Today health care is increasingly colonized by private interests, corporate agendas, and treatment programs composed of expensive therapies, high-tech interventions, surgery, and, of course, drugs, drugs, and more drugs. While drugs of every conceivable type (and for every conceivable

164   CHAPTER 7

purpose) have long saturated American society, in recent decades the political warriors have become obsessed with outlawing *selected* categories of drugs, on the basis of rather arbitrary and inconsistent criteria. For the contemporary gatekeepers of public morality, "good" drugs are those prescribed by licensed doctors, "experts" in health, medicine, and treatment. Other chemical substances are framed as illicit, addictive, even sinful—yet another source of moral panic.

In this context, Andrew Weil, Ronald K. Siegel, and kindred critics have called for urgent and thorough reassessment of the entire drug phenomenon, hoping to challenge the ideological narrowing of American medical discourse.[2] In purely economic terms, capitalist modernity advances a project of material growth through the benefits of science and technology—a project that has given rise to expanded corporate, state, and bureaucratic power. Such power is tied to an ethos of instrumental rationality and new forms of expertise, hierarchy, and professionalism that coexist with heightened mass alienation and disempowerment—beneath a façade of democratic politics. In the United States, where corporate dominion has reached its pinnacle and material abundance has delivered questionable benefits for society as a whole, the medical system—supposedly a beacon of modernity—is beset with mounting dysfunctions, reliance on illusory quick fixes, and spreading iatrogenesis (that is, causing more harm than good). Rising drug (and other) addictions—and hypermedicalized strategies of treatment—represent opposite sides of the same intensifying social crisis. Modern governance, built on a confluence of corporate, governmental, and (for the United States) military power, contains a deep authoritarian logic in which a formal liberal-democratic order is sustained alongside oligarchical and bureaucratic structures. The medical behemoth, still influenced by its Rockefeller corporate origins and close linkages to Wall Street, fits this matrix of modern domination perfectly.[3]

Here the thesis presented by Theodor Adorno and Max Horkheimer in their classic *Dialectic of Enlightenment*—where modernity is understood as a "new kind of barbarism"—might be more fully appreciated today. As Enlightenment rationality underpins expanding modes of production and consumption, systemic capacity for institutional controls and ideological hegemony deepens, allowing for the transformation of people into consumer-driven, alienated, largely impotent objects. For Adorno and Horkheimer, modernity was likened to a "totalitarian" order by its very rationalizing logic, creating a world in which "life and death, heaven and hell hang together."[4] Further, "the paradoxical nature of faith [in progress] ultimately degenerates into a swindle, and becomes the myth of the twentieth century; and its irrationality turns it into an instrument of rational administration by the wholly enlightened as they steer society toward barbarism."[5] Here domination and alienation, as twin historical modalities, represent two sides of the same trajectory: people, ideas, and goods are ritually converted into objectified entities. Viewed thusly, the present-day drug disaster—extremely high levels of consumption, nightmarish abuses and addictions, medicalized "treatment" schemes, the fears and myths that are generated—takes on special ideological meaning.

As state-corporate capitalism expands, the health of the planet deteriorates just as the health of human populations faces increasing threats—the result of heightened economic growth, widespread use of toxic chemicals, accelerated depletion of natural resources, wasteful animal-based food production, and McDonaldization of dietary patterns.[6] With US health care the most commodified and resource-depleting in the world, consuming nearly 20 percent of domestic output, the consistently high rate of deaths from cancer and other chronic diseases (perhaps one million yearly)—connected to remarkably high levels of obesity— speaks volumes about the dysfunctional, poorly accessible, and iatrogenic features of American medicine. While Big Pharma alone accounts for vast healthcare expenditures, it is easy to see how chemicalized treatment programs (to counter the deadly effects of an already toxic world) are likely to only worsen iatrogenic tendencies. The idea that healthcare outcomes can be significantly altered with more of the same—that is, more spending, more expertise, more technology, more pills—amounts to one of the grand illusions of the current period.

The corporate medical system requires, even celebrates, the power of its technical apparatus, consistent with the spread of technological rationality, often with deadly consequences.[7] While trumpeting individualism (mainly as *consumerism*), the ideology thinly conceals a technocratic instrumentalism bereft of human subjectivity and agency. In a society where personal alienation and social misery are the norm, who can be astonished to find an endless (and mounting) list of "disorders" requiring (physical or mental) treatment by chemical miracles, including "narcotic" properties found in mind-altering (or mindnumbing) drugs? Alienation ultimately gives rise to a variety of psychological coping mechanisms, including addictive behaviors in the form of shopping, food, sex, gambling, sports, the Internet, alcohol, tobacco, pharmaceuticals, and illegal drugs. Within capitalist modernity, the perpetual search for escape, for superficial and temporary meaning, produces a multitude of addictions fueled by anxiety, stress, depression, and physical disorders. Here "medicalization" and "addiction" become twin expressions of the same modern, rationalized, administered social order.[8]

166   CHAPTER 7

Corporate Medicine Today

The practice of medicine in the United States since World War II cannot be understood without discussing the rapid growth of a labyrinthine corporate network—hospitals, clinics, institutes, universities—combined with an even larger ensemble of business interests: Big Pharma, insurance companies, finance, energy, food, agriculture, and the chemical industry. This corporate empire amounts to the most costly, bureaucratic, and commodified medical system ever created—a system in which failure and iatrogenesis are built into its very modus operandi.[9] At the time of this writing (fall 2014), in the midst of heated debates over Obamacare reforms, the American demand for medical services across the board—insurance, hospitals and clinics, drugs and other medications—has skyrocketed. Drug consumption alone in the United States expanded by 3.2 percent during 2013. Chronic health problems (heart disease, diabetes, cancer, infectious diseases) have been dramatically on the rise, imposing new burdens on the healthcare system. By 2020 Americans are expected to spend nearly $5 trillion on "health care"—the total of the next ten highest-spending nations combined—at a time when chronic illnesses have reached peak levels, obesity extends to nearly 40 percent of the population, pill taking has become the norm, and ineffective or harmful medical procedures now outweigh the beneficial ones.[10]

The burdensome costs of corporate medicine have become a source of economic misery and psychological despair for tens of millions of people—especially for those suffering from chronic ailments. An exhaustive *Time* magazine report on the state of American health care, assembled by Steve Brill, points out that cancer treatment, as one example, can bring costs totaling a half million dollars (only partially covered by insurance), to one individual or family—a common source of financial and personal ruin that worsens the medical traumas.[11] A single hospital visit can cost several thousand dollars, not including expensive tests and procedures. The United States is now a nation of sick people who can expect problematic treatment at exorbitant prices, for hospital or clinic visits, doctors' fees, lab tests, drug therapies, CT scans, high-tech procedures, and surgeries.

While people suffering from chronic illnesses can spend tens of thousands of dollars for drugs and hundreds of thousands more for hospital stays of a few weeks, CEOs and hospital executives, Big Pharma, and insurance firms make huge profits and salaries: incomes of beyond $1 million yearly are common. Brill reports that fourteen high-level administrators at the Sloan Kettering Institute, a major center of cancer research and treatment, receive incomes of more than $500,000 annually, while CEO compensation at health facilities such as Cleveland

Clinic and New York Presbyterian Hospital can reach $5 million, augmented by generous benefits.[12] The CEO of the Sutter Health chain received $5.2 million in 2011, just as a ninety-year-old woman was charged $121,000 for treatment of a broken bone.[13] Hospitals, doctors, drug companies, laboratories, equipment providers, and many others within the medical establishment amass private fortunes from human misfortune and suffering. To help secure this privilege, the pharmaceutical industry spent $2.9 billion on lobbying the US Congress during 1998–2014.[14] In 2012 annual per capita healthcare spending in the United States had reached $8,000 yearly, more than double that of any other nation—a predicament the hotly debated Obama reforms were not likely to significantly alleviate. Patients with severe health problems can spend tens of thousands of dollars in a single day, especially if costly drug therapy is prescribed. Overcharges and huge markups are routine. Insurance coverage is spotty and limited by huge copays, deductibles, exemptions, and loopholes. Anyone with chronic health problems can expect a steady flow of inflated charges, what Brill calls "reams of bills to people."[15] Within corporate medicine the incentives for doctors to order drugs, testing, and procedures appear difficult to resist. With trillions of dollars spent by a public inundated with advertising, fearful of alternatives, and anxious to find ready fixes, life expectancy in the United States ranks fiftieth among nations—and overall health indicators are no more flattering, placing it near the bottom of industrialized countries.

The Many Faces of Addiction

No discussion of the medicalization of American society is possible without addressing the pervasive reality of addiction, a term that—like most linguistic constructions—has long been subject to multiple definitions and perspectives. I refer here to established, habitual patterns of behavior that can apply to most human objects and activities, from drugs to food, sex to gambling, technology to shopping. Addictive behavior varies according to duration, intensity, nature, and focus. Unfortunately, the familiar understanding of "addiction" in media, government, and medical discourse revolves around nightmarish tropes of the sort popularized on TV and in Hollywood movies, where the problem typically refers to "drugs" (illegal drugs), with occasional diversions into alcoholism—an outlook that continues to drive the War on Drugs.

Hoary stereotypes about drugs and addiction have brought untold harm to American society, yet they remain central to social policy, law enforcement, and

168   CHAPTER 7

personal treatment approaches. Few contemporary public discourses have become more ideologically hardened or politically self-defeating. A broader, more critical perspective on addictive behavior, today more urgently needed than ever, might start with the following generalizations:

- Habitual behavior patterns unfold through a dialectical interaction between personal and social life, within a complex totality involving subject, object or objects, and a range of intervening or mediating factors such as family life, work, health conditions, and culture. This helps explain why the vast majority of people who consume particular substances or engage in specific behaviors do not automatically end up habituated or dependent—or, if so, manage by means of their own resources to control potentially dysfunctional consequences. It is not the concrete *object* as such, seen in isolation, but rather *multiple* factors shaping the social context that crucially shape behavior leading (or not leading) to addiction.
- Addictions follow a continuum, with dependency spanning many possibilities, from virtually harmless to extremely destructive, most cases falling between. Many common types of habituation—daily coffee intake, regular TV watching, weekend football gambling, wine with dinner, repeated trips to McDonald's, nonstop texting—might be rather harmless even where defined as addictive. Indeed what we all-too-glibly label addictive behavior is not typically—much less innately—destructive.
- Even where addictions turn problematic or destructive, as with excessive daily consumption of drugs or alcohol, people can endure the behavior and carry on more or less "normally" with their work, careers, family, and everyday life. In regions of South America people chew coca leaves regularly; in Mediterranean countries red wine is consumed abundantly with dinner; in many American homes men drink a six-pack of beer or more daily; in modern society untold numbers of people are fixated on electronic devices; and millions of people around the world smoke pot routinely. In few of these cases is there much thought, if any, of harmful addictions requiring medical treatment. Even regular users of "hard" drugs, such as coke, heroin, and methamphetamines, can lead satisfying and productive lives, with harmful effects often controlled or minimized through human will power.
- Even in cases of severe, disabling addictions, people frequently manage to outgrow them, moving through well-known processes of adaptation to changing life situations. Youth inclined toward indulgent, outrageous

THE MEDICALIZED SOCIETY 169

behavior in their late teens and early twenties—college years when extreme use of alcohol and drugs is common—usually "mature out" of such behavior when faced with new pressures from job, career, family, health, and finances. Historical evidence suggests as much: fewer than 10 percent of long-term hospital patients dependent on painkillers remained addicted once the general *setting* had dramatically changed. The same applies to Vietnam veterans once strung out on opiates. The presumption of fixed, immutable forms of addiction—whatever the substance or behavior in question—can be dismissed as yet another myth of the drug enforcers' ideological arsenal.[16]

From the foregoing generalizations it follows that harm from addictive behavior cannot be taken for granted; worst-case scenarios are hardly inevitable, but must be determined through empirical investigation. What are the measurable consequences of daily pot consumption—or of wine, beer, cocaine, sugar, and fast foods—within a given social totality? Damaging consequences can be identified and measured according to how, and to what degree, habituation negatively influences a person's job, career, health, and finances. Scientific focus on tentative hypotheses and factual evidence appears all too forgotten when it comes to dealing with addiction or, more emphatically, "drug addiction."

As Stanton Peele and other critics argue, conventional "disease" theory, central to most medical strategies and basic to mainstream understanding of both addiction and treatment, has shaky empirical foundations, grounded as it is on oversimplified assumptions about human behavior. Habituation is better framed as a *condition* shaped by and mediated through contextual factors like those mentioned previously.[17] Proof of addiction as disease would have to depend on a range of biological variables, which have never been established through actual research that, in any event, generally ignores social, nutritional, lifestyle, and other contextual influences on patterns of human behavior.

Harmful and costly addictive behaviors actually occur at the highest rates for such legal substances as fast foods, sugar, alcohol, tobacco, and many pharmaceuticals. Those sources of habituation are so common and so thoroughly part of the culture as to be routinely overlooked as addictions—abuses and excesses perhaps, but rarely (aside from alcohol) understood as especially addictive. The potentially destructive impact of food, alcohol, cigarettes, and legal drugs should nowadays be scarcely questionable, as the evidence mounts. Matters worsen, it should be added, when individuals consume potent substances in various (and untested) combinations, such as mixing alcohol with prescribed medications or taking two or more drugs simultaneously in the form of "cocktails." Drug problems, it is often forgotten, follow multiple possible outcomes—among them adverse reactions, overdoses, drug-related accidents, and lethal episodes.

The grand myths of prevailing addiction discourse, which shape both the medical model and the War on Drugs, have in recent decades achieved something of a life of their own. Official definitions of sickness, disorder, abuse, and treatment, interwoven with the reigning medical ideology, serve to legitimate norms of technocratic intervention and quick fixes. Fixated on the discrete *objects* of behavior, such addiction theory detaches the problem from the complex totality of social life, thus diminishing the role of human agency.[18] "Addiction" results from the innate properties of substances (or activities), devaluing the immense variations in human experience, perspective, context, and volition. If certain substances or behaviors are intrinsically addictive, how is it possible—as is clearly the case—for the overwhelming majority of users to suffer few if any of the harmful outcomes so glibly imputed to those choices?

Alternatives to the dominant medical paradigm are routinely dismissed within the official discourse, riveted as it is by narratives of "disease" and "disorders" said to inhere in the *object* of individual choice. Leading sectors of the medical establishment, along with familiar twelve-step recovery programs, remain wedded to the disease model, understood as more enlightened than earlier views of addiction that focused on moral depravity and sinful behavior. The National Institute on Drug Abuse (NIDA) upholds the premise that drug abuse and addiction fit the disease model, situated within a biological framework. A recent NIDA proclamation concludes, "As a result of scientific research, we know that addiction is a disease that affects both brain and behavior." More specifically, "addiction is defined as a chronic, relapsing brain disease that is characterized by compulsive drug seeking and use, despite harmful consequences. It is considered a brain disease because drugs change the brain."[19] Generalizations about addiction refer to such determinants as the "biological makeup of the individual." Genetic variables, it is claimed, account for between 40 and 50 percent of those who experience some type of addiction.[20]

More widely circulated statements about drug addiction can be found in the *Diagnostic and Statistical Manual of Mental Disorders* (DSM-IV), which focuses more on "disorders" than on "disease"—something of an advance over NIDA—but that still imbues particular chemical substances with innately (often irresistible) addictive properties. The DSM identifies eleven classes of such disorders, among them psychotic, mood, anxiety, sleep, and sexual conditions linked to drug abuse or dependency.[21] Some disorders are associated with use of intoxicating drugs; "hallucinogenic disorders" (including maladaptive behavior), for example, are associated with consumption of LSD, mescaline, and psilocybin. Addiction means dependency, including extreme tolerance, withdrawal, persistent desire, and compulsive overindulgence, often leading to "recurrent and significant adverse consequences related to repeated use of substances," including possible social, legal, or personal difficulties.[22] The DSM emphasis on "disorders," more helpful than the NIDA model, is broad enough to apply far beyond those specific drug habituations analyzed in the manual. As for harmful consequences, the criteria for distinguishing intoxicants like cannabis and cocaine from many pharmaceuticals, as well as ordinary products like fast foods and sugar, remain vague and arbitrary.

A deeper problem is that preoccupation with "disorders" tends to stigmatize forms of behavior that, upon serious reflection, turn out to be rather common, even "normal." Conditions such as depression, anger, anxiety, shyness, and self-absorption, where not so extreme as to cause breakdown or dysfunction, can hardly be classified as distinctly medical problems—much less as something requiring expensive drug treatment. Viewed thusly, "diagnosis" emanating from the DSM and kindred psychiatric sources relies on labels best understood as moral rather than scientific. The proliferation of such "disorders," however, does ensure a steady flow of patients for the medical system and revenues for Big Pharma.[23]

By avoiding the "disease" trap, DSM manages to take into account contextual factors that contribute to addiction, though it does so as a largely peripheral concern. Referring to "substance intoxication," the manual states, "The maladaptive nature of a substance-induced change in behavior depends on the social and environmental context."[24] At other points the text refers to "cultural traditions" and "social settings" that can influence patterns of alcohol consumption.[25] While such generalizations are essentially truisms, the DSM still formulates the bulk of its addiction discourse as a more or less singular fixation on specific *objects* of abuse and dependency. Its conceptual advance beyond the disease model, therefore, remains more limited and one-dimensional than might be hoped.

The NIDA and important sectors of the medical-treatment apparatus still follow the unsupported notion that drugs (though only some categories of drugs) are immediately and inescapably addictive, transforming the user into a hopeless slave of desire and habit, powerless to change under any circumstances—at least until the experts appear on the scene. The War on Drugs is based entirely on such official fallacies. Where "disease" is the label, addiction becomes all-consuming, with a steady descent into hell being one likely outcome—a fate obviously more probable for some drugs than for others. Yet even where addictions occur at a high rate, as in stressful environments like prisons, military combat, impoverished

172   CHAPTER 7

street life, and family strife, the level and incidence of habituation usually decline, often dramatically, once the main contextual factors change.[26]

Peele refers to the disease theory of addiction as "useless folklore," a view consistent with that adopted here.[27] According to such "folklore," drug habituation is produced by an irresistible biological or medical logic—a permanent state of being created by powerful external forces. Opposition to the disease model is cavalierly dismissed as an elaborate psychological ruse, or "denial"—that is, an irrational refusal to submit to expert opinion and medical intervention. Even moderate or episodic use of (illicit) drugs is said to possibly overwhelm, even transform, the victimized user.

A crucial flaw in disease theory is that no distinct, generally agreed-upon biological or genetic mechanisms for addictive behavior have been identified—nor are they likely to be, given the complex, ever-shifting elements of individual psychology that cannot be understood apart from social factors, health and nutritional patterns, fortuitous circumstances, cultural differences, and, above all, dynamics of personal *choice*. For research on drugs to fully account for *all* such variables related to addiction—in the absence of which no biological determinants can be proven—is virtually impossible or, in any case, far too cumbersome, time-consuming, and expensive for any investigator or group of investigators to pursue. Moreover, the varieties of addictive behavior that *do not* include consumption of drugs or food, such as gambling, sex, and shopping, clearly possess no biological markers, as these are undeniably a function of social-psychological dynamics. By framing a multifaceted problem like addiction as biological and externally imposed, disease theory removes human psychology from the complexities of everyday life.

Even casual familiarity with addiction reveals a *continuum* of behavior—no different from other human problems. A common addiction is excessive fast-food consumption, typical of the McDonaldized culture. While physical and mental harm from a steady diet of fast foods is well documented, levels of dependency naturally vary, with few people consuming the amounts depicted in the film *Super Size Me*, where monthlong gorging on almost exclusively fast foods led to a near-lethal outcome. Millions of habitual fast-food patrons suffer from problems of heart disease, diabetes, cancer, and osteoporosis, but even these conditions differ widely in terms of severity. Long-term consumers of beer, wine, liquor, and cigarettes, of course, can expect above-normal serious health challenges; risks are well known, but vary according to amount and regularity of consumption, among other factors. Patterns related to food and nutrition are just as valid for products like alcohol, tobacco, and other drugs, independent of legal status. Those who abuse alcohol inevitably do so in terms of degree, with a small percentage considered extreme addicts. A person who drinks two or more glasses of wine daily with meals might be labeled an "alcoholic," yet this routine—normal for many European countries—might be perfectly functional, serving ordinary psychological needs or desires. The labeling tendency within established medicine comes easy and often, nowhere more so than for antidrug crusaders obsessed with banned substances. As for drugs, the rate of addiction among those using pot, coke, hallucinogens, and most pharmaceuticals is typically below 10 percent—among alcohol drinkers slightly higher, and among meth users still higher but not much over 15 percent.[28] Data concerning habitual gamblers and shoppers, on the other hand, are murkier as the criteria for addiction seem less well established, more vague and arbitrary.

Cocaine is one substance that the NIDA and similar official sources claim to be inherently addictive, but the reality speaks differently: just *1 percent* of coke users wind up with a daily habit, and fewer yet risk jobs, careers, health, and families to satisfy cravings. As noted, millions of people have routinely chewed coca leaves in the Andes for centuries, with few if any known problems of abuse or addiction. No evidence suggests that coke habituation, even with the more concentrated form of the drug, is more difficult to quit than, say, Valium or Vicodin dependency. Peele writes, "With cocaine as with every other illicit drug that has ever been used by large numbers of people, the majority of those who take it do not become regular users, the majority of regular users do not become addicted, and the majority of those who become addicted cease their addiction on their own without treatment."[29] Contrary to official antidrug discourse, people usually possess enough inner resources to break with dependency. The example of Vietnam veterans has been mentioned: 90 percent of returning troops hooked on cannabis or heroin soon outgrew their addictions once the social context had profoundly changed. Viewed *contextually*, therefore, hard drugs provided an escape from the stresses and horrors of combat but no longer served that function in more "normalized," less stressful civilian settings. A break with addictive behavior usually occurs with advancing age and maturity, extreme dependency becoming rare past age fifty-five. No doubt treatment can be successful, especially where it allows for self-directed change. Evidence shows that therapy for alcoholism and drug addiction is best when it focuses on self-help manuals; family and/or community reinforcement; and elevation of social, job, and communication skills—a modality far removed from a disease model that strips people of human agency.[30]

In the dominant medical ideology, the term "addict" refers to a fixed, monolithic, unchangeable state of being: once an addict, perpetually an addict. This fiction not only degrades human capacity for adaptation and change, but ignores the very *complexity* of human experience. For one individual chemical substances

174 CHAPTER 7

might serve as a medium of escape, while for others it may be a source of pain relief, a remedy for depression, a vehicle of psychological exploration, or a simple means of intoxication. The degree to which drugs can be "mind-altering" varies immensely, depending on many factors. The drug experience taps into a great variety of personal behaviors, contradicting simple notions of automatic habituation and dependency. What the drug user brings to the experience—history, age, health, nutrition, personal outlook, etc.—decisively shapes outcomes.[31]

Lost in the familiar obsession with (illegal) drug "horrors" is a far more urgent problem facing American society today—widespread and severe harm from habitual consumption of fast foods, sugar, and similar legal products that have contributed to an obesity rate in the United States of nearly 40 percent.[32] The McDonaldized diet, research shows, is largely responsible for heart disease, cancer, and diabetes—conditions leading to far more deaths than all illegal drugs combined. The fast-food culture is so deeply embedded in American life, so normalized as to be virtually invisible, yet is fully implicated in the continuing obesity "epidemic," thanks to high intakes of saturated fats and sugar. Highly popular Coca-Cola, originally laden with caffeine, cocaine, and sugar, nowadays contains up to thirty-two teaspoons of sugar per eight ounces of liquid, composed largely of high-fructose corn syrup. As tens of millions of Americans continue long-ingrained dietary patterns in the face of potentially severe harm, such habituation might well be considered addictive, at least according to the DSM criteria: dependency, loss of control, and refusal to change.

The problem here is less one of biology—"genetics" or "disease"—than of socialization processes, influence of advertising and peer communication, societal changes in food consumption, and (lest we forget) personal *choice* when faced with serious risks. With the national incidence of obesity—and associated health problems—escalating in recent decades, the idea that genetic markers (requiring *centuries* to alter even slightly) are behind this sea change is too preposterous to take seriously. That a steady increase in postwar drug consumption—and addictive behavior—could be explained in strictly biological terms makes just as little sense. What might be a problematic habit in one setting—a target of cultural taboos and legal prohibitions—can be normal, perhaps salutary, in other settings. Teenagers drinking red wine with dinner in Italy and Spain is a practice that raises few alarms, not too different from the daily chewing of coca leaves in regions of South America or regular use of cannabis in some cultures (for example, many communities and groups influenced by sixties counterculture in the United States). While marijuana is indeed liberally consumed around the world, it has long been demonized in the United States as among the most harmful of drugs. Less than a century ago in American society, liquor was savaged by moral enforcers as the devil's potion, yet today it qualifies as big business, is vigorously advertised, and is considered essential to many celebrations. Given Americans' regular intake of hundreds of potentially abused drugs, what is striking is the rather *low* rate of addiction to illegal drugs (generally less than 10 percent, as noted previously). Severe addictions to banned products, while surely too frequent, impact a relatively small percentage of drug users. Other addictions, as mentioned—to fast foods, sugar, alcohol, tobacco, and pharmaceuticals—are in fact more shockingly common today. Cigarette smoking, perhaps the most familiar of modern addictions, harms every bodily organ, contributing to many forms of cancer as well as heart disease, bronchitis, and emphysema. Tobacco is particularly harmful to reproductive health, being associated with reduced fertility, high rates of miscarriage, premature births, and even infant deaths. More than 4,000 chemicals can be found in tobacco and its smoke, including sixty substances (among them ammonia, tar, and carbon monoxide) that produce high risks of cancer. Peele, among others, has described smoking as the "toughest habit to lick."[33]

One striking reason for addictions of all sorts is that capitalist modernity is so riddled with manifestations of human misery and alienation: workplace oppression, joblessness, poverty, family crises, crime and violence, environmental problems, social disempowerment. Addictions can offer ready-made escapes from the debilitating stress, anxiety, and conflict of urban life, with its congestion, noise, pollution, economic pressures, and loss of identity that accompany steady erosion of family, work, and community. The system is virtually designed to create broken people. When this reality is combined with the aggressive marketing (and easy availability) of potent legal substances, including a cornucopia of psychotropic drugs, the spread of addictive behaviors should come as no surprise. According to some sources, no fewer than eighty-five million Americans are today impacted in some way by addictive behavior.[34]

One of the newest, reportedly widespread "diseases" manufactured by the drug industry in partnership with psychiatrists is Internet addiction, which is said to take hold once a person spends more than thirty-eight hours a week at their computer.[35] (Precisely how ordinary work activity is distinguished from compulsive behavior is never made clear.) This illness, according to the experts, can be treated by such medications as Ritalin, Valium, and Prozac, helpful in countering the (imputed) depression and "mood swings" resulting from excessive technological access. No doubt the Internet, like other parts of the technological landscape (social media, email, cell phones, texting, etc.), can be addictive, cutting off users from normal social life and generating extreme dependency. While people typically approach the Internet and kindred venues as sources of

176   CHAPTER 7

information, entertainment, research, and writing, some develop a use pattern where technology winds up all-consuming, larger than life. Reports indicate that American teenagers send and receive an average of 3,700 text messages monthly—some in dangerous situations like driving a car. Many constantly access the Internet for random, anonymous chat rooms, gaming, pornography, and sex cameras, no doubt exceeding the thirty-eight-hour threshold set by the psychiatrists. Whether such addiction frequently leads to aggressive, antisocial behavior, as is often claimed, has yet to be proven. Whatever the case, to imagine that large amounts of psychotropic drugs might remedy this problem is to partake of the most fanciful medical illusions.

Internet addiction is just the latest in a rapidly expanding list of diseases that Big Pharma and the medical profession have created to sell more pills. A strategy of medicalization is premised on the belief that millions (actually *tens* of millions) of physically sick or mentally disordered Americans will guarantee heightened drug sales—indifferent to the prospect that these drugs will give rise to new cycles of addiction, not to mention adverse reactions. For the pharmaceutical giant Roche, "social phobia" (being shy or withdrawn) is a serious illness best treated by the potent drug Manerix. At Pfizer, this same condition is rendered as "social-anxiety disorder," requiring daily use of Zoloft or other psychotropic substances. At GlaxoSmithKline, the perfect medication for individuals "allergic to other people"—a condition said to afflict millions of Americans, including children—is Seroxat, developed in 1999. Meanwhile, sexual disorders have supposedly become rampant in the United States among both men and women, generally treatable by Cialis, Viagra, and other widely advertised drugs.[36]

The medical establishment is nowadays trapped in an iron cage of hypermodernity: as health disorders multiply, pills are generously prescribed by doctors and psychiatrists as "remedies" for hundreds of problems, real or contrived.[37] Patients are expected to submit to professional authority, follow medical orders, and embrace drug therapies that often bring more harm than good. While presumably more enlightened than earlier theories emphasizing "moral" defects, the contemporary disease model, like the general medical paradigm, reinforces alienation and disempowerment while legitimating existing high levels of drug consumption the War on Drugs claims to oppose.

Obesity: Food, Drugs, Addiction

No problem better reflects the twin disasters of a medicalized society—dietary harm and its purported solution through expensive pills—than the current obesity "epidemic." In the United States, where people consume one of the heaviest meat- and fast-food-based diets in the world, excessive weight is increasingly common, indeed rather normal—a problem impacting nearly 40 percent of the population in 2014, as mentioned previously. The dramatic rise in obesity in post-WWII America stems mainly from prevailing nutritional patterns involving high consumption of fats, meat, dairy products, and sugar, most often from fast foods. The most devastating chronic diseases—cancer, atherosclerosis, and diabetes—are linked to a McDonaldized regimen that, despite even mainstream warnings of health disasters, remains popular. Meanwhile, fanciful "solutions" to obesity promised by the medical establishment—faddish diets, drugs, surgery, technical devices—have turned out to be mostly illusory.

As technocratic medicine gains legitimacy, the great challenges it sets out to overcome—obesity being at the top of the list—steadily worsen. Excessive weight in the United States stems mainly from that most tenacious of all modern addictions—food, or more accurately, fast foods and foods rich in saturated fats. With growth of the fast-food culture, obesity becomes the quintessential health condition of capitalist modernity: huge corporate sectors (agribusiness, meat and dairy interests, McDonaldized chains, grocery complexes, advertisers) generate superprofits from sales of heavy, fatty, high-calorie food products.[38] In the United States, moreover, such food products are relatively cheap, widely available to the poorest population groups (which also suffer most from obesity). Alternative food approaches have been difficult if not impossible to bring about, especially since the laissez-faire ethos regarding food is especially powerful in the United States; government rules and regulations are denounced as a source of "food fascism."

Despite an abundance of conventional arguments to the contrary, elevated rates of obesity can be traced to large-scale dietary changes going back to the 1950s, marked by an unprecedented rise in meat and dairy consumption, the upsurge of fast foods, and ubiquitous marketing campaigns touting animal-derived food choices as a sign of affluence, vitality, and progress. Beef in particular came to be associated with optimum health and power, its protein content praised as necessary for ideal physical and mental functioning—despite abundant evidence revealing just the opposite.[39] By virtue of government subsidies and sheer volume of sales, the meat-centered diet became inexpensive enough for all but the very poorest Americans to afford (though its cost advantage over healthy alternatives is usually exaggerated). The McDonaldized order, with its predictable fare, quick access, rationalized processing, and affordability fits the modality of modern capitalist production perfectly.[40] Its food choices, laden with fats, oils, meat, salt, and sugar, can be habit forming, addictive, and health depleting.[41] Fast foods are promoted as excellent choices not only by corporate lobbies and

178   CHAPTER 7

advertisers but by academic researchers and organizations like the American Public Health Association and American Dietetic Association. Food-industry guidelines, moreover, strongly encourage such unhealthy food choices in schools and other public institutions.

Foods rich in saturated fats—basic to the McDonaldized formula—are the largest contributors to obesity: compared to the Big Mac (67 percent fat content) and milk shake (64 percent), plant foods (vegetables, fruits, grains) contain negligible, if any, saturated fats. In the United States, the population consumes on average a staggering 36 percent of calories from harmful fats. As T. Colin Campbell shows in his seminal *The China Study*, the Chinese—who typically derive less than 10 percent of calories from saturated fats—experience far less obesity and, by extension, fewer chronic diseases.[42] The "diseases of modernity and affluence," Campbell notes, can be traced directly to meat-based diets with large amounts of animal proteins and fats, giving rise to a population that is "sick, overweight, and confused."[43] Further, daily habits sustained on the basis of familiarity, allure, and availability of health-damaging products are hard to break, especially as meat consumption has become something of a quasi-religious routine for most Americans.

If obesity derives mainly from eating habits, logic dictates that corrective measures to overcome it are most likely to be found in elementary dietary and related lifestyle changes. Such logic does not hold for a medicalized society, however, where the idea of changes in food consumption is dismissed or subordinated to drug treatment, consistent with the American tradition of quick and painless fixes. While at times temporarily beneficial, the overall record of expensive medical shortcuts has been less than stellar. The FDA has approved many drugs to fight obesity, but none deliver permanent reversal of the condition and all have potentially serious adverse reactions. Several of these drugs, including the widely consumed Didrex, Bontril, Xenical, and Meridia, have been placed on the "do not use" list by Sidney M. Wolfe and associates. As the authors note, "Sibutramine [Meridia] is another in the long list of diet drugs that have never been shown they can be taken safely for a long enough period of time to reduce the morbidity and mortality associated with obesity."[44]

In their general assessment of anti-obesity drugs, Wolfe and associates comment, "No diet drug . . . has ever been shown to confer a health benefit in terms of reducing the serious complications associated with long-term obesity."[45] Weight-reduction pills tend to raise blood pressure; aggravate cardiovascular disease, thyroid conditions, and glaucoma; and produce extreme addictions. Further, the magnitude of weight loss with these drugs is shown to be minuscule compared to simply taking a placebo. Many decades of experience with diet pills indicates the

THE MEDICALIZED SOCIETY   179

harm far outweighs benefits, yet tens of millions of Americans fill prescriptions each year, while the obesity "epidemic" persists. Wolfe and associates conclude, "Prevention is the best treatment for obesity. Our advice about losing weight and diet pills has been the same for 20 years: eat less, exercise more. This approach to losing weight is slow but effective. The only one who profits from it is you. That's why it isn't sold."[46]

As weight problems burden tens of millions of Americans, including 15 percent of children, the marketing activities of Big Pharma have only intensified. Advertisements for weight-loss drugs proliferate across the media landscape. Such print outlets as daily newspapers, magazines like *Time* and *People*, and tabloids like the *National Enquirer* and *Star* regularly carry ads for diet meds and "combo pilling"—mixing such drugs as Zantrex and Relacore—that overweight consumers can purchase over the counter at such outlets as Walmart, CVS, GNC, and Rite Aid. According to marketing copy for *Star*, people who are obese and tired of "dieting" can opt for magic pills that "give you power to change your life": excessive weight comes off and one's life is transformed from miserable to happy. Body fat can also be shed through use of human growth hormone (HGH), which supposedly works miracles in boosting immune-system performance and increasing strength, energy, and endurance along with weight loss. (Note: HGH is the very product antidrug warriors want to ban entirely from sports competition.)

One recurrent weight-loss advertisement in *Star* magazine calls readers' attention to "A Pill [That] Can Reshape Your Entire Body in 30 Days"—the pill touted being Vysera-CLS, sold by Bremenn Clinical. According to ad copy, "Vysera can actually reshape your entire body, dropping inch upon inch of unsightly fat from your waist, hips, thighs, and tummy . . . even if you're eating more than 2000 calories a day!"[47] (Left unsaid here is that the standard American diet—the one mostly responsible for obesity—well exceeds 2,000, or even 3,000 calories daily.) The ad continues, "The end result was that the specialized compound was shown to cause a significant reduction in body weight, fat mass, BMI, adipose tissue thickness, and waist/hip/thigh circumference while maintaining lean body mass." In other words, "It's sort of like eating a whole donut, but only absorbing a fraction of the calories."[48] There's no reference, of course, to the possibility of reducing total caloric intake, fats, and sugar.

The drug category most often prescribed to counter the effects of obesity, notably cardiovascular problems—statins—has been among the most profitable for Big Pharma, with such blockbusters as Crestor (manufactured by AstraZeneca) reaching sales of $5.3 billion in 2013.[49] Statins such as Crestor, Lipitor, and Zocor have long been among the best-selling blockbusters. Not content with

180   CHAPTER 7

this boondoggle, in November 2013 the medical establishment issued recommendations for a much wider consumption of statins, promoting low-dosage guidelines for tens of millions of Americans deemed to be at risk of heart attacks or strokes.[50] Once that guideline was adopted, the number of regular statin users was expected to reach more than seventy million people. Both the American Heart Association and the American College of Cardiology, closely aligned with the drug industry, were pushing this regimen, despite such well-known adverse reactions to statins as hemorrhaging, strokes, elevated blood sugar, muscle weakening, and loss of nutrients like coenzyme Q-10 (vital to heart function). Compared to significant dietary changes, statins have been shown to have few benefits for long-term cardiovascular health.[51]

The biomedical approach works admirably for such needs as emergency surgery and life-saving procedures. Drugs can be great miracles where injuries, wounds, toxic invasions, and severe pain occur. A problem arises when the chemical substances become everything, a source of comfort to meet every health contingency—precisely the case in the medicalized approach to obesity, implicated in untold numbers of deaths yearly. The most common health crisis resulting from obesity is some variant of heart disease, which itself kills hundreds of thousands of Americans each year. Here drugs in the category of statins are the most popular choice for Big Pharma, as sales often reach blockbuster proportions. When it comes to heart problems, the biomedical seduction looms especially large. As John Abramson notes, "The problem is that all the current medical recommendations . . . [pay] just enough lip service to preempt criticism that these issues are being ignored. The end result is that doctors and patients are being distracted from what the research really shows: physical fitness, smoking cessation, and a healthy diet trump nearly every medical intervention as the best way to keep coronary heart disease at bay."[52] As with antiobesity medications, potent drugs given for heart disease offer costly palliatives in the absence of long-term solutions.

Despite mountains of research findings, many reported and analyzed in *The China Study*, pill-based solutions to lifestyle-inflicted health problems—endorsed by medical lobbies, Big Pharma, academia, and the media—are on the upswing. In the United States, giant drugstore chains are positioned to take a more aggressive role in medicine, which means new cycles of antiobesity drugs. Hospitals, clinics, doctors, and pharmacists are becoming more aggressive in pushing weight-loss medications, on the faulty premise that diet as such has little to do with weight problems. The pharmaceutical industry is now on the leading edge of medical treatment, with sales increasing for both OTC and doctor-prescribed drugs. The industry has recently been consolidated into three major chains: Walgreens (with 8,000 stores nationwide), CVS (with 7,500 stores), and Rite Aid (with 4,600 stores), followed closely by such giant retailers as Walmart.

Where drugs and fad diets fail, there is always the lure of weight-reduction surgery—another phantom savior currently on the rise. Stomach-stapling operations, referred to as bariatric surgery, can cost upward of $25,000 despite having produced few benefits. Medical procedures to limit stomach capacity or reshape the intestinal tract were elected by 220,000 Americans in 2012. These, and kindred techniques such as liposuction, have shown few positive results for individual health (including longevity), especially in the absence of serious lifestyle alterations.[53] Surgery, like potent medications, does not remove the fundamental *causes* of obesity and heart disease; any immediate benefits quickly disappear where dietary habits remain the same, the result of what Campbell describes as a "failed treatment paradigm"—one endlessly repeated in the face of predictable futility.[54]

This paradigm, failed or not, has been endorsed by the American Medical Association (AMA) House of Delegates, which voted in June 2013 to declare the scourge of obesity a disease, lending new legitimacy to medical treatments while allowing doctors to be generously reimbursed by insurance carriers.[55] Ignoring evidence that obesity is a behavioral issue, the AMA framed it as a "complex disorder"—though the precise origins and nature of the "disease" or "disorder" were left unspecified. With this move, both the FDA and Big Pharma can more readily approve new cycles of drugs for obesity—or, more accurately, for managing the problem since it (the "disease") is regarded as permanent and irreversible. The idea that excessive weight might to some extent be the victim's *fault*, that it might be related to behavior, lifestyle, social factors, or personal choice, is soundly rejected.

Well-known diseases such as flu and pneumonia stem from pathogens that attack the body, leading to sickness, dysfunction, and possible breakdown; such pathogens are scientifically identifiable. A variety of chronic diseases (cancer, atherosclerosis, diabetes, osteoporosis, etc.)—more accurately referred to as degenerative health conditions—develop from long-term biological processes usually linked to diet and other lifestyle choices. Psychological disorders along the lines of depression, phobias, and bipolar condition occur within a matrix of complex life experiences; addictive behavior clearly fits this pattern. Viewed thusly, pathogens are determinant factors only in the first case, while obesity is best understood as overlapping the second and third patterns. No strictly biological factors—"pathogens," genetic makeup, disease—are needed to explain or treat a

182   CHAPTER 7

condition that afflicts roughly 130 million Americans who share easily identifiable food choices. (How so many human beings might presently be victims of disease, when just several decades ago there were so few, has yet to be explained.)

One problem with the disease theory, aside from its shameless rationale for costly medical interventions, is its perpetuation of an outlook in which people are detached from their social-psychological context; human capacity to make choices, to alter everyday-life circumstances, to impact health outcomes, is devalued. If obesity is a disease, afflicting its hapless victims for an entire lifetime, then the only hope is for medical intervention to help those victims manage something that will never actually vanish. Diet pills, now consumed by tens of millions of Americans, are projected to be the main option for those looking to "control" weight problems. Further, if people are either invaded by a (mysterious) pathogen or have simply inherited genes for obesity—in either case, overtaken by external forces beyond their control—they are rendered impotent, bereft of change options. The loss of human agency is preordained.

The notion within established medical-pharmaceutical circles that obesity has strict biological causes is, in fact, hardly novel; assertions to that effect were made decades ago. Peele cites one leading source as follows: "Obesity is an incurable disease. We don't know its complete etiology. We can, however, put a patient into remission for a lifetime through our weight-loss program. . . . We try to make our patients aware that their obesity is a disease, that it is incurable, and they will need maintenance assistance for the rest of their lives."[56] That individuals might be capable of making their own dietary and other lifestyle choices—leaving harmful food habits behind of their own volition, without diet pills or surgery—stands at odds with the comforts of the disease model. Yet if addictive (thus changeable) behavior can apply to such ordinary human activities as gambling, shopping, and sex, it is hard to see why it could not extend to eating—or drugs. Food is, of course, essential to life, so it can easily be overlooked in any discussion of addiction. The question here is not food as such but *harmful* food, where habit and dependency (unrelated to pathogens or genes) lead to significant weight problems. Unfortunately, health-denying food choices are not only legal but generally approved and vigorously advertised (thus invited) within the dominant culture at a time when myriad weight-reduction programs have given rise to a multibillion-dollar industry.

As obesity steadily worsens, corporations reap huge profits from the health miseries of tens of millions of people—Big Pharma in the lead. Barry Popkin notes, "Today, the drug industry dominates public expenditures and activity related to most health problems. This is as true for obesity as it is for other conditions."[57] Reliance on pill therapy allows users to embrace illusions of progress

THE MEDICALIZED SOCIETY   183

while retaining the old dietary habits. Tellingly, obesity and the rate of drug use to combat it have risen dramatically and simultaneously in recent decades. Meanwhile, champions of the biomedical model—for example, Gina Kolata of the *New York Times*—tell their large audiences that being overweight, a genetic disorder, cannot be reversed in any way apart from expert medical intervention.[58]

The endless parade of elaborate "diet" programs—books, videos, workshops, seminars, nutritional schemes—do not usually reject drug solutions, but they do, inevitably, have less reverence for the disease medical model. After all, the idea that obesity can be overcome by changing food habits implies the *possibility* of change through self-transformation, as with the famous Atkins programs and their offshoots. Such diet fads are typically based on the assumption that weight problems can be remedied by means of low-carbohydrate diets—leaving consumption of meat, fast foods, and other fatty products largely intact although those are precisely what is most responsible for obesity in the first place. The fads do nothing to permanently reverse problems they are ostensibly designed to solve. While vast evidence points to a diet of mostly plant foods as the overwhelmingly best option to fight obesity, such "low-carb" theorists as Robert Atkins and John Mansfield (in *The Six Secrets of Successful Weight Loss*) argue that people should eat animal fats and proteins without limits.[59]

Atkins and Mansfield claim that obesity rates have increased at the very time Americans are thoroughly obsessed with jettisoning high-fat diets, many turning to low-fat vegetarian or vegan alternatives—but evidence for this is lacking. On the contrary, per-capita intake of saturated fats in the United States has steadily risen as the McDonaldized regimen maintains its popularity, increasing by thirteen pounds per individual since the early 1970s.[60] Despite overwrought warnings about harmful "carbs" (ignoring the vastly different *types* of carbs), moreover, it is difficult to overlook a stark reality: vegetarians rarely have weight problems, while regular consumers of fast foods and animal products are far more likely to suffer from obesity. The claim that the real problem is too many low-fat diets runs up against a formidable McDonaldized reality. That reality has not prevented Atkins, Mansfield, and others from sticking tenaciously to their diet plans at a time when chronic diseases resulting from standard American eating habits have reached unprecedented levels.[61]

Obesity and associated health problems might be labeled "diseases of affluence"—that is, conditions of modernity and the lifestyles it favors. Solutions will be difficult to locate within the existing medical-pharmaceutical framework—or within the fast-food culture. Big Pharma offers short-term palliatives but no long-term remedies. Here observers like David Freedman argue that since the fast-food juggernaut is here to stay and those addicted to it are not likely to change, the

184 CHAPTER 7

only way to curb obesity is by improving or refining McDonaldized offerings. Most people will simply refuse the healthy alternatives that Freedman indicates, with some exaggeration, are much too expensive and inaccessible.[62] However, limits to this strategy in terms of how much the fast-food industry is willing to adapt should be obvious. However difficult, obesity will only be "solved" as an American health disaster when alternatives to both fast foods and the medicalized society achieve far greater popularity.

Modernity, Disease, Iatrogenesis

The medicalized society evolves within an ultracommodified system of production and consumption marked by the continuous growth of state-corporate power. Peter and Carole Ann Kennedy note, "With the advent of industrial capitalism and the rise to dominance of modern science, medicine became central to developing the medical model or discourse of mental illness."[63] Put differently, medicine—as both ideology and practice—colonizes broader areas of daily life, the economy, culture, and politics. Despite appearances of social and technological progress, the system turns increasingly iatrogenic at a time when sophisticated treatment methods are available to record numbers of consumers, or "patients." Gary Null characterizes this phenomenon as "death by medicine"—an advanced iatrogenic state of affairs in which the medical behemoth—including the profession, hospitals, technical devices, and drug therapies—is now a leading cause of death in the United States, with adverse reactions to legal medications near the top of the list.[64] With drugs prescribed in copious amounts, to children as well as adults, Americans now consume more than half the world total of legal drugs. By 2012, US doctors were writing some three billion prescriptions yearly for drugs that, as we have seen, often bring life-altering risk and harm. The large number of unreported adverse reactions to drugs will, of course, never be known given the difficulty of establishing clear linkages and the visceral impulse to cover up drug-related episodes owing to legal and professional fears.[65]

According to the Nutrition Institute of America, conventional medicine ranks at the top of causes of death in the United States, accounting for an estimated 700,000 fatal episodes yearly—the largest number resulting from drug problems: abuse, overuse, overdoses, accidents, severe adverse reactions, and addiction-related episodes. Antidepressants such as Halcion, Prozac, and Effexor have been known to give rise to violent impulses and outbursts, including suicide and murder. In 2013 antidepressants remained the most widely prescribed of all medications.[66] Opioids such as codeine, morphine, fentanyl, and oxycodone,

THE MEDICALIZED SOCIETY   185

prescribed for pain relief, possess enormously high abuse potential, including severe addiction, lowered blood pressure, dizziness, and comas. Popular amphetamines (Dexedrine, Adderall, Ritalin, etc.) commonly produce elevated blood pressure, heart attacks, seizures, and strokes. A frequently used muscle relaxant like Soma brings extreme risks, including vision problems, disorientation, dizziness, and strong bouts of drowsiness. Although this drug has been widely prescribed in the United States since 1959, it is located squarely on the "do not use" list by Wolfe and associates, who add that carisoprodol (Soma) is little more effective than aspirin.[67]

A mounting iatrogenic problem, in the United States and globally, concerns the precipitous overuse of antibiotics, which have now lost their capacity—first unleashed during World War II—to treat bacterial and other infections. As pathogens are increasingly widespread around the world, we are headed to a time when common bacterial afflictions resulting from ordinary injuries will become more severe, even fatal. As new classes of antibiotics have exhausted their potential over the past few decades, the overuse of antibiotics for both humans and animals has brought us into a post-antibiotic era when bacterial forms have erected massive resistance to even the most potent medications. This public-health menace, international in its dimensions, is the predictable outcome of an irrational antibiotics regimen spanning perhaps fifty years—with no strictly domestic solution in sight.[68]

Modernity, as noted, has bequeathed a flourishing medical tradition made possible by the historical triumph of science and technology, positioning an ever-growing stratum of experts—doctors, researchers, technicians, pharmacists, therapists, etc.—at the center of human problem solving. In the United States, under the aegis of Rockefeller and kindred corporate interests, this system took hold in the early twentieth century, when technocratic medicine first took its place within modern capitalism.[69] The system gained power and legitimacy through advances in biomedical science: quantitative research, biological work, genetics, varieties of germ theory, the disease model, a panoply of technical innovations. As Barbara Ehrenreich and Deirdre English show, scientific medicine took on a quasi-religious outlook that, in the United States above all, would profoundly shape healthcare structures, practices, and norms.[70] Ehrenreich and English observe that in the earliest days of technocratic medicine the experts set out to identify and label all manner of psychological conditions—most said to afflict women—as diseases that would ultimately require treatment by those same (male) experts. Even then, sickness (disorder) had become a way of life, referred to as a "medical strategy of disease by decree."[71] For women, of course, there was the familiar problem of "hysteria," along with such ailments as "nervous

186 CHAPTER 7

prostration" and "dyspepsia,"[72] and of course the list of diseases (for both males and females) would greatly multiply over the years. In this ideological milieu the (exclusively male) experts had scientific authority at their disposal while tending to the frailty, dependency, and vulnerability of growing numbers of their (mostly female) patients. An imputed biological fact, "disease" was widely understood to be a more or less fixed state, though possibly ameliorated or managed by means of expert intervention. Later the public would be warned about fearsome contagions, diseases, and epidemics requiring expensive forms of medical treatment.

Treatment programs are today a major growth industry in themselves, aligned with the medical system, corporate interests, and government programs. The recovery-treatment industry, long dominated by Alcoholics Anonymous (AA) and allied support groups, relies heavily on the disease model for addiction therapy promoted within academia, medicine, therapeutic circles, the media, and government agencies as the final word in psychological solutions. For these experts, addicts are condemned to impotence, told to submit to expert opinion and respect the mystique of "a higher power." As Jack Trimpey observes in his critique of such therapy, a great appeal of AA is that on the surface of its authoritarian structure can be found a progressive, democratic façade that celebrates virtues of personal growth, individual freedom, and human spirituality.[73]

For main currents of the American recovery business, alcoholism—arguably the most widespread of all addictions—is a permanent, incurable disease best "treated" through personal surrender to a higher force (experts, therapists, God). Lifetime abstinence is imperative. The notion that addictive behavior might be understood as a human *condition* shaped or mediated by social factors, subject to individual choice, and open to perpetual adaptation and change is rejected outright. Here Trimpey argues, with only slight exaggeration, that "our addiction treatment industry has become an American gulag that runs parallel to the former Soviet Union's past misuse of psychiatry to enforce the will of the government on its citizens."[74]

As far back as the early nineteenth century, Benjamin Rush defined "intemperance"—along with such crimes as murder—as a manifestation of "disease," a condition in which individuals had lost all will power. Rush's ideas, a mixture of religion, folklore, and pseudoscience, would strongly influence the later temperance movement, Protestant revivalism, and groups like the Anti-Saloon League that drove the prohibitionist upsurge. Today, the view of addiction caused by a brain disease involving "altered brain structure and function" has long been held by the AMA (beginning in 1956) and influential sectors of the scientific and medical communities. Disease theory has ritually invoked family patterns, where addictive tendencies are supposedly passed on from parents to children—as a set of shared illness-producing genes. Yet such "family patterns" could just as easily—more easily, even—involve long-shared eating habits and lifestyles transmitted across generations. The disease model, however, favors a medicalized strategy heavily reliant on drug therapy, which, as mentioned, brings harmful outcomes consistent with mounting iatrogenesis.

There can be little doubt: problems of substance abuse and addiction are indeed pervasive in American society, perhaps more so today than at any other time in history. The key problem is how to explain, contextualize, and treat (or, better, prevent) addictive behavior without reducing humans to passive, objectified, impotent victims—that is, without destroying their agency—as occurs within the medicalized society. As Peele writes, "The real cure for addiction lies in a social change which reorients our major institutions and the types of experience people have within them."[75] Today we are given addiction theories and recovery programs built on slogans, rituals, sound bites, and oversimplified formulas marketed as "therapy." Such programs, like so much of the medicalized society, have turned out to be widely iatrogenic. More crucially yet, they lack anything resembling a model of individual or collective empowerment. As Wendy Kaminer notes, the mainstream recovery industry upholds the virtues of individualism and self-activity but is ultimately conformist and authoritarian in its norms and practices.[76] She asks, "What are the political implications of a mass movement that counsels surrender of will and submission to a higher power describing almost everyone as hapless victims . . . ?"[77] Those implications are surely destined to carry us a great distance from the venerated legacies of personal freedom and democratic politics.

CHAPTER 8
THE GREAT POT WARS

The seemingly endless War on Drugs has long centered on marijuana, or cannabis—the most widely available and popular of all illegal substances. Oddly, what the antidrug crusaders like to call "killer weed" has no record of lethal episodes; on the contrary, in its natural state marijuana is a comparatively harmless substance that produces adverse reactions only with the kind of excessive habituation rarely found among users. A drug that dates back some 5,000 years, cannabis remains shrouded in an official discourse of myths, lies, and propaganda often masquerading as "scientific truth." While such heavily marketed legal drugs as tobacco, alcohol, and pharmaceuticals account for hundreds of thousands of deaths in the United States yearly, pot has relatively mild effects on more than 90 percent of those who consume it. Given the vast gulf between official claims and actual experience—between myth and fact—it is hardly surprising that marijuana has become a great focal point of modern-day struggles around drug warfare.

The current phase of the antidrug campaign initiated by President Nixon in the early 1970s was indeed driven by the fearsome pot menace. For Nixon and his fellow warriors the scourge of "drugs" was mainly understood to mean pot—a symbol of the counterculture, youth rebellion, social nonconformity, and, of course, crime. Pot was always something of an exotic import that, like communism and related subversive ideologies, threatened to erode the very fabric of American society; users were "addicts," "deviants," "fiends," even "vampires." For the media, politicians, and health professionals—not to mention occupants of a swollen federal drug bureaucracy—the "drug problem" aligned pot with harder drugs like cocaine and heroin, at the core of an epidemic sweeping the nation that would have to be countered by aggressive law enforcement. Warfare ideologues, led by a phalanx of Washington-based drug "czars" and their enforcers, attempted to close off public debate over prohibition, opting instead for a cycle of horror stories, phony data, name-calling, threats, and baseless claims about marijuana being a "gateway drug." The 1970s witnessed a disastrous recycling of the supermoralistic Harry Anslinger campaigns of the 1930s.[1] A crude antidrug orthodoxy refused any serious political discussion of real threats posed by an expansive marketplace of both intoxicating and medicinal substances, legal and illegal—of which pot was already scientifically proven to be among the most benign. Talk of legalization was met with apoplectic fearmongering and mythmaking combined with personal attacks, serving to undermine any prospects for a rational American drug policy.

The Cannabis Legacy

Marijuana, or cannabis sativa, has been cultivated and used for the past 5,000 years of human existence as a source not only of intoxication but of such products as rope, paper, canvas, and herbal medicine. It contains dozens of compounds, several psychoactive—the most powerful being THC, which was first synthesized in the 1980s. In China, India, and parts of Europe marijuana has been prescribed for a wide array of health problems, including insomnia, anxiety, joint pain, and other bodily pain, as a safe, inexpensive alternative to more powerful legal medications. In recent years it has been used extensively by cancer patients to ameliorate severe reactions to chemotherapy and radiation. At different times and places the herb has been viewed as something of a "miracle drug," quite at odds with the hegemonic prohibitionist agenda. While the extent of its "miraculous" properties is still open to question, the bulk of independent research indicates that marijuana (whether for recreational or medicinal purposes) is relatively harmless, especially for the kind of moderate dosages that typify common usage.[2]

Many studies have shown that pot is not a dangerous substance, tends not to create extreme dependency, never kills, and serves as a "gateway drug" no more than beer and wine.[3] Even long-term users rarely exhibit adverse reactions beyond vague feelings of lassitude—nothing compared to the hoary claims made by warriors still immersed in the "reefer madness" dogma. Extreme daily consumption has been shown to (moderately) impact the pulmonary system, but nothing compared to cigarette smoking, which kills hundreds of thousands of Americans yearly. As mentioned, no single death has ever been recorded from the intake of cannabis.

190   CHAPTER 8

The notorious "killer weed" propaganda of the early twentieth century was first directed against Mexicans, depicted as anti-American, lazy, criminal, and sexually deviant. While the outlaw image of marijuana goes back to 1914, "reefer madness" panic did not gain full attention until the 1930s, once alcohol prohibition was no longer the object of moral assault. The crusade turned to pot, despite lack of evidence supporting such demonization. In 1937 Congress passed the Marihuana Tax Act, effectively criminalizing production and consumption of the drug across the United States. This act, and the Boggs Act (named after Rep. Hale Boggs) that followed in 1951, laid the groundwork for stiff prison sentences, even for users, that would continue into the present. For Anslinger and his legion of fellow warriors, "drugs" (starting with marijuana) were associated with sinful behavior, linked to all that was subversive: Mexicans, blacks, jazz, communism, youth rebellion, and (later) the sixties counterculture.[4] It was against this historical backdrop that President Nixon launched the modern War on Drugs.

While many independent reports had shown that pot, especially consumed in its natural state and in moderation, was essentially harmless—indeed far more so than most legal drugs—such reports would have little impact on the public sphere or government policy. For prohibitionists, it was full-speed ahead. The 1972 creation of the National Commission on Marihuana and Drug Abuse, in fact, validated these reports, going so far as to suggest that pot be decriminalized under federal, state, and local laws, that mere possession no longer be treated as a crime. The commission said that the issue of marijuana abuse should be deemphasized as a social problem, scarcely worth the vast resources earmarked to combat it.[5] Obsessed with his warfare agenda, Nixon ignored these recommendations, insisting that pot was a great scourge linked to youth rebellion, the counterculture, crime, and other types of social deviance.

In 1970 marijuana was listed as a Schedule I controlled substance—that is, extremely dangerous, with no redeeming or medicinal properties, the selling and use of which merited harsh punishment. By the early 1980s President Reagan was referring to marijuana as the most dangerous drug in America, prelude to a sharp escalation of the drug war leading to the 1984 Comprehensive Crime Control Act and 1986 Anti-Drug Abuse Act, when he called for greater allocation of federal resources to eliminate the "drug menace" combined with stiffer jail sentences for users as well as sellers.[6] The first powerful federal drug czar, Carlton Turner, embraced the pot challenge with Anslinger-like fury, part of a crusade to defend "American values" from subversive forces. Drug traffickers were the personification of evil, equivalent to fascists, communists, or terrorists. The selling of just a few pounds, even ounces, of marijuana could bring a life sentence in some locales. In some states (Louisiana, Oklahoma, etc.) simple possession of demon weed could bring forty-year prison terms. From the early 1980s onward, several million Americans would be arrested on pot charges alone, 90 percent of those for simple possession. Offenders could have their property seized or driver's licenses suspended even with scanty proof that a crime had been committed. By the early 1990s, it was mainly pot offenses that fueled growth of the largest prison-industrial complex the world has ever seen.[7]

Decades of government warfare against marijuana, costing taxpayers tens of billions of dollars, have exerted little downward impact on either production or consumption, as black markets continue to thrive across the United States. One difference is that whereas in the 1960s most pot was imported from Jamaica, Mexico, and Colombia, by the early twenty-first century the majority of crop outputs were domestic, from states including Illinois, Ohio, Missouri, Kentucky, California, and Oregon. Given relatively easy money for their labors, commercial growers in the United States presently number an estimated 200,000, with untold quantities of indoor cultivators. Mexican and other foreign cartels are today less vital to the supply chain than in decades past. In any event, the most aggressive DEA operations have mattered little to the popular appetite for cannabis—or its availability. As of 2012 marijuana was consumed in the United States at a level greater than all other illegal drugs combined.[8] Meanwhile, federal power strengthened by the War on Drugs continues along its authoritarian path, as surveillance, raids, arrests, and incarceration harshly impact the lives of hundreds of thousands of Americans. The stigma of "drug offender" is usually debilitating. Despite political and media talk of fiscal deficits, budgetary crises, personal freedoms, and reduced government, the DEA—working with other federal and local agencies—maintains its aggressive warfare strategy against demon weed.[9]

As the drug war endows governing bodies with swollen powers of legal enforcement, incarceration, and social control, popular resistance has so far been rather limited. Opposition assumes diverse modalities: reform organizations like the Drug Policy Alliance and Americans for Safe Access, grassroots movements for decriminalizing or legalizing marijuana, legislative initiatives behind medical pot, and the many growers and sellers with a material interest in their besieged enterprises. Popular demand for a more rational drug policy has grown, visible in the appearance of books, websites, magazines, and films that treat marijuana consumption as a normal element of everyday life—that is, a phenomenon no longer confined to the margins of society. Prohibitionists, well funded and aided by government, corporate, and media power, have shown little readiness to

192 CHAPTER 8

back down from long-standing coercive policies, even as more than 70 percent of the American public is shown to favor a more open approach to pot (notably its medical uses).[10]

At the start of the twenty-first century the great pot wars were building across several major states, above all Colorado, Washington, California, and Oregon, where revolt against prohibition is loudest, marijuana crops are huge, and federal crackdowns on medical-pot dispensaries are most aggressive (though largely futile). Warfare seems inevitable in a political setting where antidrug fervor so totally conflicts with the actuality of drug consumption—where authoritarian policies directly clash with popular desires for freer access to intoxicating as well as medicinal substances. In his book *Reefer Madness*, Eric Schlosser aptly comments, "A society that can punish a marijuana offender more severely than a murderer is caught in the grip of a deep psychosis. It has a bad case of reefer madness. . . . We need a marijuana policy that is calmly based on the facts."[11]

The "Killer Weed" Hoax

From introduction of the 1937 Marihuana Tax Act to the present, opinion makers have endowed pot with something of a supernatural, demonic status in American culture. Despite hundreds of independent scientific findings to the contrary, cannabis is still labeled as dangerous, listed by the federal government since 1970 as a Category I drug. Its properties are said to be menacingly addictive, a source of psychological deviance and threat to the moral fabric of society. Warriors argue that heavy pot use produces "amotivational syndrome," defined by passivity, sloth, and lack of ambition, with long-term consumption reputed to cause brain damage and pulmonary disorders. In social terms pot—the most commonly used of illegal drugs—is still viewed by hard-line warriors as the stuff of a plague or scourge, demanding harsh prohibitionist measures.[12]

Studies have long contradicted such extreme propaganda, indicating few adverse effects or addictive qualities—nothing close to the harm from many legal drugs such as pharmaceuticals, taken routinely by tens of millions of people. Deaths from alcohol, tobacco, and prescribed medications count well into the hundreds of thousands yearly, while marijuana causes account for *none*.[13] Although extreme long-term pot use can surely impact pulmonary and even mental functioning, its consequences are still minimal compared to those of tobacco use. The vast majority who take cannabis, however, are *moderate* users with few if any of those horrific "syndromes" embellished by antidrug propaganda.[14] Further, the hoary notion of a marijuana plague or epidemic has never stood up to scrutiny. If it had, the most popular of all recreational drugs would have exerted a far more subversive impact on the prevailing ideology than has actually been the case.

In fact, the federal government has carried out its antipot crusade in the absence of rational argumentation. The enforcement regime has spent tens of billions of dollars to extirpate "killer weed," largely without success, ruining the careers, families, and lives of hundreds of thousands of people whose transgressions brought few if any social consequences. As discussed in earlier chapters, prohibition is enforced by a complex of agencies led by the DEA, the FDA, the FBI, the ATF, and the IRS, backed by corporate interests and their lobbies. As we have seen, pot is a key target in the "culture wars" going back to the sixties, if not earlier. The problem is that while pot and other "subversive" drugs could be associated with lawlessness, youth rebellion, and leftist politics, usage has become so pervasive as to contradict such facile myths. Still, the blind antidrug consensus held across the political spectrum has in some ways only hardened over the years, despite (or perhaps *owing to*) escalating popular and legislative challenges.

Major drug-enforcement agencies, including the DEA, the FDA, the NIDA, and the AMA, embrace a shared prohibitionism backed by recent US Supreme Court decisions.[15] The consensus is built on claims that marijuana is powerfully and innately addictive, harmful to mental and physical health, socially destructive, and a precursor to other, more horrible drugs like heroin, cocaine, and meth— the famous "gateway" thesis. Such claims generally depend on studies that are often either overstated, inconclusive, or just misleading. More problematic, the research usually assumes "heavy" and/or "long-term" consumption—measures of which are rarely defined where ordinary smokers fit neither category. As of 2012 at least seventy million Americans were reported to have smoked pot at some time (twenty million on a regular basis), for either recreational or medicinal purposes, only small numbers having experienced severe consequences of the sort presented as incontrovertible fact by such agencies as the NIDA and the DEA. Even if the bulk of warrior arguments were true, however, they would hardly justify prohibition since the adverse effects of cannabis would still fall short of what is known for most legal drugs.

The NIDA contends that research shows pot negatively impacts attention levels, memory, and learning capacity for *daily users*—though how extensively, for how long, and for what percentage of smokers is never made clear.[16] The NIDA finds "cannabis use to be associated consistently with reduced educational attainment"—few heavy cannabis users finishing college—but here again just what "heavy" is meant to convey is vague, as the text itself concedes that "a causal relationship is not yet proven between cannabis use by young people and

194   CHAPTER 8

psychosocial harm."[17] The presumed cause-and-effect relation of pot consumption to educational motivation or achievement is never clearly established.

The NIDA and other agencies mistakenly assume that marijuana *use* is equivalent to *abuse*, and that "heavy," "regular," or "daily" uses are the norm, without evidence indicating such patterns of consumption. Thus, one NIDA report states that pot addiction is extremely widespread, extending to as many as 25 to 50 percent of all smokers in the United States. Dependency is said to be strikingly common, especially since the main psychoactive element (THC) has become more potent over time.[18] The report goes on to say that "marijuana addiction is also linked to a withdrawal syndrome similar to that of nicotine withdrawal, which can make it hard to quit. People trying to quit report irritability, sleeping difficulties, craving, and anxiety."[19] Here, of course, one finds nothing remotely unique about marijuana—surely nothing that sets it apart from efforts to quit habitual consumption of tranquilizers, sleeping pills, pain relievers, antidepressants, and dozens of other *legal* drugs, not to mention such routinely consumed products as fast foods, sugar, and coffee. The NIDA unwittingly places nicotine- and cannabis-withdrawal symptoms in the same category, referring to one legal and one illegal substance. The parallel obviously contains an irrational bias against marijuana, as tobacco smokers *daily* consume a pack or more of cigarettes while the pattern for most pot smokers is more episodic, typically no more than a single joint over a similar time period. More to the point: there is no body of evidence in any NIDA report to justify classifying pot as more harmful or addictive than any legal drug, much less as a Category I substance.

The NIDA claims there is a "link between cannabis use and psychosis," but questions regarding what kind of linkage, how much consumption, and the precise character of the "psychosis" remain unresolved. Some reports suggest large doses of pot can produce hallucinations and "loss of a sense of personal identity," yet what constitutes "large doses" and whether any hallucinations might be severe or problematic are never specified.[20] Other evidence suggests that heavy, long-term pot use leads to changes in brain structure, but these too are largely nebulous and speculative. At one point the NIDA even concedes that "our understanding of marijuana's long-term brain effects is limited. Research findings on how chronic cannabis use affects brain structure, for example, have been inconsistent."[21] Nowhere does the NIDA systematically compare the long-term effects of pot smoking on mental or physical health to those of other drugs. Further, no argument is set forth to validate the criminalization of a substance responsible for no documented lethal episodes.

The FDA and the DEA, among other federal agencies, echo the long list of myths, distortions, and half-truths about marijuana. While the FDA has approved

THE GREAT POT WARS   195

synthetic THC (sold usually as Marinol) for medicinal purposes, it claims "there is currently sound evidence that smoked marijuana is harmful" and "that no sound scientific studies support medical use of marijuana for treatment in the United States, and no animal or human data support the safety or efficacy of marijuana for general medical use."[22] Since cannabis is so powerfully addictive, its legalization would pose a "mortal danger to society," according to the FDA.[23] As for the DEA, its propagandists refer to "serious mental health problems" resulting from pot, which "hastens the appearance of psychotic illnesses by up to three years."[24] They parrot the official line that long-term marijuana consumption "can lead to brain abnormalities." Much like tobacco, they add, pot smoke contains toxic properties giving rise to a variety of pulmonary ailments. Here again their language remains exceedingly vague.

Within the psychiatric establishment—its departure from the NIDA and the DEA only subtle and nuanced—one can find references to "cannabis-related" disorders that, on the whole, hardly differ from a wide range of other drug-connected problems. The DSM-IV manual, for example, speaks of the "psychoactive effects" of THC, which can include abuse, dependency, and withdrawal symptoms much like those mentioned earlier. The manual comments that "fixation" on marijuana can interfere with work, health, relationships, and family life, but again just what "abuse" and "fixation" signify regarding general pot smoking remains unclear. Likewise, mention of "psychosis" and "maladaptive behavior" is rarely clarified and, in human experience, can apply to a vast spectrum of behaviors.[25] In fairness, while the manual refers to certain psychological "disorders" associated with pot, there is considerably less discussion of its imputed harm to mind and body than what is found in NIDA literature. Moreover, DSM-IV appears far less dismissive regarding the medical properties of marijuana.

Prohibitionists claim that few drug offenders have been arrested for simple possession, yet data reveal that among more than seven million Americans busted throughout the War on Drugs more than 80 percent were just users, and the vast majority were brought up on pot charges.[26] The resulting material, social, and personal costs have been catastrophic, while hypocrisy and fearmongering corrupt the public sphere as rights and freedoms are eviscerated. How can government policy be rational or just as it demonizes and criminalizes one (relatively harmless) drug while allowing open sales and marketing of hundreds of substances that are far more risky? Nothing compelling exists in the NIDA, FDA, and DEA statements to justify a policy of marijuana criminalization; everything is based on exaggerated claims and myths. Warnings of a great pot "epidemic" among youth—intoned ritually every few years—are crudely overdrawn, with simple use of a drug defined as abuse. If more youth are now admitted into treatment, as

196   CHAPTER 8

reported by sources like DrugWarFacts.org, that is largely owing to a vast increase in court-ordered cases following arrests.[27] Whatever the shift in rhetoric toward a health-oriented approach, police charges can still bring enormous legal and social difficulties, not to mention loss of property, money, and licenses. While sentences have indeed been shortened in recent years, with treatment sometimes the preferred option, consequences for those arrested can nonetheless be ruinous.[28]

Claiming that marijuana is addictive and dangerous, the antidrug bureaucracy never tires of warning about future "nightmares" in the event of legalization. This stance ignores the experience of countries where liberalized pot laws exist: in Belgium, Holland, Germany, Spain, and Switzerland, where pot is freely and legally available and users are never thrown into jail, marijuana consumption has either declined or remained steady while law enforcement poses a far lesser burden on public spending. (The United States, in fact, continues to have much higher levels of pot use than any European country.) The fearsome "catastrophe" anticipated by the antidrug warriors has never followed adoption of rational policies around the world.

Meanwhile, no evidence can be marshaled to support the fashionable argument that pot use leads inexorably to "harder" drugs any more than beer, wine, spirits, or cigarettes do. Drug-related behavior can, of course, move simultaneously in many directions, but this proves nothing about cause-and-effect dynamics. A 1999 National Academy of Sciences report found that marijuana is "not a gateway drug to the extent it is a cause or even that it is the most significant predictor of serious drug abuse."[29] No one has suggested that drinking beer or smoking cigarettes produces such a one-way causal linkage. Correlations pertaining to drug use demonstrate nothing: anyone willing to consume an intoxicating substance is probably more inclined to try others, especially in the case of youth already predisposed to experimentation.

There remains the stubborn issue of *addiction*, but there nothing uniquely identifiable about marijuana distinguishes it from most other chemical substances, legal or illegal. The problem of dependency, as we have seen, must be understood as both *contextual* and *dialectical*: experience varies widely from person to person, time to time, setting to setting. Where pot is concerned, unfortunately, the orthodox impulse has been to conflate regular or even occasional pot smoking with abuse or addiction; dependency is simply assumed, taken for granted. It follows that the mentally dysfunctional properties ("severe psychosis," "amotivational syndrome," etc.) assigned to pot have been grossly overstated under conditions where only a tiny percentage of some seventy million users have been measurably harmed by cannabis.[30] If lethal episodes from pot smoking are zero, then its toxic properties are surely mild at worst, especially compared to the overdose risks of most pharmaceuticals. In fact the consequences of marijuana—dependency levels, potential for abuse, physical harm, withdrawal symptoms—are scarcely worse than those of caffeine, imbibed at Starbucks and other venues by tens of millions of Americans daily. When it comes to marijuana, the antidrug crusade works stealthily against basic human impulses—not to mention basic freedoms. While cannabis is among the oldest psychoactive plants and grows widely and lushly in diverse climates—and has been used for centuries with few significant problems—the hoary myth of its destructive properties lives on among the crusaders. The "delirium" it produces is in fact generally short-lived.[31] Regular (even daily) use does not typically create dependency—or, if it does, nothing uniquely debilitating—much less permanent or progressive addiction.

The NIDA and media horror stories ignore the commonly ephemeral nature of addiction and abuse: extreme indulgence, especially when resulting from youthful hedonism or experimentation, often gives way to a "maturing-out" process consistent with short-term or episodic behavior. With aging, people take on new lifestyles and commitments—jobs, careers, family, community life—that militate against the seductions of extreme or binge consumption. For pot use in particular, the pattern is typically moderate and/or temporary, contradicting those scenarios fixated on severe and permanent dependency characteristic of the disease model. The more resources available to a person in terms of education, money, work, and social supports—and the more income and status at risk—the more likely dependency will be broken or ameliorated, with or without professional help. In those small percentage of cases where use remains high with lifestyle changes or aging, effective management is usually possible.[32]

Despite such realities, the War on Drugs moves stubbornly ahead, ensuring future battles between federal agencies and local preferences for more enlightened (and democratic) approaches. The Obama administration has done little to alter this impasse: the 2008 presidential campaign initially promised some "fresh thinking" on the issue of pot, giving rise to hopes for greater tolerance of the flourishing medical dispensaries. Once in the White House, Obama and his attorney general, Eric Holder, hinted that federal priorities would mean less targeting of pot users, with greater focus on the big traffickers and cartels. The years following Obama's election, however, have brought more of the same as federal agencies stepped up their campaign against pot users and the proliferating state-empowered shops. The president, in fact, seemed determined to go after drug violators with great tenacity, as the drug war continued apace: in 2010 alone 850,000 Americans were arrested for marijuana-related offenses, most for simple possession, while Big Pharma continued to synthesize and market THC—the very substance antidrug bureaucrats had so vigorously denounced as harmful and

198   CHAPTER 8

bereft of medical benefit.[33] While the DEA raids dispensary owners and consumers, it (joined by the FDA) continues to serve as the enforcement mechanism of the pharmaceutical industry so that sector can maintain its larcenous profits.

Against the UN report findings, discussed more fully in Chapter 3, years of independent research and groundswells of public sentiment in favor of liberalized marijuana laws, a dogmatic prohibitionist mentality holds sway in Washington, DC, and most state capitols. Genuine debate around drugs remains quite limited. As of 2013 sixteen states had passed measures endorsing medical pot, two more (Colorado and Washington) had introduced full legalization, and thousands of pot dispensaries had opened across the country—yet at the federal level cannabis remained a Schedule I drug said to be as dangerous as heroin. The DEA ruled in 2012, once again, that pot had no acceptable medicinal use and should remain at the top of the threat pyramid. While the Obama administration was fighting the irrepressible medical-marijuana upsurge, DEA head Michele Leonhart was repeating the tired platitude that pot has a "high potential for abuse," which is of course a truism for virtually any chemical substance. Doctors at the Department of Veterans Affairs and other federal health centers were ordered not to use any form of medical pot for treatments.[34] From Nixon to Obama, from the 1970s to the present, the federal war on marijuana has continued to exert an authoritarian presence in American society.

Political Repression, Social Protest

By 2012 the medical-pot movement had occupied a central place within grassroots and legislative struggles for a more rational drug policy. These struggles built upon a vast store of information and awareness concerning the actual properties of cannabis, going back to the forgotten 1972 report issued by the National Commission on Marihuana and Drug Abuse. That report, issued under the aegis of the Nixon administration, concluded that marijuana possession should no longer be a crime according to federal, state, and local statutes, as its harmful potential was mild at worst; law enforcement should turn its resources to more pressing issues. Nixon, of course, rejected these findings, choosing instead to follow antipot propaganda made fashionable during the years of Harry Anslinger—propaganda that would checkmate any effort, however empirically grounded, to medicalize cannabis. That propaganda still governs federal drug policy and shapes the terrain of current pot wars.

The American public sphere has been saturated with myths and lies concerning "reefer madness" for so long that rational discourse has been blocked, above all at the summits of power. Politicians, the media, government agencies, and the medical establishment have fallen into line around the familiar linkage of pot with other "illicit" drugs, contrary to mountains of evidence. Elite consensus still views marijuana as central to an impending "drug epidemic," although that consensus is perhaps diminishing in the face of changing public opinion; the drug czars possess less credibility than in the past. Such change, however, has yet to produce a dent in the ideological armor of prohibitionists, even on the limited question of medical pot. The ghost of Anslinger still hovers over the political landscape.

One significance of the medical-pot insurgency, which took off in the mid-1990s, has been to broaden local debate over marijuana legalization and, by extension, the general War on Drugs. Equally meaningful, it has galvanized popular efforts—through organized politics, lobbies, legislative initiatives, and grassroots work—to create durable social alliances behind drug-policy liberalization. These forces have pitted scientific opinion, humane considerations, shifting public sentiment, and democratic sensibilities against a rigid federal authoritarianism. By 2013 public support for some type of decriminalization exceeded 80 percent in states like Vermont, Oregon, Washington, Colorado, and California, with youth opinion naturally running much higher; both Washington and Colorado supported full legalization with nearly 60 percent of the vote.[35] Sources of local empowerment in the great pot wars were finally gaining strength.

Many states, in fact, had long resisted federal hegemony on drug issues: laws and statutes were becoming more difficult to enforce as marijuana cultivation, sales, and use were increasingly widespread—as government and media scare tactics fell on deaf ears. The War on Drugs, especially its preoccupation with cannabis, was losing credibility among large sectors of the population; repressive tactics were backfiring. As new locales implemented workable medical-pot programs, and with adverse reactions to marijuana use milder than for most pharmaceuticals, the old debates were losing steam. Local experience was beginning to prevail over official dogma. Cannabis is far milder than opiates, which are the basis of most widely prescribed medical narcotics in the United States today. Further, marijuana had for decades and even centuries been used to treat such ailments as depression, anxiety, insomnia, headaches, and chronic pain, with at worst moderate toxicity. Positive results for these and other pot applications have been shown by reliable medical investigation over several decades.[36]

The DEA and other federal agencies still contend that marijuana is bereft of medical properties, even long after the FDA approved commercial synthesis of THC. If THC is an acceptable (though relatively expensive) medicine, how can arguments against medical pot be sustained? Of course, they cannot. A 1999

200　CHAPTER 8

review by the US-based Institute of Medicine conducted at the request of the Office of National Drug Control Policy stated, "The accumulated data indicate a potential therapeutic value of cannabinoid drugs, particularly for symptoms such as pain relief, control of nausea and vomiting, and appetite stimulation," all quite useful for cancer patients.[37] Nearly half of all American doctors favor legalizing pot as medicine, and the number is growing. There is an obvious reason why most users prefer the natural, smoked form of marijuana over its synthetic version: the latter is far more costly (fetching up to several dollars per dose).

There is mounting popular consensus that the decision to use natural cannabis for medical purposes ought to reside with individuals in need rather than government bureaucrats steeped in the old propaganda. Oddly, the biggest American drug warriors—Anslinger, Nixon, Reagan, and former drug czar William Bennett—have been strict conservatives ostensibly dedicated to "small government," individual freedoms, and rights of privacy, views that strike most critics as sheer hypocrisy. This is one reason why the DEA, the NIDA, and the FDA have suffered crushing defeats in public opinion and at the ballot box. The more federal warriors repeat their obsolete beliefs regarding pot, the more this trend is sure to accelerate, and the more the grassroots opposition is likely to be empowered. From the 1960s to the present, marijuana has become deeply embedded in American social life, "reefer madness" now being tossed into the realm of folklore, as roughly 38 percent of Americans have smoked pot at some point in their lives and perhaps twenty million do so regularly, according to a 2013 Gallup poll.[38] Many state laws have been liberalized to the degree where law enforcement at all levels has been thrown onto the defensive. The rapid increase of psychoactive drugs that accompanied the sixties youth-based counterculture bequeathed a legacy that, the tenacious drug war notwithstanding, refuses to vanish.

California alone possesses a huge pot economy and culture, with thousands of growers, yet more thousands of dispensaries, and several million regular consumers who view cannabis production, sales, and consumption as a matter of free choice and basic rights. In 2011 the underground marijuana economy fetched an estimated $14 billion in revenue, making it a leading agricultural crop.[39] Local shops took in billions more in sales. Law-enforcement crackdowns on growers and sellers have met with protracted resistance, stretching state and federal police resources to capacity. Activist groups such as the Drug Policy Alliance, Americans for Safe Access, the American Civil Liberties Union, and the National Organization for Reform of Marijuana Laws (NORML) have built a durable presence across the state. In Oakland, one center of the medical-pot movement, drug-war opponents created Oaksterdam University, the first "cannabis college" in the United States, committed to providing students with quality training in growing, processing, and selling marijuana for health purposes.[40] Inspired by the more open Dutch experience, the school even offered Freedom Fighter Scholarship funds to help counter the War on Drugs, but it was raided and closed down by federal agents in April 2012.

In the United States as a whole, marijuana as cash crop earned more than $40 billion during 2011, a major source for pot dispensaries that came to depend less and less on Mexican cartels for supplies. Increased sales were made possible by expansion of shops in new states allowing for legalized medical pot. Some states, including Colorado, Washington, Oregon, California, and Vermont, witnessed a steady rise in demand as the therapeutic benefits of pot became more widely known. A flourishing pot culture stoked popular celebrations like the annual Hempfest in Washington state, which sponsors music, videos, speeches, workshops, and other tributes to the wonderful properties of marijuana. Consensus behind pot legalization in Washington was so strong that the Hempfest could bring in such participants as professionals, academics, cultural figures, and mainstream politicians. At the 2012 event, in fact, Seattle mayor Mike McGinn said, "It [the drug war] has fueled criminal violence. Right now in this city, people are murdering each other over pot. It's time to stop. It's time to tax it, regulate it, legalize it."[41] During 2012, in Humboldt County, California, marijuana activists sponsored the widely attended play *Mary Jane: The Musical*—a melodic celebration of pot culture.

Greg Campbell's book *Pot, Inc.* explores in great detail the trend favoring medical-pot and cannabis legalization in American society.[42] As he notes, while reform sentiment in the United States has built since the 1990s, a turning point seemed to occur in October 2009 when the Justice Department issued an advisory memo to federal prosecutors urging that arrest of medical-pot-dispensary owners and patients be a low priority—an apparent ramping down of the drug war. This resonated with an Obama 2008 campaign statement indicating the War on Drugs had been an "utter failure" and that strict marijuana laws should be revisited. The memo appeared to endorse medical pot and was greeted by many activists as a major step forward; surely the tired propaganda around "killer weed" would finally be put to rest.[43] However, disillusionment soon followed hope: Obama's ascendancy to the White House did not coincide with any expected letup in federal raids on pot dispensaries and growers. Since Obama did nothing to follow up on the 2009 memo, the pot wars continued more or less on course.

At the same time, consumption of the devil weed in the United States remained at high levels: no fewer than fifteen million people admitted to being regular smokers, with probably untold millions of others unwilling to publicly

202   CHAPTER 8

divulge their preference. Demand fed an underground economy valued at tens of billions of dollars, while growers refined strains of the plant—adopting cultivation methods unknown decades ago—in the midst of police threats, governmental assaults, and financial constraints. Campbell writes, "Looking at it in terms of an actual war, the marijuana insurgency has steadily gained ground, helped immensely in recent years by pot's newly rediscovered medical wonders."[44] As Campbell adds, however, this "insurgency" was probably less interested in "medical wonders" than in the intoxicating properties of pot, which serves as a euphoric mood-altering retreat from the mundane, alienating routines of daily life.

Not only has marijuana consumption in the United States remained steady after decades of relentless fearmongering, but public attitudes have softened around prospects of full legalization, as reflected in the historic 2012 election outcomes. States moving toward liberalized policies have witnessed an ongoing flow of citizen actions and local pressures. Massive shifts in popular consciousness have not yet, unfortunately, produced corresponding alteration in official thinking at federal agencies. Still, as Campbell observes, "the question isn't if the nation will one day confront the differences between what its laws say about the subject and what science, common sense, and social culture say, but *when*."[45]

For the present, however, the pot wars show no signs of abating, even after full legalization in Colorado and Washington along with moves toward reform in several other states. A long process of implementing liberalized state and municipal laws, triggered by passage of California Proposition 215 in 1996 (the Compassionate Use Act), has inevitably run up against the federal antidrug apparatus. As of early 2013 most locales across the United States were not yet empowered to set their own rules for drug sales and use, as "drugs" remained the purview of the national government, in stark contrast to alcohol, historically deemed a matter of "states' rights." In northern California, Humboldt, Trinity, and Mendocino counties became the infamous Emerald Triangle—a sprawling region of pot farms with a vast black-market system where, as Campbell notes, "the cannabis plant became the lifeblood of the region."[46] In this and other kindred settings, law enforcement was facing a legal void, as no political entity could determine just what was "medicinal" and what was "recreational" under conditions where the two elements readily merged.

For the marijuana battles, the California predicament meant increasing chaos and confusion—but of course no letup in federal pressure on growers and dispensaries. The Compassionate Use Act did not prevent the DEA and other agencies from conducting raids and arresting people considered to be in violation of federal drug laws. Doctors writing cannabis prescriptions were threatened. Campbell and others have shown, however, that the marijuana economy and culture is now so pervasive and legitimate that no deployment of federal or local cops would suffice to monitor the vast range of growing, processing, and selling activities.[47] As in the case of Mexico, underground markets for pot remain so embedded as to thwart viable law-enforcement operations. In the Emerald Triangle, for example, arrests and prosecutions were often hardly deemed worth the time and expense.

Elsewhere, in states like Colorado and Washington, a mix of strong progressive and libertarian traditions bolstered movements for strong drug reform. Not only medical marijuana but full-scale legalization was gaining stronger popular consensus. Colorado has long had deep public sentiment hostile to federal power, as distinct from a phony libertarianism celebrating "individualism" while embracing authoritarian manifestations of corporate and military hegemony. Marijuana possession in Colorado was already decriminalized in 1975: the maximum penalty for being caught with up to an ounce of pot was a $100 fine, compared to draconian prison sentences in neighboring states such as Texas, Oklahoma, and Kansas. Colorado even boasted a medical-marijuana statute from 1979 to 1995, well before California introduced Proposition 215. It was in Colorado, moreover, that the medical-pot group Americans for Medical Rights found some of its most fertile terrain.[48]

Despite a progressive shift in public attitudes, federal crackdowns on pot gained momentum *after* passage of Proposition 215, as the clash between local preferences and national dictates heated up, giving rise to more casualties in the War on Drugs. The DEA, the FDA, and the NIDA remained out of touch with both medical evidence and common practice, stubbornly refusing to withdraw cannabis from Schedule I status. Federal law enforcers and prosecutors vowed to close pot farms and dispensaries by all means at their disposal, including raids, arrests, property seizures, and long jail sentences. No change to this authoritarian regimen was forthcoming even at a time when numerous states moved to legalize medical pot. DEA head Michele Leonhart, as late as 2011, could still insist that marijuana was uniquely dangerous, with a "high potential for abuse"—while the Obama administration, as mentioned earlier, refused to discuss the UN report advocating more liberalized drug policies.

For the US government—whoever occupies the White House—the war against pot has for decades followed a predictable enough course: crop eradications, high-tech surveillance, sting operations, nighttime raids, property seizures, dispensary closures, aggressive prosecution, and harsh jail sentences. To destroy crops in Humboldt County, for example, federal agents have used a large arsenal of weapons: helicopters, chemical sprays, surveillance devices, battalions of armed troops, undercover DEA agents, and U-2 plane overflights. Pot-eradication

204 CHAPTER 8

programs, though often futile, were for a time a centerpiece in drug warfare, just as they had been in Colombia and Mexico. Pot fields were torched and laid to waste. Local resistance, however, was so deep and resilient that the plants would soon reappear elsewhere, as they had in other parts of the world.

Federal agencies hoped to break the resistance of the medical-pot movement, thinking (rightly) that this "legitimate" form of consumption would be a precursor to broader legalization efforts. If marijuana were legalized for medical purposes, then the way toward broader reform initiatives could not be far behind. As grassroots movements gained leverage, however, the federal response stiffened. The George W. Bush years, not surprisingly, witnessed a heightened crusade against growers and dispensaries. In Oakland, San Francisco, and Los Angeles the DEA and its enforcers moved to close hundreds of legally operating marijuana shops doing solid business and injecting millions of dollars in tax revenues into the mainstream economy. Agents conducted raids, seized property, evicted tenants, harassed users, and pressured banks involved in pot financing. The Harborside Health Center in Oakland, the nation's largest medical-pot facility, was raided and closed down by federal agents in 2011.

In Los Angeles, where more than 750 registered dispensaries were doing business, in July 2012, under intense pressure from the Obama administration, the city council moved to close a majority of shops. City enforcers argued, wrongly, that marijuana outlets were cauldrons of outlawry and violence, doing great harm to local residents.[49] Shop owners and local activists fought back, aided by such politicians as city council member Bill Rosendahl, who was using marijuana in his own fight against cancer, whereupon municipal authorities repealed their ban on dozens of pot shops.[50] No evidence was furnished to support the facile argument that pot dispensaries were magnets of crime; a 2011 Rand Corporation study, in fact, found just the opposite—that legal pot outlets helped *reduce* crime in most locales where they operated.[51]

As of early 2013, a condition of stalemate persisted between federal and local venues on the question of medical pot: repression gave rise to protest and opposition in a milieu where public opinion increasingly favored some form of legalization. The old propaganda had lost its capacity to persuade, based as it was on false arguments and scare tactics. Equally important, antidrug warfare never achieved its official goal of reducing consumption, much less a "drug-free" society. If anything, pot was more widely available across the country in 2012 than it had been during the 1960s. When, in 2011, federal attorney Lena Watkins said that marijuana "is the most widely abused drug in the United States," those knowledgeable about the drug culture could only respond with derisive laughter. As for the pot dispensaries, their closing only forced drug markets further underground, part of a black market devoid of regulations, taxes, quality controls, and antitrust laws. As Jeffrey Miron points out, prohibition as social policy merely serves to transfer billions of dollars in wealth to criminal organizations while denying governments millions in tax revenues.[52]

Marijuana can be used for numerous health problems—above all pain, headaches, and anxiety—much like the synthetic form of THC happily marketed by Big Pharma. THC has proven therapeutic value but, strangely, continues to be derided as "uniquely harmful" by the same warriors who endorse its legal variant. Meanwhile, prescription meds routinely consumed for similar purposes, including OxyContin, Vicodin, and Xanax, are known to cause more severely adverse reactions, some lethal, than either the natural or synthetic form of cannabis. Fatal overdoses of medical narcotics, unheard of for marijuana, amount to tens of thousands in the United States yearly, often involving multiple-drug abuses rarely studied within orthodox medical research. Legal narcotics are aggressively marketed while the pharmaceutical giants downplay the addictive properties and health risks common to painkillers.[53] From 1999 to 2010, when American doctors wrote roughly 300 million painkiller prescriptions, the national use of painkillers *quadrupled*, OcyContin sales accounting for more than $1 billion yearly. Narcotic-based pain relievers caused three out of four overdoses in the United States during 2011, many leading to deaths. For every lethal episode attributed to legal drugs, moreover, thirty-two people went to emergency rooms—though such medical disasters received little media attention.[54]

Common pharmaceuticals used to treat pain, anxiety, and depression, including oxycodone, Fentanyl, Vicodin, Xanax, Soma, and Seroquel, together bring tens of billions of dollars yearly in revenue to Big Pharma. All can be extremely harmful and addictive, and all are prescribed for many of the same conditions as medical pot. Mixtures of these and other legal medications, which commonly lead to multiple-drug overdoses or abuses, are increasingly reported—and it is this reality instead of marijuana use that has produced the real "drug epidemic" in American society.

In the United States today, opiate-containing painkillers are sold by such companies as Merck, Pfizer, and Abbott—all, according to *Worst Pills, Best Pills*, heavily addictive and with potentially severe reactions, including hallucinations, dizziness, abnormal nervousness, swelling, sleeping problems, breathing difficulties, and sexual dysfunction *when the drugs are just taken singly*. The authors warn that such meds, when taken at all, "should be limited to the lowest dose and for the shortest period of time," which, of course, is hardly the norm.[55] One frequently prescribed narcotic painkiller is Fentanyl, applied by means of injections or patches, usually for cancer victims with chronic afflictions. It can bring

206 CHAPTER 8

"severe respiratory problems," according to Wolfe and associates, as well as chest pain, fainting, confusion, dizziness, insomnia, nervousness, and irregular heart beat, among other adverse reactions. It turns out that Fentanyl, like such pain relievers as Vicodin, OxyContin, and Percodan (all with similar risks), is usually prescribed for the same purposes as medical pot—pain and anxiety, sometimes associated with cancer.

One commonly prescribed drug for pain relief is Darvon (propoxyphene), with such potentially destructive adverse reactions that Sidney Wolfe and associates placed it on their "do not use" list. Public Citizen's Health Research Group petitioned the government as early as 1978 to remove this painkiller from the market. Wolfe and associates write, "Propoxyphene is a narcotic that relieves mild to moderate pain. For years we have recommended that you do not use it because it is no more effective than aspirin or codeine and it is much more dangerous than aspirin. . . . Most studies show that propoxyphene is less effective than aspirin and that it has a potential for addiction and overdose."[56] The drug is identified as a major cause of med-related deaths, especially when taken in combination with alcohol or other drugs; fatalities within the first hour of overdose are not uncommon. Given its extremely depressant effects, moreover, Darvon aggravates suicidal tendencies and other severe psychological disturbances.[57] For similar reasons, other pain-relieving drugs—such as Ultracet and Ultram—are located squarely in the "do not use" category. Seizures, convulsions, severe allergic reactions, and strong dependency have been reported for Ultram (tramadol) although it is not listed as a controlled drug.[58] Here it should be noted that, according to the FDA, for every report of an adverse episode at least ten go unreported.

What might be concluded about the status of medical marijuana relative to this grouping of synthetic, heavily marketed, often-harmful drugs prescribed by doctors for conditions identical to those cannabis treats? What can the prohibition agenda mean in this context? Dozens of studies, many by independent researchers, show that marijuana in its natural form can be highly useful for treating pain, anxiety, and the harsh effects of chemotherapy—without severe adverse reactions linked to those pharmaceuticals mentioned previously. Thus, in a 2008 double-blind review conducted by Dr. Ronald Ellis at UC San Diego, the researcher found that "pain relief was significantly greater with cannabis than placebo. . . . It was concluded that smoked cannabis was generally well-tolerated and effective."[59] Similar conclusions were reached by Dr. Donald Abrams at UC San Francisco in 2007; he stated, "Smoked cannabis was well tolerated and effectively relieved chronic neuropathic pain from HIV-associated sensory neuropathy. The findings are comparable to oral drugs used for chronic neuropathic pain."[60] A 2005 study by David Rog at the University of Liverpool found that "cannabis-based medicine is effective in reducing pain and sleep disturbance in patients with multiple sclerosis related central neuropathic pain and is mostly well tolerated."[61]

On the basis of this and similar research, former US surgeon general Joycelyn Elders could state that "the evidence is overwhelming that marijuana can relieve certain types of pain, nausea, vomiting, and other symptoms caused by such illnesses as multiple sclerosis, cancer, and AIDS—or by the harsh drugs used to treat them. And it can do so with remarkable safety. Indeed, marijuana is less toxic than many of the drugs that physicians prescribe every day."[62] In 2008, the American College of Physicians urged "review of marijuana's status as a Schedule I controlled substance and its reclassification into a more appropriate schedule, given the scientific evidence regarding marijuana's safety and efficacy in some clinical conditions."[63] A 2012 survey of American doctors by Medical Marijuana ProCon.org found that 54.4 percent of ninety physicians listed approved of cannabis for medical treatment, and just 27.8 percent opposed it.[64]

As synthetic THC, Marinol was approved by the FDA in 1985 to treat side effects of chemotherapy, and is now classified as a Schedule III controlled substance. Clinical studies have shown Marinol to provide relatively limited benefits with potentially more extreme reactions than cannabis in its natural state. For one thing, marijuana contains several additional cannabinoids with therapeutic properties beyond those of Marinol, which is composed only of THC. These other substances have strong anti-inflammatory and pain-relieving qualities that act in tandem, synergistically.[65] Compared to Marinol, medical marijuana—especially when smoked—is more easily controlled and less subject to unwanted psychoactive side effects such as hallucinations. Viewing Marinol as somewhat problematic, United Patients Group states, "The evidence among scientists, doctors, and patients overwhelmingly proves that natural cannabis is highly effective and superior in treating symptoms of many diseases when traditional drugs offer little to no symptomatic relief."[66]

Federal Power, Local Democracy

Despite a profound historical shift in public attitudes and sustained local efforts to counter marijuana prohibition, the federal government has scarcely budged in its hidebound crusade to stave off change. Democrats and Republicans both embrace the warfare consensus: "illicit" drugs are bad and should remain outlawed. As we have seen, the Obama presidency has closely followed the same rigid ideological narrative, apparently indifferent to scientific rationality as well

208 CHAPTER 8

as political reality. Thus, in July 2011 a deputy attorney general sent off a memo saying that "persons who are in the business of cultivating, selling, or distributing marijuana, and those who knowingly facilitate such activities, are in violation of the Controlled Substances Act, regardless of state law."[67] We have seen, further, how Obama responded to the 2012 UN report calling for drug-policy liberalization with an unyielding stance of rejectionism.

In *Pot, Inc.* Campbell writes, "No matter how far the movement has progressed [along with] the general acceptance of marijuana since the Great Green Rush of 2009—in terms of both medical efficacy and relative safety compared to the old conceptions—the war is not over." He adds, "In terms of warfare, the all-out legalization measures can be thought of as the forward lines where the pitched battles are fought. But there are other fronts being advanced that are no less important."[68] These "other fronts," of course, primarily refer to an expanding medical-pot movement that, by 2014, had secured legalization in twenty-three states, with several more states moving toward similar measures.

In this context, the November 2012 elections bringing full marijuana legalization to Colorado and Washington could turn out to be a watershed moment in the great pot wars. Voters in each state supported an end to prohibition—meaning an end to federal intervention—by an identical, decisive 55 percent. Allen St. Pierre, executive director of NORML, called this breakthrough "the beginning of the end" regarding the US pot wars, adding that "the elections have forever changed the playing field regarding cannabis prohibition in America." Indeed the contours of an entrenched federal drug policy dramatically changed overnight thanks to the voters of Colorado and Washington.[69] For Pierre, "the drug reform movement has moved from agitation to the legalization epoch" after forty years of frustrating defeats.

The key question here is, could this popular revolt against archaic federal laws pave the way toward general change? When the Colorado and Washington measures passed, thousands of jubilant people flocked into the streets of Denver, Seattle, and other cities to celebrate, many lighting up joints. Former Seattle police chief Norm Stamper exulted, "I cannot tell you how happy I am that after forty years of the racist, destructive exercise in futility that is the War on Drugs, my home state of Washington has now put us on a different path. There are people who have lost today: drug cartels, street gangs, those who profit from keeping American incarceration rates the highest in the world. For the rest of us, however, this is a win."[70] Stamper might have included among the "losers" that increasingly rigid (and obsolete) stratum of antidrug warrior in Washington and the mainstream media. At the same time, future combat between federal agencies and the locales over marijuana policy can be anticipated. Fully prepared

THE GREAT POT WARS   209

for intensified combat, Brian Vicente, an author of the Colorado initiative, remarked, "I think we are at a tipping point on marijuana policy. We are going to see whether marijuana prohibition survives, or whether we should try a new and more sensible approach."[71] Meanwhile, the DEA (backed by several federal court decisions) holds fast to the archaic notion that pot should remain a Schedule I controlled substance.

As of 2014, federal authorities still had the power—and to a lesser extent, the resources—to criminally sanction the possession and sales of cannabis, whether in Colorado, Washington, or elsewhere. Time-consuming legal challenges on both sides can be expected in coming years. Vicente says, however, that even should the feds come into Colorado and Washington with a "scorched-earth policy," it might be too late owing to the continuing shift in public sentiment toward pot legalization. Eventually, he believes, the feds will be forced to retreat, at which point a more rational approach to drugs might prevail.[72] In the 2012 election aftermath prosecutors working in the two most populous Washington counties (those including Seattle and Tacoma) indicated they were ready to drop marijuana-possession cases. In Colorado, the same was expected for Denver, Boulder, and other parts of the state.[73] If legalization is indeed allowed to proceed, then both states can expect tens of millions of dollars in tax revenues from pot sales and regulation.

The federal government is probably fighting a losing battle in its defense of untenable positions, as the War on Drugs is embraced today with far less ideological fervor than in the past. Despite the many vested interests behind prohibition, its disastrous consequences have not eluded open-minded people in law enforcement, politics, the medical establishment, and media. The medical-pot movement has contributed dramatically to this shift, despite its somewhat restricted vision of change. At the time President Nixon launched his drug war, 84 percent of Americans opposed marijuana legalization, with just 12 percent in favor. In October 2013, as noted earlier, a Gallup poll found that 58 percent backed legalization, with some other surveys reflecting approval levels of up to 73 percent.[74] As with issues like gay marriage, public opinion is sure to continue along these lines. In 2012 solid majorities among Democrats and independents favored legalization even *beyond* medical pot, while fully two-thirds of Republicans still adhered to the warfare model despite the libertarian pretenses of many. We have reached the point where candidates for political office in many districts can entertain more rational drug policies without committing electoral suicide.

The pot wars have become more incendiary in some regions of northern California, where marijuana crops are abundant and huge. Here several grass-roots organizations (Americans for Safe Access, Emerald Growers Association,

210   CHAPTER 8

and others) challenge federal prosecutors looking for records pertaining to pot cultivators, sellers, and even consumers, hoping to locate incriminating evidence. In Mendocino County, for example, reform groups have defended the rights of cannabis growers, traders, and users who, for the most part, operate fully within California state law. Federal agents, for their part, work on the premise that pot is entirely illegal, traders are outlaws, and offenders should be strictly punished. Meanwhile, the raids and arrests have continued in recent years despite some muting of antidrug rhetoric within the Obama administration. In California, as the federal-state conflict unfolds in a milieu of political and legal murkiness, most court rulings have upheld the power of locales to regulate medical dispensaries in some (ill-defined) fashion. Growers and sellers in many states, however, are left at the mercy of decision-making initiatives in Washington, DC.[75]

As of 2014 those initiatives, while fewer in number, remain ambitious, costly, and coercive: federal raids, many in search of Mexican-cartel involvement in state drug markets, have targeted marijuana fields with renewed prohibitionist zeal, even during Obama's tenure. Federal agents have employed aerial surveillance, wiretaps, GPS coordinates, subpoenaed bank records, and commando squads—typically under DEA aegis—to attack the pot trade. The federal government reported that in 2010 alone its operatives were able to destroy a record 7.1 million cannabis plants across California's Mendocino, Humboldt, Sonoma, Tulare, and Kern counties. Hundreds of growers and traders were arrested. It was jubilantly announced that the big campaign against marijuana had met with unprecedented success—yet no linkage with the feared cartels was uncovered and the pot trade was hardly weakened.[76] The most troublesome aspect of this campaign, however, is the surveillance apparatus that, once in place, has taken on a life of its own. The 2013 revelations about widespread US domestic spying programs, thanks to NSA whistle-blowers like Edward Snowden, must be at least partly understood in this context.

Despite ongoing medical-pot reform measures across the United States, the rights of local jurisdictions remain fully in limbo. In February 2013 Representative Earl Blumenauer (D-OR) authored a historic Medical Marijuana Patient Protection Act that would, finally, allow individual states to overturn prohibition by allowing them to set their own pot laws and regulations, but congressional passage would seem to have dismal prospects. Meanwhile, an Oakland challenge to federal efforts to close local medical-pot dispensaries met (in early 2013) with failure. A US magistrate judge sided with federal authorities in rejecting an Oakland lawsuit, claiming municipal right to file suit against Washington in its campaign to shut down all marijuana facilities, including the famous Harborside Health Center with its 108,000 medical-pot clients.[77]

Popular support for extensive reform of marijuana laws has, unfortunately, mattered little to those at the summits of power. Although Obama has admitted to using pot in his youth, his administration has not budged from its close-minded prohibitionism: more than 750,000 Americans are arrested yearly on pot charges, filling courtrooms, jails, and prisons with victimless offenders. The historic electoral victories in Colorado and Washington endorsing legalized marijuana have met with federal ambivalence: neither the White House nor Congress seems ready to join the democratic trend toward drug liberalization. At the same time, reform organizations like Americans for Safe Access, Marijuana Majority, and the Marijuana Policy Project—vital to the 2012 electoral breakthroughs—have been working diligently to bring the "pot issue" from demon-weed status into the mainstream consensus.[78] As of 2013, some 85 percent of the American public, in fact, favored pot for medical use, reflected in policies adopted in eighteen states.

A Great Reversal?

The stubborn reality is that marijuana—in both its economic and cultural dimensions—is a fact of American daily life, despite the relentless efforts of federal prohibitionists to stem the tide. As the cannabis plant flourishes everywhere—and with demand at consistently high levels—pot is destined to remain a big-money crop. Huge profits are to be made with legalization, especially with expansion of medical-pot markets, estimated to have reached nearly $50 billion in annual national revenue in 2012. With the election outcomes in Colorado and Washington, moreover, big investors are lining up to cash in on an increasingly lucrative drug trade that could, in time, make a serious dent in Big Pharma profits.[79] Pot legalization is likely to give rise to a new stratum of entrepreneurs, perhaps constituting a form of hipster capitalism thriving on cannabis popularity. In this setting, the great pot wars could soon tilt decisively toward popular demand, individual rights, and deference to local jurisdictions. A great reversal could be on the horizon.

The apparent sea change in American public consciousness is surely most visible in Colorado, long a haven of countercultural trends. Reporting in *Rolling Stone*, Jonathan Ringen wrote after his visit to Denver that in parts of the urban region hundreds of high-grade weed enterprises had opened, with Denver in general boasting the "highest concentration of marijuana on Earth."[80] Directly across from a police station can be found a 40,000-square-foot warehouse set up for sophisticated cannabis processing—an early outgrowth of Amendment

212   CHAPTER 8

64, which legalized pot in the state. Marijuana shops abound, provoking little opposition or controversy, with names like The Clinic and Pink House. Prices are far more reasonable than elsewhere, for typically high-quality products. It seems that Denver has surpassed Amsterdam as leading pot mecca. Legalization, of course, means taxation—which, in Colorado, is projected at 25 percent for most goods. Ringen writes, "Soccer moms and legislators alike were enticed by the high rate at which pot will be taxed, with much of that revenue going toward school construction—a precedent that can only tempt cash-strapped states from Michigan to Florida."[81]

Some estimates value the potential marijuana trade nationally at $110 billion yearly—or more. In this context, the Colorado (and Washington) electoral outcomes could provide a model for other states, especially those with already liberalized pot laws. States like Maine, Vermont, Connecticut, New York, Oregon, and California could easily follow the Colorado-Washington example in the near future. Activist groups across the United States have been emboldened, looking to build upon the 2012 political momentum. The hope is that, once a critical mass of states passes strong marijuana-friendly legislation or referenda, the federal government will be forced onto the defensive, allowing for declassification of pot and greater tolerance for local preferences. At present, however, prohibition imposes obstacles to normal business operations: obtaining loans, credit, and even bank accounts related to the drug trade is virtually impossible. Yet if the democratic upsurge of recent years can be sustained and expanded, then the famous tipping point will have been reached, with dire consequences for the War on Drugs.

As new states pass legislation allowing for medical marijuana—in the wake of the Washington and Colorado breakthroughs—a general political atmosphere favoring liberalized pot laws (and perhaps broader reforms) seems to have taken hold. Popular struggles have clearly made a difference. In early 2013 the California legislature declared the drug war a "colossal failure" and voted to give local prosecutors more flexibility in handling nonviolent drug offenses, driven in part by a move to lessen prison crowding and reduce law-enforcement costs.[82] While stiff penalties remained for traffickers, those arrested for simple possession could expect lighter sentences. In this context, marijuana possession would generally amount to nothing more than a minor citation, with no jail time. Meanwhile, in September 2013 the US attorney general announced that the federal government would be more reluctant to intervene in opposition to state laws, possibly spelling the end to DEA raids on local pot growers and shops—although the extent to which the new policy would be implemented was unclear. In Washington and Colorado, the proliferation of legal pot stores was hardly being impeded—the main resistance coming from conservative towns where city councils voted to block legalization.[83]

As this book was being completed (fall 2014), great advances being made in the pot wars—and in the drug war more generally—continue to be fiercely resisted, especially but not only within the federal government. Lightened rhetoric has not been matched by any letup in the (probably losing) warrior struggle to maintain severe bans against marijuana—still listed, after all these years, as a "dangerous drug with no redeeming properties." The political and media establishments help prop up the crusade as if nothing had happened—no historic moves toward legalizing medical pot, no efforts at full legalization across society, no massive shift in public attitudes in favor of liberal reforms. Sadly, while an entirely legal substance like alcohol was responsible for roughly 88,000 deaths in 2013, marijuana—relatively safe and never lethal—remains demonized.

Attempts to get marijuana removed from its Schedule I category, justified by mountains of research, have been rebuffed by the FDA, the NIDA, the DEA, and other federal agencies. Meanwhile, with legalization now in effect in Washington and Colorado, these agencies—fully assisted by the corporate media, which advertises such products as beer, wine, liquor, fast foods, and pharmaceuticals nonstop—regale the public with horror stories about pot and kids, pot and edible substances, pot and violence, pot and brain development. One story warned, implausibly, about the dangers of marijuana use as it enters and damages the central nervous system.[84] Horror scenarios constructed by "experts" uniformly assume both long-term and heavy usage, which is rare. These desperate ploys can be expected to proliferate in the coming period as sales of increasingly legalized pot were likely to skyrocket in 2014.

In Northern California, still an epicenter of marijuana cultivation, there has been only a slight lessening of efforts by law enforcement to uphold federal laws and pursue antipot agendas. There is the well-known Mendocino model, where arrests for possession usually result in a small fine—yet this is based on the maxim that pot can be grown or processed only for personal use. In other cases, felony prosecution can result with significant jail time, even for first-time offenders. Property and cash have been routinely seized even in this haven of progressive social values. The Mendocino model, predictably, has met with stiff resistance from both state and federal agencies.[85] Meanwhile, in July 2014, combined federal and state agents launched massive raids on marijuana-growing areas near Indian reservations, making arrests and destroying hundreds of thousands of plants. In Los Angeles, at the same time, city enforcers were busy closing down more than 200 medical-pot dispensaries that had been operating legally and openly but were being charged with minor infractions.[86]

214   CHAPTER 8

There is no way to conclude a book on drugs and politics without arguing strenuously for an end to the War on Drugs, starting with removal of all prohibitions on marijuana. What the National Commission on Marihuana and Drug Abuse found in the early 1970s—that pot is rather harmless and should be decriminalized—remains just as valid today. Public opinion now reflects an urgent need for change—its relevance going to the very core of both everyday life and democratic politics. We are presently in more favorable circumstances to insist that cultivation, sales, and possession of cannabis should be legalized, regulated, and taxed in the manner of cigarettes, beer, wine, and spirits. Liberalization of pot laws can be seen as the first step toward a more rational drug policy—one that minimizes both individual and social harm while conforming to the requirements of political democracy. The benefits would include vastly reduced government spending, freeing up of jail cells, fewer pressures on law enforcement, renewed emphasis on health concerns, transferring of profits from criminal syndicates and gangs to mainstream enterprises, and a general reversal of authoritarian and militaristic trends. The dramatic electoral shifts registered in 2012 potentially augur such far-reaching changes.

We have seen how the experience of those European nations with more open drug policies—England, Holland, Germany, Portugal, Switzerland, and others—has been overwhelmingly positive: reduced public emphasis on law enforcement, decreased crime, lessened role of criminal syndicates, and so forth. Drug-warrior predictions of skyrocketing drug use and addictions have not come to pass. People suffering from drug problems have access to better health services and more effective treatment. Politicians in these societies have come to accept as a fact of life that humans will continue to consume psychotropic drugs, for better or worse—and that no amount of coercive government policies and laws will serve to extirpate the "fourth drive."

The War on Drugs poses, perhaps more than any other set of public issues, the historic conflict between authoritarianism and democracy, between elite domination and popular freedoms and rights. Antidrug warfare in the United States consistently reinforces the former, even as it is cloaked in the guise of affirming human values and improving public health. American drug warriors, from Anslinger to Bennett and the present-day "czars," have in fact been great champions of authoritarian power, usually in the name of "American values." Even the Obama administration, with its strong rhetoric of "change" and "transparency," has resisted popular demands for drug-policy liberalization. Given an increasing concentration of power in the hands of government, corporations, and the military, ordinary people are today deeply alienated from the decision-making process, from any semblance of democratic politics—nowhere more so than in the drug war.

Despite a long history of democratic traditions and claims, American politics now resembles something of a "phantom democracy" where the *forms* of liberal politics are subverted by the everyday workings of corporate, government, and military power.[87] The War on Drugs both reflects and contributes to this intensifying dynamic in numerous ways, such as the following:

- Across the public sphere—government, media, elections, the educational system—genuine debate on drug policy has been noteworthy by its virtual absence. The warriors have long been able to shape and control discourse: prohibition is essentially a moral imperative, like the embrace of gun rights—beyond discussion.
- The drug war fuels expansion of the most coercive instruments of state power: police, surveillance, the military, prisons, and federal agencies. As antidrug warfare becomes more globalized, military force is more likely to enter the picture, as we have seen in Mexico, South American, and Afghanistan.
- Draconian law enforcement and sentencing policies—moderated somewhat in recent years but still harsh—have underpinned the largest prison complex ever, one that remains materially burdensome, socially destructive, racist, and for the most part recidivist. The lives of convicted drug offenders, especially those jailed for relatively minor charges, are often damaged or ruined. The system is driven overwhelmingly by requirements of social control; Michelle Alexander writes, "The stark and sobering reality is that, for reasons largely unrelated to actual crime trends, the American penal system has emerged as a system of social control unparalleled in world history."[88]
- In the case of both the penal system and the drug war, victims are overwhelmingly people of color, mostly blacks and Hispanics. Abundant evidence suggests that such groups are specifically targeted, as drug offenses furnish a convenient pretext for arrests. More than 70 percent of the jail/prison population—2.2 million in total—are black and Hispanic men. Alexander notes, "The racial dimension of mass incarceration is its most striking feature. No other country in the world imprisons so many of its racial or ethnic minorities."[89] In those hundreds of thousands of cases where drug violators wind up stigmatized as felons, they can face job and housing discrimination, denial of voting rights, and loss of government benefits.

216   Chapter 8

- In instances where states have liberalized marijuana statutes, democratic impulses are met with federal threats, harassment, crackdowns, and arrests. When it comes to the War on Drugs, local traditions, preferences, and decisions are routinely subverted by the national drug-enforcement apparatus, which takes for granted its supremacy over states and locales. States that have passed medical-pot initiatives find that local sellers and users are targeted by some combination of the DEA, the FDA, the FBI, and the IRS.

- Analysis of US drug policy across several decades illuminates some defining features of public life: power is more than ever located at the summit, where government, corporations, the military, and media converge within a broadening authoritarian structure. While this power structure possesses liberal-democratic forms such as elections, the party system, and legislatures, oligarchical forces nonetheless hold sway—and this is especially visible within the drug war. At the same time, the prohibition agenda destroys fictions related to both the free market and limited government in a context of expanded state power.

- The DEA, the FDA, the NIDA, and other federal agencies have long ignored persuasive studies demonstrating the relatively harmless properties of cannabis. Stonewalled too have been clinical and experimental data pointing to marijuana's several medical uses. Mindlessly repeating the "devil weed" myth to justify Schedule I listing, the antidrug warriors overlook scientific findings, including some provided by the government itself, in setting policy. Much like climate-change denial, such scientific and political obscurantism clashes with the norms of an open, democratic political process.

- Official attempts to create a "drug-free America" are not only filled with hypocrisy, but nourish trends toward coercive policies. The idea of ridding society of intoxicating substances once and for all—never remotely possible—directly contradicts an everyday reality in which large amounts of alcohol, tobacco, and other recreational drugs are routinely and legally consumed. A program of zero tolerance is innately coercive and undemocratic.

- The imposition of harsh punishment such as property seizures, long prison sentences, and denial of basic rights for relatively minor, nonviolent, usually victimless offenses such as marijuana possession amounts to what can only be defined as cruel and unusual punishment—a violation of both the US Constitution and the United Nations Universal Declaration of Human Rights. In 2014 tens of thousands of prisoners remained in American jails for minor drug offenses.

- The prevailing treatment/recovery approach to drug addiction—aligned with disease theory or its equivalent—is riddled with elements of coercion and authoritarianism. As the disease model involves submission to an external force or "higher power," individual (or collective) self-activity is inevitably devalued. As Wendy Kaminer argues, this approach "has always been covertly authoritarian and conformist, relying as it does on a mystique of expertise, encouraging people to look outside themselves for standardized instructions on how to be, teaching us that different people with different problems can easily be saved by the same techniques. It is anathema to independent thought."[90]

The War on Drugs works incessantly to undermine political values historically understood as central to American life: freedom, human rights, democracy. Those values, in theory at least, have always motivated actors within the political arena to raise questions about the nature (and limits) of both government and corporate power. A discourse of rights and freedoms, traditionally and in the present, is enough to reveal the bankruptcy of the drug war and its supporting discourses. Governments surely have license to regulate and tax economic activities, but what is the source of authority permitting the state to outlaw substances that millions of people want to purchase and consume, especially where those substances are essentially self-regarding? We have seen how the criterion of personal harm is entirely fraudulent given the large number of destructive and potentially addictive and risky products marketed and sold within the legitimate business framework. The drug war—particularly the antimarijuana crusade—reveals the futility of government policies that honor freedoms and rights in the abstract but are overridden by more pressing economic and bureaucratic agendas. Nearly all human beings at some point in their lives consume such mind-altering substances as alcohol, caffeine, and nicotine, not to mention foods like sugar or prescription drugs for depression, anxiety, pain, insomnia, and sexual dysfunction. That the rather mild cannabis plant should be outlawed against the choices of more than half the population clashes with the spirit and content of democratic politics.

NOTES

Introduction

1. On NSA domestic surveillance, see James Bamford, *The Shadow Factory: The Ultra-Secret NSA from 9/11 to the Eavesdropping on America* (New York: Doubleday, 2008), pp. 112–123.

2. See Marcia Angell, *The Truth about the Drug Companies: How They Deceive Us and What to Do About It* (New York: Random House, 2004), pp. 99–114.

3. See Gary Null, Martin Feldman, Debora Rasio, and Carolyn Dean, *Death by Medicine* (Mount Jackson, VA: Praktikos Books, 2011), p. 4.

4. Jerry Mander, "The Privatization of Consciousness," *Monthly Review* (October 2012), p. 22.

5. For US health statistics, see www.cdc.gov/nchs/hus.htm (May 2014).

6. See Null et al., *Death by Medicine*, p. 4.

7. *Los Angeles Times* (October 25, 2013).

8. See http://quotes.wsj.com/CVS (2014).

9. *Los Angeles Times* (December 11, 2012).

10. *Los Angeles Times* (July 18, 2012).

11. See Ronald K. Siegel, *Intoxication: The Universal Drive for Mind-Altering Substances* (Rochester, VT: Park Street Press, 2005).

12. For a long list of luminaries who have used psychedelic drugs extensively, see Dylan Love, "Meet the Science and Tech Geniuses Who Got High," *Business Insider* (August 22, 2013).

13. For an in-depth exploration of counterculture values, see Theodore Roszak, *The Making of a Counter Culture* (Berkeley: University of California Press, 1968), ch. 1 especially.

220 NOTES

14. Martin A. Lee, *Smoke Signals: A Social History of Marijuana—Medical, Recreational and Scientific* (New York: Simon and Schuster, 2012), p. 65.

15. Ibid., p. 66.

16. Ibid.

17. Ibid.

18. Ibid.

19. Ibid., p. 68.

20. Joel Selvin, *Summer of Love: The Inside Story of LSD, Rock & Roll, Free Love and High Times in the Wild West* (New York: Penguin Books, 1994), p. 158.

21. Ibid., p. 337.

22. See Tim Doody, "The Heretic," *Morning News* (July 26, 2012). http://www.themorningnews.org/article/the-heretic.

23. James Fadiman, *The Psychedelic Explorer's Guide: Safe, Therapeutic, and Sacred Journeys* (Rochester, VT: Park Street Press, 2011).

24. Doody, "The Heretic."

25. Lewis Lapham, in *Lapham's Quarterly* (Winter 2013), p. 18.

26. Ibid.

27. See Sven Birkerts in *Lapham's Quarterly* (Winter 2013).

28. Tom Freiling, *Cocaine Nation* (New York: Pegasus Books, 2009), p. 277.

29. Ibid., p. 282.

30. See www.drugwarfacts.org/cms/Drug_Usage.

31. Ibid.

32. Ibid., p. 283.

33. Henry Giroux, "Violence USA," *Monthly Review* (May 2013), p. 42.

34. Ibid.

35. See Dessa K. Bergen-Cico, *War and Drugs: The Role of Military Conflict in the Development of Substance Abuse* (Boulder, CO: Paradigm Publishers, 2012).

Chapter 1

1. *Los Angeles Times* (September 17, 2011).

2. Ibid.

3. See www.imshealth.com/deployedfiles/imshealth/Global/Content/Technology/Syndicated%20Analytics/Market%20Measurement/IMS_World_Review.pdf for US drug-consumption data.

4. See www.DrugWarFacts.org.

5. Mike Jay, *High Society: The Central Role of Mind-Altering Drugs in History, Science, and Culture* (Rochester, VT: Park Street Press, 2010), p. 10.

6. Andrew Weil, *The Natural Mind: A Revolutionary Approach to the Drug Problem* (Boston: Houghton Mifflin, 2004), p. 9.

7. Jay, *High Society*, p. 54.

Notes 221

8. See Ronald K. Siegel, *Intoxication: The Universal Drive for Mind-Altering Substances* (Rochester, VT: Park Street Press, 2005), p. 206.

9. Ibid., p. 208.

10. Neal Goldsmith, *Psychedelic Healing: The Promise of Entheogens for Psychotherapy and Spiritual Development* (Rochester, VT: Park Street Press, 2011), pp. 94–97.

11. Ibid., p. 121.

12. Cited in Andrew Weil, *From Chocolate to Morphine* (Boston: Houghton Mifflin, 2004), p. 244, where Weil interviews a seventy-year-old psychologist.

13. On the human capacity to contain or manage addiction, see Stanton Peele, *Diseasing of America: How We Allowed Recovery Zealots and the Treatment Industry to Convince Us We Are Out of Control* (Lexington, MA: Lexington Books, 1989), ch. 7.

14. See www.drugabuse.gov/sites/default/files/drugfactsnationwidetrends.pdf (January 2014).

15. Ibid.

16. Jay, *High Society*, pp. 127–128.

17. Ibid., pp. 71–72.

18. Ibid., p. 77.

19. See Peter Andreas, *Smuggler Nation: How Illicit Trade Made America* (Rochester, VT: Park Street Press, 2010).

20. Ibid., p. xi.

21. Ibid., p. 13.

22. Ibid., p. 184.

23. On the great failure of Prohibition, see Edward Behr, *Prohibition: Thirteen Years That Changed America* (New York: Arcade Publishing, 1996), ch. 12.

24. See Theodore Roszak, *The Making of a Counter Culture* (Berkeley: University of California Press, 1968), p. 155.

25. See www.imshealth.com/deployedfiles/imshealth/Global/Content/Technology /Syndicated%20Analytics/Market%20Measurement/IMS_World_Review.pdf for US drug-consumption data.

26. For the Pfizer data, see www.cnbc.com/id/100413694; for AstraZeneca data, see www.fiercepharmamarketing.com.

27. Sidney Wolfe et al., *Worst Pills, Best Pills: A Consumer's Guide to Avoiding Drug-Induced Death or Illness* (New York: Pocket Books, 2005), pp. xxiii–xxv.

28. See Kathryn Stone, "The Over-the-Counter Drug Industry," cited in http:// pharma.about.com/od/Over-the-Counter-Medicine/a/The-Over-the-counter-Drug -Industry.htm.

29. See Karen Kaplan, "Death Toll from Alcohol Tallied," *Los Angeles Times* (February 22, 2014).

30. Reported for 2012 by the Centers for Disease Control and Prevention, www .cdc.gov/nchs/fastats/alcohol.htm.

31. On US cigarette consumption, see www.cdc.gov/tobacco/data_statistics/ (2012).

32. See www.rand.org/news/press/2014/03/10.html.

222 NOTES

33. See www.businessweek.com/debateroom/archives/2010/03/legalize_mariju
.html.

34. Estimates on the value of marijuana as a cash crop in California vary immensely. According to the Marijuana Policy Project, the figure for 2012 was $14 billion.

35. On prohibitionist ideology, see Behr, *Prohibition*, ch. 2.

36. The prohibitionist link to anti-German sentiment is explored in ibid., pp. 60, 71.

37. Mike Gray, *Drug Crazy* (New York: Random House, 1998), p. 17.

38. See Behr, *Prohibition*, ch. 1.

39. See Jeffrey Miron, *Drug War Crimes: The Consequences of Prohibition* (Oakland, CA: Independent Institute, 2004), pp. 8–12.

40. Ibid., pp. 10–12.

41. On "reefer madness" and the Harry Anslinger crusade, see David F. Musto, *The American Disease: Origins of Narcotic Control* (New York: Oxford University Press, 1999), pp. 219–229.

42. Miron, *Drug War Crimes*, p. 38.

43. See Moisés Naim, *Illicit* (New York: Anchor Books, 2005), p. 2.

44. See Steven Brill, "Bitter Pill: Why Medical Bills Are Killing Us," *Time* magazine (April 4, 2013) for a lengthy discussion. http://time.com/198/bitter-pill -why-medical-bills-are-killing-us/.

45. See www.DrugWarFacts.org (2010).

46. Gray, *Drug Crazy*, p. 94.

47. *Los Angeles Times* (November 18, 2011).

48. On the national culture of fear as it influences social and foreign policy, see Tom Engelhardt, *The United States of Fear* (Chicago: Haymarket Books, 2011), chs. 1 and 6.

49. Ziauddin Sardar and Merryl Wyn Davies, *Why Do People Hate America?* (New York: Disinformation, 2002), p. 21.

50. Ibid., p. 29.

51. Ibid., p. 48.

52. *Los Angeles Times* (June 3, 2012).

53. See Gray, *Drug Crazy*, p. 100.

54. See www.drugfree.org.

55. On the growth of authoritarian politics generally in the United States across recent decades, see Carl Boggs, *Phantom Democracy: Corporate Interests and Political Power* (New York: Palgrave, 2011).

56. C. Wright Mills, *The Power Elite* (New York: Oxford University Press, 1956), ch. 1.

Chapter 2

1. On the early history of prohibition and antidrug warfare, see David F. Musto, *The American Disease: Origins of Narcotic Control* (New York: Oxford University Press, 1999), chs. 1, 3.

NOTES 223

2. Mike Gray, *Drug Crazy* (New York: Random House, 1999), chs. 9 and 10. See also Dan Baum, *Smoke and Mirrors: The War on Drugs and the Politics of Failure* (Boston: Little, Brown, and Co., 1997); and Arthur Benavie, *Drugs: America's Holy War* (New York: Routledge, 2009), ch. 2.

3. See Mike Jay, *High Society: The Central Role of Mind-Altering Drugs in History, Science, and Culture* (Rochester, VT: Park Street Press, 2010), pp. 158–171.

4. This is the central motif of Edward J. Epstein's *Agency of Fear: Opiates and Political Power in America* (London: Verso, 1990). See also Tom Engelhardt, *The United States of Fear* (Chicago: Haymarket Books, 2011), ch. 1.

5. For an excellent overview of early drug-war ideology, see Benavie, *Drugs*, ch. 2.

6. Musto, *The American Disease*, p. 5.

7. On the linkage of drug warfare and racism in American society, see Michelle Alexander, *The New Jim Crow: Mass Incarceration in the Age of Colorblindness* (New York: The New Press, 2012), introduction.

8. See Gray, *Drug Crazy*, chs. 4 and 5.

9. Steven Wisotsky, *Beyond the War on Drugs: Overcoming a Failed Public Policy* (Buffalo, NY: Prometheus Books, 1990), p. 201.

10. Baum, *Smoke and Mirrors*, p. 72.

11. Ibid., p. 165.

12. Ibid., pp. 203–205.

13. Alexander, *The New Jim Crow*, p. 98.

14. Ibid., p. 7.

15. See the National Survey on Drug Use and Health at https://nsduhweb.rti.org /respweb/homepage.cfm.

16. Benavie, *Drugs*, p. 68.

17. Alexander, *The New Jim Crow*, pp. 93–96.

18. Ibid., introduction.

19. Ibid., p. 12.

20. Benavie, *Drugs*, p. 4.

21. Edward Behr, *Prohibition: Thirteen Years That Changed America* (New York: Arcade, 1996), ch. 12.

22. Ibid., ch. 16.

23. See Musto, *The American Disease*, ch. 11.

24. Ibid., p. 222.

25. Gray, *Drug Crazy*, p. 78.

26. Ibid., p. 84.

27. Musto, *The American Disease*, p. 242.

28. Epstein, *Agency of Fear*, ch. 1.

29. Baum, *Smoke and Mirrors*, p. 72.

30. Ibid., p. 152.

31. Musto, *The America Disease*, pp. 265–267.

32. For Bennett's fanatical approach to drugs, see William J. Bennett, John J. Dilulio

224 NOTES

Jr., and John P. Walters, *Body Count: Moral Poverty . . . And How to Win America's War against Crime and Drugs* (New York: Simon and Schuster, 1996).

33. Cited in Baum, *Smoke and Mirrors*, p. 264.

34. See the critique of Bennett set forth by Benavie in *Drugs*, pp. 88–90.

35. Bennett, Dilulio, and Walters, *Body Count*, chs. 1 and 2.

36. Cited in Baum, *Smoke and Mirrors*, p. 334.

37. Jeffrey Miron, *Drug War Crimes: The Consequences of Prohibition* (Oakland, CA: Independent Institute, 2004), ch. 2.

38. Carl Elliott, "Making a Killing," *Mother Jones* (September/October 2010), pp. 78–82.

39. On the manufacture of synthetic cannabis—one example being Marinol—by Big Pharma, and its suffering by comparison to natural cannabis, see Martin A. Lee, *Smoke Signals* (New York: Scribner's, 2012), pp. 169–170.

40. Gray, *Drug Crazy*, p. 75.

41. Ibid.

42. Ibid.

43. On the exaggerated dangers of marijuana use, both short-term and long-term (including supposed links to cancer), see the website Partnership for Drug-Free Kids, at www.drugfree.org/drug-guide/marijuana (2012).

44. John Stuart Mill, "On Liberty," in Mill, *Utilitarianism on Liberty, Essay on Bentham* (New York: World Publishing, 1962), pp. 205–225.

45. See Ronald K. Siegel, *Intoxication: The Universal Drive for Mind-Altering Substances* (Rochester, VT: Park Street Press, 2005).

46. On the McDonaldized food regimen in the United States, see George Ritzer, *The McDonaldization of Society* (Thousand Oaks, CA: Pine Forge Press, 2000) and Eric Schlosser, *Fast Food Nation: The Dark Side of the All-American Meal* (Boston: Houghton Mifflin, 2001).

47. For obesity data, see www.epidemicobesity.com/statistics/html.

48. On growth in popularity of the McDonald's brand, see Schlosser, *Fast Food Nation*, pp. 49–51.

49. See Barry Popkin, *The World Is Fat: The Fads, Trends, Policies, and Products That Are Fattening the Human Race* (New York: Avery, 2009), ch. 6.

50. Nancy Appleton and G. N. Jacobs, *Suicide by Sugar: A Startling Look at Our #1 National Addiction* (Garden City Park, NJ: Square One, 2009), pp. 92–99.

51. On the power of the sugar lobby, see Popkin, *The World Is Fat*, ch. 6, and Appleton and Jacobs, chs. 1–3.

52. Wisotsky, *Beyond the War on Drugs*, p. 214.

53. Norm Stamper, "Drug Warrior No More," *YES!* (June 3, 2011). www.yesmagazine.org/issues/beyond-prisons/drug-warrior-no-more.

Notes 225

Chapter 3

1. A short version of the United Nations World Drug Report 2012 (released June 2, 2012) is available at www.globalcommissionondrugs.org. It is this version, referred to as "the UN report," that is cited throughout this chapter. The full report is available at www.unodc.org/unodc/data-and-analysis/WDR-2012.html.

2. Ibid., pp. 1–4.

3. Ibid., pp. 9–10.

4. Ibid., p. 12.

5. Ibid., p. 6.

6. Ibid., p. 13.

7. Ibid., p. 3.

8. Ibid., p. 8.

9. Ibid., p. 5.

10. Ibid.

11. Ibid., p. 15.

12. Ibid., pp. 14–15.

13. Ibid., p. 15.

14. Ibid., p. 16.

15. Ibid., p. 9.

16. Ibid., p. 4.

17. Ibid., p. 11.

18. Ibid.

19. Ibid., p. 15.

20. Ibid., p. 13.

21. Ibid.

22. Ibid., p. 4.

23. Ibid., p. 8.

24. Ibid., p. 13.

25. Ibid., p. 14.

26. Ibid.

27. Ibid., p. 16.

28. Ibid.

29. Ibid.

30. Ibid., p. 15.

31. Ibid., p. 11.

32. Ibid., p. 17.

33. Ibid.

34. Ibid., p. 5.

35. Ibid., p. 17.

36. Ibid.

226 NOTES

37. Caitlin Elizabeth Hughes and Alex Stevens, "A Resounding Success of a Disastrous Failure: Re-examining the Interpretation of Evidence on the Portuguese Decriminalization of Illicit Drugs," *Drug and Alcohol Review* (January 2012), pp. 101–113. This article shows how most criticisms of liberalized drug policies in nations like Portugal are biased and simplistic.

38. Responding to the UN report, Rafael Lemaitre, communications director of the Office of National Drug Control Policy, said that making any illegal drug more available would simply make American communities less healthy and safe. In response to the UN report, Lemaitre offered a "third way" in drug policy—between continued outright warfare and full-scale legalization. See www.whitehouse.gov/ondcp/news-releases-remarks /statement-lemaitre-directors-visit-guatemala.

39. For Obama's response here, see the interview with Barbara Walters for ABC News (December 14, 2012), at http://abcnews.go.com/Politics/OTUS/president -obama-marijuana-users-high-priority-drug-war/story?id=17946783.

40. *Time* (June 2, 2011).

41. For President Obama's views on pot here, see http://marijuana.com/news /2014/01/president-obama-marijuana-less-dangerous-than-alcohol-legalization-in -wa-and-co-important/.

42. Michelle Alexander, "Obama's Drug War," *The Nation* (December 27, 2010), p. 26.

43. See Obama's interview with Barbara Walters at http://abcnews.go.com/Politics /OTUS/president-obama-marijuana-users-high-priority-drug-war/story?id=17946783.

44. Reported in *Daily Mail* Online (May 10, 2012).

Chapter 4

1. See Edward Behr, *Prohibition: Thirteen Years That Changed America* (New York: Arcade, 1996), chs. 12–14.

2. On Nixon's antidrug initiatives, see Dan Baum, *Smoke and Mirrors: The War on Drugs and the Politics of Failure* (Boston: Little, Brown, and Co.), chs. 1–4.

3. See Joel Dyer, *The Perpetual Prisoner Machine: How America Profits from Crime* (Boulder, CO: Westview Press, 2000), p. 178.

4. On President Clinton's antidrug policies, see Steven Wisotsky, *Beyond the War on Drugs: Overcoming a Failed Public Policy* (Buffalo, NY: Prometheus Books, 1990), pp. 126–127.

5. Dyer, *The Perpetual Prisoner Machine*, pp. 182–183.

6. Wisotsky, *Beyond the War on Drugs*, p. 125.

7. On the linkage between a militarized foreign policy and growing domestic violence in the United States, see Henry Giroux, "Violence USA," *Monthly Review* (May 2013), pp. 37–54.

Notes 227

8. An excellent treatment of the rise of the national-security state in post-WWII US history is Garry Wills, *Bomb Power: The Modern Presidency and the National Security State* (New York: Penguin, 2010), chs. 4–6.

9. For an extensive discussion of the harsh penal consequences of the antidrug crusade, see Michelle Alexander, *The New Jim Crow: Mass Incarceration in the Age of Colorblindness* (New York: The New Press, 2010), ch. 2.

10. On the impact of forfeiture laws in drug cases, see Martin A. Lee, *Smoke Signals: A Social History of Marijuana—Medical, Recreational and Scientific* (New York: Scribner, 2012), pp. 160–161, 205–206.

11. On sentencing for marijuana offenses particularly, see Eric Schlosser, *Reefer Madness* (Boston: Houghton Mifflin, 2003), pp. 42–48 especially.

12. See Lee, *Smoke Signals*, pp. 160–162.

13. Schlosser, *Reefer Madness*, pp. 26–29.

14. On the federal move toward a drug-free workplace, see ibid., p. 50.

15. Isabel Macdonald, "The GOP's Drug-Testing Dragnet," *The Nation* (April 22, 2013), www.thenation.com/article/173654/gops-drug-testing-dragnet.

16. See The Daily Take Team, "It's Time to End All Drug Testing," *Truthout* (March 12, 2014). See www.truth-out.org/opinion/item/22434-its-time-to-end-all-drug-testing.

17. The Supreme Court has been a particular offender of individual rights. See, among others, Lee, *Smoke Signals*, pp. 160–161.

18. Mattelart refers to the "globalization of surveillance." See Armand Mattelart, *The Globalization of Surveillance* (Cambridge, MA: Polity Press, 2007).

19. Ray Pratt, *Projecting Paranoia: Conspiratorial Visions in American Film* (Lawrence, KS: University Press of Kansas, 2001), p. 26.

20. Ibid., pp. 235–237.

21. On the DEA modus operandi, see Alexander, *The New Jim Crow*, pp. 70–72.

22. Ibid., p. 61.

23. Ibid., p. 67.

24. See Maureen Webb, *Illusions of Security* (San Francisco: City Lights Books, 2007), ch. 8.

25. Nick Turse, *The Complex: How the Military Invades Our Everyday Lives* (New York: Henry Holt and Co., 2008), p. 270.

26. Ibid., pp. 262–263.

27. On the sharing of accumulated data by federal agencies, see James Bamford, *The Shadow Factory: The Ultra-Secret NSA from 9/11 to the Eavesdropping on America* (New York: Doubleday, 2008), pp. 331–345.

28. See Nancy Chang, *Silencing Political Dissent: How Post–September 11 Anti-Terrorism Measures Threaten Our Civil Liberties* (New York: Seven Stories, 2002), pp. 43–46.

29. James Bamford, *Body of Secrets: Anatomy of the Ultra-Secret National Security Agency* (New York: Anchor Books, 2002), p. 650.

228 NOTES

30. On heightened *domestic* surveillance activities by federal agencies, including the NSA, see Alfred W. McCoy, "Obama's Expanding Surveillance Universe," Tom Dispatch.com, www.tomdispatch.com/blog/175724/ (July 14, 2013). See also Kate Epstein, "Total Surveillance," *CounterPunch* (June 28, 2013), www.counterpunch.org/2013/06/28/total-surveillance/.

31. *Los Angeles Times* (August 1, 2013).

32. *Los Angeles Times* (August 17, 2013).

33. On government tracking of personal electronic transactions, see Webb, *Illusions of Security*, chs. 6–9.

34. See Drug War Chronicle at http://stopthedrugwar.org/chronicle.

35. On the DEA's heavy-handed tactics over the years, see Alexander, *The New Jim Crow*, pp. 80–84.

36. John Shiffman, Reuters (August 11, 2013). Shiffman provided a full airing of his views during an interview by Amy Goodman (August 6, 2013). See www.democracynow.org/2013/8/6/a_domestic_surveillance_scandal_at_the.

37. Ibid.

38. For an extensive general treatment of drone use in surveillance, see Medea Benjamin, *Drone Warfare: Killing by Remote Control* (New York: ORBooks, 2012), pp. 55–81.

39. www.faa.gov/news/fact_sheets/news_story.cfm?newsId=14153.

40. On the expansion of drone technology, including its use on US borders with Mexico and in the drug war, see "Emerging Drone Culture," *Miami Herald* (August 6, 2012), and Ryan Gallagher, "Mexico Turns to Surveillance Technology to Help Fight the Drug War," *Slate* (August 3, 2012). www.slate.com/blogs/future_tense/2012/08/03/surveillance_technology_in_mexico_s_drug_war_.html. On the three basic types of drones being made available to law enforcement—mini, tactical, and strategic—see Asawin Suebsaeng, "Drones: Everything You Ever Wanted to Know but Were Always Afraid to Ask," *Mother Jones* (March 5, 2013).

41. Benjamin, *Drone Warfare*, p. 33.

42. Christian Parenti, *The Soft Cage: Surveillance in America from Slavery to the War on Terror* (New York: Basic Books, 2003).

43. Alfred W. McCoy, "Surveillance Blowback," *Nation* (July 16, 2013). www.thenation.com/article/175280/surveillance-blowback.

44. On the threat of domestic surveillance activities to democratic politics, see Webb, *Illusions of Security*, ch. 13. See also Norman Pollack, "Obama's Fanaticism over Secrecy: Surveillance and Repression," *CounterPunch* (July 27, 2013), www.counterpunch.org/2013/07/24/obamas-fanaticism-over-secrecy-surveillance-and-repression/.

45. *Los Angeles Times* (October 25, 2013).

46. See Julia Angwin, *Dragnet Nation: A Quest for Privacy, Security, and Freedom in a World of Relentless Surveillance* (New York: Times Books, 2014).

47. On the worsening situation under Obama, See Pollack, "Obama's Fanaticism over Secrecy," and Epstein, "Total Surveillance."

Notes   229

48. See Get the Facts, "Crime, Arrests, and US Law Enforcement," at www.drug warfacts.org/cms/crime.

49. On the US drive toward criminalization of petty offenses, especially directed against people of color, see Alexander, *The New Jim Crow*, introduction.

50. Dyer, *The Perpetual Prisoner Machine*, p. 142.

51. Ibid., p. 182.

52. On the state of American prisons, see Shane Bauer, "Solitary in Iran Nearly Broke Me. Then I Went Inside America's Prisons," *Mother Jones* (November–December 2012). www.motherjones.com/politics/2012/10/solitary-confinement-shane-bauer.

53. Christian Parenti, *Lockdown America: Police and Prisons in the Age of Crisis* (London: Verso, 2008), pp. 67–68.

54. Ibid., p. 241.

55. Alexander, *The New Jim Crow*, pp. 58–61.

56. Ibid., p. 89.

57. Ibid., p. 94.

58. On the systematic use of drugs on prisoners, see Lisa M. Hammond, "Drug War Policy and the Prison-Industrial Complex," Terri Gorski's Blog (2013), http://terrygorski .com/2014/07/29/drug-war-policy-and-the-prison-industrial-complex/.

59. C. Wright Mills, *The Power Elite* (New York: Oxford University Press, 1956), ch. 1.

Chapter 5

1. Ziauddin Sardar and Merryl Wyn Davies, *Why Do People Hate America?* (New York: Disinformation, 2002), p. 59.

2. On the consequences of prohibition for crime, violence, and corruption, see Jeffrey Miron, *Drug War Crimes: The Consequences of Prohibition* (Oakland, CA: Independent Institute, 2004), ch. 4.

3. For an excellent historical overview of global drug trades, see Mike Jay, *High Society: The Central Role of Mind-Altering Drugs in History, Science, and Culture* (Rochester, VT: Park Street Press, 2010), pp. 108–167.

4. Ibid., p. 148.

5. See Moisés Naim, *Illicit: How Smugglers, Traffickers, and Copycats Are Hijacking the Global Economy* (New York: Anchor Books, 2005), p. 2.

6. Ibid., p. 22.

7. Ibid., p. 265.

8. Peter Andreas, *Smuggler Nation: How Illicit Trade Made America* (New York: Oxford University Press, 2013), p. 351.

9. According to the 2014 World Drug Report issued by the United Nations, an estimated 167 to 315 million people worldwide between the ages of fifteen and sixty-four had used illegal drugs in 2011—as much as 6.9 percent of the adult population.

230 NOTES

The report emphasized that such usage has remained more or less stable across the past several years. See www.unodc.org/wdr2014/.

10. For the White House statement, see www.cadca.org/resources/detail/white-houseresponds.

11. On President Obama's drug policy, see Michelle Alexander, "Obama's Drug War," *The Nation* (December 27, 2010). www.thenation.com/article/156997/obamas-drug-war.

12. See Anabel Hernández, interview by Nick Alexandrov in *CounterPunch* (May 16, 2014). www.counterpunch.org/2014/05/16/a-war-on-drugs-would-be-a-good-idea/#.U3Z5Z-UYJTB.twitter.

13. Ioan Grillo, *El Narco: Inside Mexico's Criminal Insurgency* (New York: Bloomsbury Press, 2011), p. 5.

14. Ibid., p. 138.

15. On the tight connection between the criminal underground and elements of the power structure in Mexico, see Anabel Hernández, *Narcoland: The Mexican Drug Lords and Their Godfathers* (London: Verso, 2013), especially ch. 1.

16. Whatever political grouping rules Mexico, the cartel-based killings continue at a gruesome pace. The number of murders spanning December 1, 2012, and April 1, 2013, was 4,249, with no signs of letup. See www.borderlandbeat.com/2013.

17. One of the most gripping accounts of the narco wars in Mexico is Howard Campbell's *Drug War Zone: Frontline Dispatches from the Streets of El Paso and Juárez* (Austin: University of Texas Press, 2009), p. 6.

18. Ibid., introduction.

19. On the great resiliency and capacity to adapt of the Mexican cartels, see Grillo, *El Narco*, chs. 14 and 15.

20. See Campbell, *Drug War Zone*, pp. 97–105.

21. On the role of the CIA in post-WWII drug trafficking, see Alexander Cockburn and Jeffrey St. Clair, *Whiteout: The CIA, Drugs, and the Press* (London: Verso, 1998), chs. 4, 9, and 12.

22. Fariba Nawa, *Opium Nation: Child Brides, Drug Lords, and One Woman's Journey through Afghanistan* (New York: Harper Perennial, 2011), p. 35.

23. Ibid., p. 100.

24. Ibid., ch. 9.

25. Ibid., pp. 142–144. The Afghan opium markets reap as much as $400 million yearly.

26. Ibid., p. 144.

27. Ibid., p. 199.

28. Ibid., ch. 6.

29. Ibid., pp. 223–224.

30. Ibid., p. 243.

31. Cockburn and St. Clair, *Whiteout*, p. 260.

32. Ibid., pp. 267–270.

33. See Naim, *Illicit*, ch. 4.

34. Jay, *High Society*, p. 128.

35. On lawlessness generated by prohibition, see Edward Behr, *Prohibition: Thirteen Years That Changed America* (New York: Arcade, 1996), chs. 12, 13.

36. Mike Gray, *Drug Crazy* (New York: Random House, 1998), p. 17.

37. Behr, *Prohibition*, chs. 10 and 11.

38. Ibid., p. 95.

39. Ibid., pp. 133–134.

40. Jay, *High Society*, pp. 164–165.

41. See Eric Hobsbawm, *Primitive Rebels* (New York: W. W. Norton and Co., 1959), pp. 43–47.

42. Ibid., p. 56.

43. Ibid., p. 47.

44. Ibid., p. 33.

45. Ibid., p. 38.

46. Cockburn and St. Clair, *Whiteout*, p. 359.

47. On the role of local gangs, see Grillo, *El Narco*, pp. 164–166.

48. Ibid., p. 261.

49. On the globalization of drug smuggling, see Naim, *Illicit*, ch. 2.

50. *Los Angeles Times* (September 28, 2012).

51. On the oligopolistic character of organized crime in Mexico, see Grillo, *El Narco*, chs. 4 and 5.

52. David Rothkopf, *Superclass: The Global Power Elite and the World They Are Making* (New York: Farrar, Strauss, and Giroux, 2008), pp. 34–36.

53. On the Hobbesian features of drug-war zones, see Campbell, *Drug War Zone*, pp. 30–33. These features are often limited through the convergence of syndicate and established leadership.

54. On the development of *maquiladora* economic activity in the border regions of Mexico, which has taken off in recent years (amounting to $324 billion in exports in 2013). See www.abqjournal.com/179611/biz/nm-enjoying-boom-in-crossborder -trade.html.

55. Nelson Lichtenstein, *The Retail Revolution: How Wal-Mart Created a Brave New World of Business* (New York: Henry Holt and Co., 2009).

56. See Ethan Rome, "Big Pharma Pockets $711 Billion in Profits by Robbing Seniors, Taxpayers," *Huffington Post* (April 8, 2013). www.huffingtonpost.com/ethan-rome /big-pharma-pockets-711-bi_b_3034525.html.

57. *Los Angeles Times* (October 11, 2012).

58. Donald L. Bartlett and James B. Steele, *Critical Condition: How Health Care in America Became Big Business—and Bad Medicine* (New York: Doubleday, 2004), p. 158.

59. On the topic of adverse reactions to prescription drugs, see Sidney Wolfe et al., *Worst Pills, Best Pills* (New York: Pocket Books, 2005), pp. xxii–xxvii.

232   NOTES

60. The 2008 Mérida Initiative, often referred to as Plan Mexico, was eventually meant to extend to Central America as well. See the US Department of State, http://www.state.gov/j/inl/merida/.

61. See Paul Rexton Kan, *Drugs and Contemporary Warfare* (Washington: Potomac Books, 2009), ch. 1.

62. Ibid., p. 118.

63. Ibid., pp. 107–109.

64. See the excellent account of drug warfare in Mexico in Cecilia Ballí, "Calderón's War," *Harper's* (January 2012). http://harpers.org/archive/2012/01/calderons-war/.

65. Ibid., pp. 34–35.

66. On Governor Rick Perry's stance on drugs related to border issues, see On the Issues, "Rick Perry on Drugs," www.ontheissues.org/governor/Rick_Perry_Drugs.htm.

67. On the merger of counternarcotics operations and general US foreign policy objectives, see Peter Dale Scott, *Drugs, Oil, and War: The United States in Afghanistan, Colombia, and Indochina* (Lanham, MD: Rowman and Littlefield, 2003), introduction.

68. Ibid., pp. 70–75.

69. On Plan Colombia, see Kan, *Drugs and Contemporary Warfare*, pp. 86 and 108, and Scott, *Drugs, Oil, and War*, pp. 97–102.

70. See Scott, *Drugs, Oil, and War*, chs. 4 and 5.

71. On human-rights violations in drug warfare, see Kan, *Drugs and Contemporary Warfare*, pp. 42–43, 96–97.

72. *Los Angeles Times* (October 16, 2012).

73. See Dawn Paley, "Off the Map in Mexico," *The Nation* (May 23, 2011). www.thenation.com/article/160436/map-mexico.

74. On revelations that the National Security Agency had become deeply involved in surveillance of cartel activity in Mexico, see Stewart M. Powell, "NSA Keeps Its Eyes and Ears Turned Toward Latin America," *San Antonio Express-News* (June 29, 2013), www.expressnews.com/news/local/article/NSA-keeps-its-eyes-and-ears-turned-toward-Latin-4637904.php.

75. *Los Angeles Times* (February 23, 2014).

76. *Los Angeles Times* (July 31, 2012).

77. Scott, *Drugs, Oil, and War*, chs. 2, 4, 5.

78. Nawa, *Opium Nation*, ch. 16.

79. Scott, *Drugs, Oil, and War*, ch. 7.

80. See Gary Webb, *Dark Alliance: The CIA, the Contras, and the Crack Cocaine Explosion* (New York: Seven Stories Press, 1998), ch. 5. See also the excellent account of the Webb story in Cockburn and St. Clair, *Whiteout*, ch. 1.

81. Cockburn and St. Clair, *Whiteout*, ch. 12.

82. Ibid., chs. 9–11.

83. Webb, *Dark Alliance*, pp. 154–155.

84. Ibid., p. 184.

85. Ibid., p. 175.

86. Tom Engelhardt, "An America Eternally 'at War,'" *Los Angeles Times* (October 9, 2012). http://articles.latimes.com/2012/oct/09/opinion/la-oe-engelhardt-military-spending-20121009.

87. On drug use in military combat, see Kan, *Drugs and Contemporary Warfare*, ch. 3.

88. For an excellent overview of the problem of drugs in the US military, especially under combat conditions, see Dessa K. Bergen-Cico, *War and Drugs: The Role of Military Conflict in the Development of Substance Abuse* (Boulder, CO: Paradigm Publishers, 2012). See also Kan, *Drugs and Contemporary Warfare*, chs. 2 and 3.

89. On drug use in Vietnam, see James William Gibson, *The Perfect War: Technowar in Vietnam* (New York: Atlantic Monthly Press, 1986), pp. 262–268. Some reports indicated that perhaps 50 percent of US military personnel in Vietnam smoked pot in a given year.

90. Ibid., pp. 222–223.

91. On CIA involvement in the drug trade in Vietnam and beyond, see Alfred McCoy, *The Politics of Heroin in Southeast Asia* (New York: Harper and Row, 1972).

92. On the capacity of Vietnam veterans to mature out of their drug addictions, see Stanton Peele, *Diseasing of America: How We Allowed Recovery Zealots and the Treatment Industry to Convince Us We Are Out of Control* (Lexington, MA: Lexington Books, 1989), pp. 149–150.

93. *New York Times* (October 14, 2010).

94. Research has shown that widely prescribed psychotropic drugs, mostly antidepressants, are responsible for up to ten times the number of violent episodes of other pharmaceuticals. See Gary G. Kohls, "Many Psychotropic Drugs Are Strongly Associated with Violence," *Duluth Reader* (April 5, 2012).

95. *Los Angeles Times* (April 3, 2012).

96. Gary Null, Martin Feldman, Debora Rasio, and Carolyn Dean, *Death by Medicine* (Mount Jackson, VA: Praktikos Books, 2011), pp. 23–24.

97. See Peele, *Diseasing of America*, pp. 255–256.

Chapter 6

1. Mike Jay, *High Society: The Central Role of Mind-Altering Drugs in History, Science, and Culture* (Rochester, VT: Park Street Press, 2010), p. 10.

2. www.cancer.org/research/cancerfactsstatistics/cancerfactsfigures2014/.

3. By 2011 domestic pharmaceutical sales annually had reached $330 billion, accounting for roughly 40 percent of global sales. See www.statista.com/markets/412/topic/456/pharmaceutical-products-market/.

4. On the failed US corporate model of medicine, see Donald L. Bartlett and James B. Steele, *Critical Condition: How Health Care in America Became Big Business—And Bad Medicine* (New York: Doubleday, 2004), chs. 3–5.

234 NOTES

5. See John Abramson, *Overdosed America: The Broken Promise of American Medicine* (New York: HarperCollins, 2004).

6. Ivan Illich, *Medical Nemesis: The Expropriation of Health* (New York: Vintage, 1978) and Otis Webb Brawley, *How We Do Harm: A Doctor Breaks Ranks about Being Sick in America* (New York: St. Martin's, 2011).

7. Marcia Angell, *The Truth about the Drug Companies: How They Deceive Us and What to Do about It* (New York: Random House, 2004). See also Bartlett and Steele, *Critical Condition*.

8. E. Richard Brown, *Rockefeller Medicine Men: Medicine and Capitalism in America* (Berkeley: University of California Press, 1979), p. 8.

9. Ibid., p. 52.

10. On the critical Bayh-Dole Act and its consequences, see Angell, *The Truth about Drug Companies*, pp. 7–8, 68–72.

11. On the dramatic rise of biotechnology in the United States, see Peter Kennedy and Carole Ann Kennedy, *Health, Medicine, and Society* (Portland, OR: Policy Press, 2010), chs. 1 and 2.

12. See Harriet A. Washington, *Deadly Monopolies: The Shocking Corporate Takeover of Life Itself—And the Consequences for Your Health and Our Medical Future* (New York: Doubleday, 2011), ch. 4, and Abramson, *Overdosed America*, ch. 9.

13. Angell, *The Truth about Drug Companies*, p. 169.

14. See Bartlett and Steele, *Critical Condition*, ch. 5.

15. For an overview of easily available pain drugs, see Sidney M. Wolfe et al., *Worst Pills, Best Pills: A Consumer's Guide to Avoiding Drug-Induced Death or Illness* (New York: Pocket Books, 2005), pp. 279–287.

16. *Los Angeles Times* (March 2, 2012).

17. On serious problems with Celebrex, see Angell, *The Truth about Drug Companies*, pp. 108–109.

18. On the phenomenon of "pill tourism," see Matt Taibbi in *Rolling Stone* (February 24, 2005).

19. *Los Angeles Times* (March 26, 2013).

20. See Wolfe et al., *Worst Pills, Best Pills*, p. 10.

21. *Los Angeles Times* (February 7, 2005).

22. See Washington, *Deadly Monopolies*, ch. 4.

23. Wolfe et al., *Worst Pills, Best Pills*, p. xxiv.

24. Ibid., p. xxiii.

25. On the medical scandal that is HRT, see Abramson, *Overdosed America*, pp. 55–71.

26. Ibid., p. 97.

27. See Washington, *Deadly Monopolies*, pp. 149–154.

28. See the *Los Angeles Times* (October 1, 2014).

29. On problems with statins, see Wolfe et al., *Worst Pills, Best Pills*, pp. 109–116, and Abramson, *Overdosed America*, pp. 13–22.

30. Wolfe et al., *Worst Pills, Best Pills*, pp. 113–115.

NOTES   235

31. On the issue of obesity, see Abramson, *Overdosed America*, pp. 229–230.

32. On the corporate domination of medicine in the United States, see Bartlett and Steele, *Critical Condition*, ch. 2.

33. On Big Pharma lobbying power, see Angell, *The Truth about Drug Companies*, ch. 11, and T. Colin Campbell, *The China Study* (Dallas: BenBella Press, 2006), ch. 17.

34. The sprawling American medical empire is analyzed in Bartlett and Steele, *Critical Condition*, ch. 4.

35. For data on pharmaceutical sales, see www.statista.com/markets/412/topic/456/pharmaceutical-products-market/.

36. On Big Pharma spending for nonresearch priorities, see Angell, *The Truth about Drug Companies*, ch. 3.

37. Ibid., ch. 7.

38. Washington, *Deadly Monopolies*, p. 326.

39. Angell, *The Truth about Drug Companies*, p. 43.

40. Ibid., p. 66.

41. Washington, *Deadly Monopolies*, p. 269.

42. Ibid., p. 274.

43. Ibid., pp. 266–267.

44. Ibid., p. 268.

45. Angell, *The Truth about Drug Companies*, p. 201.

46. On the FDA Modernization Act of 1997, see ibid., pp. 203–204.

47. For a critique of the Medicare Reform Act of 2003, see Bartlett and Steele, *Critical Condition*, p. 70. They write that the measure "might more aptly be called the Pharmaceutical Company and Health Care Industry Welfare Act," p. 70.

48. Philip Selznick, *TVA and the Grassroots: A Study of Politics and Organization* (Berkeley: University of California Press, 1949).

49. Angell, *The Truth about Drug Companies*, pp. 210–211.

50. See Bartlett and Steele, *Critical Condition*, p. 66.

51. Wolfe et al., *Worst Pills, Best Pills*, p. 6.

52. Ibid., p. 6.

53. For an excellent overview of issues surrounding research on Vioxx, see Todd Zwillich, "How Vioxx Is Changing U.S. Drug Regulations," *Lancet* 366, no. 949 (2005).

54. On the Vioxx scandal, see Abramson, *Overdosed America*, pp. 33–38.

55. Wolfe et al., *Worst Pills, Best Pills*, p. 302.

56. Abramson, *Overdosed America*, pp. 25–37.

57. *New York Times* (February 22, 2005).

58. Donald L. Bartlett and James B. Steele, "Deadly Medicine," *Vanity Fair* (January 2011), p. 59.

59. Ibid., p. 63.

60. On Monsanto's aggressive lobbying efforts, see Washington, *Deadly Monopolies*, pp. 276–285.

61. Carl Elliott, "Making a Killing," *Mother Jones* (October 2010), p. 58.

236 NOTES

62. See the *Los Angeles Times* (July 19, 2014).

63. Celia Wexler, "Money Talks and What It Says May Hurt the FDA," *Union of Concerned Scientists Bulletin* (March 29, 2012).

64. *Los Angeles Times* (May 22, 2014).

65. *Los Angeles Times* (April 7, 2014).

66. Wolfe et al., *Worst Pills, Best Pills*, pp. 420–421.

67. For data on yearly cancer deaths in the United States, see www.cancer.org /research/cancerfactsstatistics/cancerfactsfigures2014/.

68. Ralph W. Moss, *The Cancer Industry* (New York: Equinox Press, 1996). Before writing his series of books dealing with the cancer industry, Moss worked as a researcher at Sloan Kettering Institute in New York City.

69. Ibid., chs. 17, 18.

70. Devra Davis, *The Secret History of the War on Cancer* (New York: Basic Books, 2007).

71. On the deep flaws of establishment cancer research, see Campbell, *The China Study*, chs. 3, 14.

72. See Davis, *The Secret History*, p. 4.

73. For a critique of Sloan Kettering, see Moss, *The Cancer Industry*, pp. 441–450.

74. See Campbell, *The China Study*, ch. 3.

75. John Robbins, *The Food Revolution: How Your Diet Can Help Save Your Life and Our World* (Berkeley: Conari Press, 2001), ch. 3.

76. Campbell, *The China Study*, pp. 163–164.

77. Robbins, *The Food Revolution*, pp. 37–38.

78. Campbell, *The China Study*, ch. 7.

79. Ibid., p. 258.

80. Ibid., pp. 261–264.

81. Ibid., p. 265.

82. Ibid., p. 312.

83. Moss, *The Cancer Industry*, pp. 82–88.

84. On severe problems—and fallacies—associated with chemotherapy treatments of cancer, see Gary Null, Martin Feldman, Debora Rasio, and Carolyn Dean, *Death by Medicine* (Mount Jackson, VA: Praktikos Books, 2011), pp. 82–88.

85. Moss, *The Cancer Industry*, p. 83.

86. Null et al., *Death by Medicine*, p. 159.

87. On the extensive and worrisome side effects, including secondary cancer episodes, resulting from these and related chemo agents, see www.cancer.net/survivorship.

88. Campbell, *The China Study*, p. 318.

89. Angell, *The Truth about Drug Companies*, p. 237.

90. See Bartlett and Steele, *Critical Condition*, ch. 5.

91. On the influence of Big Pharma within the Obama administration, see Peter Baker, "Obama Was Pushed by the Drug Industry," *New York Times* (June 8, 2012).

92. *Los Angeles Times* (August 16, 2010).

93. *Los Angeles Times* (November 17, 2009).

NOTES 237

94. *Los Angeles Times* (July 23, 2009).

95. On the soaring cost of medicine in the United States, see Steven Brill, "Bitter Pill: Why Medical Bills Are Killing Us," *Time* (April 4, 2013). http://time.com/198 /bitter-pill-why-medical-bills-are-killing-us/.

96. See Ethan Rome, "Big Pharma Pockets $711 Billion in Profits by Robbing Seniors, Taxpayers," *Huffington Post* (April 8, 2013). www.huffingtonpost.com/ethan-rome /big-pharma-pockets-711-bi_b_3034525.html.

97. See Ivan Illich et al., *Disabling Professions* (New York: Marion Boyars, 1987), pp. 14 and 17.

Chapter 7

1. On the motif of technological rationality as a form of ideological hegemony, see Antonio Gramsci, "Americanism and Fordism," in *Selections from the Prison Notebooks*, ed. Quintin Hoare and Geoffrey Nowell Smith (New York: International Publishers, 1971), pp. 271–318; Max Horkheimer and Theodor W. Adorno, *Dialectic of Enlightenment* (New York: Continuum, 1995), pp. 3–42; and Herbert Marcuse, *One-Dimensional Man* (Boston: Beacon Press, 1964), pp. 1–120.

2. See Ronald K. Siegel, *Intoxication: The Universal Drive for Mind-Altering Substances* (Rochester, VT: Park Street Press, 2005), and Andrew Weil, *Chocolate to Morphine: Everything You Need to Know about Mind-Altering Drugs* (Boston: Houghton Mifflin, 2004) and *The Natural Mind: A Revolutionary Approach to the Drug Problem* (Boston: Houghton Mifflin, 2004) for more in-depth, complex, and balanced treatments of the drug phenomenon than is usually available from mainstream sources.

3. On the Rockefeller-corporate origins of American medicine, see E. Richard Brown, *Rockefeller Medicine Men: Medicine and Capitalism in America* (Berkeley: University of California Press, 1979), ch. 3.

4. Horkheimer and Adorno, *Dialectic of Enlightenment,* p. 14.

5. Ibid., p. 20.

6. See George Ritzer, *The McDonaldization of Society* (Thousand Oaks, CA: Pine Forge Press, 2000). See also Eric Schlosser, *Fast Food Nation: The Dark Side of the All-American Meal* (Boston: Houghton Mifflin, 2001).

7. See Harriet A. Washington, *Deadly Monopolies: The Shocking Corporate Takeover of Life Itself—And the Consequences for Your Health and Our Medical Future* (New York: Doubleday, 2011), especially the introduction.

8. On the connection between the medicalization of society and approaches to addiction, see Stanton Peele, *The Diseasing of America: How We Allowed Recovery Zealots and the Treatment Industry to Convince Us We Are Out of Control* (Lexington, MA: Lexington Books, 1989), chs. 3 and 5.

9. On the phenomenon of iatrogenesis in American medicine, see Ivan Illich, *Medical Nemesis: The Expropriation of Health* (New York: Pantheon, 1976), and Otis Webb

238 NOTES

Brawley, *How We Do Harm: A Doctor Breaks Ranks about Being Sick in America* (New York: St. Martin's, 2011).

10. Gary Null, Martin Feldman, Debora Rasio, and Carolyn Dean, *Death by Medicine* (Mt. Jackson, VA: Praktikos Books, 2011), chs. 1–3.

11. See Steven Brill, "The High Cost of American Medicine," *Time* magazine (March 4, 2013), p. 20.

12. Ibid., p. 20.

13. Ibid., p. 49.

14. See www.opensecrets.org/orgs/list.php.

15. Ibid., p. 50.

16. Peele, *The Diseasing of America*, ch. 4.

17. Stanton Peele, *The Truth about Addiction and Recovery* (New York: Fireside, 1991), part 1. See also Jack Trimpey, *Rational Recovery: The New Cure for Substance Addiction* (New York: Pocket Books, 1996).

18. On the authoritarian implications of prevailing addiction theory, see Peele, *The Diseasing of America*, ch. 9, and Wendy Kaminer, *I'm Dysfunctional, You're Dysfunctional: The Recovery Movement and Other Self-Help Fashions* (New York: Vintage, 1993), conclusion.

19. For the NIDA statement on drug abuse and addiction, see www.drugabuse.gov /publications/drugfacts/understanding-drug-abuse-addiction.

20. See, for example, statements made by AddictionsAndRecovery.org, at www .addictionandrecovery.org/is-addiction-a-disease.htm.

21. *Diagnostic and Statistical Manual of Mental Disorders* (DSM-IV) (published by the American Psychiatric Association, 2000), pp. 210–114.

22. Ibid., p. 198.

23. For a penchant critique of the DSM approach, see Eugenia Tsao, "Inside the DSM: The Drug Barons' Campaign to Make Us All Crazy," *CounterPunch* (June 16–30, 2009). www.counterpunch.org/2009/08/20/the-drug-barons-campaign-to-make-us-all -crazy/.

24. DSM-IV, p. 200.

25. Ibid., p. 219.

26. On the capacity of humans to control and escape addiction, see Peele, *The Diseasing of America*, ch. 7.

27. Peele, *The Truth about Addiction*, p. 21.

28. According to the US Department of Health and Human Services, fewer than 10 percent of users of any drug wind up with severe addictions; see www.enterhealth .com/docs/FactSheet-AlcoholandDrugAddiction (2012). See also Stanton Peele, "The Deluded Mantras of Addiction," *Huffington Post* (October 11, 2012).

29. Peele, *The Truth about Addiction*, p. 76.

30. This point is thoroughly developed, with practical implications, in Trimpey, *Rational Recovery*, chs. 20 and 21.

31. On the dialectics of addictions and recovery, see Peele, *The Truth about Addiction*, part III.

NOTES **239**

32. For data on obesity rates in the United States, see reports of the Centers for Disease Control and Prevention, which have found that (in 2013) 35 percent of adults over age twenty in the United States are obese while 69 percent are classified as overweight. See www.cdc.gov/obesity/data/facts.html.

33. See Peele, *The Truth about Addiction*, p. 95.

34. *Los Angeles Times* (September 28, 2013).

35. On the dynamics of "Internet Addiction" disorder, described as an "impulse-control disorder," see information from the Illinois Institute for Addiction Recovery, at www.addictionrecov.org/internet.htm.

36. According to some research, no fewer than 43 percent of women and 31 percent of men report some type of sexual dysfunction. See https://my.clevelandclinic.org/health/diseases_conditions/hic_An_Overview_of_Sexual_Dysfunction.

37. On the iatrogenic dysfunctions of modern medicine, see Null et al., *Death by Medicine*, chs. 1–3.

38. On the evolution of obesity-inducing dietary patterns within the context of the food industry, see Schlosser, *Fast Food Nation*, chs. 5 and 9.

39. On the sordid history of beef production and consumption, see Jeremy Rifkin, *Beyond Beef: The Rise and Fall of the Cattle Culture* (New York: Penguin, 1992).

40. George Ritzer, *The McDonaldization of Society* (Thousand Oaks, CA: Pine Forge Press, 2000), ch. 9.

41. Barry Popkin, *The World Is Fat: The Fads, Trends, Policies, and Products That Are Fattening the Human Race* (New York: Penguin, 2010), p. 90.

42. T. Colin Campbell, *The China Study* (Dallas: BenBella Books, 2006), pp. 99–101. This work, the most scientifically comprehensive of its kind, explores nutritional patterns far beyond China itself.

43. Ibid., p. 110.

44. Wolfe et al., *Worst Pills, Best Pills*, p. 434.

45. Ibid., p. 431.

46. Ibid., p. 430.

47. Advertisement in *Star* magazine (September 2, 2013).

48. Ibid.

49. See the overview on drug sales by Megan Brooks, "Top 100 Selling Drugs of 2013," *Medscape* (January 30, 2014).

50. *Los Angeles Times* (November 19, 2013).

51. See John Abramson, *Overdosed America* (New York: HarperCollins, 2004), pp. 235–237.

52. Ibid., p. 222.

53. *Los Angeles Times* (February 21, 2013).

54. Campbell, *The China Study*, p. 124.

55. *Los Angeles Times* (June 19, 2013).

56. Cited in Peele, *The Diseasing of America*, p. 118.

57. Popkin, *The World Is Fat*, p. 162.

240 NOTES

58. Gina Kolata, *Rethinking Thin: The New Science of Weight Loss* (New York: Farrar, Strauss, and Giroux, 2007).

59. On the "low-carb" approach to weight loss, see Robert Atkins, *Dr. Atkins' New Diet Revolution* (New York: Avon Books, 2002), and John Mansfield, *The Six Secrets of Successful Weight Loss* (London: Hammersmith Heath Books, 2012).

60. Campbell, *The China Study*, p. 95.

61. For a critique of the Atkins diet and kindred programs, see ibid., pp. 95–102.

62. See David H. Freedman, "How Junk Food Can End Obesity," *Atlantic* (July/August, 2013). www.theatlantic.com/magazine/archive/2013/07/how-junk-food-can-end-obesity/309396/.

63. Peter Kennedy and Carole Ann Kennedy, *Health, Medicine, and Society* (Portland, OR: Policy Press, 2010), p. 110.

64. Null et al., *Death by Medicine*, p. 59.

65. According to Wolfe and associates, the yearly toll of adverse reactions to drugs is horrific: it includes 61,000 people with drug-induced parkinsonism, 16,000 with injuries from car crashes, 32,000 with hip fractures, and 41,000 hospitalizations resulting from anti-inflammatory drugs. See Wolfe et al., *Worst Pills, Best Pills*, p. xxii.

66. According to the National Center for Health Statistics, the rate of prescriptions for antidepressants in the United States skyrocketed by 400 percent from 1988 to 2008. See Peter Wehrwein, "Astounding Increase in Antidepressant Use by Americans," *Harvard Health Publication* (October 20, 2011).

67. Wolfe et al., *Worst Pills, Best Pills*, p. 484.

68. See *Guardian* (May 9, 2014).

69. Brown, *Rockefeller Medicine Men*, chs. 2 and 3.

70. Barbara Ehrenreich and Deirdre English, *For Her Own Good: Two Centuries of the Experts' Advice to Women* (New York: Anchor Books, 1979), pp. 71–73.

71. Ibid., p. 134.

72. Ibid., p. 102.

73. Trimpey, *Rational Recovery*, p. 308.

74. Ibid., p. 58.

75. Peele, *The Diseasing of America*, p. 223.

76. See Kaminer, *I'm Dysfunctional, You're Dysfunctional*, p. 6.

77. Ibid., p. 152.

Chapter 8

1. For an excellent overview on the closed nature of public discourse on drugs in the United States, see Arthur Benavie, *Drugs: America's Holy War* (New York: Routledge, 2009), especially pp. 8–20.

2. The website for Americans for Medical Rights shows no fewer than 105 peer-reviewed studies indicating the generally positive medical benefits—along with relatively

Notes   241

harmless effects—of cannabis in its different forms. Hundreds of other studies, reported in different venues, have largely validated these conclusions. See www.drugpolicy.org /doc1uploads/AMR (2009). See also assembled reports comparing the health effects of both marijuana and its synthetic equivalent, Marinol, at www.unitedpatientsgroup .com/resources (2012), and the discussion of marijuana versus Marinol in Martin A. Lee, *Smoke Signals: A Social History of Marijuana—Medical, Recreational and Scientific* (New York: Scribner, 2012), pp. 169–170.

3. On the familiar "gateway" myth, see Eric Schlosser, *Reefer Madness: Sex, Drugs, and Cheap Labor in the American Black Market* (Boston: Houghton Mifflin, 2004), pp. 14–16.

4. On the Anslinger crusade, see David F. Musto, *The American Disease: Origins of Narcotic Control* (New York: Oxford University Press, 1999), ch. 9.

5. On the 1972 Marijuana Commission Report, see Lee, *Smoke Signals*, pp. 121–122.

6. See Michelle Alexander, *The New Jim Crow: Mass Incarceration in the Age of Colorblindness* (New York: The New Press, 2012), pp. 53–54.

7. On the growth of the American prison complex, see Joel Dyer, *The Perpetual Prisoner Machine* (Boulder, CO: Westview Press, 2000), introduction, and Alexander, *The New Jim Crow*, ch. 2.

8. According to the 2013 Gallup survey cited previously, 38 percent of Americans over age twenty have tried marijuana—a pattern that has been fairly stable since the late 1980s.

9. On *recent* DEA aggressive tactics in tracking and arresting even casual drug users, see Alexander, *The New Jim Crow*, pp. 50–54.

10. Schlosser, *Reefer Madness*, p. 67.

11. Ibid., p. 74.

12. On the question of "amotivational syndrome," a supposed long-term effect of smoking pot hypothesized by most within the antidrug establishment, see www .rightdiagnosis.com/a/amotivational_syndrome/intro.htm for more information on the "syndrome" and its consequences.

13. For many reasons, no conclusive data regarding lethal episodes for particular drugs can be established. What is clear, however, is that year after year no deaths have been attributed to pot intake. For rough estimates, which presented (in 2010) 435,000 deaths from tobacco, 85,000 deaths from alcohol, 17,000 deaths from all illegal drugs combined, and *none* for marijuana, see www.drugwarfacts.org (2011).

14. For a comprehensive overview of studies on marijuana, which overwhelmingly point toward the relatively benign properties of the drug, see Lester Grinspoon and James B. Bakalar, *Marihuana: The Forbidden Medicine* (New Haven: Yale University Press, 1997), chs. 2 and 3.

15. In June 2005 the Supreme Court ruled against the case involving Angel Raich and Diane Monson, affirming in certain terms that marijuana must be declared an illegal drug. See Lee, *Smoke Signals*, pp. 333–334.

16. NIDA is very clear about its position on the dangers of marijuana. Statements abound at its website. For example, "Marijuana overactivates the cannabinoid system,

242 NOTES

causing the 'high' and other effects that users experience. These effects include altered perceptions and mood, impaired coordination, difficulty with thinking and problem solving, and disrupted learning and memory." See "DrugFacts: Marijuana," at www.drugabuse.gov/publications/drugfacts/marijuana. The fraudulent character of such glib statements is easy enough to detect. Aside from the nebulous nature of the supposed effects, neither the amount of marijuana consumed nor the intensity of these effects is ever specified.

17. Ibid.

18. Ibid.

19. Ibid.

20. Ibid.

21. Ibid.

22. According to a January 2011 statement by the DEA, "Specifically, smoked marijuana has not withstood the rigors of science—it is not medicine, and it is not safe." The DEA goes on to warn that, while some people think the federal government has relaxed its policy on medical pot, this is manifestly not the case. It makes clear that investigations, raids, and prosecutions will continue full-force. This sentiment has been repeated continuously since medical marijuana dispensaries became legal in many states. See *The DEA Position on Marijuana*, at www.justice.gov/dea/docs/marijuana_position _2011.pdf.

23. Ibid.

24. Ibid.

25. *Diagnostic and Statistical Manual of Mental Disorders* (DSM-IV) (published by the American Psychiatric Association, 2000), p. 236.

26. According to the Marijuana Policy Project, no fewer than 87 percent of those arrested on pot charges were simple casual users—750,000 total in 2010. See www.mpp .org/about/.

27. See "Substance Use Treatment Data, Research, and Policies," www.drugwarfacts .org/cms/Treatment.

28. On the impact of mass incarceration, see Paul Street, "American Justice: Marijuana Convicts Scarred While BP Execs Untouched," *Truthout* (September 2013). http://truth-out.org/opinion/item/13120-the-artificial-felon-british-petroleum-bp -the-earth-and-american-justice.

29. A 2002 Rand Corporation study thoroughly debunked the old drug-warrior myth that marijuana opens the "gate" to harder and more destructive substances. See http:// norml.org/library/item/your-government-is-lying-to-you-again-about-marijuana.

30. While the medicinal and intoxicating properties of cannabis are many, extremely harmful effects rarely occur—and then typically when the user takes in very large amounts. The plant can exert widely different outcomes for different consumers. See Lee, *Smoke Signals*, pp. 5–9, and Schlosser, *Reefer Madness*, pp. 17–18.

31. See Grinspoon and Bakalar, *Marihuana*, pp. 242–243.

Notes 243

32. On the topic of managing addictive impulses or tendencies, see Stanton Peele, *The Truth about Addiction and Recovery* (New York: Fireside, 1991), ch. 8.

33. On Obama's drug-policy agenda, see Fred Gardner, "How Cannabis Works," *CounterPunch* (October 16–31, 2011). www.counterpunch.org/2011/07/14/how-cannabis-works/.

34. *Los Angeles Times* (October 17, 2012).

35. Public attitudes regarding marijuana have been shifting rapidly in the United States. According to an October 2013 Gallup poll, 58 percent of Americans say pot should be fully legalized—up from 44 percent in 2010. See Art Swift, "For First Time, Americans Favor Legalizing Marijuana," Gallup (October 22, 2013). www.gallup.com/poll/165539/first-time-americans-favor-legalizing-marijuana.aspx.

36. On testing results for medical marijuana related to a wide range of health problems, see Grinspoon and Bakalar, *Marihuana,* chs. 2 and 3.

37. See the reports on medical marijuana contained in www.unitedpatientsgroup.com/resources (2012).

38. See Lydia Saad, "In U.S., 38% Have Tried Marijuana, Little Changed since '80s," Gallup (August 2, 2013). www.gallup.com/poll/163835/tried-marijuana-little-changed-80s.aspx.

39. While the marijuana crop in California has been reported to be valued as high as $36 billion yearly, more reliable 2013 estimates placed the value at $31 billion, still enormous. See http://marijuana.com/news/2014/06/report-californias-marijuana-is-worth-a-cool-31-billion/.

40. www.oaksterdamuniversity.com.

41. *Los Angeles Times* (August 3, 2012).

42. Greg Campbell, *Pot, Inc.: Inside Medical Marijuana, America's Most Outlaw Industry* (New York: Sterling, 2013).

43. Ibid., pp. xiv–xv.

44. Ibid., p. xxiii.

45. Ibid., p. xxvi.

46. Ibid., pp. 7–8.

47. Ibid., pp. 9–10.

48. On the important medical-pot group Americans for Medical Rights, see www.drugpolicy.org/doc1uploads/AMR (2013). This site provides an enormously wide range of scientific evidence available on medical marijuana—precisely the evidence that NIDA and the DEA claim does not exist.

49. *Los Angeles Times* (July 25, 2012).

50. *Los Angeles Times* (October 3, 2012).

51. *Los Angeles Times* (October 5, 2012).

52. See Jeffrey Miron, *Drug War Crimes: The Consequences of Prohibition* (Oakland, CA: Independent Institute, 2004), pp. 12–19.

53. *Los Angeles Times* (November 11, 2012).

244 NOTES

54. *Los Angeles Times* (November 11, 2012).

55. Sidney Wolfe et al., *Worst Pills, Best Pills: A Consumer's Guide to Avoiding Drug-Induced Death or Illness* (New York: Pocket Books, 2005), pp. 311–313.

56. Ibid., p. 325.

57. Ibid., p. 324.

58. Ibid., pp. 325–326.

59. http://medicalmarijuana.procon.org/view.resource.php?resourceID=000884.

60. Ibid.

61. Ibid.

62. Ibid.

63. Ibid.

64. Ibid.

65. On the medical properties and other features of Marinol, see Lee, *Smoke Signals*, pp. 169–170.

66. Ibid.

67. See Ryan Grim, "Medical Marijuana Memo: DOJ Cracks Down on Pot Shops," *Huffington Post* (July 1, 2011). www.huffingtonpost.com/2011/07/01/medical-marijuana-memo-doj_n_888995.html.

68. Campbell, *Pot, Inc.*, pp. 250–251.

69. See Allen St. Pierre, "Making History in Colorado and Washington," *Huffington Post* (November 8, 2012). St. Pierre is executive director of NORML, the leading organization pushing for marijuana legalization.

70. Ibid.

71. Ibid.

72. On Brian Vicente's opinions regarding pot legalization, see the wide-ranging interview with him in *Marijuana Business Daily* (November 4, 2013), titled "Q&A with Cannabis Attorney Brian Vicente on Colorado's Recreational Marijuana Tax Proposal," http://mmjbusinessdaily.com/qa-with-cannabis-attorney-brian-vicente-on-colorados-recreational-marijuana-tax-proposal/.

73. According to a report in the *Denver Post* (January 12, 2014), marijuana-related cases filed in Colorado state courts declined by 77 percent from 2012 to 2013.

74. According to the Gallup survey of October 2013 mentioned previously, 58 percent of Americans favor legalization of marijuana, the first time this outlook registered majority support.

75. *Los Angeles Times* (January 27, 2013).

76. *Los Angeles Times* (December 26, 2012).

77. *Los Angeles Times* (February 17, 2013).

78. See Kristen Gwynne, "Turning the Tide on Drug Reform," *The Nation* (February 18, 2013).

79. *Los Angeles Times* (March 24, 2013).

80. Jonathan Ringen, "Too High to Fail: Inside Denver's Weed Boom," *Rolling Stone* (June 20, 2013), p. 48.

81. Ibid., p. 49.

82. On the California legislature's departure from the drug-war norm here, see the report in the *Los Angeles Times* (September 8, 2013).

83. *Los Angeles Times* (November 1, 2013).

84. *Los Angeles Times* (April 17, 2014).

85. *Los Angeles Times* (May 26, 2014).

86. *Los Angeles Times* (July 22, 2014).

87. This is the central thesis in my book *Phantom Democracy: Corporate Interests and Political Power* (New York: Macmillan, 2012).

88. Alexander, *The New Jim Crow*, p. 8.

89. Ibid., p. 6.

90. Wendy Kaminer, *I'm Dysfunctional, You're Dysfunctional: The Recovery Movement and Other Self-Help Fashions* (New York: Vintage, 1993), p. 6.

INDEX

AA (Alcoholics Anonymous), 186
Abbott, 89, 153
Abrams, Donald, 206
Abramson, John, 138, 140, 144, 145, 180
ACS (American Cancer Society), 155, 157
Actos, 154
Addiction: to cocaine, 173; as complex process, 62–64; context for, 175; as continuum of behavior, 172–173; critical perspective on, 168–169, 172, 173–174; definition of, 167; dietary patterns and, 64–65; disease model of, 63, 169–170, 171–172, 186–187; DSM perspective on, 170–171; to food, 64–65, 172, 174; of GIs, 133, 134, 173; in Holland, 78; to Internet, 175–176; to marijuana, 193–194, 196–197; recovery-treatment industry and, 186–187; stereotypes of, 167–168; to sugar, 66; to tobacco, 175; treatment for, 173; UN report on, 70–71, 75
Adorno, Theodor, 164–165
Adverse reactions, 142–143, 184–185
Advertising of drugs: alcoholic beverages, 29; anti-obesity, 179; by Big Pharma, 7–8, 82–83, 122, 139–140; FDA and, 151; tobacco, 29
Affluence, diseases of, 183–184

Afghanistan: opium in, 111–113, 129; war in, 133–134
AICR (American Institute for Cancer Research), 156, 157
Alcoholic beverages: consumption of, 28–29; moralism and, 55; outlawing of, 30–32; prohibition on, 51–52
Alcoholics Anonymous (AA), 186
Alexander, Michelle, 49, 50, 81, 92, 101, 215
AMA (American Medical Association), 181, 186
American Cancer Society (ACS), 155, 157
American Civil Liberties Union, 95, 200
American Council on Science and Health, 157
American Institute for Cancer Research (AICR), 156, 157
American Medical Association (AMA), 181, 186
American Society of Addiction Medicine, 90
Americans for Safe Access, 191, 200, 209–210, 211
Andean Counterdrug Initiative, 126
Andreas, Peter, 26, 107
AndroGel, 153
Angell, Marcia, 139, 140, 144, 147, 148, 149, 150, 160
Angwin, Julia, 98

247

248 INDEX

Anslinger, Harry, 6, 33, 52–53, 59
Antibiotics: cost of, 141–142; overuse of, 9, 185
Anti-Drug Abuse Act of 1986, 190
Antidrug warfare. *See* War on Drugs; Warfare, motif of
Anti-obesity drugs, 178–179, 180–181, 182–183
AstraZeneca, 58, 134, 146, 153, 156
Atkins, Robert, 183
Authoritarianism: in American society, 84; of corporate power, 120; of modern governance, 164–165; of prison system, 99–103; of prohibition, 61–62, 66; of Prohibition, 31–32; of recovery-treatment industry, 186–187; of War on Drugs, 1, 2, 10–11, 44, 131, 214–217
Avandia, 152
Ayahuasca plant, 148

Balli, Cecelia, 125
Balloon effect, 72
Bamford, James, 3, 93, 94
Bariatric surgery, 181
Bartlett, Donald L., 122, 139, 146, 152, 160
Bayh-Dole Act of 1984, 139, 146, 150
Beat generation, 11–13
Behr, Edward, 115
Bell, Terrence, 55
Benavie, Arthur, 50
Benjamin, Mark, 79
Bennett, William, 55–56
Big Pharma: advertising by, 7–8, 82–83, 122, 139–140; cartels compared to, 121; Congress and, 149, 161, 167; defrauding of federal government by, 153; in drug war, 8; federal government and, 7, 57–60, 149; harmful impact of, 121–122; healthcare reform and, 160–161; influence of, 4, 146; as oligopoly, 6–7, 139; power of, 149–154; profits of, 162; rise of, 139–149; sales of, 28, 146; as sector of economy, 58; state-capitalist apparatus and, 57–60
Binney, William, 3

"Blockbuster" drugs, 140
Blumenauer, Earl, 210
Boggs Act of 1951, 190
Bolivia, coca-leaf chewing in, 71
Borders: Afghan-Iran, 112; as porous, 106; US-Mexican, 97, 117, 121
Brill, Steve, 166, 167
Bristol-Myers Squibb, 59, 146, 147–148
Brown, E. Richard, 139
Bureau of Narcotics, 52. *See also* Anslinger, Harry
Burroughs, William, 12–13
Burzynski: The Movie (film), 159
Bush, George W., antidrug policy of, 124, 126, 204

Calderón, Felipe, 2, 19, 97, 108, 110, 123
California: DEA in, 204; Emerald Triangle in, 202–203; law enforcement efforts in, 213; lawsuits by counties in, against narcotics producers, 153; medical marijuana in, 82; pot economy and culture in, 200, 202–203, 209–210; spending on prisons in, 100
Campbell, Greg, 201, 202, 208
Campbell, Howard, 109
Campbell, T. Colin, 155, 156–157, 159, 178, 181
Cancer: chemotherapy for, 157–159; contexts of disease formation, 154–157; cost of treatment for, 166; deaths from, 138; drugs for, 147–148, 154; marijuana for, 189, 200
Cannabis. *See* Marijuana
Capitalism: of drug syndicates, 113–122; mafia, 108–109; underground, 105, 106. *See also* Capitalist modernity; State-capitalist apparatus
Capitalist modernity, 163–165, 176–177, 184–187
Capone, Al, 115
Cardosa, Fernando Henrique, 68
Celebrex, 141, 152
CEO compensation, 166–167
Chemotherapy, 157–159
Chen, Li-Chuan, 159–160

INDEX 249

Choice, personal, limitations on, 10–11, 61–62
CIA and drug trade, 129, 130–131, 133
Cisplatin, 158–159
Citizens for Better Medicare, 149
Civil liberties/rights: antidrug mania and, 44; in Declaration of Independence, 10–11; post-9/11, 93; privacy, 98; Prohibition and, 32; prohibition of marijuana and, 200; as under siege, 87–90; to substances of individual preference, 61–62; UN report on, 72
Clinton, Bill, 56–57, 86
Closed Circuit (film), 98, 103
Coca-Cola, 174
Cocaine: addiction to, 173; CIA and, 129, 130–131; consumption of, 29, 107; moral panic fixated on, 38, 54–55; production of, 128–129; war on, 15–16
Coca-leaf chewing, 16, 71
Cockburn, Alexander, 129, 130
"Cocktails," 140
Coenzyme Q-10, 180
Colombia, antidrug efforts in, 74, 125–127
Colorado, legalization of marijuana in, 199, 202, 203, 208, 211–212
Comcast, 59–60
Communism, 53
Community Oriented Police Services, 80–81
Comprehensive Crime Control Act of 1984, 190
Comprehensive Drug Abuse Prevention and Control Act of 1970, 85
Congress and Big Pharma, 149, 161, 167
Consciousness, pursuit of noninstrumental modes of, 13–14, 15, 23
Constitutional rights. *See* Civil liberties/rights
Consumption of drugs: modalities of, 22–23; in U.S., 81–82, 107–108. *See also specific drugs*
Contra operations, 129–131
Corporate-medical complex, 138–139, 159–162, 166–167

Corporations: boundary between government and, 42; cartels compared to, 118–121; in Mexico, 120; oligopolistic power of, 57–60. *See also* Corporate-medical complex; *specific corporations*
Corruption: in Afghanistan, 113, 129; forfeiture laws and, 88–89; mafia capitalism and, 108–109; in Mexico, 108–110, 117–118, 128
Costa, Antonio Maria, 73
Costs: of antibiotics, 141–142; of health care, 8, 162, 166–167; of legal drugs, 122; of Prohibition, 33, 105; UN report on, 73, 77; of War on Drugs, 2
Counter Narco-Terrorism Program Office, 124
Criminal subculture and Prohibition, 31, 33
Criminal syndicates: in Afghanistan, 111–113; capitalism of, 113–122; in Latin America, 108–111; overview of, 105–108
Culture wars and drug hysteria, 50–57, 193
Customs and Border Patrol, drones of, 3, 96–97
CVS, 9, 181

Darvon, 206
Davies, Merryl Wyn, 36, 104
Davis, Devra, 155, 157
DEA: budget of, 91; in California, 203–204; drones of, 3; GPS and, 95; marijuana and, 195; Mexican cartels and, 108–109; surveillance by, 95–96; "zero-tolerance" goals and, 47
Deaths: from cancer, 138, 154; of celebrities, 143; from legal drugs, 9, 20, 34, 81, 142, 144, 184; from obesity, 145; from painkillers, 153–154, 205; from Vioxx, 151
Debate: on healthcare reform, 145; on marijuana legalization, 199; need for, UN report on, 77; on War on Drugs, 5–6, 16, 18

250 INDEX

Decriminalization: of drugs, 66; of marijuana, 58–59, 191–192, 196, 199, 209, 214; in Portugal, 77–78; UN report on, 75–76

Democracy: coercive underpinnings of drug war and, 62; corporate-medical complex and, 159–162; surveillance and, 98; War on Drugs and, 214–217. *See also* Civil liberties/rights

Department of Homeland Security, 92

Diagnostic and Statistical Manual of Mental Disorders (DSM-IV), 63, 170–171, 195

Diet and cancer, 156–157

Direct-to-consumer advertising, 82–83

Disease model of addiction, 63, 169–170, 171–172, 186–187

Domestic surveillance, 3–4

Doxorubicin, 158–159

Drones, 3, 96–97

Drug Abuse Policy Office, 54

Drug czars, 53, 55–57, 86, 189, 199

Drug testing in workplace, 89–90

"Drug-free society": achievability of, 66; commitment to, 16, 43; as official dogma, 34; Reagan on, 54; search for, 1–2

Drug-Free Workplace Program, 89

Drugs: commodification of, 26–27; consumption of, in US, 81–82; dual properties of, 5; experience of, 11–14, 15, 23, 60; federal mobilization against, 33–34; historical and contextual framework for, 21–30; as source of taboos, fears, and myths, 20–21. *See also* Alcoholic beverages; Drugs, illegal; Drugs, legal; Global drug trade; Tobacco; *specific drugs*

Drugs, illegal: addiction to, 175; attraction of, 11, 107; as competition for legal drugs, 57–58; consumption of, 16, 20, 24, 29, 75, 81–82, 107–108; legalization of, 58–59, 66, 76; popularity of, 47; social consequences of, 64. *See also* Cocaine; Marijuana

Drugs, legal: abuse of, 142; administered in prisons, 102; consumption of, 28–29, 184; cost of, 122; deaths from, 9, 20, 34, 81; generic, 141–142; harmful effects of, 5, 58–59, 142–143, 184–185; in Iraq and Afghanistan wars, 133–134; medical iatrogenesis and, 8–9. *See also* Advertising of drugs

DSM-IV (*Diagnostic and Statistical Manual of Mental Disorders*), 63, 170–171, 195

Dyer, Joel, 100

Easy medical fixes, fashion of, 65

Economics of prohibition, 57–58

Ehrenreich, Barbara, 185

Eighth Amendment, infringements on, 88

Elders, Joycelyn, 207

Electronic Privacy Information Center, 95

Eli Lilly, 58, 59, 147, 153, 154

Ellis, Ronald, 206

Employee-at-will doctrine, 89

Enemy of the State (film), 103

Engelhardt, Tom, 132

England, decriminalization in, 78

English, Deirdre, 185

Epstein, Edward J., 53–54

Epstein, Samuel, 155

Ethnicity: drug offenses and, 86; of prison population, 99–101, 215

Etoposide, 158–159

Experience of drugs: existential mode of, 11–14, 15; factors in, 60; framework of, 23

Fadiman, James, 13, 14

FARC (Revolutionary Armed Forces of Colombia), 125, 126, 127

Fast foods: addiction to, 172, 174; cancer and, 156; globalization of, 120; heart disease and, 145; obesity and, 65, 176–178

Fats, saturated, 178, 183

FBI, surveillance by, 3, 94

FDA: as colonized by corporate interests, 150; marijuana and, 194–195; pharmaceutical industry and, 4, 140, 141; standing advisory committees of, 150–151; Vioxx and, 151–152

INDEX 251

FDA Modernization Act of 1997, 149–150

Fearmongering: Marihuana Tax Act and, 35; moral panic and, 37–42; popular culture and, 36–37, 39–42; threat, motif of, 45–50; War on Drugs and, 36

Federal government: agencies in antidrug warfare, 84, 86; antidrug policy of, 203–204; Big Pharma and, 7, 57–60, 149, 161, 167; defrauding of, 153; growth of, 55–56; local governments and, 209–211; psychedelic substances and, 13–14. *See also* National-security state; War on Drugs; *specific presidents*

Fentanyl, 205–206

Food: addiction to, 64–65; personal choice and, 61; sugar, consumption of, 65–66. *See also* Fast foods

Food and Drug Administration. *See* FDA

Foreign Intelligence Surveillance Act, 94

Forfeiture laws, 88–89

Fourth Amendment, infringements on, 88, 89, 98

"Fourth drive," 11–13, 14, 15, 22, 62

Freedman, David, 183–184

Freiling, Tom, 16–17

Gabler, Neal, 37

Gates, Daryl, 35, 56

Generic drugs, 141–142

Gingrich, Newt, 35, 56

Giroux, Henry, 17

GlaxoSmithKline, 150, 152, 176

Global drug trade: Afghanistan in, 111–113; as alternative capitalism, 113–122; criminal syndicates in, 105–113; dark side of, 34; expansion of battle zones on, 122–131; history of, 25–26; Latin America in, 108–111; in 1960s, 115–116; Obama on, 79; rights violations in war on, 72. *See also* United Nations World Drug Report

Global-positioning systems, 95

Goldsmith, Neal, 23

Government: boundary between corporations and, 42; local,

208–211. *See also* Federal government

Graham, David, 151

Gray, Mike, 31, 53, 59, 114

Grillo, Ioan, 109

Guadalajara cartel, 106, 109

Gulf cartel, 118

Guzmán, Joaquín, 128

Habituation, 167, 168, 169. *See also* Addiction

Hallucinogenic plants, 23

Harm, measurement of, 60–61, 62–64, 70

Harm-reduction programs, 70, 71, 74–75

Harrison Narcotics Tax Act of 1914, 45, 61

Hatch-Waxman Act of 1984, 141

Health care: as colonized, 163–164; corporate takeover of, 138–139, 159–162, 166–167; cost and outcomes of, 8, 162, 166–167; deregulation and, 138; as "free market," 145–146; indicators or outcomes of, 137–138, 159; medical model of, 4–5, 9–11, 63, 185–186; tyranny within, 159–162; as Wall Street operation, 146

Healthcare reform, 145, 160–162

Hearst, William Randolph, 52

Heart disease, 179–180

Hernández, Anabel, 108–109

Hobsbawm, Eric, 116

Hoffman-LaRoche, 59, 89

Holder, Eric, 197

Holland, decriminalization in, 78

Homeland Security, 3

Horkheimer, Max, 164–165

Hormone-replacement therapy (HRT), 143–144

House I Live In, The (film), 6, 42, 83

Human growth hormone, 179

Ignani, Karen, 161

Illich, Ivan, 138, 162

Import restrictions, 141

Incarceration rates and ethnicity, 49–50. *See also* Prison-industrial complex

252 INDEX

"Information centers," regional, 3–4
Institute of Medicine, 200
Insurance companies and The Partnership for a Drug-Free America, 59
International Narcotics Control Board, 71
Internet: addiction to, 175–176; as source for drugs, 141
Iran, prohibitionism in, 112
Iraq War, 133–134

Jarecki, Eugene, 6, 83
Jay, Mike, 20, 106, 114, 137
Jazz music, 12, 32, 46–47
Johnson & Johnson, 59, 146
Joint Task Force Six, 93
"Just Say No" slogan, 48, 54

Kaminer, Wendy, 187, 217
Karzai, Hamid, 111, 113
Kennedy, Peter and Carole Ann, 184
Kerlikowske, Gil, 81–82
Kerouac, Jack, 11–12
Kolata, Gina, 183

LabCorp, 89
Lapham, Lewis, 14–15
Latin America: antidrug policy in, 74, 80, 95, 125–127, 128–129; drug cartels in, 110–111; foreign policy toward, 48. *See also* Mexico
Lazcano, Heriberto, 127
Lee, Martin A., 12
Legality, as socially constructed concept, 63–64
Legalization, moves toward, 16. *See also* Decriminalization
Lemaitre, Rafael, 79
Leonhart, Michele, 203
Lichtenstein, Nelson, 120
Lifestyle changes, long-term medications compared to, 144–145
Lifestyle issues: in cancer, 155–157; in obesity, 176–184. *See also* Fast foods
Local government, 208–211
Local police operations: antidrug policy and, 49; Community Oriented Police Services, 80–81; Mexican

cartels and, 108–109; national intelligence agencies and, 3–4; surveillance, 98
Low-carb diets, 183
Lowe, James, 161
LSD, 13–14

Mafia structure, 116
Mallinckrodt, 59
Mander, Jerry, 7
Mansfield, John, 183
Manufacturing of drugs, 147
Marihuana Tax Act of 1937, 33, 35, 190
Marijuana: arrests for possession of, 43, 56, 195–196, 197–198; Bennett and, 55–56; as cash crop, 201; civil forfeiture statutes and, 88; consumption of, 29, 82, 107, 108, 191, 201–202; as controlled substance, 190–191, 192, 213; dependency on, 196–197; effects of use of, 193–195; eradication efforts, 203–204; as "gateway" drug, 54–55, 189, 193, 196; Hispanics and, 46; history of, 188–189; as "killer weed," 190, 192–198; local governments and, 208–211; medical use for, 81–82, 195, 198, 199–200, 206–207; Nixon and, 54; Obama on, 80, 201; political repression, social protest, and, 198–207; popularity and availability of, 52–53; prohibition on use of, 27, 33, 52; reversal of policy on, 211–217; as social phenomenon, 12; sources for, 191; support for decriminalization of, 58–59, 191–192, 196, 199, 209, 214; uses of, 189
Marinol, 195, 207
Market exclusivity, 149
McCaffrey, Barry, 56–57
McCoy, Alfred W., 97
McDonaldized diet, 65, 120, 174, 177, 178
McDougall, John, 155
McGinn, Mike, 201
McGovern Report, 156–157, 159
Measurement of harm, 60–61, 62–64, 70

INDEX

Meat-centered diet, 177–178
Media: coverage of alternative treatments in, 158; coverage of drug violence in, 19–20; coverage of drugs in, 7–8; fearmongering and, 37–38; moral panic and, 37–38; on UN report, 79
Medical iatrogenesis, increase in, 8–9, 134–135, 138
Medical model of health care, 4–5, 9–11, 63, 185–186
Medicalization of society: addiction and, 167–176; modernity, disease, iatrogenesis and, 184–187; obesity and, 176–184; overview of, 163–165
Medical-pharmaceutical-industrial complex. *See* Big Pharma; Pharmaceutical industry
Medical-pot insurgency, 198–202, 204, 208
Medicare Modernization Act of 2003, 150
Medication. *See* Drugs, legal
Mefloquine, 135
Merck, 59, 121, 146, 151, 152
Mérida Initiative, 123, 124, 128
Meridia, 178
Methamphetamine, moral panic fixated on, 39
Mexican cartels: antidrug warfare and, 108–111, 117–119; borders and, 106; corporations compared to, 118–121; as ideal nemesis, 2–3; media coverage of, 19–20; survival of, 127–128
Mexico: antidrug efforts in, 72, 74, 105, 108–109, 123–125; drug war zone (DWZ) in, 109–110, 124; relations with US, 123; surveillance by, 97; transnational companies in, 120. *See also* Mexican cartels
Militarization of antidrug politics: in Andean region, 126; in Colombia, 125–127; in Latin America, 95, 128–129; in Mexico, 123–125, 127–128; overview of, 2–3, 48, 84
Military: drones of, 3; drug use by members of, 132–135, 173; medical iatrogenesis and, 134–135;

national-security state and, 86–87; US, reach of, 131–132. *See also* Militarization of antidrug politics
Military-industrial complex, post-9/11, 92
Mill, John Stuart, 61, 62
Miller, Loren, 148
Mills, C. Wright, 42, 102
Miron, Jeffrey, 34, 57, 105, 205
Mitotane, 158
Monsanto, 152
Moral panic, 37–42, 54–55
Moralism: Prohibition and, 30–31; War on Drugs and, 35, 50–57
Moss, Ralph, 154–155, 157, 158
Movies, drug-related motifs in, 39–42
Mujahideen, 113, 129
Myers, Dee Dee, 56

Naim, Moisés, 34, 106
Naked Lunch (Burroughs), 12–13
Naltrexone, 10
Narco culture, 110
Narcoterrorism, 95, 123–124
Narcotic Control Act of 1956, 53
Narcotics, marketing and use of, 205–206
National Academy of Sciences, 157
National Cancer Institute, 156
National Commission on Marihuana and Drug Abuse, 190, 198, 214
National Institute on Drug Abuse (NIDA), 63, 170, 193–194
National Institutes of Health (NIH), 146, 157
National Organization for Reform of Marijuana Laws (NORML), 200
National Security Agency (NSA): DEA and, 96; domestic surveillance by, 3; surveillance power of, 93–94, 98
National-security state (NSS): Department of Homeland Security and, 92; military actions and, 86–87, 132; surveillance and, 91
Nawa, Fariba, 111, 113
Neoliberal economic model, War on Drugs as, 131
NIDA (National Institute on Drug Abuse), 63, 170, 193–194

254 INDEX

NIH (National Institutes of Health), 146, 157
Nixon, Richard: antidrug policy of, 47, 53–54, 85, 188; foreign policy of, 48; War on Drugs and, 1, 35
NORML (National Organization for Reform of Marijuana Laws), 200
North American Free Trade Agreement, 117
Novartis, 121, 146
NSA. *See* National Security Agency
NSS. *See* National-security state
Null, Gary, 158, 184

Oaksterdam University, 200–201
Obama, Barack: antidrug policy of, 57, 77, 79–81, 197, 207–208; healthcare reform of, 160–161; marijuana and, 80, 201; PATRIOT Act and, 99; UN report and, 78–79, 108
Obesity: deaths due to, 145; disease model of, 181–182, 183; drugs for, 178–179, 180–181, 182–183; epidemic of, 176–177; fast foods and, 174; management of, 10; rise of, 65, 177–178; sugar consumption and, 66; surgery for, 181
Office of National Intelligence, 3
Oil conglomerates, 120
Olmstead, Roy, 115
Omnibus Crime Bill of 1984, 49
Omnibus Crime Bill of 1994, 86
On the Road (Kerouac), 12
Opiates, 45–46, 199, 205–206
Opioids, 143
Organization of American States, 80
OTC (over-the-counter) drug sales, 28, 179, 180–181
"Others," targeting of with antidrug policy, 81. *See also* Racism
Overmedicated, society as, 140
OxyContin, 205

Painkillers, 153–154, 205–206
Pakistan, 113
Paley, Dawn, 128
Parenti, Christian, 97, 100–101
Parke-Davis, 59

Partnership at Drugfree.org, The, 39, 59
Partnership for a Drug-Free America, The, 39, 56, 59–60
Patent controls, 150
Patents, 146, 147, 148–149
Paul, Ron, 6
Paxil, 150
Peele, Stanton, 169, 172, 173, 175, 182, 187
Peña Nieto, Enrique, 109
Perry, Rick, 125
Pfizer, 59, 121, 146, 147, 176
Pharmaceutical industry: Anslinger and, 53; influence of, 4, 6; lobbying by, 167; Partnership for a Drug-Free America and, 39; sales of, 138; World War II and, 27. *See also* Big Pharma; *specific corporations*
Phenomenology of drugs, 23–24
PhRMA, 149
Physician Payments Sunshine Act of 2010, 144
Plan Colombia, 125–126, 127, 128
Plants, drugs from, 148–149
Popkin, Barry, 182
Popular opinion, 44
Portugal, decriminalization in, 77–78
Post-traumatic stress disorder in GIs, 134
Pot. *See* Marijuana
Power Geyser, 93
Pratt, Ray, 91
Premarin, 143–144
Prescription Drug User Fee Act of 1992, 150
Prescription drugs. *See* Drugs, legal
Prevention: Obama and, 79; UN report on, 76
Prices of drugs, 141–142. *See also* Costs
Prison-industrial complex: antidrug mania and, 34, 44, 49–50, 56; authoritarianism and, 99–103
Procter and Gamble, 59
Prohibition: conflict between consumption and, 26–27; consequences of, 62, 64, 85, 205; costs of, 33, 105; economics of, 57–58; history of, 30–34, 66; in Iran, 112; marijuana and, 192–198;

INDEX 255

moralizing and, 24; UN report on, 72–73; underground economy and, 114–115. *See also* War on Drugs
Prohibitionist ideology, framing of, 45
Prozac, 147
Psychedelic substances, 13–14, 23, 27–28
Psychotropic drugs: administered in prisons, 102; administered to GIs, 134–135
Public sphere: closing of, 5–6; colonization of, for commercial messages, 7; diminishment of, 42
Puritanism and appetite for drugs, 25, 30. *See also* Moralism

Qsymia, 10

Racial profiling, 92
Racism: incarceration and, 215; Prohibition and, 30–31; War on Drugs and, 36, 46–47, 49–50
Rationality, technological, 163
Reagan, Nancy, 38, 54
Reagan, Ronald: antidrug policy of, 38, 48–49, 54–55, 95, 190; Colombia and, 125; military-industrial complex and, 56
Recreational consumption of drugs, 22–23
"Reefer madness," 52–53, 190
Remus, George, 115
Reports of harm, 61
Research: biomedical, 152–153; commercially-sponsored, 144; corporate influence over, 157
Research and development (R&D), 146–147
Revolutionary Armed Forces of Colombia (FARC), 125, 126, 127
Rights. *See* Civil liberties/rights
Rimbaud, Arthur, 12, 15
Ringen, Jonathan, 211, 212
Rite-Aid, 181
Robbins, John, 155, 156
Roche, 146, 176
Rog, David, 206–207
Rohack, J. James, 161
Rosendahl, Bill, 204

Roszak, Theodore, 12, 14, 28
Rush, Benjamin, 186

Saloon culture, 30–31, 32, 51
Sardar, Ziauddin, 36, 104
Savagery, images of, and antidrug campaign, 53
Savages (film), 41
Schering-Plough, 59
Schlosser, Eric, 192
Scott, Peter Dale, 129
Security and Prosperity Partnership of North America, 124
"Self-regarding" category, 61, 62
Selvin, Joel, 13
Selznick, Phillip, 150
Seniors, targeting of, 153
Sentencing Reform Act of 1984, 85–86
Seroquel, 153
Seroquel cocktails, 134, 135
Shiffman, John, 96
Shultz, George, 79
Side Effects (film), 42
Siegel, Ronald K., 11, 22, 62, 164
Sinaloa cartel, 128
Sixties era, 13, 27–28, 49, 188–189
Sloan Kettering Institute, 154, 155, 166
Smuggling subculture, 26
Snowden, Edward, 3, 93
Social consequences of illegal drugs, 64
Social phobia, 176
"Society of security," 97
Soma, 185
Squibb, 59
St. Clair, Jeffrey, 129, 130
St. Pierre, Allen, 208
Stamper, Norm, 66, 208
State-capitalist apparatus: authoritarianism and, 102; expansion of, 165; medicalization of society and, 184–187; overview of, 57–60
Statin drugs, 65, 144–145, 179–180
Steele, James B., 122, 139, 140, 146, 152, 160
Substance Abuse and Mental Health Services Administration, 81–82
Substance-abuse disorders, 10

256 INDEX

Sugar, consumption of, 65–66
Surgery for weight reduction, 181
Surveillance complex, 90–99, 102–103, 210
Switzerland, decriminalization in, 78

Takeda, 154
Taliban, 111
Tamoxifen, 156
Tauzin, Billy, 161
Taxol, 147–148
Taylor, Michael, 152
Temperance movement, 30–32, 51–52
Terrorism: narcoterrorism, 95, 123–124; war against, 94–95, 98
Testing of drugs, 152
THC, 189, 194, 205
THC, synthetic, 195, 197–198, 207
Threat, motif of, 45–50. *See also* Fearmongering
Tobacco: addiction to, 175; consumption of, 29, 82; effects of withdrawal from, 194
Tobacco companies and The Partnership for a Drug-Free America, 59
Transnational corporate hegemony, globalization in form of, 123
Treatment of addiction, 186–187
Trimpey, Jack, 186
Turner, Carlton, 54, 190
Turse, Nick, 92

Ultram, 206
Underground commerce/capitalism, 105, 106, 113–122
United Nations Global Commission on Drug Policy, 68
United Nations Office on Drugs and Crime, 73
United Nations Single Convention on Narcotic Drugs, 52
United Nations Universal Declaration of Human Rights, 62, 71–72
United Nations World Drug Report (2012): alternative path suggested by, 73–78; conclusions of, 69–73; overview of, 6, 68–69; political reaction to, 78–83

United States: consumption of drugs in, 81–82, 107–108; drugs in, 24–30; global ambitions of, 104, 129–130; postwar global ascendancy of, 97–98; UN report on, 77. *See also* Civil liberties/rights; Democracy; Federal government; Military
Urine testing, 89–90
USA PATRIOT Act, 93, 99

Vicente, Brian, 209
Vietnam War, 132–133, 173
Violent crime and antidrug policy, 72
Vioxx, 151–152
Vivus, Inc., 10
Volcker, Paul, 79
Volstead Act, 27, 30, 31–32, 33, 85

Walgreens, 9, 181
Wal-Mart, 120
War on Drugs: admission of failure of, 78–79; argument for end to, 214–217; authoritarian logic of, 1, 2, 10–11, 44, 131, 214–217; budget for, 79–80; consequences of, 73, 142; cost of, 2; damage done by, 1–2, 66–67; debate on, 5–6, 18, 36; history of, 43–44; irrationality of, 16–18; Nixon and, 35; racism of, 36, 46–47, 49–50; resources for, 17; stigma and, 35–36; tropes of, 6; US imperial power and, 104, 129–130; as working against "fourth drive," 14. *See also* "Drug-free society"
Warfare: motif of, 2, 36–37; myths and illusions of, 60–67; US, protracted legacy of, 104–105. *See also* War on Drugs
Warfare state, 17–18, 36, 86–87, 91
Washington: Hempfest in, 201; legalization of marijuana in, 199, 202, 203, 208
Washington, Harriet, 140, 144, 148–149
Watkins, Lena, 204
Webb, Gary, 129, 130, 131
Weil, Andrew, 21, 164
Willful ignorance, 65
Wisotsky, Steven, 47, 66, 86

Wolfe, Sidney, 28, 143, 144, 151, 154, 178–179, 185, 206
Workplace drug testing, 89–90
World Cancer Research Fund, 156
World Health Organization, 16, 29, 73
Wyeth-Ayerst, 144

Xenophobia and War on Drugs, 36, 45–46, 49

Youth cultures, 27

Zedillo, Ernesto, 79
Zetas syndicate, 118, 127–128
Zyprexa, 153

ABOUT THE AUTHOR

After receiving his PhD in political science from UC Berkeley, **Carl Boggs** taught at Washington University (in St. Louis), Carleton University (in Ottawa), UCLA, USC, Antioch University (in Los Angeles), and, currently, National University in Los Angeles. His most recent book is *Ecology and Revolution: Global Crisis and the Political Challenge* (Macmillan, 2012). Boggs's previous books include *Empire versus Democracy: The Triumph of Corporate and Military Power* (Routledge, 2012); *Phantom Democracy: Corporate Interests and Political Power in America* (Macmillan, 2011); *The Crimes of Empire: The History and Politics of an Outlaw Nation* (Pluto, 2010); *The Hollywood War Machine: U.S. Militarism and Popular Culture*, with Tom Pollard (Paradigm, 2007); *Imperial Delusions: American Militarism and Endless War* (Rowman and Littlefield, 2006); *The End of Politics: Corporate Power and Decline of the Public Sphere* (Guilford, 2000); *The Socialist Tradition: From Crisis to Decline* (Routledge, 1996); *Social Movements and Political Power: Emerging Forms of Radicalism in the West* (Temple University Press, 1986); and *The Two Revolutions: Gramsci and the Dilemmas of Western Marxism* (South End Press, 1984). In 2007 he received the Charles A. McCoy Career Achievement Award from the American Political Science Association. He has written more than 300 articles along with numerous book and film reviews, and has had three radio programs at KPFK in Los Angeles. He is on the editorial board of several journals, including *Theory and Society* (where he is book-review editor) and *New Political Science*.

CPSIA information can be obtained at www.ICGtesting.com
Printed in the USA
BVOW02*1945061016

464370BV00007B/154/P